Basic Facts about the United Nations

Basic Facts
about the
United Nations

United Nations Department of Public Information
New York

Basic Facts about the United Nations

Published by the United Nations Department of Public Information
New York, New York 10017, United States of America

Revised edition
Copyright © 2011 United Nations
All rights reserved

ISBN: 978-92-1-101235-4
eISBN: 978-92-1-054807-6
United Nations publication
Sales no. E.11.I.2

Front cover: Dust rises as a helicopter of the UN Mission in Sudan (UNMIS) takes off, carrying voting materials to Tali Payam for Southern Sudan's referendum on self-determination (2 January 2011, UN Photo/Tim McKulka).

Cover design: Graphic Design Unit, United Nations, New York

Printed at the United Nations, New York

FOREWORD

The United Nations was founded on the conviction that the nations of the world can and should cooperate to resolve conflicts peacefully and change people's lives for the better. More than 65 years later, and with a record of genuine accomplishments, we remain fully committed to these principles.

Much has changed since the United Nations was founded. The Organization's membership has nearly quadrupled, while decolonization, population growth and globalization have each contributed to the redrawing of our modern landscape. As our world has evolved, so have the challenges. Advances in technology are connecting and affecting us all in ways we could not have imagined even a decade ago; financial, food, health and energy crises have shown no respect for national borders; and climate change and other ecological threats have highlighted that sustainable development depends equally on three component pillars: social development, economic growth and environmental protection.

In meeting these challenges, multilateral collaboration is more critical than ever, and the most effective venue for action remains the United Nations. Only by working together can we harness the opportunities presented by these monumental shifts and avert the risks they pose. This century began with a breakthrough. In 2000, the Millennium Development Goals (MDGs) gave us a blueprint with an achievable timetable for meeting people's most critical needs. We now have real results. With a growing number of development success stories—dramatic increases in school enrolment, expanded access to clean water, better control of disease, the growth of green technology—the transformative impact of the MDGs is undeniable.

Equally influential is the unquenchable desire of ordinary people everywhere to see the fundamental values of the *Charter of the United Nations* realized in their daily lives. From Southern Sudan to Timor-Leste, from Tunisia to Kyrgyzstan, we have seen people longing for democratic accountability, freedom and human rights. The United Nations will continue to articulate and stand up for universal values and work through its system to embed them in the fabric of national and international life.

Basic Facts about the United Nations, first issued in 1947, presents the history, goals, structure and most recent developments of the Organization. As new challenges emerge in politics, economics, technology and human rights, the United Nations continues to evolve to meet them. A notable example is the establishment, in 2010, of UN-Women, meant to help advance the benefits of gender equality and women's empowerment across the whole of the UN agenda. At the same time, the ongoing process of change management at the UN is helping us to deliver more, and more effectively.

I recommend this publication to anyone interested in this unique, invaluable and indispensable Organization, both as a reference for what has been achieved and a guide to what remains to be accomplished.

Ban Ki-moon
Secretary-General of the United Nations
New York, April 2011

CONTENTS

II. INTERNATIONAL PEACE AND SECURITY

III. ECONOMIC AND SOCIAL DEVELOPMENT

IV.   HUMAN RIGHTS

V.   HUMANITARIAN ACTION

VI.   INTERNATIONAL LAW

VII.   DECOLONIZATION

APPENDICES

LIST OF ACRONYMS

CTBTO	Preparatory Commission for the Comprehensive Nuclear-Test-Ban Treaty Organization
DESA	Department of Economic and Social Affairs
DFS	Department of Field Support
DGACM	Department for General Assembly and Conference Management
DM	Department of Management
DPA	Department of Political Affairs
DPI	Department of Public Information
DPKO	Department of Peacekeeping Operations
DSS	Department of Safety and Security
ECA	Economic Commission for Africa
ECE	Economic Commission for Europe
ECLAC	Economic Commission for Latin America and the Caribbean
ECOSOC	Economic and Social Council
ESCAP	Economic and Social Commission for Asia and the Pacific
ESCWA	Economic and Social Commission for Western Asia
FAO	Food and Agriculture Organization of the United Nations
IAEA	International Atomic Energy Agency
IASC	Inter-Agency Standing Committee
IBRD	International Bank for Reconstruction and Development
ICAO	International Civil Aviation Organization
ICSID	International Centre for Settlement of Investment Disputes
IDA	International Development Association
IDPs	Internally displaced persons
IFAD	International Fund for Agricultural Development
IFC	International Finance Corporation
ILO	International Labour Organization
IMF	International Monetary Fund
IMO	International Maritime Organization
IPCC	Intergovernmental Panel on Climate Change
ITC	International Trade Centre
ITU	International Telecommunication Union
MDGs	Millennium Development Goals
MIGA	Multilateral Investment Guarantee Agency
NEPAD	New Partnership for Africa's Development
NGOs	non-governmental organizations
OCHA	Office for the Coordination of Humanitarian Affairs
OHCHR	Office of the United Nations High Commissioner for Human Rights
OIOS	Office of Internal Oversight Services
OLA	Office of Legal Affairs
OPCW	Organisation for the Prohibition of Chemical Weapons
UNAIDS	Joint United Nations Programme on HIV/AIDS
UNCDF	United Nations Capital Development Fund

UNCTAD	United Nations Conference on Trade and Development
UNDP	United Nations Development Programme
UNEP	United Nations Environment Programme
UNESCO	United Nations Educational, Scientific and Cultural Organization
UNFPA	United Nations Population Fund
UN-HABITAT	United Nations Human Settlements Programme
UNHCR	Office of the United Nations High Commissioner for Refugees
UNICEF	United Nations Children's Fund
UNICRI	United Nations Interregional Crime and Justice Research Institute
UNIDIR	United Nations Institute for Disarmament Research
UNIDO	United Nations Industrial Development Organization
UNITAR	United Nations Institute for Training and Research
UNODA	United Nations Office for Disarmament Affairs
UNODC	United Nations Office on Drugs and Crime
UN-OHRLLS	Office of the High Representative for the Least Developed Countries, Landlocked Developing Countries and Small Island Developing States
UNOPS	United Nations Office for Project Services
UNOWA	United Nations Office for West Africa
UNRISD	United Nations Research Institute for Social Development
UNRWA	United Nations Relief and Works Agency for Palestine Refugees in the Near East
UNSSC	United Nations System Staff College
UNU	United Nations University
UNV	United Nations Volunteers
UN-Women	United Nations Entity for Gender Equality and the Empowerment of Women
UNWTO	World Tourism Organization
UPU	United Nations Postal Union
WFP	World Food Programme
WHO	World Health Organization
WIPO	World Intellectual Property Organization
WMO	World Meteorological Organization
WTO	World Trade Organization

ABOUT THIS EDITION

Published regularly since 1947—including under the title *The United Nations Today* in 2008—*Basic Facts about the United Nations* serves as a UN primer, describing in a comprehensive yet succinct fashion what the Organization does and how it functions, setting out its structure and goals in the context of its history and recent developments.

This 2011 edition of *Basic Facts* explains the role played by each of the principal UN organs and provides an overview of the family of related UN institutions and agencies (Chapter I). It also highlights the Organization's manifold efforts to promote and support international peace and security (Chapter II); enhance economic and social development through environmentally sustainable means (Chapter III); protect human rights and eliminate discrimination (Chapter IV); provide humanitarian relief to refugees, displaced persons and victims of natural disasters (Chapter V); advance the formulation and application of international law (Chapter VI); and foster the movement towards decolonization (Chapter VII). The portrait that emerges from these pages is one of a dynamic institution unique in its ability to meet, through international cooperation, the profound challenges of our age that affect all the world's peoples without respect for national borders—that no single country can resolve on its own. The appendices document current UN membership; growth in UN membership since the founding of the Organization; UN peacekeeping missions: past and present; UN decades, years, weeks and days observed; contact information for UN information centres, services and offices; and selected UN websites.

The work of the United Nations reaches every corner of the globe. This edition of *Basic Facts* has been substantially revised to take account of many significant recent developments in the world and within the UN itself. All data are current as of December 2010, unless otherwise noted. For the latest in all areas of UN involvement, please visit the official website of the Organization (*www.un.org*) and especially the UN News Centre (*www.un.org/news*). A thematic view of the United Nations' engagement in global affairs can be found in the magazine *UN Chronicle* (*www.un.org/wcm/content/site/chronicle*). For an in-depth presentation of UN activities and concerns, please consult the authoritative reference work on the activities and concerns of the Organization, the *Yearbook of the United Nations* (*unyearbook.un.org*).

The United Nations System

UN Principal Organs

General Assembly

Security Council

Economic and Social Council

Secretariat

International Court of Justice

Trusteeship Council[4]

Subsidiary Bodies

Main and other sessional committees

Disarmament Commission

Human Rights Council

International Law Commission

Standing committees and ad hoc bodies

Subsidiary Bodies

Counter-terrorism committees

International Criminal Tribunal for Rwanda (ICTR)

International Criminal Tribunal for the former Yugoslavia (ICTY)

Military Staff Committee

Peacekeeping operations and political missions

Sanctions committees (ad hoc)

Standing committees and ad hoc bodies

Programmes and Funds

UNCTAD United Nations Conference on Trade and Development

- **ITC** International Trade Centre (UNCTAD/WTO)

UNDP United Nations Development Programme

- **UNCDF** United Nations Capital Development Fund

- **UNV** United Nations Volunteers

UNEP United Nations Environment Programme

UNFPA United Nations Population Fund

Functional Commissions

Crime Prevention and Criminal Justice

Narcotic Drugs

Population and Development

Science and Technology for Development

Social Development

Statistics

Status of Women

Sustainable Development

United Nations Forum on Forests

Other Bodies

Committee for Development Policy

Committee of Experts on Public Administration

Committee on Non-Governmental Organizations

Permanent Forum on Indigenous Issues

United Nations Group of Experts on Geographical Names

Other sessional and standing committees and expert, ad hoc and related bodies

Departments and Offices

EOSG Executive Office of the Secretary-General

DESA Department of Economic and Social Affairs

DFS Department of Field Support

DGACM Department for General Assembly and Conference Management

DM Department of Management

DPA Department of Political Affairs

DPI Department of Public Information

DPKO Department of Peacekeeping Operations

DSS Department of Safety and Security

OCHA Office for the Coordination of Humanitarian Affairs

NOTES:

1 UNRWA and UNIDIR report only to the General Assembly.

2 IAEA reports to the Security Council and the General Assembly.

3 Specialized agencies are autonomous organizations working with the UN and each other through the coordinating machinery of ECOSOC at the intergovernmental level, and through the Chief Executives Board for Coordination (CEB) at the inter-secretariat level. This section is listed in order of establishment of these organizations as specialized agencies of the United Nations.

4 The Trusteeship Council suspended operation on 1 November 1994 with the independence of Palau, the last remaining United Nations Trust Territory, on 1 October 1994.

This is not an official document of the United Nations, nor is it intended to be all-inclusive.

UN-HABITAT United Nations Human Settlements Programme

UNHCR Office of the United Nations High Commissioner for Refugees

UNICEF United Nations Children's Fund

UNODC United Nations Office on Drugs and Crime

UNRWA[1] United Nations Relief and Works Agency for Palestine Refugees in the Near East

UN-Women United Nations Entity for Gender Equality and the Empowerment of Women

WFP World Food Programme

Research and Training Institutes

UNICRI United Nations Interregional Crime and Justice Research Institute

UNIDIR[1] United Nations Institute for Disarmament Research

UNITAR United Nations Institute for Training and Research

UNRISD United Nations Research Institute for Social Development

UNSSC United Nations System Staff College

UNU United Nations University

Other Entities

UNAIDS Joint United Nations Programme on HIV/AIDS

UNISDR United Nations International Strategy for Disaster Reduction

UNOPS United Nations Office for Project Services

Related Organizations

CTBTO Preparatory Commission for the Comprehensive Nuclear-Test-Ban Treaty Organization

IAEA[2] International Atomic Energy Agency

OPCW Organisation for the Prohibition of Chemical Weapons

WTO World Trade Organization

Advisory Subsidiary Body

UN Peacebuilding Commission

Specialized Agencies[3]

ILO International Labour Organization

FAO Food and Agriculture Organization of the United Nations

UNESCO United Nations Educational, Scientific and Cultural Organization

WHO World Health Organization

World Bank Group

- **IBRD** International Bank for Reconstruction and Development
- **IDA** International Development Association
- **IFC** International Finance Corporation
- **MIGA** Multilateral Investment Guarantee Agency
- **ICSID** International Centre for Settlement of Investment Disputes

IMF International Monetary Fund

ICAO International Civil Aviation Organization

IMO International Maritime Organization

ITU International Telecommunication Union

UPU Universal Postal Union

WMO World Meteorological Organization

WIPO World Intellectual Property Organization

IFAD International Fund for Agricultural Development

UNIDO United Nations Industrial Development Organization

UNWTO World Tourism Organization

Regional Commissions

ECA Economic Commission for Africa

ECE Economic Commission for Europe

ECLAC Economic Commission for Latin America and the Caribbean

ESCAP Economic and Social Commission for Asia and the Pacific

ESCWA Economic and Social Commission for Western Asia

OHCHR Office of the United Nations High Commissioner for Human Rights

OIOS Office of Internal Oversight Services

OLA Office of Legal Affairs

OSAA Office of the Special Adviser on Africa

SRSG/CAAC Office of the Special Representative of the Secretary-General for Children and Armed Conflict

UNODA Office for Disarmament Affairs

UNOG United Nations Office at Geneva

UN-OHRLLS Office of the High Representative for the Least Developed Countries, Landlocked Developing Countries and Small Island Developing States

UNON United Nations Office at Nairobi

UNOV United Nations Office at Vienna

I. UN CHARTER, STRUCTURE AND SYSTEM

United Nations flag
The United Nations flag flies on the opening day of the general debate of the sixty-fifth session of the General Assembly at UN Headquarters in New York (23 September 2010, UN Photo/Mark Garten).

I. UN CHARTER, STRUCTURE AND SYSTEM

The struggle for peace is an enduring one. More than a century ago, in 1899, the first International Peace Conference was held in The Hague to elaborate multilateral instruments for settling crises peacefully, preventing wars and codifying rules of warfare. It adopted the *Convention for the Pacific Settlement of International Disputes* and established the Permanent Court of Arbitration, which began its work in 1902. Subsequently, in 1919, the League of Nations, conceived during the First World War, was established under the *Treaty of Versailles* "to promote international cooperation and to achieve peace and security". While the League of Nations ceased activities after failing to prevent the Second World War, the need for peaceful resolution of conflicts through international collaboration and dialogue continued to grow.

The term 'United Nations' was coined by United States President Franklin D. Roosevelt during the Second World War. It first appeared in the *Declaration by United Nations* of 1 January 1942, which put forth a pledge by 26 nations to fight together against the Axis powers. Following deliberations in 1944 by representatives from China, the Soviet Union, the United Kingdom and the United States in Washington, D.C., delegates from 50 countries met the next year in San Francisco at the United Nations Conference on International Organization. There, with a firm commitment to end "the scourge of war", they drew up the *Charter of the United Nations*, signed on 26 June 1945. (Poland, which was not represented at the Conference, signed the *Charter* later and so became one of the original 51 member states.)

Headquartered in New York, the United Nations officially came into existence on 24 October 1945 with the ratification of the *Charter* by China, France, the Soviet Union, the United Kingdom, the United States and a majority of other signatories. In commemoration of this historic pledge for world peace, **United Nations Day** is celebrated on 24 October each year. Despite the sharp divisions from which it arose in the Second World War and those of the ensuing cold war that marked many of its deliberations, the UN continues to grow in remaining true to this pledge—one all the more relevant in the face of the tremendous global transformations that, at the beginning of the 21st century, are confronting the world and its peoples.

The Charter of the United Nations

The *Charter of the United Nations* (*www.un.org/aboutun/charter*) is the constitutive instrument of the UN, setting out the rights and obligations of member states, and establishing its principal organs and procedures. An international treaty, the *Charter* codifies basic tenets of international relations—from the sovereign equality of states to prohibition of the use of force in any manner inconsistent with the purposes of the United Nations.

The *Charter* consists of a Preamble and 111 articles grouped into 19 chapters. Of these, Chapter 1 sets forth the purposes and principles of the United Nations; Chapter 2 establishes the criteria for UN membership; Chapter 3 names the six principal UN organs; Chapters 4–15 define the functions and powers of these organs; Chapters 16–17 relate the United Nations to extant international law; and Chapters 18–19 define the amendment and ratification of the *Charter*.

The Preamble to the *Charter* expresses the shared ideals and common aims of all the peoples whose governments joined together to form the United Nations:

WE THE PEOPLES OF THE UNITED NATIONS

DETERMINED

prevent war
protect human right

to save succeeding generations from the scourge of war, which twice in our lifetime has brought untold sorrow to mankind, and

to reaffirm faith in fundamental human rights, in the dignity and worth of the human person, in the equal rights of men and women and of nations large and small, and

to establish conditions under which justice and respect for the obligations arising from treaties and other sources of international law can be maintained, and

to promote social progress and better standards of life in larger freedom,

AND FOR THESE ENDS

to practice tolerance and live together in peace with one another as good neighbours, and

to unite our strength to maintain international peace and security, and

to ensure, by the acceptance of principles and the institution of methods, that armed force shall not be used, save in the common interest, and

to employ international machinery for the promotion of the economic and social advancement of all peoples,

HAVE RESOLVED TO COMBINE OUR EFFORTS

TO ACCOMPLISH THESE AIMS

Accordingly, our respective Governments, through representatives assembled in the city of San Francisco, who have exhibited their full powers found to be in good and due form, have agreed to the present Charter of the United Nations and do hereby establish an international organization to be known as the United Nations.

Purposes and principles

As set forth in the *Charter*, the *purposes* of the United Nations are:

- to maintain international peace and security;
- to develop friendly relations among nations based on respect for the principle of equal rights and self-determination of peoples;
- to cooperate in solving international economic, social, cultural and humanitarian problems and in promoting respect for human rights and fundamental freedoms;
- to be a centre for harmonizing the actions of nations in attaining these common ends.

In turn, the United Nations acts in accordance with the following *principles*:

- It is based on the sovereign equality of all its members;
- All members are to fulfil in good faith their *Charter* obligations;
- They are to settle their international disputes by peaceful means and without endangering international peace and security and justice;
- They are to refrain from the threat or use of force against any other state;

Amendments to the Charter

The *Charter* may be amended by a vote of two thirds of the members of the General Assembly and ratification by two thirds of the members of the United Nations, including the five permanent members of the Security Council. So far, four Articles of the *Charter* have been amended, one of them twice:

- In 1965, the membership of the Security Council was increased from 11 to 15 states (Article 23) and the number of affirmative votes needed for a decision was increased from seven to nine, including the concurring vote of the five permanent members for all matters of substance rather than procedure (Article 27).
- In 1965, the membership of the Economic and Social Council was increased from 18 to 27 states, and again in 1973 to 54 (Article 61).
- In 1968, the number of votes required in the Security Council to convene a General Conference to review the *Charter* was increased from seven to nine (Article 109).

- They are to give the United Nations every assistance in any action it takes in accordance with the *Charter*;
- Nothing in the *Charter* is to authorize the United Nations to intervene in matters which are essentially within the domestic jurisdiction of any state.

Membership and official languages

Membership in the United Nations is open to all peace-loving nations that accept the obligations of the *Charter* and are willing and able to carry out these obligations. The General Assembly admits new member states on the recommendation of the Security Council. The *Charter* provides for the suspension or expulsion of a member for violation of the principles of the *Charter*, but no such action has ever been taken. Under the *Charter*, the official languages of the United Nations are Chinese, English, French, Russian and Spanish. Arabic was added as an official language in 1973.

UN structure

The *Charter* establishes six principal organs of the United Nations: the General Assembly, the Security Council, the Economic and Social Council, the Trusteeship Council, the International Court of Justice and the Secretariat. The United Nations family, however, is much larger, encompassing 15 specialized agencies and numerous programmes and funds as well as other entities.

General Assembly

The **General Assembly** (*www.un.org/ga*) is the main deliberative organ of the United Nations. It is composed of representatives of all member states, each of which has one vote. Decisions on important questions (such as those on peace and security, admission of new members and budgetary matters) require a two-thirds majority. Decisions on other questions take place by simple majority.

Functions and powers

Under the *Charter*, the functions and powers of the General Assembly include:

- considering and making recommendations on the principles of cooperation in the maintenance of international peace and security, including the principles governing disarmament and arms regulation;
- discussing any question relating to international peace and security and, except where a dispute or situation is being discussed by the Security Council, making recommendations on it;
- discussing and, with the same exception, making recommendations on any question within the scope of the *Charter* or affecting the powers and functions of any organ of the United Nations;
- initiating studies and making recommendations to promote international political cooperation, the development and codification of international law, the realization of human rights and fundamental freedoms for all, and international collaboration in the economic, social, cultural, educational and health fields;
- making recommendations for the peaceful settlement of any situation, regardless of origin, which might impair friendly relations among nations;
- receiving and considering reports from the Security Council and other United Nations organs;
- considering and approving the United Nations budget and apportioning the contributions among members;
- electing the non-permanent members of the Security Council, the members of the Economic and Social Council and additional members of the Trusteeship Council (when necessary); electing jointly with the Security Council the judges of the International Court of Justice; and, on the recommendation of the Security Council, appointing the Secretary-General.

Under the "Uniting for peace" resolution, adopted by the General Assembly in November 1950, the Assembly may take action if the Security Council, because of lack of unanimity of its permanent members, fails to act where there appears to be a threat to international peace, a breach of the peace or an act of aggression. The Assembly is empowered to consider the matter immediately with a view to making recommendations to members for collective measures, including, in the case of a breach of the peace or an act of aggression, the use of armed forces when necessary to maintain or restore international peace and security.

Sessions

The General Assembly's regular session begins each year on Tuesday in the third week of September, counting from the first week that contains at least one working day. The election of the President of the Assembly, as well as its 21 Vice-Presidents and the Chairpersons of its six main committees, takes place at least three months before the start of the regular session. To ensure equitable geographical representation, the presidency of the Assembly rotates each year among five groups of states: African, Asian, Eastern European, Latin American and Caribbean, and Western European and other states. In addition, the Assembly may meet in special sessions at the request of the Security Council, of a majority of member states or of one member, if the majority of members concur. Emergency special sessions may be called within 24 hours of a request by the Security Council on the vote of any nine Council members, or by a majority of the members of the United Nations, or by one member if the majority of members concur. At the beginning of each regular session, the Assembly holds a general debate—often addressed by heads of state and government—in which member states express their views on the most pressing international issues.

Year-round, the work of the United Nations derives largely from the mandates given by the General Assembly—that is to say, the will of the majority of the members as expressed in the resolutions and decisions adopted by the Assembly. That work is carried out:

- by committees and other bodies established by the Assembly to study and report on specific matters such as disarmament, peacekeeping, development and human rights;
- in international conferences called for by the Assembly; and
- by the Secretariat of the United Nations—the Secretary-General and his staff of international civil servants.

Most questions are discussed in one of the six **Main Committees** of the Assembly:

- First Committee (Disarmament and International Security);
- Second Committee (Economic and Financial);
- Third Committee (Social, Humanitarian and Cultural);
- Fourth Committee (Special Political and Decolonization);
- Fifth Committee (Administrative and Budgetary);
- Sixth Committee (Legal).

While some issues are considered directly in plenary meetings, most are allocated to one of these committees. Resolutions and decisions, including those recommended by the committees, may be adopted—with or without a vote—in plenary meetings, usually before the recess of the regular session in December.

The Assembly normally adopts its resolutions and decisions by a majority of members present and voting. Important questions—including recommendations on international peace and security, the election of members to some principal organs and budgetary matters—must be decided by a two-thirds majority. Voting may be conducted as a recorded vote, a show-of-hands or a roll-call vote. While the decisions of the Assembly have no legally binding force for governments, they carry the weight of world opinion and the moral authority of the world community.

Security Council

The **Security Council** (*www.un.org/docs/sc*) of the United Nations—one of its key distinctions from the League of Nations being the ability to enforce its decisions—has primary responsibility, under the *Charter*, for the maintenance of international peace and security. It has 15 members: five permanent members (China, France, the Russian Federation, the United Kingdom and the United States), and 10 members elected by the General Assembly for two-year terms. Each member has one vote. Decisions on procedural matters are made by an affirmative vote of at least 9 of the 15 members. Decisions on substantive matters require nine votes and the absence of a negative vote (veto) by any of the five permanent members. All five permanent members have exercised the right of veto at one time or another. If a permanent member does not fully agree with a proposed resolution but does not

Current members of the Security Council (2011–2012)

Permanent members
  China
  France
  Russian Federation
  United Kingdom
  United States
Non-permanent members (with year of term's end)
  Bosnia and Herzegovina (2011)
  Brazil (2011)
  Colombia (2012)
  Gabon (2011)
  Germany (2012)
  India (2012)
  Lebanon (2011)
  Nigeria (2011)
  Portugal (2012)
  South Africa (2012)

wish to cast a veto, it may choose to abstain, thus allowing the resolution to be adopted if it obtains the required number of nine favourable votes. The presidency of the Council is held by each of the members in turn for one month, following alphabetical order.

The composition of the Council, as well as its procedures, are the subject of a working group of the General Assembly considering Security Council reform, especially the addition of permanent seats or enlarging non-permanent member-ship. At issue is the notion of the equitable representation of member states in addressing matters of global consequence. Seventy-three UN member states have never sat on the Council. All members of the United Nations, however, agree to accept and carry out the decisions of the Security Council. While other organs of the United Nations make recommendations to member states, only the Security Council has the power to make decisions that member states are then obligated to implement under the *Charter*.

Functions and powers

The functions and powers of the Security Council include the following:
- maintaining international peace and security in accordance with the principles and purposes of the United Nations;
- formulating plans for establishing a system to regulate armaments;
- calling upon the parties to a dispute to settle it by peaceful means;
- investigating any dispute or situation that might lead to international friction, and recommending methods of adjustment or terms of settlement;
- determining the existence of a threat to the peace or act of aggression and recommending what action should be taken;

- calling upon the parties concerned to comply with such provisional measures as it deems necessary or desirable to prevent an aggravation of the situation;
- calling upon members of the United Nations to apply measures not involving the use of armed force—such as sanctions—to give effect to the Council's decisions;
- resorting to or authorizing the use of force to maintain or restore international peace and security;
- encouraging the peaceful settlement of local disputes through regional arrangements and using such regional arrangements for enforcement under its authority;
- recommending to the General Assembly the appointment of the Secretary-General and, together with the Assembly, electing the judges of the International Court of Justice;
- requesting the International Court of Justice to give an advisory opinion on any legal question;
- recommending to the General Assembly the admission of new members to the United Nations.

The Security Council is organized in such a way that it can function continuously. A representative of each of its members must be present at all times at UN Headquarters. The Council may meet elsewhere: in 1972 it held a session in Addis Ababa, Ethiopia; in 1973 it met in Panama City, Panama; and in 1990 it met in Geneva.

When a complaint concerning a threat to peace is brought before it, the Council's first action is usually to recommend that the parties try to reach agreement by peaceful means. The Council may set forth principles for such an agreement. In some cases, the Council itself undertakes investigation and mediation. It may dispatch a mission, appoint special envoys or request the Secretary-General to use his good offices to achieve a pacific settlement of the dispute.

When a dispute leads to hostilities, the Council's primary concern is to bring them to an end as soon as possible. It may issue ceasefire directives that can help prevent an escalation of the conflict. The Council may also dispatch military observers or a peacekeeping force to help reduce tensions, separate opposing forces and establish a calm in which peaceful settlements may be sought. Beyond this, the Council may opt for enforcement measures, including economic sanctions, arms embargoes, financial penalties and restrictions, and travel bans; severance of diplomatic relations; blockade; or even collective military action. A chief concern is to focus action on those responsible for the policies or practices condemned by the international community, while minimizing the impact of the measures taken on other parts of the population and economy.

Following the terrorist attacks on the United States on 11 September 2001, the Council established the Counter-Terrorism Committee as a subsidiary organ. The Peacebuilding Commission, established by the Council in 2005, supports peace efforts in countries emerging from conflict. The Military Staff Committee helps plan UN military measures and regulate armaments.

Tribunals and courts

Over the past two decades, the Council has established, as subsidiary organs, two ad hoc, territorially specific, international criminal tribunals to prosecute crimes against humanity in the former Yugoslavia and in Rwanda. There are also three 'hybrid' courts established by Cambodia, Lebanon and Sierra Leone, respectively, with substantial help from the United Nations. These are not permanent and will cease to exist once their business draws to a close.

International Criminal Tribunal for the former Yugoslavia (ICTY)

Established by the Security Council in 1993, the International Criminal Tribunal for the former Yugoslavia (*www.icty.org*) is mandated to prosecute persons responsible for genocide, war crimes and crimes against humanity committed in the former Yugoslavia since 1991. Its organizational components are its Chambers, Registry and the Office of the Prosecutor. It has 16 permanent judges, 12 *ad litem* judges (of whom it can call upon up to 12 at any given time) and a staff of 1,039 representing 83 nationalities. Its 2010–2011 regular budget was $301.9 million. The Tribunal has indicted 161 accused for crimes committed against many thousands of victims during the conflicts in Croatia (1991–1995), Bosnia and Herzegovina (1992–1995), Kosovo (1998–1999) and The former Yugoslav Republic of Macedonia (2001). By holding individuals accountable regardless of their position, the Tribunal has substantially contributed to further dismantling impunity for war crimes.

President: Patrick L. Robinson (Jamaica)
Prosecutor: Serge Brammertz (Belgium)
Registrar: John Hocking (Australia)
Headquarters: Churchillplein 1, 2517 JW The Hague, The Netherlands
Tel.: (31-70) 512-5000; Fax: (31-70) 512-5355

International Criminal Tribunal for Rwanda (ICTR)

Created by the Security Council in 1994, the International Criminal Tribunal for Rwanda (*www.ictr.org*) has the mandate to prosecute persons responsible for genocide and other serious violations of international humanitarian law committed in Rwanda during 1994, as well as Rwandan citizens responsible for such violations committed in the territory of neighbouring states. Its three Trial Chambers and one Appeals Chamber are composed of 16 independent judges. No two of them may be nationals of the same state. Three judges sit in each of the Trial Chambers and five judges sit in the Appeals Chamber, which is shared with the International Criminal Tribunal for the former Yugoslavia. It also has a pool of 18 *ad litem* judges (of whom it can call upon up to nine at any given time) and 693 staff posts for 2010, among which were represented some 77 nationalities. Its 2010–2011 budget was $245.3 million. As of July 2010, the ICTR had completed 51 cases, while 23 cases were still in progress and three were awaiting trial. Those convicted include Jean Kambanda, Prime Minister of Rwanda during the genocide—the first head of government to be arrested and subsequently convicted for genocide.

President: Charles Michael Dennis Byron (Saint Kitts and Nevis)
Prosecutor: Hassan B. Jallow (Gambia)
Registrar: Adama Dieng (Senegal)
Headquarters: Arusha International Conference Centre, P.O. Box 6016, Arusha, Tanzania
Tel.: (255-27) 250 27 4207-4211 or (via New York) (1-212) 963 2850; Fax: (255-27) 250 4000 or (via New York) (1-212) 963 2848

Special Court for Sierra Leone

The Special Court for Sierra Leone (*www.sc-sl.org*) was set up jointly by Sierra Leone and the United Nations in 2002, as requested by the Security Council in 2000. It is mandated to try those who bear the greatest responsibility for serious violations of international humanitarian law and Sierra Leonean law committed in the territory of Sierra Leone since 30 November 1996. The Special Court consists of three organs, including the Chambers (Appeals Chamber, Trial Chamber I and Trial Chamber II), the Registry (including the Defence Office) and the Office of the Prosecutor. The Special Court is the first international criminal tribunal to be funded entirely from voluntary contributions from governments. As of 2010, it had received contributions from over 40 states in all world regions.

President: Jon Kamanda (Sierra Leone)
Prosecutor: Brenda Hollis (United States)
Registrar: Binta Mansaray (Sierra Leone)
Headquarters: Jomo Kenyatta Road, New England, Freetown, Sierra Leone
Tel.: (232-22) 297 000 or (via Italy) (39) 831-257000; Fax: (232-22) 297 001 or (via Italy) (39) 831-257001

Extraordinary Chambers in the Courts of Cambodia (ECCC)

The Extraordinary Chambers in the Courts of Cambodia for the Prosecution of Crimes Committed during the Period of Democratic Kampuchea (*www.eccc.gov.kh*), is a national court established in 2006 pursuant to an agreement between Cambodia and the United Nations to try senior members of the Khmer Rouge for serious violations of international humanitarian law and Cambodian law during the period between 17 April 1975 and 6 January 1979, including crimes against humanity, war crimes and genocide. The Trial Chamber is composed of five judges, three of whom are Cambodian and one of these President. The Supreme Court Chamber has seven judges, four of whom are Cambodian and one of these President. International judges are appointed by the Cambodian Supreme Council of the Magistracy upon nomination by the Secretary-General of the United Nations. The United Nations Assistance to the Khmer Rouge Trials (UNAKRT) (*www.unakrt-online.org*) provides technical assistance to the ECCC.

Headquarters: National Road 4, Chaom Chau Commune, Dangkao District, Phnom Penh, Cambodia
Tel.: (855) 23 219814; Fax: (855) 23 219841

Special Tribunal for Lebanon (STL)

In 2005, the Lebanese government requested that the United Nations establish an international tribunal to try persons alleged responsible for the attack of 14 February 2005 in Beirut that killed former Lebanese Prime Minister Rafiq Hariri and 22 other persons. Pursuant to a Security Council resolution, the United Nations and Lebanon negotiated an agreement on the Special Tribunal for Lebanon (*www.stl-tsl.org*). The Special Tribunal, established following a further Security Council resolution in 2007 and officially opened in 2009, sits in Leidschendam-Voorburg, near the Hague—not in Lebanon, principally for reasons of security and fairness. The first indictments were announced by the Prosecutor in January 2011. The Chambers of the Special Tribunal consist of one international Pre-Trial Judge; a Trial Chamber (with three judges: one Lebanese and two international, plus two alternate judges: one Lebanese and one international); and an Appeals Chamber (five judges: two Lebanese and three international). The Secretary-General appoints the judges in consultation with the Lebanese government.

President: Antonio Cassese (Italy)
Prosecutor: Daniel A. Bellemare (Canada)
Registrar: Herman von Hebel (The Netherlands)
Headquarters: Dokter van der Stamstraat 1, 2265 BC, Leidschendam, The Netherlands
Tel.: (31-70) 800 3400

Economic and Social Council (ECOSOC)

The *Charter of the United Nations* establishes the **Economic and Social Council** (*www.un.org/ecosoc*) as the principal organ to coordinate the economic, social and related work of the United Nations and the specialized agencies and other bodies. The 54 members of the Council serve for three-year terms. Seats on the Council are allocated based on geographical representation, with 14 allocated to African states, 11 to Asian states, 6 to Eastern European states, 10 to Latin American and Caribbean states, and 13 to Western European and other states. Voting in the Council is by simple majority, with each member having one vote.

Functions and powers

ECOSOC is tasked with:

- serving as the central forum for discussing international economic and social issues, and for formulating policy recommendations addressed to member states and the United Nations system;
- making or initiating studies and reports and making recommendations on international economic, social, cultural, educational, health and related matters;
- promoting respect for, and observance of, human rights and fundamental freedoms;
- assisting in preparing and organizing major international conferences in the economic, social and related fields and promoting a coordinated follow-up to these conferences;
- coordinating the activities of the specialized agencies through consultations with and recommendations to them as well as to the General Assembly.

Through its discussion of international economic and social issues and its policy recommendations, ECOSOC plays a key role in fostering international cooperation for development and in setting priorities for action throughout the UN system.

Sessions and subsidiary bodies

The Council normally holds several short sessions and many preparatory meetings, roundtables and panel discussions throughout the year with members of civil society dealing with the organization of its work. It also holds a four-week substantive session in July, alternating annually between New York and Geneva. That session includes a high-level segment, attended by cabinet ministers and other officials, to discuss major economic, social and humanitarian issues. The Council also cooperates with, and to a certain extent coordinates the work of, United Nations programmes (such as UNDP, UNEP, UNFPA, UN-HABITAT and UNICEF) and the

2005 World Summit

At the 2005 World Summit, held at UN Headquarters, world leaders committed themselves to take action on a range of global challenges, including:

- *development:* achieving the Millennium Development Goals (MDGs) by 2015; contributing $50 billion a year by 2010 to fight poverty; cancelling 100 per cent of the official multilateral and bilateral debt of heavily indebted poor countries;
- *terrorism:* unqualified condemnation by all governments of terrorism "in all its forms and manifestations, committed by whomever, wherever and for whatever purposes";
- *peacebuilding, peacekeeping and peacemaking:* creating a Peacebuilding Commission to help countries successfully make the transition from war to peace, backed by a support office, funds and police capacity for UN peacekeeping operations;
- *responsibility to protect:* unambiguous acceptance of collective international responsibility to protect populations from genocide, war crimes, ethnic cleansing and crimes against humanity;
- *human rights, democracy and rule of law:* strengthening the UN human rights machinery; doubling the budget of the Office of the High Commissioner for Human Rights; establishing a Human Rights Council; reaffirming democracy as a universal value; welcoming a new Democracy Fund; eliminating pervasive gender discrimination, including inequalities, violence against women and girls, and impunity. Ratifications during the Summit triggered the entry into force of the *Convention against Corruption;*
- *management reform:* strengthening UN oversight capacity and expanding oversight to additional agencies;
- *environment:* recognizing the serious issue of climate change; acting through the *UN Framework Convention on Climate Change;* assisting vulnerable small island developing states; creating a global early warning system for all natural hazards;
- *international health:* scaling up response to HIV/AIDS, TB and malaria through prevention, care, treatment and support; full implementation of the new International Health Regulations, and support for the WHO Global Outbreak Alert and Response Network;
- *humanitarian assistance:* improving the Central Emergency Response Fund, so that relief is immediate when disasters occur; recognizing the Guiding Principles on Internal Displacement as an important framework for protecting the internally displaced;
- *updating the Charter:* winding up the Trusteeship Council and deleting the *Charter's* anachronistic references to "enemy states".

Many of these commitments have already been accomplished, and many others are well under way.

---

specialized agencies (such as the FAO, ILO, WHO and UNESCO), all of which report to the Council and make recommendations for its substantive sessions.

The year-round work of the Council is carried out in its subsidiary and related bodies. These include:

- eight functional commissions—deliberative bodies whose role is to consider and make recommendations on issues in their areas of responsibility and expertise: the Statistical Commission, Commission on Population and Development, Commission for Social Development, Commission on the Status of Women, Commission on Narcotic Drugs, Commission on Crime Prevention and Criminal Justice, Commission on Science and Technology for Development, Commission on Sustainable Development, as well as the United Nations Forum on Forests;

- five Regional Commissions: Economic Commission for Africa (Addis Ababa, Ethiopia), Economic and Social Commission for Asia and the Pacific (Bangkok, Thailand), Economic Commission for Europe (Geneva), Economic Commission for Latin America and the Caribbean (Santiago, Chile), Economic and Social Commission for Western Asia (Beirut, Lebanon);
- three standing committees: Committee for Programme and Coordination, Committee on Non-Governmental Organizations, Committee on Negotiations with Intergovernmental Agencies;
- expert bodies on such topics as geographical names, public administration, international cooperation in tax matters, and the transport of dangerous goods;
- other bodies, including the Permanent Forum on Indigenous Issues.

Regional commissions

The regional commissions of the United Nations report to ECOSOC, and their secretariats are under the authority of the Secretary-General. Their mandate is to initiate measures that promote the economic development of each region, and strengthen the economic relations of the countries in that region, both among themselves and with other countries of the world. They are funded under the regular UN budget.

Economic Commission for Africa (ECA)

Established in 1958, the Economic Commission for Africa (*www.uneca.org*) encourages the growth of the economic and social sectors of the continent. The ECA promotes policies and strategies to increase economic cooperation and integration among its 53 member countries, particularly in the production, trade, monetary, infrastructure and institutional fields. It focuses on information and analysis on economic and social issues; food security and sustainable development; development management; the information revolution for development; and regional cooperation and integration. The Commission pays special attention to improving the condition of women, enhancing their involvement and decision-making in development, and ensuring that women and gender equity are key elements in national development.

Executive Secretary: Abdoulie Janneh (Gambia)
Address: P.O. Box 3001, Addis Ababa, Ethiopia
Tel.: (251-11) 551-7200; Fax: (251-11) 551-0365; E-mail: *ecainfo@uneca.org*

Economic Commission for Europe (ECE)

Created in 1947, the Economic Commission for Europe (*www.unece.org*) is the forum at which the countries of North America, Europe (including Israel) and Central Asia forge the tools of their economic cooperation. The ECE has 56 member countries. Priority areas include economic analysis, environment and human settlements, statistics, sustainable energy, trade, industry and enterprise development, timber and transport. It pursues its goals primarily through policy analysis and debates, as well as conventions, regulations, standards and harmonization. Such instruments help eliminate obstacles and simplify procedures for trade in the region and with the rest of the world. Others aim at improving the environment. The ECE contributes to their implementation by providing technical assistance, in particular to countries with economies in transition.

Executive Secretary: Ján Kubiš (Slovakia)
Address: Palais des Nations, CH-1211 Geneva 10, Switzerland
Tel.: (41-22) 917-4444; Fax: (41-22) 917-0505; E-mail: *info.ece@unece.org*

Economic Commission for Latin America and the Caribbean (ECLAC)

Established in 1948, the Economic Commission for Latin America and the Caribbean (*www.eclac.org*) coordinates policies for promoting sustainable economic and social development in the region. The 33 countries of Latin America and the Caribbean are members of ECLAC, together with 11 North American, Asian and European nations that have historical, economic and cultural ties with the region. Nine non-independent Caribbean territories are associate members of the Commission. It works especially on agricultural development; economic and social planning; industrial, technological and entrepreneurial development; international trade, regional integration and cooperation; investment and financing; social development and equity; integration of women in development; natural resources and infrastructure; environment and human settlements; statistics; administrative management; and demography and population policies.

Executive Secretary: Alicia Bárcena Ibarra (Mexico)
Address: Avenida Dag Hammarskjöld 3477, Casilla 179-D, Santiago de Chile
Tel.: (56-2) 210-2000; Fax: (56-2) 208-0252; E-mail: *secepal@cepal.org*

Economic and Social Commission for Asia and the Pacific (ESCAP)

Created in 1947, the Economic and Social Commission for Asia and the Pacific (*www.unescap.org*) has a mandate to address the economic and social issues of the region. ESCAP is the only intergovernmental forum for all the countries of Asia and the Pacific. Its 53 member states and 9 associate member states represent some 60 per cent of the world's population. ESCAP gives technical support to governments for social and economic development. This assistance takes the form of advisory services to governments, training, and information-sharing through publications and inter-country networks. The Commission aims to improve socio-economic conditions and help build the foundations of modern society in the region. Four research and training institutions—for agricultural development, agricultural machinery and engineering, statistics, and technology transfer—operate under its auspices. Current priority areas are poverty reduction, globalization and emerging social issues.

Executive Secretary: Noeleen Heyzer (Singapore)
Address: United Nations Building, Rajadamnern Nok Avenue, Bangkok 10200, Thailand
Tel.: (66-2) 288-1234; Fax: (66-2) 288-1000; E-mail: *escap-registry@un.org*

Economic and Social Commission for Western Asia (ESCWA)

Established in 1973, the Economic and Social Commission for Western Asia (*www.escwa.un.org*) facilitates concerted action for the economic and social development of the countries of the region by promoting economic cooperation and integration. Comprised of 13 member states, ESCWA serves as the main general economic and social development forum for Western Asia in the United Nations system. Its focal areas are sustainable development and productivity; social development; economic development and globalization; information and communications technologies; statistics; women's empowerment; and conflict-related issues.

Executive Secretary: Rima Khalaf (Jordan)
Address: P.O. Box 11-8575, Riad el-Solh Square, Beirut, Lebanon
Tel.: (961-1) 98-1301 or (via New York) (1-212) 963-9731; Fax: (961-1) 98-1510

Relations with non-governmental organizations

Non-governmental organizations (NGOs) are seen by the United Nations as important partners and valuable links to civil society. Consulted regularly on matters of mutual concern in policy and programme, NGOs in growing numbers around the world collaborate daily with the UN community to help achieve its objectives. Indeed, under the *Charter of the United Nations*, the Economic and Social Council may consult not only with member states, but also with NGOs concerned with matters within its competence. At the end of 2010, 3,051 NGOs had consultative status with the Council. The Council recognizes that these organizations should have the opportunity to express their views, and that they possess special experience or technical knowledge valuable for its work.

The Council classifies NGOs into three categories: *general* organizations are those concerned with most of the Council's activities; *special* organizations are those offering competence in particular areas corresponding to the concerns of the Council; and *roster* organizations are those that can contribute to the Council when consulted on an ad hoc basis. NGOs with consultative status may send observers to meetings of the Council and its subsidiary bodies and may submit written statements relevant to its work.

Trusteeship Council

The **Trusteeship Council** (*www.un.org/en/mainbodies/trusteeship*) was originally established by the *Charter* to provide international supervision for 11 Trust Territories placed under the administration of seven member states, and to ensure that adequate steps were taken to prepare the Territories for self-government or independence. It carried out this work for forty-nine years. By a 1994 resolution, the Council amended its rules of procedure to drop the obligation to meet annually and agreed to meet as occasion required—by its decision or the decision of its President, or at the request of a majority of its members or the General Assembly or the Security Council. Subsequently, on 1 November 1994, the Trusteeship Council suspended operation following the independence of Palau, the last remaining UN trust territory, on 1 October of that year.

International Court of Justice

The **International Court of Justice** (*www.icj-cij.org*) is the principal judicial organ of the United Nations. Located at The Hague (The Netherlands), it is the only one of the six principal organs not located in New York. The Court is charged with settling legal disputes between states and giving advisory opinions to the United Nations and its specialized agencies. The General Assembly and the Security Council can ask the Court for such an opinion on any legal question. Other organs of the United Nations and the specialized agencies, when authorized by the Assembly, can ask for advisory opinions on legal questions within the scope of their activities. The *Statute* of the Court is an integral part of the *Charter of the United Nations*. The Court is open to all states that are parties to its *Statute*, which includes all members of the United Nations. Only states, however, may be parties in contentious cases before the Court and submit disputes to it. The Court is not open to private persons and entities or other international organizations. A civil tribunal, it does not have criminal jurisdiction to prosecute individuals.

Jurisdiction

The Court's jurisdiction covers all questions referred to it by states and all matters provided for in the *Charter* or in international treaties and conventions. States may bind themselves in advance to accept the jurisdiction of the Court, either by signing a treaty or convention that provides for referral to the Court or by making a declaration to that effect. Such declarations accepting compulsory jurisdiction often contain reservations excluding certain classes of disputes. In accordance with its *Statute*, the Court decides disputes by applying the following: international conventions establishing rules expressly recognized by the contesting states; international custom, as evidence of a general practice accepted as law; the general principles of law recognized by nations; and judicial decisions and the teachings of the most qualified scholars of the various nations.

Membership

The Court is composed of 15 judges elected by the General Assembly and the Security Council, voting independently. They are chosen on the basis of their qualifications. Care is taken to ensure that the principal legal systems of the world are represented in the Court. In 2010, the geographical distribution of judges was as follows: three from Africa, two from Latin America and the Caribbean, three from Asia, five from Western Europe and other states, and two from Eastern Europe—corresponding to the current membership of the Security Council. Although there is no entitlement to membership on the part of any country, the Court has always included judges of the nationality of the permanent members of the Security Council. The Court also has a Chamber for Environmental Matters.

President: Hisashi Owada (Japan)
Registrar: Philippe Couvreur (Belgium)
Headquarters: Peace Palace, Carnegieplein 2, 2517 KJ The Hague, The Netherlands
Tel.: (31-70) 302 23 23; Fax: (31-70) 364 99 28

Secretariat

The **UN Secretariat** (*www.un.org/en/mainbodies/secretariat*)—consisting of staff representing all nationalities working in duty stations around the world—carries out the diverse day-to-day work of the Organization. Calling upon some 44,000 staff members worldwide, the Secretariat services the other principal organs of the United Nations and administers the programmes and policies established by them. At its head is the Secretary-General, who is appointed by the General Assembly on the recommendation of the Security Council for a renewable five-year term.

Previous Secretaries-General

Under the *Charter*, the Secretary-General is appointed by the General Assembly upon the recommendation of the Security Council. Ban Ki-moon's predecessors were: Kofi Annan (Ghana), January 1997 to December 2006; Boutros Boutros-Ghali (Egypt), January 1992 to December 1996; Javier Pérez de Cuéllar (Peru), January 1982 to December 1991; Kurt Waldheim (Austria), January 1972 to December 1981; U Thant (Burma, now Myanmar), November 1961, when he was appointed acting Secretary-General (he was formally appointed Secretary-General in November 1962) to December 1971; Dag Hammarskjöld (Sweden), who served from April 1953 until his death in a plane crash on mission in Africa in September 1961—the only Secretary-General to die in office; and Trygve Lie (Norway), who held office from February 1946 to his resignation in November 1952.

The United Nations, while headquartered in New York, maintains a significant presence in Addis Ababa, Bangkok, Beirut, Geneva, Nairobi, Santiago de Chile and Vienna, and has other offices around the globe. The United Nations Office at Geneva (UNOG) (*www.unog.ch*) is a centre for conference diplomacy and a forum for disarmament and human rights. The United Nations Office at Vienna (UNOV) (*www.unvienna.org*) is the headquarters for activities in the fields of international drug-abuse control, crime prevention and criminal justice, the peaceful uses of outer space and international trade law. The United Nations Office at Nairobi (UNON) (*www.unon.org*) is the headquarters for activities in the fields of environment and human settlements.

The duties carried out by the Secretariat are as wide-ranging and varied as the manifold concerns and activities of the United Nations itself. These extend from administering peacekeeping operations, mediating international disputes and organizing humanitarian relief programmes to surveying economic and social trends, preparing studies on human rights and sustainable development and laying the groundwork for international agreements. Secretariat staff also inform the world—the media, governments, NGOs, research and academic networks and the general public—about the work of the United Nations. They organize international conferences on issues of global significance; interpret speeches and translate documents into the Organization's official languages; and establish clearing-houses of information, making possible international collaboration in all areas of science and technology, as well as cultural, economic and social activities.

As international civil servants, staff members and the Secretary-General answer to the United Nations alone for their activities, not to any member state or other organization, even as they serve the community of nations. They pledge not to seek or receive instructions from any government or outside authority. In turn, under the *Charter*, each member state undertakes to respect the exclusively international character of the responsibilities of the Secretary-General and staff members, and to refrain from seeking to influence them improperly.

Secretary-General

The **Executive Office of the Secretary-General**, comprising the Secretary-General and his senior advisers, establishes general policies and provides overall guidance to the Organization. Equal parts diplomat and advocate, civil servant and chief executive officer, the Secretary-General (*www.un.org/sg*) is a symbol of UN ideals and a spokesperson for the interests of the world's peoples, above all the poor and vulnerable. The eighth Secretary-General, Ban Ki-moon of the Republic of Korea, took office in 2007.

The *Charter* describes the Secretary-General as "chief administrative officer" of the Organization, who acts in that capacity and performs such other functions as are entrusted to him or her by the Security Council, General Assembly, Economic and Social Council and other United Nations organs. The *Charter* also empowers the Secretary-General to bring to the attention of the Security Council any matter which might threaten the maintenance of international peace and security. These guidelines both define the functions and powers of the office and grant it considerable leeway for action. The Secretary-General would fail if he did not take careful account of the needs and concerns of individual member states, but he would also be remiss if he did not uphold the values and moral authority of the United Nations, and speak and act independently for peace—even at the risk of challenging or disagreeing with those same member states.

This creative tension accompanies the Secretary-General throughout each day—in attendance at sessions of United Nations bodies as well as consultations with world leaders, government officials, civil society representatives, members of the private sector and private individuals—and drives the search for solutions to problems that acknowledge the perspective of individual member states in the context of the needs of the world at large. At the same time, the travels of the Secretary-General allow him to keep in touch with the citizens of member states and be informed at first-hand about how issues occupying the international agenda concretely affect the lives of people everywhere.

The Secretary-General issues an annual report on the work of the Organization that appraises its activities and outlines future priorities. One of the most vital roles played by the Secretary-General, however, is the use of his good offices—steps taken publicly and in private, drawing upon his independence, impartiality and integrity—to prevent international disputes from arising, escalating or spreading. Over the years, the good offices of the Secretary-General—including the work of his special and personal representatives and envoys—have proven beneficial in a wide range of situations, including those involving Cyprus, East Timor, Iraq, Libya, the Middle East, Nigeria and Western Sahara.

Each Secretary-General defines his role within the context of his particular time in office. Overall, Ban Ki-moon's priorities include: climate change; disarmament; combating the global financial crisis and poverty; health; peace and security; women's rights and empowerment; protecting all the world's peoples from genocide, war crimes, ethnic cleansing and crimes against humanity; and UN reform. With demands for UN peacekeeping having grown at an unprecedented rate in recent years, the Secretary-General proposed at the beginning of his term basic structural reforms to enable the Organization to keep pace. In response, the General Assembly approved the creation of a Department of Field Support to take over the day-to-day management of peacekeeping operations, leaving the Department of Peacekeeping Operations free to focus on overall strategy, planning and deployment. The Secretary-General has also been particularly outspoken on climate change, describing it as a defining issue of our time, one exemplifying why the formidable cross-border challenges of our

Reform and Revitalization:
Peacekeeping and Disarmament

Already during the first months of his tenure as Secretary-General, in 2007, Ban Ki-moon proposed a number of basic reforms aimed at strengthening the capacity of the United Nations to carry out its mission in the world. These reforms, meant to respond to the growing demand for UN peacekeeping, aimed to improve the ability of the Organization to manage and sustain such operations. Anticipating the need for a considerable increase in the number of personnel in UN peace operations, the Secretary-General favoured the creation of a new Department of Field Support to handle the planning, deployment and support of peacekeeping operations. It was formally established that same year by the General Assembly. Under the new arrangement, DPKO became responsible for strategic oversight and operational political guidance, while DFS was charged with planning, deployment and maintenance. Also in 2007, the Assembly endorsed the Secretary-General's proposal to foster progress on the disarmament agenda—particularly entry into force of the *Comprehensive Nuclear-Test-Ban Treaty* of 1996—by transforming the Department of Disarmament Affairs into the Office for Disarmament Affairs led by the High Representative for Disarmament Affairs, who reports directly to the Secretary-General.

---

times are best addressed collectively through the United Nations. His UNiTE to End Violence against Women campaign aims to prevent and eliminate violence against women and girls in all parts of the world. He has also promoted the establishment of a new hybrid peacekeeping mission in the Sudan and brought the UN disarmament machinery into closer relationship with his office, creating the United Nations Office for Disarmament Affairs and appointing a High Representative for Disarmament Affairs.

Ban Ki-moon's actions build on earlier efforts aimed at helping the UN adapt to a new era in global affairs. For example, the Global Compact, launched in July 2000, is a network-based initiative that brings private corporations together with UN agencies, governments, labour and non-governmental organizations to advance universally recognized principles in the areas of human rights, labour, the struggle against corruption and the environment. By July 2010, it had over 7,700 participants, including more than 5,300 businesses, as well as international and national labour groups and hundreds of civil society organizations in 130 countries, mostly in the developing world. Two major gatherings of world leaders also outlined the direction of the UN in the 21st century. The 2000 Millennium Summit brought forth the *Millennium Declaration* with its series of specific goals and targets—including the Millennium Development Goals (MDGs) (*www.un.org/millenniumgoals*)—in matters of poverty and hunger, universal education, gender equality, child health, maternal health, HIV/AIDS, environmental sustainability, and global partnership. Its five-year review, the 2005 World Summit, voiced bold decisions in the areas of development, security, human rights and UN reform.

Deputy Secretary-General. Louise Fréchette of Canada was appointed as the first Deputy Secretary-General in 1998. She was succeeded in 2006 by Mark Malloch Brown of the United Kingdom and in 2007 by Asha-Rose Migiro of Tanzania.

Departments and Offices

Department of Economic and Social Affairs (DESA)
Under-Secretary-General: Sha Zukang (China)

The mission of the Department of Economic and Social Affairs (*www.un.org/en/ development/desa*) is to promote development for all. DESA's work is far-reaching, covering such issues as poverty reduction, population, gender equality and indigenous rights, macroeconomic policy, development finance, public sector innovation, forest policy, climate change and sustainable development. To this end, DESA

- analyses, generates and compiles a wide range of data and information on development issues;
- brings together the international community at conferences and summits to address economic and social challenges;
- supports the formulation of development policies, global standards and norms;
- monitors and supports the implementation of international agreements;
- assists states in meeting their development challenges through a variety of capacity-development initiatives.

In carrying out its work, DESA engages with a variety of stakeholders around the world, NGOs, civil society, the private sector, research and academic organizations and intergovernmental organizations, as well as partner organizations in the United Nations system.

Department of Field Support (DFS)
Under-Secretary-General: Susana Malcorra (Argentina)

The Department of Field Support (*www.un.org/en/peacekeeping/dfs.shtml*) deals with matters of finance; logistics; information and communication technology (ICT); and human resources and general administration to help missions promote peace and security. Supporting field missions entails such things as providing rations to feed troops, air transport to move people around in places where there are almost no roads or infrastructure, and well-trained staff with the full range of skills required to deliver on Security Council mandates. To do this, DFS liaises with member states and commercial partners. In order to help ensure unity of command in UN peacekeeping, the head of the Department, in a unique structure, reports to and receives direction from the Under-Secretary-General for Peacekeeping Operations.

Department for General Assembly and Conference Management (DGACM)
Under-Secretary-General: S. Muhammad Shaaban (Egypt)

The Department for General Assembly and Conference Management (*www.un.org/ depts/DGACM*) provides technical and secretariat support services to the General Assembly, the Security Council, the Economic and Social Council, and their committees and other subsidiary bodies, as well as to conferences held away from UN Headquarters. It is responsible for processing and issuing at Headquarters all official documents in the official languages of the Organization, and providing interpretation services for these languages to intergovernmental meetings. In addition, it produces the official records of the United Nations, including summary and verbatim records of meetings. Responsible for UN conference-management policies, the Under-Secretary-General for DGACM advises the President of the General Assembly on all matters relating to the work of the General Assembly.

Department of Management (DM)
Under-Secretary-General: Angela Kane (Germany)

The Department of Management (*www.un.org/en/hq/dm*) provides strategic policy guidance and support to all entities of the Secretariat in three management areas: finance, human resources and support services. These fall under the purview of the Offices of Programme Planning, Budget and Accounts; Human Resources Management; and Central Support Services, respectively. DM is responsible for formulating and implementing improved management policies in the Secretariat; the management and training of staff; and programme planning, budgetary, financial and human resources management along with technological innovations. It also provides technical servicing for the General Assembly's Fifth (Administrative and Budgetary) Committee, as well as servicing for the Committee for Programme and Coordination. The head of the Department provides policy guidance, coordination and direction for the preparation of UN budgets; represents the Secretary-General on matters relating to management; monitors emerging management issues; and ensures the efficient implementation of the Organization's internal system of justice.

Department of Political Affairs (DPA)
Under-Secretary-General: B. Lynn Pascoe (United States)

The Department of Political Affairs (*www.un.org/depts/dpa*) plays a central role in the efforts of the United Nations to prevent and resolve conflict around the world and to consolidate peace in the aftermath of war. To that end, DPA

- monitors, analyses and assesses political developments throughout the world;
- identifies potential or actual conflicts in whose control and resolution the United Nations could play a useful role;
- recommends to the Secretary-General appropriate action in such cases and executes the approved policy;
- assists the Secretary-General in carrying out political activities decided by him, the General Assembly and the Security Council in the areas of preventive diplomacy, peacemaking, peacekeeping and peacebuilding;
- advises the Secretary-General on requests for electoral assistance received from member states and coordinates programmes established in response to such requests;
- advises and supports the Secretary-General in the political aspects of his relations with member states;
- services the Security Council and its subsidiary bodies, as well as the Committee on the Exercise of the Inalienable Rights of the Palestinian People and the Special Committee of 24 on Decolonization.

The head of the Department also undertakes consultations and negotiations relating to peaceful settlement of disputes, and is the focal point for UN electoral assistance activities.

Department of Public Information (DPI)
Under-Secretary-General: Kiyo Akasaka (Japan)

The Department of Public Information raises global awareness of the activities and concerns of the United Nations and promotes understanding of its work. DPI uses outreach programmes, information campaigns, news and feature services, radio and television programmes, press releases, publications, documentary videos and special events to communicate the Organization's messages. DPI spearheads the UN's international campaigns; engages prominent personalities as UN Messengers of Peace; and organizes exhibits, concerts, seminars and other events to mark occasions of international importance. It also provides library and knowledge-sharing services. In addition to its staff at UN Headquarters, DPI has 63 UN information centres, or UNICs, worldwide (*http://unic.un.org*) and a regional information centre (UNRIC) in Brussels (*www.unric.un.org*).

The Department consists of three divisions. Its Strategic Communications Division develops communication strategies and campaigns to promote United Nations priorities. The News and Media Division produces and distributes UN news and information to the media, including daily press briefings and statements by the Office of the Spokesperson for the Secretary-General, the UN websites, radio broadcasts and live TV feeds. The Outreach Division, which includes the Dag Hammarskjöld Library, publishes books, notably the *Yearbook of the United Nations*, and periodicals such as the *UN Chronicle* and *Africa Renewal*; works with NGOs and educational institutions; organizes special events and exhibitions on priority issues; and offers an annual training programme for journalists from developing countries. It also develops partnerships with the private and public sector to advance UN goals.

Department of Peacekeeping Operations (DPKO)
Under-Secretary-General: Alain Le Roy (France)

The Department of Peacekeeping Operations (*www.un.org/en/peacekeeping*) is responsible for assisting member states and the Secretary-General in their efforts to maintain, achieve and sustain international peace and security. It does this by planning, preparing and conducting United Nations peacekeeping operations, in accordance with mandates provided by member states. To this end, DPKO

- undertakes contingency planning for possible new peacekeeping operations;
- secures, through negotiations with member states, the civilian, military and police personnel, the military units, and the equipment and services required to accomplish the mandate;
- provides political and executive guidance, direction and support to peacekeeping operations;
- maintains contact with parties to conflicts and with members of the Security Council on the implementation of Council resolutions;
- manages integrated operational teams to direct and supervise all peacekeeping operations;
- advises the Security Council and member states on key peacekeeping issues, including security sector reform, the rule of law, and the disarmament, demobilization and reintegration of former combatants;
- analyses emerging policy questions and best practices related to peacekeeping, and formulates policies, procedures and general peacekeeping doctrine;
- coordinates all UN activities related to landmines, and develops and supports mine-action programmes in peacekeeping and emergency situations.

The head of the Department directs peacekeeping operations on behalf of the Secretary-General; formulates policies and guidelines for operations; and advises the Secretary-General on all matters relating to peacekeeping and mine action.

Department of Safety and Security (DSS)
Under-Secretary-General: Gregory B. Starr (United States)

The Department of Safety and Security (*http://dss.un.org/public*) provides leadership, operational support and oversight of the security management system for the United Nations, ensuring the maximum security for staff and their dependants as well as enabling the safest and most efficient conduct of its programmes and activities throughout the world. Responsible for the safety of UN staff and consultants around the world, DSS was established by the General Assembly in 2005 to meet the need for a unified and strengthened security management system. The Department brings together under a single structure three previously separate entities: the Office of the UN Security Coordinator, the security and safety services at each headquarters location, and the civilian security component of the Department of Peacekeeping Operations.

Office for the Coordination of Humanitarian Affairs (OCHA)
Under-Secretary-General for Humanitarian Affairs and Emergency Relief Coordinator: Valerie Amos (United Kingdom)

The Office for the Coordination of Humanitarian Affairs (*http://ochaonline.un.org*) mobilizes and coordinates humanitarian action in partnership with national and international actors to alleviate human suffering in disasters and emergencies. Through its network of field offices, humanitarian coordinators and country teams, OCHA works to ensure the coherence of relief efforts. It supports the efforts of its humanitarian coordinators and of UN agencies that deliver assistance through needs assessments, contingency planning and the formulation of humanitarian programmes. OCHA also advocates for the rights of people in need (notably with political organs such as the Security Council), promotes preparedness and prevention as well as policy development, and facilitates the implementation of sustainable solutions to humanitarian problems.

The Emergency Relief Coordinator chairs the Inter-Agency Standing Committee (IASC), an umbrella organization that comprises all major humanitarian actors—including the Red Cross and Red Crescent Movement and consortia of other NGOs. By developing common policies, guidelines and standards, the Committee ensures a coherent interagency response to complex emergencies and natural and environmental disasters.

Office of the United Nations High Commissioner for Human Rights (OHCHR)
High Commissioner: Navanethem Pillay (South Africa)

The United Nations High Commissioner for Human Rights is the official with principal responsibility for UN human rights activities and is charged with promoting and protecting civil, cultural, economic, political and social rights for all. The Office of the High Commissioner for Human Rights (*www.ohchr.org*) prepares reports and undertakes research at the request of the General Assembly and other policy-making bodies. It cooperates with governments and international, regional and non-governmental organizations. It acts as the secretariat for the meetings of UN human rights bodies. OHCHR's 2010–2011 budget requirement was $399.3 million—$141.5 million from the UN regular budget and $257.8 million from voluntary contributions. OHCHR, with some 960 staff, is organized into four divisions:

- The Human Rights Treaties Division supports nine human rights treaty bodies and the UN Voluntary Fund for Victims of Torture. It assists in the preparation and submission of documents for review by these independent expert bodies, processes communications submitted to them under optional procedures, follows-up on recommendations and decisions taken at treaty-body meetings, and helps build national capacities to implement these recommendations. It also supports field visits by one of the treaty bodies, the Subcommittee on Prevention of Torture.
- The Human Rights Council and Special Procedures Division supports the Human Rights Council, the Council's Universal Periodic Review process and its fact-finding and investigatory mechanisms—including special rapporteurs, special representatives and thematic working groups—with a view to documenting human rights violations worldwide, enhancing the protection of victims, and promoting their rights.
- The Research and Right to Development Division is responsible for promoting and protecting the right to development. It conducts research, supports the Working Group on the Right to Development, and seeks to incorporate human rights in development activities. It services the UN Voluntary Trust Fund on Contemporary Forms of Slavery and the UN Voluntary Fund for Indigenous Populations.
- The Field Operations and Technical Cooperation Division develops, implements, monitors and evaluates advisory services and technical-assistance projects at the request of governments. It lends support to fact-finding missions and investigations.

Office of Internal Oversight Services (OIOS)
Under-Secretary-General: Carman Lapointe-Young (Canada)

The Office of Internal Oversight Services (*www.un.org/depts/oios*) provides independent, professional and timely internal audit, monitoring, inspection, evaluation and investigation services. It promotes responsible administration of resources, a culture of accountability and transparency, and improved programme performance. OIOS assists the Organization and member states in protecting UN assets and ensuring the compliance of programme activities with regulations, rules and policies, as well as the more efficient and effective delivery of UN activities; and detecting fraud, waste, abuse, malfeasance or mismanagement. The Under-Secretary-General is appointed by the Secretary-General and approved by the General Assembly for one five-year term without possibility of renewal.

Office of Legal Affairs (OLA)
Under-Secretary-General: Patricia O'Brien (Ireland)

The Office of Legal Affairs (*http://untreaty.un.org/ola*) is the central legal service of the Organization. It also contributes to the progressive development and codification of international public and trade law. Among its chief responsbilities, OLA

- provides legal advice to the Secretary-General, Secretariat departments and offices and principal and subsidiary organs of the United Nations in the field of public and private international law;
- performs substantive and secretariat functions for legal organs involved in public international law, the law of the sea and international trade law; and

- carries out the functions conferred on the Secretary-General as depositary of multilateral treaties.

OLA also

- deals with legal questions relating to international peace and security; the status, privileges and immunities of the United Nations; and the credentials and representations of member states;
- prepares drafts of international conventions, agreements, rules of procedure of United Nations organs and conferences, and other legal instruments; and
- provides legal services and advice on issues of international private and administrative law and on UN resolutions and regulations.

Office of the Special Adviser on Africa (OSAA)
Special Adviser: Cheick Sidi Diarra (Mali)

The Office of the Special Adviser on Africa (*www.un.org/africa/osaa*) was established in 2003. OSAA enhances international support for Africa's development and security through its advocacy and analytical work; assists the Secretary General in improving coherence and coordination of the UN system support to Africa; and facilitates inter-governmental deliberations on Africa at the global level, in particular relating to the New Partnership for Africa's Development (NEPAD). OSAA takes the lead in the preparation of Africa-related reports and inputs on NEPAD. The Office also convenes an inter-departmental Task Force on African Affairs to improve coherence in UN support to Africa.

Office of the Special Representative of the Secretary-General for Children and Armed Conflict (SRSG/CAAC)
Special Representative: Radhika Coomaraswamy (Sri Lanka)

The Office of the Special Representative for Children and Armed Conflict (*www. un.org/children/conflict*) promotes and protects the rights of all children affected by armed conflict. The Special Representative serves as a moral voice and independent advocate for the protection and well-being of boys and girls affected by armed conflict; works with partners to propose ideas and approaches that enhance protection; advocates, raises awareness and gives prominence to issues of rights and protection; and undertakes humanitarian and diplomatic initiatives to facilitate the work of those acting on the ground for the sake of children in armed conflict.

Office of the High Representative for the Least Developed Countries, Landlocked Developing Countries and Small Island Developing States (UN-OHRLLS)
Under-Secretary-General and High Representative for the Least Developed Countries, Landlocked Developing Countries and Small Island Developing States: Cheick Sidi Diarra (Mali)

UN-OHRLLS (*www.un.org/ohrlls*) was established by the General Assembly in 2001 to help mobilize international support for implementation of the *Brussels Declaration* and Programme of Action for the Least Developed Countries for the Decade 2001–2010. It assists the Secretary-General in ensuring mobilization and coordination of international support for the effective implementation of the Brussels Programme of Action and related international commitments. The Office also works to ensure implementation of the 1994 Barbados Programme of Action for the Sustainable Development of Small Island Developing States and the 2005 Mauritius

Strategy for carrying out the Barbados Programme. The Office facilitates coordination within the UN system with regard to these programmes and supports the Economic and Social Council and the General Assembly in assessing progress made. It also promotes global awareness of issues affecting these countries in partnership with UN bodies, civil society, the media, academia and foundations.

Office for Disarmament Affairs (UNODA)
High Representative for Disarmament: Sergio de Queiroz Duarte (Brazil)

Part of the Secretary-General's efforts to bring new momentum into the United Nations disarmament agenda, the Office for Disarmament Affairs (*www.un.org/ disarmament*) works towards nuclear disarmament and non-proliferation along with the strengthening of disarmament regimes with respect to other weapons of mass destruction, including chemical and biological weapons. UNODA also promotes disarmament in the area of conventional weapons, especially action against illicit trade in small arms—weapons of choice in many contemporary conflicts. Its purview includes:

- arms collection and stockpile management programmes;
- transparency in military matters, including the UN Register of Conventional Arms and standardized reporting on military expenditures;
- the disarmament and demobilization of former combatants and their reintegration into civil society; and
- restrictions on and eventual disarmament of anti-personnel landmines.

UNODA provides substantive and organizational support for norm-setting in disarmament through the work of the General Assembly and its First Committee, the Disarmament Commission, the Conference on Disarmament and other bodies. It encourages regional disarmament efforts, including nuclear-weapon-free zones and regional and subregional transparency regimes. UNODA also supports educational initiatives on UN disarmament efforts.

Budget

The regular budget of the United Nations is approved by the General Assembly for a two-year period. The budget is initially submitted by the Secretary-General and then reviewed by the Advisory Committee on Administrative and Budgetary Questions. The Advisory Committee consists of 16 experts, nominated by their governments and elected by the General Assembly, who serve in their personal capacity. Programmatic aspects of the budget are reviewed by the Committee for Programme and Coordination, which is made up of 34 experts who are elected by the General Assembly and represent the views of their governments. The budget reflects the main priorities of the Organization, as set out in its strategic framework for each biennium. During the biennium, the approved budget can be adjusted by the General Assembly to reflect changing circumstances.

The main source of funds for the budget lies in the contributions of member states. These are assessed on a scale approved by the General Assembly on the recommendation of the Committee on Contributions, made up of 18 experts serving in their personal capacity and selected by the Assembly on the recommendation of its Administrative and Budgetary (Fifth) Committee. The scale is based on the capacity of countries to pay. This is determined by considering their relative shares of total gross national product, adjusted to take into account a number of factors, including per capita income. The Committee reviews the scale every three years in light of the latest national income statistics in order to ensure that assessments are fair and accurate. There is a fixed maximum of 22 per cent of the budget for any one contributor.

Budget of the United Nations for the biennium 2010–2011

	Main categories of expenditure	US dollars
1.	Overall policymaking, direction and coordination	777,439,800
2.	Political affairs	1,248,438,400
3.	International justice and law	96,855,200
4.	International cooperation for development	434,311,700
5.	Regional cooperation for development	526,456,100
6.	Human rights and humanitarian affairs	301,937,600
7.	Public information	186,707,400
8.	Common support services	577,969,100
9.	Internal oversight	39,438,800
10.	Jointly financed administrative activities and special expenses	125,248,200
11.	Capital expenditures	61,265,500
12.	Safety and security	239,288,500
13.	Development account	23,651,300
14.	Staff assessment	517,021,500
	Total:	**5,156,029,100**

The regular budget approved for the biennium 2010–2011 amounts to $5.156 billion, including provision for special political missions expected to be extended or approved during the course of the biennium. The budget for such missions—mandated by the Security Council and/or the General Assembly—has evolved from $100.9 million in 2000 to $1 billion in 2010–2011. The budget also covers the costs of UN programmes in areas such as development, public information, human rights and humanitarian affairs. The regular budget does not cover peacekeeping operations or international tribunals, which have their own separate budgets. Member states are also separately assessed for the costs of the international tribunals and peacekeeping operations.

The financial position of the regular budget of the Organization on 5 October 2010 represented an improvement compared to the previous year. Unpaid assessed contributions, at $787 million, were $43 million lower than a year earlier. At the same time, the budget for 2010–2011 entailed an increase of less than one per cent over against the appropriations for 2008–2009.

Global approved peacekeeping resources have grown from $2.8 billion in 2001–2002 to $7.3 billion in 2010–2011, although the latter amount is less overall than the $8 billion approved budget for 2009–2010. This growth has resulted mainly from an almost 200 per cent increase in military and police staff, from 38,100 in 2001–2002 to approximately 111,300 in 2010–2011. During the same period, the number of civilian staff on mission increased only 67 per cent, from approximately 16,800 to 28,100. The UN mission in the Democratic Republic of the Congo and the hybrid United Nations-African Union mission in Darfur consume much of the 2010–2011 peacekeeping budget: $3.2 billion. (Noteworthy is the fact that the total amount spent on UN peacekeeping annually represents less than 1 per cent of world military spending of more than $1 trillion per year.)

Peacekeeping budgets are approved by the General Assembly for a one-year period beginning on 1 July. The Assembly apportions the costs based on a special scale of assessment applicable to peacekeeping. This scale takes into account the relative economic wealth of member states, with the permanent members of the Security Council paying a larger share because of their special responsibility for the maintenance of international peace and security. Non-payment of assessed contributions delays reimbursements to those member states that contribute troops, equipment and logistical support. Outstanding assessed contributions for peacekeeping operations in October 2010 totalled $3.2 billion. (That same month, assessed contributions in the amount of $50 million were outstanding for the international tribunals, as well as some $84 million towards the much-needed renovation of UN Headquarters.)

United Nations funds, offices and programmes—among them the United Nations Children's Fund (UNICEF), the United Nations High Commissioner for Refugees (UNHCR) and the United Nations Development Programme (UNDP)—have separate budgets as well. The bulk of their resources is provided by governments on a voluntary basis, but a portion also comes from individuals and institutions. Specialized agencies of the United Nations—like UNESCO and the WHO—also have separate budgets supplemented through voluntary state contributions.

UN system

The United Nations system (*www.unsystem.org*) consists of the United Nations family of organizations. It includes the Secretariat, the United Nations funds and programmes, the specialized agencies and other related organizations. The funds, offices and programmes are subsidiary bodies of the General Assembly. The specialized agencies are linked to the United Nations through individual agreements and report to the Economic and Social Council and/or the Assembly. The related organizations—including IAEA and the World Trade Organization—address particular areas of activity and have their own legislative bodies and budgets. Together, the family members of the UN system address all areas of cultural, economic, scientific and social endeavour.

The **United Nations System Chief Executives Board for Coordination (CEB)** (*www.unsystemceb.org*) is the UN system's highest coordinating mechanism. Chaired by the Secretary-General, its members are the leaders of the main parts of the UN system. The CEB aims to coordinate UN action in the pursuit of the common goals of member states. It meets twice a year, and is supported in its work by a high-level committee on programmes and a high-level committee on management. Its 28 members include the United Nations, FAO, IAEA, ICAO, IFAD, ILO, IMF, IMO, ITU, UNCTAD, UNDP, UNEP, UNESCO, UNFPA, UN-HABITAT, UNHCR, UNICEF, UNIDO, UNODC, UNRWA, UNWTO, UPU, WFP, WHO, WIPO, WMO, World Bank and WTO.

Programmes and funds, research and training institutes, and other entities

United Nations Conference on Trade and Development (UNCTAD)

Established in 1964 as a permanent intergovernmental body and subsidiary of the General Assembly, the United Nations Conference on Trade and Development (*www.unctad.org*) is the UN focal point for the integrated treatment of trade and

The United Nations and the Nobel Peace Prize

The United Nations family and its associates have been awarded the Nobel Peace Prize numerous times in recognition of their contributions to the cause of world peace. UN-related Nobel Peace Prize laureates since the establishment of the Organization include:

- Cordell Hull—United States Secretary of State instrumental in establishing the United Nations (1945)
- John Boyd Orr—founding Director-General of the Food and Agriculture Organization of the United Nations (1949)
- Ralph Bunche—UN Trusteeship Director and principal secretary of the UN Palestine Commission, leader of mediation efforts in the Middle East (1950)
- Léon Jouhaux—a founder of the International Labour Organization (1951)
- Office of the United Nations High Commissioner for Refugees (1954)
- Lester Bowles Pearson—General Assembly President in 1952 honoured for trying to end the Suez conflict and solve the Middle East question through the UN (1957)
- Secretary-General Dag Hammarskjöld—one of only two posthumous awards (1961)
- United Nations Children's Fund (1965)
- International Labour Organization (1969)
- Sean MacBride—UN Commissioner for Namibia and promoter of human rights (1974)
- Office of the United Nations High Commissioner for Refugees (1981)
- United Nations Peacekeeping Forces (1988)
- United Nations and Secretary-General Kofi A. Annan (2001)
- International Atomic Energy Agency and its Director-General Mohamed ElBaradei (2005)
- Intergovernmental Panel on Climate Change (IPCC) and former United States Vice President Albert Arnold (Al) Gore, Jr. (2007)

This list does not include the many Nobel laureates who have worked closely with the United Nations or at common purpose with it in making their contribution to peace.

---

development and related issues of finance, investment, technology and sustainable development. UNCTAD's main goal is to help developing countries and transition economies use trade and investment as an engine for development, poverty reduction and integration into the world economy. It works in three main areas: research and analysis; consensus-building through intergovernmental deliberations; and technical cooperation projects carried out with various partners. It also contributes to international debate on emerging issues related to developing countries and the world economy through major reports, policy briefs and contributions to international meetings.

UNCTAD's highest decision-making body is its ministerial conference, at which the organization's 193 member states debate international economic issues and set UNCTAD's mandate. The most recent—twelfth—conference in 2008 placed particular emphasis on commodity markets and the need to highlight links between international commodity trade and national development, particularly pov-

A World of Support for the United Nations

The entire UN family benefits from the energy and enthusiasm of grassroots organizations and movements that help give the high ideals of the *Charter* practical form. The United Nations also benefits from its partnership with various members of civil society, including the business and labour communities and international charitable organizations, as well as the support of prominent figures in all fields of endeavour. From the children who "Trick-or-Treat for UNICEF" to the educational activities of some 5,000 UNESCO Clubs in more than 120 countries and thousands of NGOs on the ground, people everywhere are engaged in helping the United Nations make this world a better place:

- *United Nations Associations.* Inspired by the opening words of the *Charter*, "We the Peoples ...", a 'People's Movement for the United Nations' was born in 1946, one year after the organization itself. UN Associations in over 100 member states bring the power and energy of hundreds of thousands of individuals to bear in a global network of support for the aims and purposes of the *Charter*.

- *Non-governmental organizations.* The World Federation of UN Associations is only one of thousands of NGOs that have enlisted in the cause of the United Nations—including some 3,294 in consultative status with the Economic and Social Council and 1,549 with strong information programmes that work in partnership with the UN Department of Public Information. NGOs are active across the broad spectrum of UN issues, including peacebuilding, disarmament, outer space affairs, AIDS, malaria prevention, agriculture, food aid, sustainable development, information and communication technologies, disaster reduction, desertification, human rights, the global drug problem, and the environment—to name but a few.

- *The Global Compact.* Over 7,700 participants, including more than 5,300 businesses, as well as international and national labour groups and hundreds of civil society organizations in 130 countries, work with the United Nations to advance universally recognized principles in the areas of human rights, labour and the environment.

- *Public Charities.* The United Nations Foundation is among a number of public charities which support the work of the United Nations. It was created in 1998 with an historic $1 billion gift in support of UN causes and activities by entrepreneur/philanthropist Ted Turner—named an Advocate for the Millennium Development Goals by Ban Ki-moon in 2010. The UN Fund for International Partnerships (UNFIP) acts within the United Nations to coordinate, channel and monitor the Foundation's contributions.

---

erty reduction. Based in Geneva, UNCTAD has 510 staff members and an annual regular budget of approximately $70 million. Its technical cooperation activities, financed from extra-budgetary resources, amount to some $36 million, with more than 250 technical assistance projects ongoing in about 100 countries. UNCTAD's main publications are: the *Trade and Development Report, World Investment Report, Economic Development in Africa Report, Least Developed Countries Report, UNCTAD Handbook of Statistics, Information Economy Report,* and *Review of Maritime Transport.*

Secretary-General: Supachai Panitchpakdi (Thailand)
Headquarters: Palais des Nations, CH-1211 Geneva 10, Switzerland
Tel.: (41-22) 917-5809; Fax: (41-22) 917-0051; E-mail: *info@unctad.org*

International Trade Centre (ITC)

The International Trade Centre (*www.intracen.org*) is the joint agency of the World Trade Organization and the United Nations. As the development partner for small business export success, the ITC helps developing and transition countries achieve sustainable development through exports. The ITC has two mutually reinforcing functions. Affiliation with the WTO vests the ITC with the role of helping its clients benefit from the opportunities created by the WTO framework. As a UN development organization, the ITC's role is to promote the fulfilment of the Millennium Development Goals.

The ITC budget has two parts: the regular budget, which is provided equally by the WTO and UNCTAD, and extrabudgetary funds, which are provided by donors as voluntary contributions. Measured by extrabudgetary expenditure, 2009 saw an increase in net project expenditure from $33.3 million to $34.6 million, focusing on regionally structured solutions and global public goods. The organization's priority is to meet the needs of some 101 countries categorized as least developed countries, landlocked developing countries, small island developing states and sub-Saharan Africa. Total expenditure in these areas was $15.2 million in 2009. The ITC has a headquarters staff of around 280, as well as some 800 consultants in the field.

Executive Director: Patricia R. Francis (Jamaica)
Headquarters: Palais des Nations, CH-1211 Geneva 10, Switzerland
Tel.: (41-22) 730-0111; Fax: (41-22) 733-4439; E-mail: *itcreg@intracen.org*

United Nations Development Programme (UNDP)

The United Nations Development Programme (*www.undp.org*) leads the UN's global development network. With activities in more than 160 countries, UNDP works throughout the developing world helping countries meet their development goals. Its mandate is to work with countries to reduce poverty, promote democratic governance, prevent and recover from crises, protect the environment and combat climate change. The UNDP network seeks to ensure that developing countries have access to resources and knowledge to meet the Millennium Development Goals.

UNDP is governed by a 36-member Executive Board, representing both developing and developed countries. Its flagship publication is the annual *Human Development Report*, which focuses on key development issues and provides measurement tools, innovative analysis and policy proposals. UNDP is funded entirely by voluntary contributions from member states; its budget is approximately $5 billion per annum.

Administrator: Helen Clark (New Zealand)
Headquarters: 1 UN Plaza, New York, NY 10017, USA
Tel.: (1-212) 906-5000; Fax: (1-212) 906-5364

United Nations Volunteers (UNV)

The United Nations Volunteers programme (*www.unv.org*) is the volunteer arm of the UN system, supporting peace, relief and development initiatives in more than 130 countries. Created by the General Assembly in 1970, it is administered by UNDP, reports to the UNDP/United Nations Population Fund (UNFPA) Executive Board and works through UNDP country offices. As a volunteer-based programme, UNV is unique both within the United Nations family and in its scale as an international undertaking. Assisting in sectoral and community-based development projects, humanitarian aid activities, the protection of refugees and the promotion of human rights and democracy, UNV mobilizes more than 7,500 volunteers every year. Some 80 per cent of UNV volunteers come from developing countries, and more than 30 per cent volunteer in their own countries. The UNV budget increased to $427 million in 2008–2009, compared to $367 million in the previous biennium. Its funding comes from UNDP, partner UN agencies and donor contributions to the UNV Special Voluntary Fund.

Executive Coordinator: Flavia Pansieri (Italy)
Headquarters: Hermann-Ehlers-Str. 10, 53113 Bonn, Germany
Tel.: (49-228) 815-2000; Fax: (49-228) 815-2001; E-mail: *information@unv.org*

United Nations Capital Development Fund (UNCDF)

The United Nations Capital Development Fund (*www.uncdf.org*) is the UN's capital investment agency for the world's 49 least developed countries. It creates new opportunities for poor people and their communities by increasing access to microfinance and investment capital. UNCDF focuses on Africa and the poorest countries of Asia, with a special commitment to countries emerging from conflict or crisis. It provides seed capital—grants and loans—and technical support to help microfinance institutions reach more poor households and small businesses. It also helps local governments finance the capital investments—water systems, feeder roads, schools, irrigation schemes—that improve the lives of the poor. Over 50 per cent of the clients of UNCDF-supported microfinance institutions are women. All UNCDF support is provided via national systems, in accordance with the 2005 *Paris Declaration* concerning aid. UNCDF programmes are designed to catalyze larger investment flows from the private sector, development partners and national governments. Established by the General Assembly in 1966 and headquartered in New York, UNCDF is an autonomous UN organization affiliated with UNDP. In 2009 total income of the Fund was about $40 million. Fund balances at the end of the year were approximately $53 million. UNCDF employs 150 staff.

Executive Secretary: David Morrison (Canada)
Headquarters: 2 UN Plaza, New York, NY 10017, USA
Tel.: (1-212) 906-6565; Fax: (1-212) 906-6479; E-mail: *info@uncdf.org*

United Nations Environment Programme (UNEP)

Founded in 1972, the United Nations Environment Programme (*www.unep.org*) provides leadership and encourages partnerships in caring for the environment—enabling nations and peoples to improve their quality of life without compromising that of future generations. As the principal UN body in the field of the environment, UNEP sets the global environmental agenda, promotes implementation of the environmental dimension of sustainable development in the UN system, and serves as an authoritative advocate of the global environment.

During 2010–2013, UNEP is focusing on six priorities:

- climate change: strengthening the ability of countries—in particular developing countries—to integrate climate change responses into national development processes;

- ecosystem management: ensuring that countries manage land, water and living resources holistically in a manner conducive to conservation and sustainable use;

- environmental governance: ensuring that environmental governance and interactions at the country, regional and global levels are strengthened to address environmental priorities;
- harmful substances and hazardous waste: minimizing their impact on the environment and people;
- disasters and conflicts: minimizing threats to human well-being from the environmental causes and consequences of natural and man-made disasters;
- resource efficiency: ensuring that natural resources are produced, processed and consumed in a more environmentally sustainable way.

UNEP's mandate and focus are determined by its Governing Council, a body of 58 government representatives elected by the General Assembly taking into account equitable regional representation. Its 2010–2011 approved budget is $495 million. UNEP's main voluntary funding mechanism is the Environment Fund. Additional funds are provided by the UN regular budget as well as those mobilized by UNEP in the form of trust funds and earmarked contributions. UNEP has a global staff of approximately 1,000.

Executive Director: Achim Steiner (Germany)
Headquarters: United Nations Avenue, Gigiri, P.O. Box 30552, 00100, Nairobi, Kenya
Tel.: (254-20) 762-1234; Fax: (254-20) 762-4489, 4490; E-mail: *unepinfo@unep.org*

United Nations Population Fund (UNFPA)

Established in 1969 at the initiative of the General Assembly, the United Nations Population Fund (*www.unfpa.org*) is the largest internationally funded source of population assistance to developing countries and those with economies in transition. It assists countries in improving reproductive health and family planning services on the basis of individual choice, as well as in formulating population policies for sustainable development. It is a subsidiary organ of the General Assembly and has the same Executive Board as UNDP. With headquarters in New York and a global network of 129 offices, UNEP supported the development priorities of 155 countries, territories and areas in 2009. Income totalled $783.1 million, including $469.4 million in voluntary contributions from governments and private donors. That same year, UNFPA provided $160.9 million in assistance for reproductive health—including safe motherhood, family planning and sexual health—to refine approaches to adolescent reproductive health, reduce maternal disabilities such as obstetric fistula, address HIV/AIDS, and give assistance in emergencies. UNFPA devoted $94.6 million to population and development strategies. Also in 2009, $46.3 million was provided for gender equality and women's empowerment. UNFPA has decentralized its programmes to bring staff closer to the people it serves. Over 80 per cent of UNFPA's 1,119 staff members work in regional, subregional or country offices.

Executive Director: Babatunde Osotimehin (Nigeria)
Headquarters: 220 East 42nd Street, New York, NY 10017, USA
Tel.: (1-212) 297-5000

United Nations Human Settlements Programme (UN-HABITAT)

The United Nations Human Settlements Programme (*www.unhabitat.org*), established in 1978, promotes sustainable human settlements development through advocacy, policy formulation, capacity-building, knowledge creation and the strengthening of partnerships between governments and civil society. UN-HABITAT is responsible for helping the world meet the Millennium Development Goal of improving the lives of at least 100 million slum dwellers by 2020, and reducing by half those without sustainable access to safe drinking water and basic sanitation. The Programme works in partnership with other agencies, governments, local authorities, NGOs and the private sector. Its technical programmes and projects focus on slum upgrading, urban poverty reduction, post-disaster reconstruction, the provision of urban water and sanitation and the mobilization of domestic financial resources for shelter delivery.

UN-HABITAT is governed by a 58-member Governing Council. Expenditures of $356.0 million were approved for 2010–2011, $310.9 million (88 per cent) of which being reserved for programme activities, with the remaining $45.1 million going for support activities and policy-making organs. The Programme produces two flagship publications: the *Global Report on Human Settlements*, a complete review of human settlements conditions worldwide, and the *State of the World's Cities*.

Executive Director: Joan Clos (Spain)
Headquarters: P.O. Box 30030, Nairobi 00100, Kenya
Tel.: (254-20) 762-3120; Fax: (254-20) 762-3477; E-mail: *infohabitat@unhabitat.org*

Office of the United Nations High Commissioner for Refugees (UNHCR)

The Office of the United Nations High Commissioner for Refugees (*www.unhcr.org*)—set up in 1951 to help more than 1 million people still uprooted after the Second World War—was initially given a three-year mandate later prolonged by successive five-year terms until 2003, when the General Assembly extended the mandate "until the refugee problem is solved". UNHCR provides international protection to refugees, guaranteeing respect for their basic human rights, including the ability to seek asylum, and to ensure that no person is returned involuntarily to a country where he or she has reason to fear persecution. It monitors government compliance with international law, and provides emergency and material assistance to those under its care, collaborating with many partners. It seeks long-term solutions for refugees through voluntary repatriation, integration in countries where they first sought asylum, or resettlement in third countries. By the end of 2010, UNHCR was looking after some 36.5 million people, including refugees, returnees, people displaced within their own countries, and stateless people.

Some 86.7 per cent of UNHCR staff, including UN Volunteers, are field-based. There are currently around 6,800 staff members, including 900 at the Geneva Headquarters, working in more than 118 countries. The Office has been recognized with two Nobel Peace Prizes, in 1954 and in 1981. UNHCR works within the UN inter-agency framework and cooperates with a wide range of external partners, including intergovernmental and voluntary organizations, as well as governments. Its Executive Committee is composed of 79 member states. UNHCR is funded almost entirely by voluntary contributions, with 93.5 per cent coming from governments and intergovernmental organizations. A further 3.5 per cent comes from pooled funding mechanisms, including the UN Central Emergency Response Fund, and the remaining 3 per cent from the private sector. In addition, the Office receives a limited subsidy from the UN regular budget for administrative costs. UNHCR also accepts 'in-kind' contributions, including relief items such as tents, medicine, trucks and air transport. Its budget for 2010 was $3.2 billion.

High Commissioner: António Guterres (Portugal)
Headquarters: Case Postale 2500, CH-1211 Geneva 2, Switzerland
Tel.: (41-22) 739-8111

United Nations Children's Fund (UNICEF)

United Nations Children's Fund (*www.unicef.org*) was created in 1946 to provide emergency food and health care to children in countries that had been ravaged by World War II. The Fund provides long-term humanitarian and developmental assistance to children and mothers in developing countries. It has evolved from an emergency fund to a development agency, committed to protecting the rights of every child to survival, protection and development. UNICEF works in partnership with governments, civil society and other international organizations to prevent the spread of HIV/AIDS and helps affected children and families live with dignity. It also promotes quality education for girls and boys. UNICEF advocates for a pro-tective environment for children, especially in emergencies, to prevent and re-spond to violence, exploitation and abuse. The UNICEF Innocenti Research Centre in Florence, Italy, facilitates implementation of the *Convention on the Rights of the Child* in all industrialized and developing countries.

UNICEF is governed by an Executive Board with delegates from 36 countries. It has more than 9,000 employees working in more than 150 countries and territories. The Fund is supported entirely by voluntary contributions; its programme expendi-tures in 2009 totalled $3.14 billion. While most support comes from governments (60 per cent in 2009), UNICEF also receives considerable aid from the private sector and NGOs—$916 million—and from some six million people who give through 36 National Committees. In 1965, UNICEF was awarded the Nobel Peace Prize. Its flagship publication, *The State of the World's Children*, is released annually.

Executive Director: Anthony Lake (United States)
Headquarters: UNICEF House, 3 United Nations Plaza, New York, NY 10017, USA
Tel.: (1-212) 326-7000; Fax: (1-212) 888-7465

United Nations Office on Drugs and Crime (UNODC)

Established in 1997, the United Nations Office on Drugs and Crime (*www.unodc. org*) is a global leader in the struggle against illicit drugs and transnational organ-ized crime. It is committed to achieving health, security and justice for all, and to delivering legal and technical assistance to prevent terrorism. With its portfolios expanding through the strengthening of concerted international action and the rule of law, its mission involves: research and analysis to produce authoritative re-ports; technical assistance to states in ratifying and implementing international treaties on drugs, crime and terrorism; developing domestic legislation consistent with these treaties; and training judicial officials. Other focuses include preven-tion, treatment and reintegration, along with the creation of sustainable alterna-tive livelihoods for drug-crop farmers. These measures aim at reducing incentives for illicit activities and addressing drug abuse, the spread of HIV/AIDS and drug-related crime.

UNODC has over 1,500 staff working through a network of 54 field and project offices, as well as liaison offices in New York and Brussels. In its two-year budget for 2008–2009, the General Assembly allocated $41 million to UNODC, which ac-counted for 7.5 per cent of total UNODC income. In 2009, voluntary contributions were pledged in the amount of $214.2 million. Overall voluntary funding for the two-year budget period 2008–2009 totalled $491.6 million.

Executive Director: Yury Fedotov (Russian Federation)

Headquarters: Vienna International Centre, Wagramerstrasse 5, P.O. Box 500, A-1400 Vienna, Austria

Tel.: (43-1) 26060-0; Fax: (43-1) 263-3389; E-mail: *unodc@unodc.org*

United Nations Relief and Works Agency for Palestine Refugees in the Near East (UNRWA)

The United Nations Relief and Works Agency for Palestine Refugees in the Near East (*www.unrwa.org*) was established by the General Assembly in 1949 to carry out relief work for Palestine refugees. It began operations in May 1950. In the absence of an agreed solution to the refugee problem, its mandate has been periodically renewed; it was most recently extended until 30 June 2011. The Agency is the main provider of basic services—education, health, relief and social welfare—to 4.8 million registered Palestine refugees in the Middle East, including some 1.4 million in 58 refugee camps in Jordan, Lebanon and Syria, as well as the Gaza Strip and the West Bank, including East Jerusalem. It manages a microfinance programme and undertakes infrastructure works inside officially designated camp areas. UNRWA has been providing emergency humanitarian assistance to mitigate the effects of the ongoing crisis on the most vulnerable refugees in Gaza and the West Bank since 2000. It has also responded to the emergency needs of conflict-affected refugees in Lebanon since 2006.

UNRWA's operations are supported by its two headquarters in Gaza and Amman, Jordan. The Commissioner-General, who reports to the General Assembly, is assisted by a 23-member Advisory Commission composed of Australia, Belgium, Canada, Denmark, Egypt, Finland, France, Germany, Ireland, Italy, Japan, Jordan, Lebanon, the Netherlands, Norway, Saudi Arabia, Spain, Sweden, Switzerland, Syria, Turkey, the United Kingdom and the United States. The European Union, the League of Arab States and Palestine are observers. UNRWA employs more than 30,000 local staff and 133 international staff. The Agency depends almost entirely on voluntary contributions from donor states for its regular and emergency operations; approximately 2.5 per cent of its current biennium budget requirements are met by the UN regular budget. Most voluntary contributions are in cash, but some are in kind—mostly food for needy refugees. UNRWA's core activities budget in 2010 totalled $863.9 million, including $262 million for projects.

Commissioner-General: Filippo Grandi (Italy)

Headquarters (Gaza): Gamal Abdul Nasser Street, Gaza City, P.O. Box 61 Gaza City

Tel.: (972-8) 288 7333; Fax: (972-8) 288 7555

Headquarters (Amman, Jordan): Bayader Wadi Seer, P.O. Box 140157, Amman 11814, Jordan

Tel.: (962-6) 580 8100; Fax: (962-6) 580-8335; E-mail: *HQ-PIO@unrwa.org*

World Food Programme (WFP)

The World Food Programme (*www.wfp.org*) is the world's largest humanitarian organization and the UN frontline agency in the fight against global hunger. Since its founding in 1963, the WFP has fed more than 1.6 billion of the world's poorest people, and invested more than $41.8 billion in development and emergency relief. Over the years, the Programme has reached hundreds of millions of people in more than 80 countries, using food assistance to meet emergency needs and support economic and social development. At any given time, the WFP has 30 ships at sea, 70 aircraft in the sky and 5,000 trucks on the ground, moving food and other assistance to where it is needed most. Through its global school meals campaign, the WFP supplies daily meals to 22 million school children in 60 countries. In 2009—when the number of hungry people worldwide grew to more than one billion—the WFP delivered an unprecedented 4.6 million metric tons of food to 101.8 million people in 75 countries. During that same year, it provided nearly 70 per cent of the world's emergency food aid. The Programme mounted the most complex emergency operation in its history following the catastrophic Haiti earthquake of January 2010. Within hours it was providing food to thousands in very precarious conditions.

The WFP is funded completely by voluntary donations from nations, private donors and individuals. In 2009, it raised $4.2 billion. More than 90 per cent its staff of 10,200 are field-based. The WFP is governed by a 36-member Executive Board. It works closely with its two Rome-based sister organizations, the Food and Agriculture Organization of the United Nations and the International Fund for Agricultural Development. The WFP also partners with more than 2,800 NGOs to distribute food.

Executive Director: Josette Sheeran (United States)
Headquarters: Via C.G. Viola 68, Parco dei Medici, 00148 Rome, Italy
Tel.: (39-06) 65131; Fax: (39-06) 6590632; E-mail: *wfpinfo@wfp.org*

United Nations Interregional Crime and Justice Research Institute (UNICRI)

The United Nations Interregional Crime and Justice Research Institute (*www.unicri.it*) carries out action-oriented research, training and technical cooperation projects. It supports governments and the international community at large in tackling the threats that crime poses to social peace, development and political stability and in fostering the development of just and efficient criminal justice systems. Established in 1967, UNICRI supports the formulation and implementation of improved policies in the field of crime prevention and criminal justice, the promotion of national self-reliance and the development of institutional capabilities. It does so by advancing the understanding of crime-related problems, supporting respect for international instruments and standards, and facilitating the exchange and dissemination of information, cooperation in international law enforcement and judicial assistance.

UNICRI's activities are entirely financed through voluntary contributions. The Institute enjoys the support of member states, international and regional organizations, charities and foundations, as well as financial and in-kind contributions from public and private sector organizations. In the biennium 2008–2009, UNICRI expenditures amounted to $23.4 million, while the total value of contributions and donations to the UNICRI Trust Fund was $18.3 million.

Director: Carlos Lopes (Guinea Bissau)
Headquarters: Viale Maestri del Lavoro 10, 10127 Turin, Italy
Tel.: (39-011) 653-7111; Fax: (39-011) 631-3368; E-mail: *information@unicri.it*

United Nations Institute
for Disarmament Research (UNIDIR)

Established in 1980, the United Nations Institute for Disarmament Research (*www.unidir.org*) is an autonomous institute that conducts research on disarmament and security, with the aim of assisting the international community in its disarmament thinking, decisions and efforts. Through its research projects, publications, meetings and expert networks, UNIDIR promotes creative thinking and dialogue on disarmament and security challenges. The Institute explores both current and future security issues, examining topics as varied as tactical nuclear weapons, refugee security, computer warfare, regional confidence-building measures, and small arms. It organizes expert-level meetings and discussions, implements research projects, and publishes books, reports and papers, as well as the quarterly journal *Disarmament Forum*. UNIDIR relies predominantly on voluntary contributions from governments and private funders. It received nearly $3.6 million in 2010: $2 million from governments and $1.6 in public donations. The Institute's staff of 20 is supplemented by visiting fellows and research interns.

Director: Theresa A. Hitchens (United States)
Headquarters: Palais des Nations, CH-1211 Geneva 10, Switzerland
Tel.: (41-22) 917-3186; Fax: (41-22) 917-0176; E-mail: *unidir@unog.ch*

United Nations Institute
for Training and Research (UNITAR)

An autonomous UN body established in 1965, the United Nations Institute for Training and Research (*www.unitar.org*) has the mandate to enhance the effectiveness of the UN through training and research. UNITAR provides training and capacity development to assist mainly developing and in-transition countries in meeting the challenges of the 21st century. It conducts research on innovative training and capacity-development methodologies with a people-centered approach based on knowledge transfer and leadership promotion. In 2008–2009, UNITAR offered over 700 courses, seminars and workshops benefiting over 73,000 participants—mainly from developing countries and countries in transition. Some 5,000 trainees also profited from its e-learning courses. UNITAR is governed by a Board of Trustees. The Institute is fully self-funded and is sponsored by voluntary contributions from governments, intergovernmental organizations, foundations and other non-governmental sources. UNITAR's activities are conducted from its headquarters in Geneva, as well as through its New York, Brasilia and Hiroshima offices. It has a staff of 55 and a budget of $50.7 million.

Executive Director: Carlos Lopes (Guinea-Bissau)
Headquarters: International Environment House, Chemin des Anémones 11-13,
    CH-1219 Châtelaine, Geneva, Switzerland
Tel.: (41-22) 917-8400; Fax: (41-22) 917-8047

United Nations Research Institute
for Social Development (UNRISD)

Established in 1963, the United Nations Research Institute for Social Development (*www.unrisd.org*) is an autonomous institution within the UN system that carries out multidisciplinary research on the social dimensions of contemporary development issues such as gender equality, social policy, poverty reduction, governance and politics, and corporate social responsibility. The Institute provides the UN system, governments, development agencies, civil society organizations and scholars with a better understanding of how development policies and processes of economic and social change affect different social groups. UNRISD relies wholly on voluntary contributions for financing its activities and has an average annual operating budget of approximately $4 million. Responsibility for approving the research programme and budget of the Institute is vested in a Board composed of experts nominated by the UN Commission for Social Development and confirmed by ECOSOC.

Director: Sarah Cook (United Kingdom)
Headquarters: Palais des Nations, CH-1211 Geneva 10, Switzerland
Tel.: (41-22) 917-3020; Fax: (41-22) 917-0650; E-mail: *info@unrisd.org*

United Nations University (UNU)

The United Nations University (*www.unu.edu*), established in 1975 in Tokyo, is an international community of academics engaged in research, policy study, institutional and individual capacity development, as well as the dissemination of knowledge to further the UN's aims of peace and progress. UNU has a worldwide network of 13 research and training centres and programmes. Its aim is to contribute to solving the pressing global problems of human survival, development and welfare that are the concern of the UN, its member states and their peoples. The University is financed entirely by voluntary contributions from states, agencies, foundations and individual donors. Receiving no funds from the United Nations budget, its basic annual income for operating expenses comes from investment income derived from its Endowment Fund. UNU's budget for the biennium 2008–2009 was $101.8 million, with its 559 staff members representing both developing and developed countries. UNU has a 24-member Governing Council. Its members are appointed for six-year terms by the Secretary-General of the United Nations and by the Director-General of UNESCO. United Nations University Press is its publishing division.

Rector: Konrad Osterwalder (Switzerland)
Headquarters: 5-53-70 Jingumae, Shibuya-ku, Tokyo 150-8925, Japan
Tel.: (81-3) 5467 1212; Fax: (81-3) 3499-2828; E-mail: *mbox@hq.unu.edu*

Joint United Nations Programme on HIV/AIDS (UNAIDS)

Active since 1996, UNAIDS (*www.unaids.org*) is the UN entity that spearheads the struggle against HIV worldwide, advocating for accelerated, comprehensive and global action against the epidemic. UNAIDS leads a response that includes preventing transmission, providing care and support to those infected, reducing the vulnerability of persons and communities to HIV, and alleviating the manifold impacts of the epidemic. It works to prevent the epidemic from becoming a severe pandemic and strives to eliminate all forms of discrimination against those infected. UNAIDS provides information and technical support to guide efforts against AIDS and tracks, monitors and evaluates the epidemic and responses to it. The Programme represents a combined effort of 10 other UN entities: the ILO, UNDP, UNESCO, UNFPA, UNHCR, UNICEF, UNODC, the WHO, the WFP and the World Bank. Together with the UNAIDS Secretariat, these form the Committee of Cosponsoring Organizations, which serves as the standing committee of the Programme Coordinating Board.

Executive Director: Michel Sidibé (Mali)
Headquarters: 20 Avenue Appia, CH 1211 Geneva 27, Switzerland
Tel.: (41-22) 791-3666; Fax: (41-22) 791-4187; E-mail: *communications@unaids.org*

United Nations Office for Project Services (UNOPS)

The mission of the United Nations Office for Project Services (*www.unops.org*) is to expand the capacity of the UN system and its partners to implement peacebuilding, humanitarian and development operations that matter for people in need. Core services include project management, procurement, human resources management, financial management and UN common services. Focus areas include support to partners in physical infrastructure, public order and security, census and elections, environment and health—all areas where UNOPS has the ability to enhance the capacities of UN agencies and other partners. UNOPS employs almost 6,000 personnel annually, and on behalf of its partners creates thousands more work opportunities in local communities. With its headquarters in Copenhagen, Denmark, a network of five regional offices and a further 20 operations and project centres, UNOPS oversees activities in more than 60 countries. During 2009 UNOPS delivered $1.1 billion in project management services in approximately 1,000 projects around the world.

Executive Director: Jan Mattsson (Sweden)
Headquarters: Midtermolen 3, P.O. Box 2695, DK-2100 Copenhagen, Denmark
Tel.: (45-3) 546-7000; Fax: (45-3) 546-7508; E-mail: *hq@unops.org*

United Nations Entity for Gender Equality and the Empowerment of Women (UN-Women)

In 2010, the General Assembly voted unanimously to create the United Nations Entity for Gender Equality and the Empowerment of Women (*www.unwomen.org*). UN-Women aims to accelerate progress in meeting the needs of women and girls worldwide. Equality for women and girls is not only a basic human right, it is a social and economic imperative. Where women are educated and empowered, economies are more productive and stronger, and societies are more peaceful and stable. The establishment of UN-Women consolidated the existing mandate and functions of four UN agencies and offices: the United Nations Development Fund for Women, the Division for the Advancement of Women, the Office of the Special Adviser on Gender Issues, and the United Nations International Research and Training Institute for the Advancement of Women.

"By bringing together four parts of the UN system dedicated to women's issues, member states have created a much stronger voice for women and for gender equality at the global level", declared Secretary-General Ban Ki-moon on the founding of UN-Women. The entity has an initial annual budget of $500 million. It supports the Commission on the Status of Women and other intergovernmental bodies in devising policies and member states in implementing standards relevant to women's issues. It also holds the UN system accountable for its own commitments on gender equality, including regular monitoring of system-wide progress.

Executive Director: Michelle Bachelet (Chile)
Headquarters: 304 East 45th Street, 15th Floor, New York, NY 10017, USA
Tel.: (1-212) 906-6400; Fax: (1-212) 906-6705

Specialized agencies and related organizations

International Labour Organization (ILO)

The International Labour Organization (*www.ilo.org*) promotes social justice and human and labour rights. Established in 1919, it became the first specialized agency of the United Nations in 1946. On its fiftieth anniversary, in 1969, the ILO was awarded the Nobel Peace Prize. The ILO formulates international policies and programmes to help improve working and living conditions; creates international labour standards to serve as guidelines for national authorities in putting these policies into action; carries out an extensive programme of technical cooperation to help governments in making these policies effective; and engages in training, education and research to help advance these efforts. The ILO is unique among world organizations in that workers' and employers' representatives have an equal voice with those of governments in formulating its policies. It is composed of three bodies:

- The International Labour Conference brings together government, employer and worker delegates from member countries every year. It sets international labour standards and acts as a forum where social and labour questions of importance to the entire world are discussed.
- The Governing Body directs ILO operations, prepares the programme and budget and examines cases of non-observance of ILO standards.
- The International Labour Office is the permanent secretariat of the Organization.

In addition, opportunities for study and training are offered at the International Training Centre in Turin, Italy. The ILO's International Institute for Labour Studies works through research networks; social policy forums; courses and seminars; visiting scholar and internship programmes; and publications. The ILO employs 2,500 staff at its Geneva headquarters and in 40 field offices around the world. Its budget for the 2010–2011 biennium amounted to $594.3 million.

Director-General: Juan Somavía (Chile)
Headquarters: 4, route des Morillons, CH-1211 Geneva 22, Switzerland
Tel.: (41-22) 799-6111; Fax: (41-22) 798-8685; E-mail: *ilo@ilo.org*

Food and Agriculture Organization of the United Nations (FAO)

The Food and Agriculture Organization of the United Nations (*www.fao.org*) is the lead agency for agriculture, forestry, fisheries and rural development in the UN system. World Food Day, observed annually on 16 October, marks the founding of the FAO on that date in 1945. The FAO works to alleviate poverty and hunger by promoting agricultural development, improved nutrition and the pursuit of food security. Such security exists when all people at all times have physical and economic access to sufficient, safe and nutritious food to meet their dietary needs and food preferences for an active and healthy life. Present in over 130 countries, the FAO offers development assistance; provides policy and planning advice to governments; collects, analyses and disseminates information; and acts as an international forum for debate on food and agriculture issues. Special programmes help countries prepare for emergency food crisis and provide relief assistance. During 2009, FAO-assisted projects applied $647.1 million from donor agencies and governments for agricultural and rural development projects and emergencies. Some 82.1 per cent of field programme finances were taken from national trust funds.

During that same year, the FAO itself contributed 9.2 per cent (or $66.4 million) to its field programme.

The FAO is governed by its Conference of member nations. Its 49-member elected Council serves as the governing body between sessions of the Conference. The FAO has a staff of 3,641 working at headquarters and in the field. Its regular programme budget for 2010–2011 was $1.005 billion.

Director-General: Jacques Diouf (Senegal)
Headquarters: Viale delle Terme di Caracalla, 00153 Rome, Italy
Tel.: (39-06) 5705-1; Fax: (39-06) 5705-3152; E-mail: *FAO-HQ@fao.org*

United Nations Educational, Scientific and Cultural Organization (UNESCO)

Created in 1946, UNESCO (*www.unesco.org*) works to create the conditions for dialogue among civilizations, cultures and peoples, based upon respect for commonly shared values and geared towards sustainable development, a culture of peace, observance of human rights and the alleviation of poverty. UNESCO's areas of work are education, natural sciences, social and human sciences, culture, and communication and information. Specific concerns include: achieving education for all; promoting natural and social science research through international and intergovernmental scientific programmes; supporting the expression of cultural identities; protecting and enhancing the world's natural and cultural heritage; and promoting the free flow of information and press freedom, as well as strengthening the communication capacities of developing countries. The Organization also has two global priorities, namely Africa and gender equality.

UNESCO maintains a system of 193 National Commissions and is supported by some 3,800 UNESCO associations, centres and clubs. It enjoys official relations with hundreds of NGOs and a range of foundations and similar institutions. It also works with a network of 9,000 educational institutions in 180 countries. UNESCO's governing body—the General Conference—is made up of its 193 member states. The Executive Board, consisting of 58 members elected by the Conference, is responsible for supervising the programme adopted by the Conference. UNESCO has a staff of 2,149 from some 170 countries—more than 1,100 of whom work in 53 field offices and 11 institutes and centres worldwide, including four regional bureaux for education in Bangkok, Beirut, Dakar and Santiago de Chile. Its approved budget ceiling for 2010–2011 is $653 million.

Director-General: Irina Bokova (Bulgaria)
Headquarters: 7, place de Fontenoy, 75352 Paris 07-SP, France
Tel.: (33) 14568-1000; Fax: (33) 14567-1690; E-mail: *info@unesco.org*

World Health Organization (WHO)

Established in 1948, the World Health Organization (*www.who.int*) is the directing and coordinating authority within the United Nations system for health. The WHO is responsible for providing leadership on global health matters; shaping the health research agenda; setting norms and standards; articulating evidence-based policy options; providing technical support to countries; and monitoring and assessing health trends. Its decision-making body is the World Health Assembly, which meets annually and is attended by delegations from all 193 Member States. The Executive Board is composed of 34 members technically qualified in the health field. Nearly 7,000 people from more than 150 countries work for the

United Nations Messengers of Peace and Goodwill Ambassadors

From the earliest days of the United Nations, actors, artists, football and tennis players, gymnasts, designers, composers, ballet dancers, astronauts, entrepreneurs, scientists, writers, singers, philosophers, models, and other talented and compassionate women and men from around the world have lent their names and public recognition in support of the United Nations' work for a better world. Today, there are 12 United Nations Messengers of Peace (*www.un.org/sg/mop*) appointed by the Secretary-General. These are: Princess Haya Bint Al Hussein, Daniel Barenboim, George Clooney, Paulo Coelho, Michael Douglas, Jane Goodall, Midori Goto, Yo-Yo Ma, Wangari Maathai, Charlize Theron, Elie Wiesel and Stevie Wonder.

The ideals and objectives of the specialized agencies and funds, offices and programmes of the UN system are supported by the public appearances, contacts with international media and humanitarian work of some 200 Goodwill Ambassadors:

United Nations: Edward Norton (*Biodiversity*)

Food and Agricultural Organization of the United Nations (FAO): the Magida Al Roumi, Anggun, Roberto Baggio, Dee Dee Bridgewater, Raoul Bova, Pierre Cardin, Al Bano Carrisi, Margarita Cedeño de Fernández, Celine Dion, Beatrice Faumuina, Deborah Ferguson, Carla Fracci, Gilberto Gil, Raúl González Blanco, the Italian Singers' Soccer Team, Mory Kanté, Ronan Keating, Khaled, Rai Singer, Carl Lewis, Gong Li, Gina Lollobrigida, Fanny Lu, Maná, Rita Levi Montalcini, Youssou N'Dour, Noa, Justine Pasek, María Gloria Penayo de Duarte, Massimo Ranieri, Lea Salonga, Oumou Sangaré, Susan Sarandon, Chucho Valdés, Patrick Vieira, Dionne Warwick

Joint United Nations Programmes on HIV/AIDS (UNAIDS): Emmanuel Adebayor, Michael Ballack, Toumani Diabaté, Annie Lennox, Lebo M, H.R.H. Crown Princess Mette-Marit, Her Serene Princess Stephanie, Naomi Watts

United Nations Children's Fund (UNICEF): Lord Richard Attenborough, Amitabh Bachchan, Ismael Beah, David Beckham, Harry Belafonte, the Berliner Philharmoniker, Orlando Bloom, Jackie Chan, Myung-Whun Chung, Judy Collins, Mia Farrow, Danny Glover, Whoopi Goldberg, Maria Guleghina, Angélique Kidjo, Yuna Kim, Tetsuko Kuroyanagi, Femi Kuti, Leon Lai, Lang Lang, Ricky Martin, Shakira Mebarak, Lionel Messi, Sir Roger Moore, Nana Mouskouri, Youssou N'Dour, HM Queen Rania, Vanessa Redgrave, Sebastião Salgado, Susan Sarandon, Maxim Vengerov

United Nations Development Programme (UNDP): Antonio Banderas, Iker Cassillas, Didier Drogba, Misako Konno, Ronaldo, Maria Sharapova, Marta Vieira da Silva, Zinédine Zidane, Crown Prince Haakon Magnus of Norway

United Nations Educational, Scientific and Cultural Organization (UNESCO): Ara Abramian, Valdas Adamkus, Mehriban Aliyeva, Alicia Alonso, Ivonne A. Baki, Patrick Baudry, Pierre Bergé, Chantal Biya, Montserrat Caballé, Pierre Cardin, Claudia Cardinale, H. R. H. the Princess of Hanover, Esther Coopersmith, Cheick Modibo Diarra, Miguel Angel Estrella, Vigdís Finnbogadóttir, H. R. H. Princess Firyal of Jordan, Christine Hakim, Bahia Hariri, Vitaly Ignatenko, Jean Michel Jarre, Marc Ladreit de Lacharrière, H. R. H. Princess Lalla Meryem of Morocco, Omer Zülfü Livaneli, H. R. H. Princess Maha Chakri Sirindhorn, Jean Malaurie, Nelson Mandela, H. R. H. the Grand Duchess María Teresa of Luxembourg, Rigoberta Menchu Túm, Kitín Muñoz, Ute-Henriette Ohoven, Cristina Owen-Jones, Kim Phuc Phan Thi, Yazid Sabeg, H. E. Sheikh Ghassan I. Shaker, Madanjeet Singh, Zurab Tsereteli, Marianna Vardinoyannis

---

United Nations Entity for Gender Equality and the Empowerment of Women (UN-Women): Hon. Mrs. Phoebe Asiyo, Nicole Kidman, H.R.H. Princess Bajrakitiyabha Mahidol, H.R.H. Princess Basma bint Talal

United Nations Environment Programme (UNEP): Yann Arthus-Bertrand, Don Cheadle, Gisele Bündchen, Sachin Tendulkar

United Nations High Commissioner for Refugees (UNHCR): Giorgio Armani, Julien Clerc, George Dalaras, Muazzez Ersoy, Barbara Hendricks, Adel Imam, Angelina Jolie, Osvaldo Laport, Jesús Vázquez Martínez

United Nations Industrial Development Organization (UNIDO): Mansour Cama, Reinosuke Hara, Rajendra K. Pachauri, Peter Sutherland

United Nations Office on Drugs and Crime (UNODC): Ross Bleckner, Nicholas Cage, Igor Cassina, Mira Sorvino

United Nations Population Fund (UNFPA): Catarina Furtado, Goedele Liekens, Princess Basma Bint Talal, Ashi Sangay Choden Wangchuck

United Nations World Food Programme (WFP): George McGovern

World Health Organization (WHO): Nancy Goodman Brinker, Liya Kebede, Jet Li, Yohei Sasakawa, Vienna Philharmonic Orchestra; Craig David, Luis Figo (*Stop TB Partnership*)

WHO in 145 country offices, its headquarters in Geneva, and the six regional offices in Brazzaville, Congo; Washington, D.C.; Cairo, Egypt; Copenhagen, Denmark; New Delhi, India; and Manila, the Philippines. The programme budget for the biennium 2010–2011 was over $4.5 billion, of which $928 million was financed by the assessed contributions from member states (regular budget), with the remainder coming from voluntary contributions.

Director-General: Margaret Chan (China)
Headquarters: 20 Avenue Appia, CH-1211 Geneva 27, Switzerland
Tel.: (41-22) 791-2111; Fax: (41-22) 791-3111; E-mail: *inf@who.int*

World Bank Group

The World Bank Group (*www.worldbankgroup.org*) consists of five institutions:

- the International Bank for Reconstruction and Development (IBRD, founded in 1944);
- the International Finance Corporation (IFC, 1956);
- the International Development Association (IDA,1960);
- the Multilateral Investment Guarantee Agency (MIGA,1988); and
- the International Centre for Settlement of Investment Disputes (ICSID, 1966).

The term 'World Bank' itself refers specifically to two of the five institutions: the IBRD and the IDA. The goal of the Bank is to reduce poverty around the world by strengthening the economies of poor nations; and improving people's living standards by promoting economic growth and development. The Bank orients its lending and capacity-building activities on two pillars for development: building a climate for investment, jobs and sustainable growth; and investing in poor people and empowering them to participate in development.

The World Bank is owned by its 187 member countries, which constitute its Board of Governors. General operations are delegated to a smaller group, the Board of Executive Directors, with the President of the Bank serving as Chairman of the Board. It has a staff of about 10,000 employees working at headquarters and in over 100 offices. In 2010, the World Bank Group provided $46.9 billion for 303 projects in developing countries, with its financial and/or technical expertise aimed at helping those countries reduce poverty. The Bank is involved in more than 1,800 projects in virtually every sector and developing country. Projects are as diverse as providing microcredit in Bosnia and Herzegovina, raising AIDS-prevention aware-ness in Guinea, supporting education of girls in Bangladesh, improving health care delivery in Mexico, and helping Timor-Leste rebuild following its independence. Among its major publications is the annual *World Development Report*.

President: Robert B. Zoellick (United States)
Headquarters: 1818 H Street NW, Washington, D.C. 20433, USA
Tel.: (1-202) 473-1000; Fax: (1-202) 477-6391; E-mail: *pic@worldbank.org*

International Bank for Reconstruction and Development (IBRD)

The International Bank for Reconstruction and Development (*www.worldbank.org*), the original institution of the World Bank Group, seeks to reduce poverty in middle-income and creditworthy poorer countries by promoting sustainable development through loans, guarantees, risk management products, and analytical and advisory services. The IBRD is structured like a cooperative owned and operated for the ben-efit of its 187 member countries. It raises most of its funds on the world's finan-cial markets. The income that the Bank has generated over the years has allowed it to fund development activities and ensure its financial strength, which enables it to borrow at low cost and offer good borrowing terms to its clients. The amount paid in by countries when they join the Bank constitutes less than 5 per cent of the IBRD's funds, but it has been leveraged into hundreds of billions in loans since the Bank was established. In fiscal 2010, the IBRD's new loan commitments amounted to $44.2 billion, covering 164 new operations in 46 countries.

International Development Association (IDA)

The International Development Association (*www.worldbank.org/ida*) is the World Bank's Fund for the poorest. One of the world's largest sources of aid, the IDA, counting 170 member states, provides support for health and education, infra-structure and agriculture, and economic and institutional development to the world's 79 poorest countries. About one fifth of IDA funding is provided as grants; the rest is in the form of interest-free, long-term credits. Since its establishment in 1960, IDA has provided $221.9 billion in cumulative commitments. Almost fifty per cent of the lending in fiscal year 2010, or $7.1 billion out of $14.5 billion, went to Africa, reflecting the fact that half of IDA-eligible countries are situated on that continent. The IDA is replenished every three years by both developed and devel-oping country donors, as well as by two other World Bank Group organizations—the International Bank for Reconstruction and Development and the International Finance Corporation. Forty-five countries contributed to the last IDA replenish-ment of some $42 billion.

International Finance Corporation (IFC)

The International Finance Corporation (*www.ifc.org*) is the largest global develop-ment institution focused on the private sector in developing countries. It provides financing to help businesses employ more people and supply essential services;

mobilizes capital in the international financial markets; and delivers advisory services to ensure sustainable development. In a time of global economic uncertainty, the IFC's new investments climbed to a record $18 billion in fiscal 2010. The IFC, which has 182 member countries, promotes development by encouraging the growth of productive enterprise and efficient capital markets. It joins in an investment only when it can make a special contribution that complements the role of market investors. It also plays a catalytic role, stimulating and mobilizing private investment in developing countries by demonstrating that investments there can be profitable. During the fiscal year ending in mid-2010, the IFC had an authorized borrowing programme of up to $9.5 billion. Its total capital amounted to $18.4 billion.

Multilateral Investment Guarantee Agency (MIGA)

The mandate of the Multilateral Investment Guarantee Agency (*www.miga.org*) is to promote foreign direct investment in developing countries by providing guarantees (political risk insurance) to investors and lenders. Its subscribed capital comes from its 175 member countries. The agency's strategy focuses on supporting investment in the world's poorest countries, investment in conflict-affected countries, complex deals in infrastructure and the extractive industries, and South-South investments. Since its inception in 1998, the MIGA has issued guarantees worth more than $22 billion for more than 600 projects in 100 developing countries.

International Centre for Settlement of Investment Disputes (ICSID)

The International Centre for the Settlement of Investment Disputes (*www.worldbank.org/icsid*) aims to foster increased flows of international investment by providing a neutral international forum for the resolution of disputes between governments and foreign investors. To date, 144 countries are ICSID members. The ICSID administers procedures for the settlement of such disputes by conciliation and arbitration in cases where both the host and the home country of the investor are ICSID members. The ICSID also administers certain types of proceedings between governments and foreign nationals, and appoints arbitrators and administers proceedings conducted under the Arbitration Rules of the UN Commission on International Trade Law. In addition to its dispute settlement activities, the ICSID has a publications programme in the area of foreign investment law. Its governing body, the Administrative Council, is composed of one representative of each ICSID member state and is chaired by the President of the World Bank Group.

International Monetary Fund (IMF)

Established at the Bretton Woods Conference in 1944, the International Monetary Fund (*www.imf.org*) facilitates international monetary cooperation; promotes exchange rate stability and orderly exchange arrangements; assists in the establishment of a multilateral system of payments and the elimination of foreign exchange restrictions; and assists members by temporarily providing financial resources to correct maladjustments in their balance of payments. The IMF has authority to create and allocate to its members international financial reserves in the form of Special Drawing Rights—the IMF's unit of account. The Fund's financial resources consist primarily of the subscriptions ('quotas' determined by a formula based upon the relative economic size of the members) of its 187 member countries, which totalled about $328 billion as of August 2010. A core responsibility of the IMF is to provide loans to countries experiencing balance-of-payment problems. This financial assistance enables such countries to rebuild their international reserves, stabilize their currencies, continue paying for imports, and restore conditions for strong economic growth. In return, members borrowing from the Fund agree to undertake policy reforms to correct the problems that underlie these difficulties. The amounts that IMF members may borrow are limited in proportion to their quotas. The Fund also offers concessional assistance to low-income member countries.

Its Board of Governors includes all member states. Daily work is led by the 24-member Executive Board. The IMF has a staff of more than 2,400 from over 140 countries, headed by a Managing Director selected by the Executive Board. The administrative budget (net of receipts) for the financial year ending 30 April 2011 was $891 million, and the capital budget $48 million. The IMF publishes the *World Economic Outlook* and the *Global Financial Stability Report,* along with a variety of other studies.

Managing Director: Dominique Strauss-Kahn (France)
Headquarters: 700 19th Street NW, Washington, D.C. 20431, USA
Tel.: (1-202) 623-7300; Fax: (1-202) 623-6278; E-mail: *publicaffairs@imf.org*

International Civil Aviation Organization (ICAO)

The International Civil Aviation Organization (*www.icao.int*) promotes the safe and orderly development of international civil aviation throughout the world. It sets standards and develops regulations necessary for aviation safety, security, efficiency and regularity, as well as for environmental protection. To achieve safe, secure and sustainable development of civil aviation, it relies on the cooperation of its 190 member states. The ICAO has an Assembly—its policymaking body—comprising delegates from all Contracting States, and a Council of representatives of 36 nations elected by the Assembly. The Council is the executive body, and carries out Assembly directives.

President of the Council: Roberto Kobeh González (Mexico)
Secretary General: Raymond Benjamin (France)
Headquarters: 999 University Street, Montreal, Quebec H3C 5H7, Canada
Tel.: (1-514) 954-8219; Fax: (1-514) 954-6077; E-mail: *icaohq@icao.int*

International Maritime Organization (IMO)

The International Maritime Organization (*www.imo.org*), which began functioning in 1959, is responsible for the safety and security of shipping in international trade and for preventing marine pollution from ships. The IMO helps governments cooperate in formulating regulations and practices relating to technical matters affecting international shipping; facilitates the adoption of the highest practicable standards of maritime safety and efficiency in navigation; and helps protect the marine environment through the prevention and control of pollution from ships. Some 50 conventions and agreements and some 1,000 codes and recommendations have been adopted by IMO. In 1983, it established the World Maritime University in Malmö, Sweden, which provides advanced training for administrators, educators and others involved in shipping at the senior level. The IMO International Maritime Law Institute (Valletta, Malta) was established in 1989 to train lawyers in international maritime law. The Assembly—the IMO's governing body—consists of all 169 Member States and three Associate Members (Faroe Islands, Denmark; Hong Kong, China; and Macau, China). It elects the 40-member Council, the IMO's executive organ. The IMO's budget for 2011 stood at £30,860,300. It has a staff of about 300.

Secretary-General: Efthimios E. Mitropoulos (Greece)
Headquarters: 4 Albert Embankment, London SE1 7SR, United Kingdom
Tel.: (44-207) 735-7611; Fax: (44-207) 587-3210; E-mail: *infor@imo.org*

International Telecommunication Union (ITU)

The International Telecommunication Union (*www.itu.int*) coordinates global tele-communication networks and services for governments and the private sector. The Union is also responsible for the management of the radio-frequency spectrum and satellite orbits. The ITU is at the forefront of work to achieve safe and reliable interoperability of networks and equipment amid the rapid advance of information and communication technologies. It puts priority on fostering the deployment of telecommunications in developing countries by advising on policy and regulatory frameworks, and by providing specialized technical assistance and training in such areas as cybersecurity, network installation and maintenance, and early warning and mitigation systems for natural disasters. Founded in Paris in 1865 as the International Telegraph Union, the ITU took its present name in 1932 and became a UN specialized agency in 1949. It has a membership of 192 countries and more than 700 sector members and associates (scientific and industrial bodies, public and private companies, and regional and international organizations). The ITU's governing body, the Plenipotentiary Conference, elects its senior officials, as well as the 46-member ITU Council representing all regions of the world. Based in Geneva, the ITU has around 850 staff members of some 85 nationalities. It had a budget of CHF 332,639,000 for the biennium 2010–2011.

Secretary-General: Hamadoun I. Touré (Mali)
Headquarters: Place des Nations, CH-1211 Geneva 20, Switzerland
Tel.: (41-22) 730-5111; Fax: (41-22) 733-7256; E-mail: *itumail@itu.int*

Universal Postal Union (UPU)

Comprising 191 member states, the Universal Postal Union (*www.upu.int*) regulates international postal services. Established in 1874, it became a UN specialized agency in 1948. The UPU advises, mediates and renders technical assistance for postal services. Its objectives include the promotion of a universal postal service linking all the nations of the world; growth in mail volume through the provision of up-to-date postal products and services; and improvement in the quality of postal service for customers. The Universal Postal Congress is the supreme authority of the UPU, whose annual budget is approximately $36 million. Some 250 staff, drawn from more than 50 countries, work at the UPU International Bureau in Berne, Switzerland. The UPU has regional coordinators in San José, Costa Rica; Harare, Zimbabwe; Cairo, Egypt; Castries, Saint Lucia; Cotonou, Benin; Bangkok, Thailand; and Berne.

Director-General: Edouard Dayan (France)
Headquarters: Weltpoststrasse 4, Case Postale 3000, Berne 15, Switzerland
Tel.: (41-31) 350-3111; Fax: (41-31) 350-3110; E-mail: *info@upu.int*

World Meteorological Organization (WMO)

The World Meteorological Organization (*www.wmo.int*), a United Nations special-ized agency since 1951, provides authoritative scientific information on the state and behaviour of the Earth's atmosphere, its interaction with the oceans, the cli-mate it produces and the resulting distribution of water resources, and related en-vironmental issues. The WMO operates a global observing system and a network of global, regional and national centres providing weather, climate and hydrologi-cal forecasting services. The WMO Information System makes possible the rapid exchange of weather, climate and water information, and promotes its application. Its major programmes provide the basis for better preparation and forewarning of most natural hazards. The WMO has 189 members, all of which maintain their own meteorological and hydrological services. Its governing body is the World Mete-orological Congress. The WMO has a staff of around 300. Its budget for 2008–2011 was CHF 269.8 million.

Secretary-General: Michel Jarraud (France)
Headquarters: 7 bis, avenue de la Paix, Case postale No. 2300, CH-1211 Geneva 2, Switzerland
Tel.: (41-22) 730-8111; Fax: (41-22) 730-8181; E-mail: *wmo@wmo.int*

World Intellectual Property Organization (WIPO)

The World Intellectual Property Organization (*www.wipo.int*) was established in 1970 and became a UN specialized agency in 1974. Its mandate is to promote the protection of intellectual property (IP) through cooperation among states and in collaboration with other international organizations. It is dedicated to developing a balanced and accessible international IP system that rewards creativity, stimu-lates innovation and contributes to economic development while safeguarding the public interest. The strategic goals of the WIPO include: the balanced evolution of the international normative IP framework; facilitating the use of IP for develop-ment; providing global IP services; building respect for IP; developing global IP in-frastructure; becoming a world reference source for IP information; and addressing IP in relation to global policy challenges such as climate change, public health and food security. The WIPO has 184 member states and administers 24 international treaties on IP and copyright. It is unique among the family of UN organizations in that it is largely self-financing. Over 90 per cent of the Organization's budget of CHF 618 million for the 2010–2011 biennium comes from earnings derived from services which it provides to industry and the private sector. The remainder of the budget is made up mainly of revenue generated by its Arbitration and Mediation Centre, the sale of publications and contributions from member states.

Director-General: Francis Gurry (Australia)
Headquarters: 34 chemin des Colombettes, P.O. Box 18, CH-1211 Geneva 20, Switzerland
Tel.: (41-22) 338-9111; Fax: (41-22) 733-5428

International Fund for Agricultural Development (IFAD)

Established in 1977, the International Fund for Agricultural Development (*www. ifad.org*) is dedicated to eradicating poverty in the rural areas of developing coun-tries. IFAD mobilizes resources from its 165 member countries to provide low-interest loans and grants to middle- and lower-income members to finance poverty

Intergovernmental Panel on Climate Change (IPCC)

The Intergovernmental Panel on Climate Change (*www.ipcc.ch*) is the leading body for the assessment of climate change. It was established by the United Nations Environment Programme (UNEP) and the World Meteorological Organization (WMO) to provide a clear scientific view on the state of climate change and its potential environmental and socioeconomic consequences. Its secretariat is hosted by the WMO at its Geneva headquarters. It shared the Nobel Peace Prize in 2007. The IPCC reviews and assesses scientific, technical and socioeconomic information produced worldwide that is relevant to the understanding of climate change. It does not conduct research, nor does it monitor data or parameters. Thousands of scientists contribute voluntarily. Review is an essential part of the process, ensuring an objective and complete assessment of current information. The IPCC aims to reflect a range of views and expertise. Its work is policy-relevant and yet policy-neutral, never policy-prescriptive. The IPCC is open to all UN and WMO member countries. States can participate in the review process and in IPCC plenary sessions, where the main decisions about the IPCC work programme are taken and reports accepted, adopted and approved. The IPCC Bureau and Chair are also elected in plenary sessions. In 2010, the secretariat had a staff of 10. That same year, 831 experts were selected to conduct the Fifth Assessment Report.

Chair: Rajendra K. Pachauri (India)
Head of Secretariat: Dr. Renate Christ (Austria)
Secretariat: c/o World Meteorological Organization, 7 bis, Avenue de la Paix, C.P. 2300, CH-1211 Geneva 2, Switzerland
Tel.: (41-22) 730-8208; Fax: (41-22) 730-8025; E-mail: *IPCC-Sec@wmo.int*

---

reduction programmes and projects in the poorest communities. It gives grants instead of loans to poor countries unable to sustain debt to ensure that essential financial assistance does not cause undue financial hardship for those most in need. From its inception, IFAD has worked in partnership with governments, other UN agencies, international financial institutions, research institutions and the private sector. It also has strong relationships with national partners, including farmers' organizations and NGOs. The Fund is financed by voluntary contributions from governments, special contributions, loan repayments and investment income. Since 1978, it has invested $11.5 billion in over 800 projects and programmes that have reached more than 350 million poor rural people. Governments and other financing sources in recipient countries, including project participants, have contributed $10.1 billion, and multilateral, bilateral and other donors approximately another $8.2 billion in co-financing. IFAD's Governing Council is made up of all 165 member states. The Executive Board, which consists of 18 members and 18 alternates, oversees operations and approves loans and grants.

President: Kanayo F. Nwanze (Nigeria)
Headquarters: Via del Serafico 107, 00142 Rome, Italy
Tel.: (39-06) 54-591; Fax: (39-06) 504-3463; E-mail: *ifad@ifad.org*

United Nations Industrial Development Organization (UNIDO)

The mandate of the United Nations Industrial Development Organization (*www.unido.org*) is to promote industrial development and cooperation. Established by the General Assembly in 1966, it became a United Nations specialized agency in

1985. UNIDO helps improve the living conditions of people and promote global prosperity by offering tailor-made solutions for the sustainable industrial development of developing countries and countries in transition. It cooperates with governments, business associations and the private industrial sector to build industrial capabilities for meeting the challenges and spreading the benefits of the globalization of industry. UNIDO has engineers, economists, and technology and environment experts in Vienna, as well as professional staff in its network of Investment Promotion Service offices and field offices. Field offices are led by UNIDO regional and country representatives.

UNIDO's 173 member states meet at its General Conference to approve the budget and work programme. The Industrial Development Board, comprising 53 member states, makes recommendations relating to the planning and implementation of the programme and budget. In 2010, UNIDO had 651 staff members working at headquarters and worldwide in 11 regional offices (including its Regional Centre in Turkey) and 37 country offices. It also had 13 Investment and Technology Promotion Offices, 43 National Cleaner Production Centres, 14 International Technology Centres, 32 subcontracting and partnership exchanges offices, and two South-South Cooperation Centres. The preceding year, UNIDO delivered technical cooperation valued at over $139 million.

Director-General: Kandeh K. Yumkella (Sierra Leone)
Headquarters: Vienna International Centre, Wagramerstrasse 5, P.O. Box 300, A-1400 Vienna, Austria
Tel.: (43-1) 26026-0; Fax: (43-1) 269-2669; E-mail: *unido@unido.org*

World Tourism Organization (UNWTO)

The World Tourism Organization (*www.unwto.org*) is the leading international organization responsible for promoting the development of responsible, sustainable and universally accessible tourism. Established in 1975, the UNWTO became a UN specialized agency in 2003. It serves as a global forum for tourism policy issues and a practical source of tourism know-how. Its membership includes 154 countries, seven territories, two permanent observers and over 400 affiliate members, including local governments, educational institutions, tourism associations and private sector firms. Through tourism, the UNWTO aims to stimulate economic growth, job creation and development, and promote peace and understanding among nations. The UNWTO encourages the implementation of the Global Code of Ethics for Tourism, which sets a frame of reference for the responsible and sustainable development of world tourism. The code aims to minimize the negative impacts of tourism on the environment and on cultural heritage while maximizing the benefits for residents of tourism destinations.

The UNWTO's General Assembly—its supreme body made up of full, associate and affiliate members—approves the budget and the programme of work, and debates major topics in the tourism sector. The Executive Council is its governing board, composed of 29 full members elected by the Assembly, and a permanent member, Spain (the host country). In 2010–2011, the UNWTO had a staff of 106 and a budget of €28 million.

Secretary-General: Taleb D. Rifai (Jordan)
Headquarters: Capitán Haya 42, 28020 Madrid, Spain
Tel.: (34-91) 567-8100; Fax: (34-91) 571-3733; E-mail: *omt@unwto.org*

Preparatory Commission for the Comprehensive Nuclear-Test-Ban Treaty Organization (CTBTO)

The *Comprehensive Nuclear Test-Ban Treaty* was adopted and opened for signature in 1996. It prohibits all nuclear explosions. At the end of 2010, 181 States had signed, and of these 153 had also ratified, the *Treaty*. Of the 44 nuclear-technology-holding States whose ratification is needed for the *Treaty's* entry into force, nine have yet to ratify: China, the Democratic People's Republic of Korea (DPRK), Egypt, Indonesia, India, Iran, Israel, Pakistan and the United States. India, the DPRK and Pakistan have also yet to sign the *Treaty*. The Vienna-based Preparatory Commission for the Comprehensive Nuclear-Test-Ban Treaty Organization (*www.ctbto.org*) is tasked with building up the CTBT verification regime so that it will be fully operational when the *Treaty* enters into force. Its mandate also includes promoting the signature and ratification of the *Treaty*. The CTBT verification regime consists of a globe-spanning network of 337 facilities monitoring the Earth for signs of a nuclear explosion; an International Data Centre for processing and analysis; and on-site inspections to collect evidence on the ground in the case of a suspicious event. The organization's budget for 2010 was $115,579,600. It employs some 260 staff from 74 countries.

Executive Secretary: Tibor Tóth (Hungary)
Headquarters: Vienna International Centre, P.O. Box 1200, A-1400 Vienna, Austria
Tel.: (43-1) 26030-6200; Fax: (43-1) 26030-5823; E-mail: *info@ctbto.org*

International Atomic Energy Agency (IAEA)

The International Atomic Energy Agency (*www.iaea.org*) promotes the peaceful uses of nuclear energy for the benefit of humanity and guards against its use for military purposes. It is the world's foremost intergovernmental forum for scientific and technical cooperation in the peaceful uses of nuclear energy, and the international inspectorate for the application of nuclear safeguards covering civilian nuclear programmes. The Agency is also at the centre of efforts to promote international cooperation on nuclear safety and security-related matters. Established in 1957 as an autonomous agency under the aegis of the United Nations, it had 151 member states in November 2010. The IAEA provides technical assistance to member states in need, focusing on the application of nuclear science and technology to sustainable development, according to priorities set by the states themselves—in areas including food and agricultural production, health, industry, water management, improvement of the marine environment, generation of electricity, and nuclear safety and security. The IAEA monitors and verifies states' compliance with their non-proliferation obligations pursuant to bilateral agreements and international treaties meant to ensure that nuclear materials and facilities are not diverted for military purposes. The 2005 Nobel Peace Prize was awarded to the IAEA and its Director General Mohamed ElBaradei.

Over 250 IAEA inspectors regularly carry out inspections in more than 900 installations and other locations covered under the IAEA Safeguards Programme. The Agency's governing bodies are the General Conference, in which all member states are represented, and the Board of Governors, with 35 member states. The IAEA has a staff of 2,200 from more than 90 countries. Its regular budget for 2010 was €315.4 million; the target for additional, voluntary contributions to its Technical Cooperation Fund was $85 million.

Director General: Yukiya Amano (Japan)
Headquarters: P.O. Box 100, Wagramerstrasse 5, A-1400 Vienna, Austria
Tel.: (43-1) 2600-0; Fax: (43-1) 2600-7; E-mail: *Official.Mail@iaea.org*

Organisation for the Prohibition of Chemical Weapons (OPCW)

The Organisation for the Prohibition of Chemical Weapons (*www.opcw.org*) is an independent international organization in close working relationship with the United Nations. It monitors the implementation of the *Convention on the Prohibition of the Development, Production, Stockpiling and Use of Chemical Weapons and on their Destruction*. The *Convention*, which entered into force in 1997, is the first multilateral disarmament and non-proliferation agreement that provides for the global elimination of an entire category of weapons of mass destruction, under stringent international verification and within prescribed timelines.

The OPCW is composed of 188 member states. Since 1997, member states have verifiably destroyed more than 43,000 metric tons of chemical agents—over 60 per cent of the total declared quantity of more than 71,000 metric tons. OPCW inspectors have conducted over 4,000 inspections at military and industrial plants in 81 countries. These missions ensure that chemical weapons production facilities are deactivated and destroyed or verifiably converted to permitted purposes. Inspectors also verify the destruction of chemical weapons through their presence at destruction facilities. All OPCW member states are obliged to assist one another if they are threatened or attacked with chemical weapons. To handle such a contingency, OPCW regularly tests and enhances its capacity to coordinate a swift and effective international response aimed at protecting lives, as well as to efficiently investigate any alleged use of chemical weapons. The OPCW also has a range of international cooperation programmes to facilitate the peaceful uses of chemistry. The OPCW Technical Secretariat, based in The Hague, Netherlands, has a staff of over 500, representing some 80 nationalities. Its budget for 2010 was €75 million.

Director-General: Ahmet Uzümcü (Turkey)
Headquarters: Johan de Wittlaan 32, 2517 JR, The Hague, The Netherlands
Tel.: (31-70) 416-3300; Fax: (31-70) 306-3535; E-mail: *media@opcw.org*

World Trade Organization (WTO)

The World Trade Organization (*www.wto.org*) replaced the General Agreement on Tariffs and Trade (GATT) in 1995 as the only international organization dealing with multilateral rules governing trade between nations. It works closely with the UN and its agencies. The WTO helps trade flow smoothly in a system based on multilateral rules agreed to by all its members; to impartially settle trade disputes between governments; and to provide a forum for trade negotiations. At its heart are some 60 WTO agreements, annexes, decisions and understandings—the legal ground rules for international commerce and trade policy. The principles on which these agreements are based include: non-discrimination (the 'most-favoured nation' clause and the national treatment provision), more open trade, encouraging competition, and special provisions for less developed countries. One of the WTO's objectives is to gradually open trade for the benefit of all.

The WTO is the forum for negotiations to open markets in telecommunications, information technology equipment and financial services. Over 400 trade disputes have been brought to the WTO's dispute settlement mechanism. The WTO continues to oversee implementation of the agreements reached in the 1986–1994 Uruguay Round of world trade talks. In 2001, the WTO launched a new round of multilateral trade negotiations known as the Doha Development Agenda. Ministerial discussions have taken place since then but they have not yet resulted in the necessary breakthroughs to conclude the negotiations.

The WTO has 153 members. Its governing body is the Ministerial Conference; the General Council carries out the day-to-day work. The WTO's budget for 2010 was CHF 194 million. At the end of 2009, the WTO had 621 staff on its regular budget.

Director-General: Pascal Lamy (France)

Headquarters: Centre William Rappard, Rue de Lausanne 154, CH-1211 Geneva 21, Switzerland

Tel.: (41-22) 739-5111; Fax: (41-22) 731-4206; E-mail: *enquiries@wto.org*

II. INTERNATIONAL PEACE AND SECURITY

UN officers discover unexploded bomb in Darfur area
Personnel from the African Union-United Nations Hybrid Operation in Darfur (UNAMID) mark the location of an unexploded bomb near Shangel Tubaya, North Darfur, warning local villages and beginning the process for its destruction (27 March 2011, UN Photo/ Albert Gonzalez Farran).

II. INTERNATIONAL PEACE AND SECURITY

One of the primary purposes of the United Nations is the maintenance of international peace and security. Since its creation, the UN has often been called upon to prevent disputes from escalating into war, to persuade opposing parties to use the conference table rather than force of arms, or to help restore peace when armed conflict does break out. Over the decades, the UN has helped end numerous conflicts, often through actions of the Security Council—the primary organ for dealing with issues of international peace and security. The Security Council, the General Assembly and the Secretary-General, however, all play major, complementary roles in fostering peace and security. United Nations activities cover the principal areas of conflict prevention, peacemaking, peacekeeping, enforcement and peacebuilding (see *www.un.org/peace*). These types of engagement must overlap or take place simultaneously if they are to be effective.

During the 1990s, the end of the cold war led to an entirely new global security environment, one marked by a focus on internal rather than inter-state wars. In the 21st century, new global threats have emerged. During the same period, civil conflicts raised complex issues regarding the adequate response of the international community, including the question of how best to protect civilians in conflicts. The attacks of 11 September 2001 on the United States, followed by the atrocities committed in Bali (2002), Madrid (2004), London (2005), and Mumbai (2008), clearly demonstrated the challenge of international terrorism. In parallel, other events heightened concern about the proliferation of nuclear weapons and the dangers from other non-conventional weapons.

The United Nations mobilized immediately to step up action against terrorism. On 28 September 2001, the Security Council adopted a wide-ranging resolution under the enforcement provisions of the *Charter* to prevent the financing of terrorism, criminalize the collection of funds for such purposes, and immediately freeze terrorist financial assets—establishing a Counter-Terrorism Committee to oversee its implementation. The Council also acted to impose sanctions on suspected leaders of Al Qaeda and the Taliban.

The UN has reshaped and considerably enhanced the range of instruments at its command, strengthening its peacekeeping capacity to meet new challenges, increasingly involving regional organizations, and enhancing its post-conflict peacebuilding capability, as well as reviving use of preventive diplomacy. In addressing civil conflicts, the Security Council has authorized complex and innovative peacekeeping operations. These have provided the time and space for building the bases of sustainable peace, enabled millions of people in dozens of countries to participate in free and fair elections, and helped disarm half a million ex-combatants in the past decade alone. Since 1948, the UN has played a major role in ending conflict and fostering reconciliation, including successful missions in Cambodia, El Salvador, Guatemala, Liberia, Mozambique, Namibia, Sierra Leone, Tajikistan and Timor-Leste. Other conflicts, however—such as in the Democratic Republic of the Congo (DRC), Rwanda, Somalia and the former Yugoslavia in the early 1990s—often characterized by ethnic violence and the lack of internal power structures to deal with security issues, have brought new challenges to UN peacemaking and peacekeeping.

The essential role of UN peacekeeping was dramatically reaffirmed at the end of the 1990s, as continuing crises in the Central African Republic, the DRC, Kosovo, Sierra Leone and Timor-Leste led the Council to establish five new missions. The surge in peacekeeping reached an apex in 2009–2010, when more than 100,000 blue helmets were deployed globally. Recurring conflicts over recent years have brought the United Nations to focus increasingly on peacebuilding, with targeted efforts to reduce a country's risk of lapsing or relapsing into conflict by strengthening national capacities for conflict management, and by laying the foundations for sustainable peace and development. Experience has indicated that the creation of lasting peace depends upon pulling together all resources to help countries foster economic development, social justice, respect for human rights and good governance.

No other institution has the global legitimacy, multilateral experience, competence, coordinating ability and impartiality that the UN brings in support of these tasks. The UN has established special political missions and peacebuilding support offices in a number of countries, including Afghanistan, Burundi, the Central African Republic, Guinea-Bissau, Iraq and Sierra Leone. There are also UN political offices for Central Asia, Lebanon, the Middle East, Nepal, Somalia and West Africa.

The **Peacebuilding Commission**, which became operational in 2006, is an intergovernmental advisory body of the United Nations specifically dedicated to helping countries in transition from war to lasting peace. It brings together all relevant peacebuilding actors, including international donors and financial institutions, governments, troop-contributing countries and representatives of civil society; proposes integrated strategies for post-conflict peacebuilding and recovery; helps ensure predictable financing for early recovery activities and sustained financial investment; extends the period of attention by the international community to post-conflict recovery; and develops best practices on issues that require collaboration among political, military, humanitarian and development actors.

The concurrent General Assembly and Security Council resolutions establishing the Peacebuilding Commission also provided for the establishment of a **Peacebuilding Fund** (*www.unpbf.org*) and a **Peacebuilding Support Office** (*www.un.org/peace/peacebuilding*). In 2010, the position of Special Representative against Sexual Violence in Conflict was created, following a decade-long effort on the part of the Security Council to address and condemn all acts of sexual violence committed during times of armed conflict against civilians, especially women and children.

Security Council

The *Charter of the United Nations*—an international treaty—obligates member states to settle their disputes by peaceful means, in such a manner that international peace and security and justice are not endangered. They are to refrain from the threat or use of force against any state, and may bring any dispute before the Security Council: the UN organ with primary responsibility for maintaining peace and security. Under the *Charter*, member states are obliged to accept and carry out its decisions. Recommendations of other United Nations bodies do not have the mandatory force of Security Council decisions, but can influence situations by expressing the opinion of the international community.

When a dispute is brought to its attention, the Council usually urges the parties to settle it by peaceful means. The Council may make recommendations to the par-

Peacebuilding architecture

The UN peacebuilding architecture comprises the Peacebuilding Commission, the Peacebuilding Fund and the Peacebuilding Support Office. These three bodies work together to:

- design and coordinate peacebuilding strategies;
- sustain peace in conflict-affected countries by garnering international support for nationally owned and led peacebuilding efforts;
- provide effective support to countries in the transition from war to lasting peace.

The Peacebuilding Commission, a 31-member intergovernmental body, is charged with bringing together all relevant actors to advise on and propose integrated strategies for post-conflict peacebuilding and recovery. Its standing organizational committee consists of members of the Security Council, the Economic and Social Council, the General Assembly and top providers of contributions, military personnel and civilian police to UN missions.

The Peacebuilding Fund, a multi-year standing fund for post-conflict peacebuilding, funded by voluntary contributions, aims to ensure the immediate release of resources needed to launch peacebuilding activities, as well as the availability of appropriate financing for recovery. The Fund, which provides initial seed money for peacebuilding, had nearly $331.5 million in commitments as of February 2010, towards an initial target of $250 million. At a high-level stakeholders meeting held the following November, the Fund was commended as a fast, relevant, and catalytic resource for supporting peacebuilding initiatives in countries emerging from conflict, and $53 million were pledged for the 2011–2013 Business Plan from 21 member states.

The Peacebuilding Support Office assists and supports the Peacebulding Commission, administers the Peacebuilding Fund, and serves the Secretary-General in coordinating UN agencies in their peacebuilding efforts.

---

ties for a peaceful settlement, appoint special representatives, ask the Secretary-General to use his good offices, and undertake investigation and mediation. When a dispute leads to fighting, the Council seeks to bring it to an end as quickly as possible. Often the Council has issued ceasefire directives that have been instrumental in preventing wider hostilities. In support of a peace process, the Council may deploy military observers or a peacekeeping force to an area of conflict.

Under Chapter VII of the *Charter*, the Council is empowered to take measures to enforce its decisions. It can impose embargoes and sanctions, or authorize the use of force to ensure that mandates are fulfilled. In some cases, the Council has authorized the use of military force by a coalition of member states or by a regional organization or arrangement. However, the Council takes such action only as a last resort, when peaceful means of settling a dispute have been exhausted, and after determining that a threat to the peace, a breach of the peace or an act of aggression actually exists. Many of the recently established peacekeeping operations have been authorized by the Council in this way, meaning that the peacekeepers may use force if needed to implement their mandates. Also under Chapter VII of the *Charter*, the Council has established international tribunals to prosecute those accused of gross violations of human rights and serious breaches of international humanitarian law, including genocide.

General Assembly

Article 11 of the *Charter of the United Nations* empowers the General Assembly to "consider the general principles of cooperation in the maintenance of international peace and security" and "make recommendations … to the Members or to the Security Council or to both". The Assembly offers a means for finding consensus on difficult issues, providing a forum for the airing of grievances and diplomatic exchanges. To foster the maintenance of peace, it has held special sessions or emergency special sessions on such issues as disarmament, the question of Palestine and the situation in Afghanistan. The General Assembly considers peace and security issues in its First Committee (Disarmament and International Security) and in its Fourth Committee (Special Political and Decolonization). Over the years, the Assembly has helped promote peaceful relations among nations by adopting declarations on peace, the peaceful settlement of disputes and international cooperation.

The Assembly in 1980 approved the establishment in San José, Costa Rica, of the **University for Peace**, an international institute for studies, research and dissemination of knowledge on peace-related issues. The Assembly has designated 21 September each year as the **International Day of Peace**.

Conflict prevention

The main strategies for preventing disputes from escalating into conflict, and for preventing the recurrence of conflict, are *preventive diplomacy* and *preventive disarmament*.

Preventive diplomacy refers to action taken to prevent disputes from arising or from escalating into conflicts, and to limit the spread of conflicts when they occur. It may take the form of mediation, conciliation or negotiation. Early warning is an essential component of prevention, and the United Nations carefully monitors developments around the world to detect threats to international peace and security, thereby enabling the Security Council and the Secretary-General to carry out preventive action. Envoys and special representatives of the Secretary-General are engaged in mediation and preventive diplomacy throughout the world. In some trouble spots, the mere presence of a skilled envoy can prevent the escalation of tension. This work is often undertaken in cooperation with regional organizations.

Complementing preventive diplomacy is preventive disarmament, which seeks to reduce the number of small arms in conflict-prone regions. In El Salvador, Liberia, Sierra Leone, Timor-Leste and elsewhere, this has entailed demobilizing combat forces, as well as collecting and destroying their weapons as part of an overall peace agreement. Destroying yesterday's weapons prevents their being used in tomorrow's wars.

The Secretary-General plays a central role in peacemaking, both personally and by dispatching special envoys or missions for specific tasks, such as negotiation or fact-finding. Under the *Charter*, the Secretary-General may bring to the attention of the Security Council any matter that might threaten the maintenance of international peace and security.

Peacekeeping

United Nations peacekeeping operations (*www.un.org/en/peacekeeping*) are a vital instrument employed by the international community to advance peace and secu-

Responsibility to protect

Should the international community intervene in a country to stop gross, systematic and widespread violations of human rights? The question was raised in 1998 by Secretary-General Kofi Annan, generating wide debate. In the wake of genocide, crimes against humanity, and war crimes in Central Africa, the Balkans and elsewhere, he argued for agreement on legitimate and universal principles, within the framework of international law, for protecting civilians against gross human rights violations. Today, the question is no longer whether, but when and how the international community should intervene to protect populations against these crimes.

World leaders gathered in New York for the 2005 World Summit addressed the responsibility to protect in their comprehensive "Outcome Document". They declared that:

"Each individual state has the responsibility to protect its populations from genocide, war crimes, ethnic cleansing and crimes against humanity. This responsibility entails the prevention of such crimes, including their incitement, through appropriate and necessary means. We accept that responsibility and will act in accordance with it. The international community, through the United Nations, also has the responsibility to use appropriate diplomatic, humanitarian and other peaceful means, in accordance with Chapters VI and VIII of the *Charter*, to help to protect populations from [these crimes].

"In this context, we are prepared to take collective action, in a timely and decisive manner, through the Security Council, in accordance with the *Charter*, including Chapter VII, on a case-by-case basis and in cooperation with relevant regional organizations as appropriate, should peaceful means be inadequate and national authorities are manifestly failing to protect their populations from genocide, war crimes, ethnic cleansing and crimes against humanity."

They also highlighted the need to help states build capacity to protect their populations from these crimes, and to assist states that are under stress before crises and conflicts break out. (See General Assembly resolutions 60/1 and 63/308, and Security Council resolutions 1674(2006) and 1894(2009) addressing the protection of civilians in armed conflict and endorsing these principles.)

In 2009, Secretary-General Ban Ki-moon issued a report entitled *Implementing the Responsibility to Protect*, which outlined relevant principles to this end. The Special Adviser responsible for the conceptual, political and institutional development of the responsibility to protect, appointed by the Secretary-General in 2008, works in close collaboration with the Office of the Special Adviser on the Prevention of Genocide, established in 2004.

---

rity. The role of the UN in peacekeeping was recognized in 1988, when the United Nations peacekeeping forces received the Nobel Peace Prize. While not specifically envisaged in the *Charter*, the UN pioneered peacekeeping in 1948 with the establishment of the United Nations Truce Supervision Organization in the Middle East. Since then, it has established a total of 67 operations. At the beginning of 2011, there were 14 active peacekeeping operations.

Peacekeeping operations are deployed with the authorization of the Security Council and the consent of the host government and/or the main parties to the conflict. Peacekeeping has traditionally involved a primarily military model of observing ceasefires and the separation of forces after inter-state wars. Today, it has evolved into a complex model of many elements—military, police and civilians—working together to help lay the foundations of a sustainable peace.

Who commands peacekeeping operations?

Peacekeeping operations are established by the Security Council and directed by the Secretary-General, usually through a special representative. Depending on the mission, a Force Commander is responsible for the operation's military aspects, although military contingents answer to their own national defence entities. The United Nations has no military force of its own, and member states provide the military and police personnel required for each operation, while civilians are recruited or volunteer from around the world. Peacekeepers wear their country's uniform with a UN blue helmet or beret and a badge.

In recent years, the Council has introduced the practice of invoking the enforcement provisions in Chapter VII of the *Charter* when authorizing the deployment of certain UN peacekeeping operations, or mandating them to perform tasks which may require the use of force—such as the protection of civilians under imminent threat of physical violence. Traditionally, UN peacekeepers could only use their weapons in self-defence, but the more 'robust' mandates under Chapter VII enable them to use force, for example, to protect civilians.

The military personnel of peacekeeping operations are voluntarily provided by member states and are financed by member states, which are assessed under the peacekeeping budget. Troop-contributing states are compensated at a standard rate from that budget. The approved peacekeeping budget for 2010–2011 was approximately $7.3 billion—which represents less than 0.5 per cent of global military spending. Operations are financed through the peacekeeping budget and include troops from many countries. This worldwide 'burden-sharing' can offer extraordinary efficiency in human, financial and political terms.

Since 1948, more than 2,800 peacekeepers have lost their lives in the line of duty. As 2011 began, more than 100,000 military and police personnel from 115 countries were serving in UN peacekeeping operations.

Conflicts today are a complex mix. Their roots may be internal, but they are complicated by cross-border involvement, either by states or by economic interests and other non-state actors. Recent conflicts in Africa, for example, have involved a deadly mix of civil strife and illegal export of natural resources—such as diamonds, coltan (used in cell phones and electronic devices) and gold—which fuel arms purchases, terrorism, drug trafficking, refugee flows and environmental degradation. The response must be equally multifaceted. The Kimberley Process Certification Scheme (KPCS)—to name just one instance—was introduced by the General Assembly in 2000 to prevent diamond sales from financing conflict and human rights violations. The certification scheme aims at preventing 'blood diamonds' from entering the mainstream market.

United Nations operations, because of their universality, offer a unique legitimacy as a means of addressing conflicts. Their universality adds to their legitimacy and limits the implications for the host country's sovereignty. Peacekeepers from outside a conflict can foster discussion among warring parties while focusing global attention upon local concerns—opening doors that would otherwise remain closed for collective peace efforts. Prerequisites for the success of an operation include a genuine desire on the part of the opposing forces to resolve their dif-

United Nations peacekeeping operations*

- United Nations Truce Supervision Organization (UNTSO, est. 1948), in the Middle East (military 150; civilian 210)
- United Nations Military Observer Group in India and Pakistan (UNMOGIP, est. 1949) (military 44; civilian 71)
- United Nations Peacekeeping Force in Cyprus (UNFICYP, est. 1964) (military 857; civilian police 69; civilian 151)
- United Nations Disengagement Observer Force (UNDOF, est. 1974) in the Syrian Golan Heights (military 1,037; civilian 143)
- United Nations Interim Force in Lebanon (UNIFIL, est. 1978) (military 11,713; civilian 966)
- United Nations Mission for the Referendum in Western Sahara (MINURSO, est. 1991) (military 218; police 6; civilian 258; UN Volunteers 20)
- United Nations Interim Administration Mission in Kosovo (UNMIK, est. 1999) (military 8; police 6; civilian 417; UN Volunteers 20)
- United Nations Mission in Liberia (UNMIL, est. 2003) (military 9,369; police 1,364; civilian 1,429; UN Volunteers 213)
- United Nations Operation in Côte d'Ivoire (UNOCI, est. 2004) (military 7,385; police 1,169; civilian 1,153; UN Volunteers 273)
- United Nations Stabilization Mission in Haiti (MINUSTAH, est. 2004) (military 8,603; police 2,965; civilian 1,708; UN Volunteers 193)
- United Nations Mission in the Sudan (UNMIS, est. 2005) (military 9,938; police 665; civilian 3,556; UN Volunteers 364)
- United Nations Integrated Mission in Timor-Leste (UNMIT, est. 2006) (military 34; police 1,473; civilian 1,261; UN Volunteers 168)
- African Union-United Nations Hybrid Operation in Darfur (UNAMID, est. 2007) (military 16,997; military observers 242; police 4,577; civilian 3,750; UN Volunteers 445)
- United Nations Mission in the Central African Republic and Chad (MINURCAT, est. 2007) (military 1327; military observers 20; police 109). (The Mission completed its mandate on 31 December 2010.)
- United Nations Organization Stabilization Mission in the Democratic Republic of the Congo (MONUSCO, est. 2010) (military 18,461; police 1,224; civilian 3,180; UN Volunteers 589)

*as of 31 December 2010.

ferences peacefully, a clear peacekeeping mandate, strong political support by the international community, and the provision of the financial and human resources necessary to achieve the operation's objectives. Most importantly, peacekeeping must accompany a political process; it should not and cannot substitute for one.

The international community has drawn lessons from past operations and is working to strengthen the United Nations peacekeeping capacity in a number of areas. A blueprint for reform was provided by the 2000 report of the Secretary-General's Panel on Peace Operations, which aimed to make possible launching one new multidisciplinary peace mission per year. In effect, the decade ending in 2010 witnessed the start-up or expansion of 11 peacekeeping operations, as well as of a number of special political missions, including in Afghanistan and Iraq.

MISSIONS ADMINISTERED BY THE DEPARTMENT OF PEACEKEEPING OPERATIONS

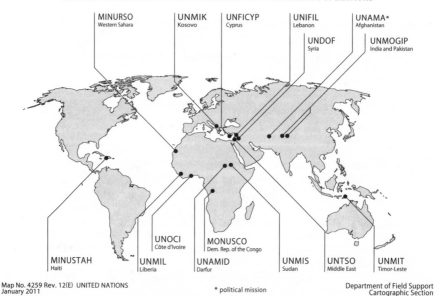

| MINURSO | UNMIK | UNFICYP | UNIFIL | UNAMA* |
| Western Sahara | Kosovo | Cyprus | Lebanon | Afghanistan |

UNDOF — Syria
UNMOGIP — India and Pakistan

UNOCI — Côte d'Ivoire
MONUSCO — Dem. Rep. of the Congo

| MINUSTAH | UNMIL | UNAMID | UNMIS | UNTSO | UNMIT |
| Haiti | Liberia | Darfur | Sudan | Middle East | Timor-Leste |

Map No. 4259 Rev. 12(E) UNITED NATIONS
January 2011

* political mission

Department of Field Support
Cartographic Section

At the instigation of Secretary-General Ban Ki-moon, a major restructuring of the UN peacekeeping apparatus took place in 2007, through the creation of a **Department of Field Support (DFS)**. While the **Department of Peacekeeping Operations (DPKO)** and the **Department of Political Affairs (DPA)** give political and executive direction, respectively, to peacekeeping operations and special political and peacebuilding missions, DFS provides dedicated support and guidance to all UN field peace operations in the areas of finance, logistics, information, communications and technology, human resources and general administration. In 2009, DPKO and DFS launched the 'New Horizon' process designed to assess the major policy and strategy dilemmas facing UN peacekeeping and to reinvigorate the dialogue with stakeholders on possible solutions, so that UN peacekeeping can meet current and future requirements.

Peacekeeping operations continuously evolve in light of changing circumstances. The tasks discharged by peacekeepers over the years have included:

- maintaining ceasefires and separation of forces. By providing 'breathing space', an operation based on a limited agreement between parties can foster an atmosphere conducive to negotiations;
- protecting humanitarian operations. In many conflicts, civilian populations have been deliberately targeted as a means to gain political ends. In such situations, peacekeepers have been asked to provide protection and support for humanitarian operations. However, such tasks can place peacekeepers in difficult political positions, and can lead to threats to their security;
- implementing a comprehensive peace settlement. Complex, multidimensional operations, deployed on the basis of comprehensive peace agreements, can assist in such diverse tasks as providing humanitarian assistance, monitoring human rights, observing elections and coordinating support for economic reconstruction;

- leading states or territories through a transition to stable government, based on democratic principles, good governance and economic development;
- protecting civilians. Non-combatants, women and children have all too often been the direct or collateral victims of recent conflicts.

Cooperation with regional and collective security organizations. The United Nations has been increasingly cooperating with regional organizations and other actors and mechanisms provided for in Chapter VIII of the *Charter*. It has worked closely with the Organization of American States (OAS) in Haiti; the European Union (EU) in the former Yugoslavia and the Democratic Republic of the Congo; the Economic Community of West African States (ECOWAS) in Liberia and Sierra Leone; and the African Union (AU) in Western Sahara, the Great Lakes region and Darfur—to name just a few. United Nations military observers have cooperated with peacekeeping forces of regional organizations in Georgia, Liberia, Sierra Leone and Tajikistan; the North Atlantic Treaty Organization (NATO) works alongside UN personnel in Afghanistan and Kosovo. This is a welcome development, insofar as the global demand for peace operations now outstrips the capacity of any single actor, including the UN. Efforts by regional actors to develop their own abilities to plan, manage and sustain peace operations give a greater depth to response options, thus spawning a more flexible and responsive system that is better able to face complex challenges posed by internal conflict.

Enforcement

Under Chapter VII of the *Charter*, the Security Council can take enforcement measures to maintain or restore international peace and security. Such measures range from economic sanctions to international military action.

Sanctions

The Security Council has resorted to mandatory sanctions as an enforcement tool when peace was threatened and diplomatic efforts had failed. Sanctions have been imposed in recent years on Afghanistan, the Democratic People's Republic of Korea, Eritrea, Ethiopia, Haiti, Iran, Iraq, Liberia, Libya, Rwanda, Sierra Leone, Somalia, the Sudan, UNITA forces in Angola and the former Yugoslavia. The range of sanctions has included comprehensive economic and trade sanctions, or more specific measures such as arms embargoes, travel and sport bans, as well as financial or diplomatic restrictions.

The point of sanctions is to apply pressure on a state or entity to comply with the objectives set by the Council without resorting to the use of force. Sanctions offer the Council an important tool to enforce its decisions. The universal character of the UN makes it an appropriate body to establish and monitor sanctions. Yet many states and humanitarian organizations have expressed concerns at the possible adverse impact of sanctions on the most vulnerable segments of the civilian population, such as the elderly, the disabled, refugees or mothers with children. Concerns also exist about the negative economic, social and even political impact sanctions can have on the economies of third or neighbouring countries, where trade and economic relations with the sanctioned state are interrupted.

It is increasingly accepted that the design and application of sanctions need to be improved. The negative effects of sanctions can be reduced either by incorpo-

Current United Nations Political and Peacebuilding Missions*

- United Nations Political Office for Somalia (UNPOS, 1995) (civilian 53)
- Office of the United Nations Special Coordinator for the Middle East (UNSCO, 1999) (civilian 58)
- United Nations Office for West Africa (UNOWA, 2001) (civilian 25; military advisers 4)
- United Nations Assistance Mission in Afghanistan (UNAMA, 2002) (military observers 12; police 4; civilian 1,973; UN Volunteers 56)
- United Nations Assistance Mission for Iraq (UNAMI, 2003) (military 235; civilian 818) (Authorized strength: 1,014)
- United Nations Integrated Office in Burundi (BINUB, 2007) (military observers 4; civilian 347; UN Volunteers 43)
- United Nations Mission in Nepal (UNMIN, 2007) (military observers 72; civilian 159; UN Volunteers 19)
- Office of the United Nations Special Coordinator for Lebanon (UNSCOL, 2007) (civilian 76)
- United Nations Integrated Peacebuilding Office in Sierra Leone (UNIPSIL, 2008) (civilian 66; UN Volunteers 6)
- United Nations Regional Centre for Preventive Diplomacy for Central Asia (UNRCCA, 2008) (civilian 20)
- United Nations Integrated Peacebuilding Office in the Central African Republic (BINUCA, 2009) (military advisers 5; police 6; civilian 105; UN Volunteers 4)
- United Nations Integrated Peace-building Office in Guinea-Bissau (UNIOGBIS, 2010) (military adviser 1; civilian 90)

* as of 31 December 2010.

rating humanitarian exceptions into Security Council resolutions, or by better targeting them. So-called 'smart sanctions'—which seek to pressure those in power rather than the population at large, thus reducing humanitarian costs—have been gaining support. Smart sanctions may, for instance, involve freezing assets and blocking the financial transactions of elites or other political entities whose illicit activities triggered action in the first place.

Authorizing military action

When peacemaking efforts fail, stronger action by member states may be authorized under Chapter VII of the *Charter*. The Security Council has authorized coalitions of member states to use "all necessary means", including military action, to deal with a conflict—as it did to restore the sovereignty of Kuwait after its invasion by Iraq (1991); to establish a secure environment for humanitarian relief operations in Somalia (1992); to contribute to the protection of civilians at risk in Rwanda (1994); to restore the democratically elected government in Haiti (1994); to protect humanitarian operations in Albania (1997); to restore peace and security in East Timor (1999 and 2006); and to protect civilians in Libya (2011). These actions, though authorized by the Security Council, were entirely under the control of the participating states. They were not UN peacekeeping operations—which are established by the Council and directed by the Secretary-General.

Peacebuilding

For the United Nations, peacebuilding refers to efforts to assist countries and regions in their transitions from war to peace, including activities and programmes to support and strengthen these transitions. A peacebuilding process normally begins with the signing of a peace agreement by former warring parties and a United Nations role in facilitating its implementation. This may include a continued diplomatic role for the UN, to ensure that difficulties are overcome through negotiation rather than a resort to arms. It may also include various types of assistance—such as the deployment of peacekeepers; the repatriation and reintegration of refugees; the monitoring of elections; and the disarmament, demobilization and reintegration of combatants. At the heart of peacebuilding is the attempt to build a new and legitimate state that will have the capacity to peacefully manage disputes, protect its civilians and ensure respect for human rights.

Peacebuilding involves action by a wide array of organizations of the UN system, including the World Bank, regional economic commissions, NGOs and local citizens' groups. Peacebuilding has played a prominent role in UN operations in Bosnia and Herzegovina, Cambodia, El Salvador, Guatemala, Kosovo, Liberia and Mozambique, as well as more recently in Afghanistan, Burundi, Iraq, Sierra Leone and Timor-Leste. An example of inter-state peacebuilding has been the UN Mission in Ethiopia and Eritrea.

Electoral assistance

The United Nations broke new ground in 1989, when it supervised the entire election process that led to the independence of Namibia. Since then, the United Nations, at the request of governments, has assisted with elections in countries such as Nicaragua (1990), Angola (1992), Cambodia (1993), El Salvador, South Africa and Mozambique (1994), Eastern Slavonia (Croatia) (1997), the Central African Republic (1998, 1999), Afghanistan (2004, 2005, 2010), Iraq (2005, 2010), Liberia (2005), Haiti (2006, 2010), the Democratic Republic of the Congo (2006) and Côte d'Ivoire (2010). It observed the 1993 referendum in Eritrea, and organized and conducted the 1999 popular consultation in East Timor and its 2001 and 2002 elections, which led to the independence of East Timor as Timor-Leste, as well as its elections in 2007.

The degree and type of United Nations involvement depends upon such factors as the requests received from governments, provisions of peace agreements, or mandates from the General Assembly or the Security Council. The UN has played a variety of roles, ranging from technical assistance to the actual conducting of the electoral process. In some cases, the UN coordinates the activities of international observers. Typically, such observers follow the registration of voters, the electoral campaign and the organization of the polls. When requested to step in after a conflict, the Organization has carried out wide-ranging tasks in this new form of peacebuilding—on occasion taking up the full range of government powers while working with local political and civil leaders to build a self-sustaining government.

Since 1992, the United Nations has provided various forms of electoral assistance to more than 100 countries—including advisory services, logistics, training, civic education, computer applications and short-term observation. The **Electoral Assistance Division** in the Department of Political Affairs (*www.un.org/depts/dpa/ead*) is the focal point for electoral affairs within the UN system. The Division has

ONGOING POLITICAL AND PEACEBUILDING MISSIONS

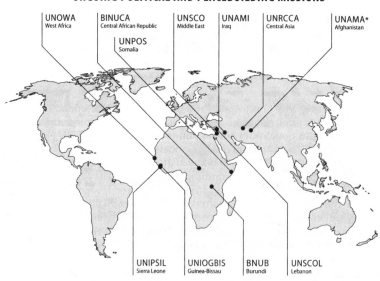

| UNOWA | BINUCA | UNSCO | UNAMI | UNRCCA | UNAMA* |
| West Africa | Central African Republic | Middle East | Iraq | Central Asia | Afghanistan |

UNPOS
Somalia

| UNIPSIL | UNIOGBIS | BNUB | UNSCOL |
| Sierra Leone | Guinea-Bissau | Burundi | Lebanon |

Map No. 4147 Rev. 35(E) UNITED NATIONS   * Mission directed and supported by the   Department of Field Support
January 2011   Department of Peacekeeping Operations   Cartographic Section

increasingly been called upon to provide support and guidance for electoral processes as key elements of UN-brokered peace negotiations, or in the context of peacekeeping and peacebuilding efforts. The UNDP provides technical support to the election process, helps countries establish electoral structures, and often coordinates UN electoral assistance in the field. The OHCHR helps to train election officials, establish guidelines for drafting electoral laws and procedures, and sets up information activities on human rights and elections.

Building peace through development

The United Nations aims to consolidate peace through development assistance. Organizations including the UNDP, UNICEF, WFP, and UNHCR play key roles in the recovery stage, which is crucial for providing opportunities for displaced persons and restoring confidence in national and local institutions. The United Nations can help repatriate refugees, clear landmines, repair infrastructure, mobilize resources and stimulate economic recovery. While war is the worst enemy of development, a healthy and balanced development is the best form of conflict prevention.

Action for peace
Africa

Africa is an area of major focus and action for the United Nations (see *www.un.org/africa/osaa*). The Organization has addressed the challenges posed by protracted conflicts and longstanding disputes on the continent in innovative ways and at the highest level. In their *Millennium Declaration* in September 2000, world leaders resolved to give full support, including special measures to help Africa tackle its peace and development issues.

Africa: a UN priority

UN action for Africa over the years has included its campaign against apartheid in South Africa, active support for Namibia's independence, and some 25 peacekeeping operations in various areas on the continent.

In a 1998 report on the causes of conflict in Africa, the Secretary-General urged African nations to rely on political rather than military responses; embrace good governance, respect for human rights, democratization and accountability; and enact reforms to promote growth. The Security Council has adopted resolutions on the destabilizing effects of illicit arms flows, on arms embargoes, and on conflict prevention. In 2010, the Council extended the mandate of the African Union mission in Somalia; and extended the mandates of UN missions, among others, in Côte d'Ivoire, the DRC, Guinea-Bissau, Sierra Leone and the Sudan. It also re-authorized states to intervene in acts of piracy off the coast of Somalia

The Secretary-General and his special representatives, advisers and envoys all remain deeply engaged in UN action for Africa, and the UN continues to act in close collaboration with the African Union and subregional organizations, such as the Economic Community of West African States (ECOWAS) and the Southern African Development Community (SADC).

The Office of the Special Adviser on Africa (*www.un.org/africa/osaa*) works to enhance international support for African development and security, improve coordination of UN system support, and facilitate global deliberations on Africa, particularly with respect to the long-term strategic framework adopted by African leaders in 2001—the New Partnership for Africa's Development (NEPAD).

Southern Africa

At the end of the 1980s, with the cold war waning, the United Nations was able to reap the fruits of many years of efforts aimed at ending wars that had plagued southern Africa. The demise of the apartheid regime in South Africa, whose influence extended to the bordering 'frontline' states, and which had supported opposition combat forces in Angola and Mozambique, was a major factor in these efforts. In 1988, South Africa agreed to cooperate with the Secretary-General to ensure the independence of Namibia.

In 1992, the government of Mozambique and the Mozambican National Resistance (RENAMO) signed a peace agreement to end a long and debilitating civil war. As part of the agreement, the **United Nations Operation in Mozambique**, deployed in 1993, successfully monitored the ceasefire, the demobilization of forces and the country's first multiparty elections, held in 1994.

An intermittent yet devastating civil war in Angola, between the government and the National Union for the Total Independence of Angola (UNITA), had plagued the country since its independence from Portugal in 1975. The UN played an active role in ending the conflict—through mediation by the Secretary-General and his envoys, the organization of peace talks, the imposition of a Security Council arms and oil embargo and travel restrictions against UNITA, and the monitoring of national elections. The Security Council established several successive peacekeeping and political missions in Angola from 1989 to 2003. After many years of proactive involvement by the UN and the international community to promote peace in the country, the protracted war in Angola came to an end when UNITA founder and leader Jonas Savimbi was killed in combat in February 2002. UNITA and the government agreed to a ceasefire in March of that year. The following August, the **United Nations Mission to Angola (UNMA)** was mandated to assist the government with elections, promoting human rights, enhancing the rule of law, supporting reintegration of demobilized soldiers and promoting economic recovery. In December 2002, the Security Council lifted all sanctions it had imposed on UNITA. By early 2003, UNMA was dissolved, and responsibility for its remaining activities was transferred to a strengthened office of the UN Resident Coordinator.

Great Lakes region

Rwanda. The involvement of the United Nations in Rwanda began in 1993, when Rwanda and Uganda requested the deployment of military observers along their common border to prevent military use of the area by the Rwandese Patriotic Front (RPF). The Security Council established the **United Nations Observer Mission Uganda-Rwanda (UNOMUR).**

Fighting had broken out in Rwanda in 1990 between the mainly Hutu government and the Tutsi-led RPF, operating from Uganda. A 1993 peace agreement provided for a transitional government and for elections. At the parties' request, the Security Council set up the **United Nations Assistance Mission for Rwanda (UNAMIR)** to help them implement it. But in April 1994, the death of the Presidents of Burundi and Rwanda (both Hutus) in a plane crash caused by rocket fire ignited weeks of intense and systemic waves of massacres by the Hutu-dominated army and militias, aimed at exterminating Tutsis and moderate Hutus. UNAMIR sought to arrange a ceasefire, without success, and when some countries unilaterally withdrew their contingents, the Security Council reduced UNAMIR's strength from 2,548 to 270. Nevertheless, UNAMIR managed to shelter thousands of Rwandans. In May, the Council imposed an arms embargo against Rwanda and increased UNAMIR's strength to up to 5,500 troops, but it took months for member states to provide those additional troops. In July, RPF forces took control of Rwanda, ending the civil war and establishing a broad-based government.

From a population of 7.9 million, approximately 800,000 people had been murdered, some 2 million fled to other countries, and up to 2 million were internally displaced. A UN appeal raised $762 million to address the enormous humanitarian challenge.

The ending of the civil war led large numbers of Rwandese Hutus to take refuge in eastern Zaire—now the Democratic Republic of the Congo (DRC). Among them were elements that had been involved in the genocide, and these armed groups began launching attacks into adjacent Rwanda. Eventually, Uganda and Rwanda intervened in the DRC, claiming security concerns over sanctuary being given there to former Hutu militias responsible for the 1994 genocide. After intensive diplomatic efforts by the United Nations, the OAU and the region, the 1999 Lusaka Ceasefire Agreement was signed. The Security Council subsequently established the **United Nations Mission in the Democratic Republic of the Congo (MONUC).**

In July 2002, Rwanda and the DRC agreed on the withdrawal of Rwandese troops from the DRC and the dismantling of the Hutu militias—a major turning point towards peace and stability in the region. In 2003, MONUC voluntarily repatriated some 900 Rwandese combatants and their dependants. That same year, a new constitution was adopted by referendum, and the first multiparty parliamentary elections were held since independence in 1962. To mark the tenth anniversary of the genocide, the General Assembly declared 7 April 2004 as the International Day of Reflection on the 1994 Genocide in Rwanda.

The **International Criminal Tribunal for Rwanda (ICTR)**, established by the Security Council, is tasked with prosecuting those responsible for genocide and war crimes. By the end of 2010, the ICTR had indicted 92 individuals, handing down 42 judgements involving 52 accused. There were 22 detainees on trial, two awaiting trial, and 10 whose cases were pending appeal; 11 accused remained at large. Former President Jean Kambanda was convicted and sentenced to life imprisonment.

Burundi. The United Nations participated in efforts to resolve the crisis in that country, where a long-standing internal conflict led in 1993 to a coup attempt in which the first democratically elected President, a Hutu, and six ministers were killed. This ignited factional fighting in which scores died in the following three years.

In 1996, the government—put in place by a 1994 agreement between the Hutu majority and Tutsi minority—was deposed by a Tutsi-led military coup. As fighting intensified between the largely Tutsi army and Hutu rebels, some 500,000 people were forcibly transferred to 'regroupment camps', while 300,000 fled to Tanzania. After the establishment in 1998 of a transitional constitution based on political partnership between Hutus and Tutsis, a transitional government and parliament were installed in November 2001. By mid-2003, ceasefire agreements had been signed with three major factional groups, and the AU had authorized deployment of the African Mission in Burundi (AMIB), comprising up to 3,500 troops. By the end of April, half-way through the transitional period, a Hutu President and Tutsi Vice-President were sworn in. However, deadly attacks continued to take place in Bujumbura, Burundi's capital. Sixteen of Burundi's 17 provinces were subject to sporadic fighting, looting and armed banditry, forcing the UN to withdraw its non-essential staff from Bujumbura.

Sustained efforts by South Africa and other countries in the region resulted in a ceasefire agreement in November 2003. There was real hope that peace would emerge from a decade of civil strife that had left between 250,000 and 300,000 people dead, and the presence of AMIB had played a key role in making it possible. The Mission suffered from a serious lack of funds and logistics support, however, and the AU requested that AMIB be taken over by the United Nations. In May 2004, acting under the enforcement provisions of the *Charter*, the Security Council authorized the deployment of the **United Nations Operation in Burundi (ONUB)**—to be composed, initially, of AMIB forces. More than 2,000 AMIB troops were re-branded as UN forces. In 2005, a referendum on Burundi's post-transitional constitution was held, followed by communal elections in June, and the election of the country's first post-transitional president in August. A ceasefire agreement was signed in September, which the UN helped implement.

In January 2007, ONUB was replaced by the **United Nations Integrated Office in Burundi (BINUB)**, to support the peace consolidation process and assist the government in strengthening national institutions, training the police, professionalizing the national defence force, completing demobilization and reintegration of former combatants, protecting human rights, reforming the justice and legal sector, and promoting economic growth and poverty reduction. In January 2011, the UN Office in Burundi (BNUB) replaced BINUB.

Democratic Republic of the Congo (DRC). Following the 1994 genocide in Rwanda and the establishment of a new government there, some 1.2 million Rwandese Hutus—including elements who had taken part in the genocide—fled to the neighbouring Kivu provinces of the DRC, formerly Zaïre. A rebellion began in those provinces in 1996, pitting the forces led by Laurent Désiré Kabila against the army of President Mobutu Sese Seko. Kabila's forces, aided by Rwanda and Uganda, took the capital city of Kinshasa in 1997 and renamed the country the Democratic Republic of the Congo. In 1998, a rebellion against the Kabila government, led by the Congolese Rally for Democracy (RCD), started in the Kivu regions. Within weeks, the rebels had seized large areas of the country. Angola, Chad, Namibia and Zimbabwe promised President Kabila military support, but the rebels maintained their grip on the eastern regions. Rwanda and Uganda supported the rebel movement. The Security Council called for a ceasefire and the withdrawal of foreign forces. In early 1999, the DRC, along with Angola, Namibia, Rwanda, Uganda and Zimbabwe, signed the Lusaka Ceasefire Agreement, which also provided for the holding of an inter-Congolese dialogue. The RCD and the Mouvement de Libération du Congo signed it in August. The Council subsequently established the **United Nations Mission in the Democratic Republic of the Congo (MONUC)** to assist in implementing the agreement.

In January 2001, President Kabila was assassinated. He was succeeded by his son Joseph. In April, an expert panel established by the Security Council reported that the DRC conflict was mainly about access by foreign armies to the country's rich mineral resources. Five key minerals—diamonds, copper, cobalt, gold and coltan (a component of electronic chips used in mobile devices)—were being exploited by those armies, while a number of companies had been trading arms for natural resources. In May, President Joseph Kabila announced that he was lifting the ban on political parties, and in October, the long-awaited inter-Congolese dialogue began in Addis Ababa, Ethiopia.

In July 2002, an agreement was signed by the DRC and Rwanda on the withdrawal of Rwandan combatants from the DRC. In September, a similar agreement was reached between the DRC and Uganda. However, by October, renewed fighting in the eastern part of the DRC threatened to destabilize the entire country. By the end of the year, the parties to the conflict, under UN and South African mediation, agreed to form a transitional government. The Security Council enlarged MONUC to 8,700 military personnel and expanded its presence eastward, but fighting erupted again in the South Kivu, generating massive refugee flows. Finally, in May 2003, the parties signed a ceasefire agreement for the Ituri region. MONUC continued to patrol Bunia, the capital city of the Ituri province, trying to ease ethnic tensions and reassure the terrified local population—the brutal interethnic power struggle had been marked by the systematic use of rape and murder.

Following the ceasefire, the Security Council authorized deployment of an **Interim Emergency Multinational Force (IEMF)** to Bunia to help stabilize the situation. In June of that year, the government and the country's main opposition factions signed an agreement on military and security arrangements, and subsequently, a power-sharing government of national unity and transition was installed—led by President Kabila. The Council increased MONUC's military strength to 10,800. Acting under Chapter VII of the *Charter*, it authorized the mission to use force to fulfill its mandate in Ituri and North and South Kivu. In September, IEMF handed over its security responsibilities to MONUC.

The country's first free and fair elections in 46 years were held in July 2006, with voters electing a 500-seat National Assembly. Following a run-off election for the presidency in October, Joseph Kabila was declared the winner. The electoral process represented one of the most complex votes the UN had ever helped organize.

Through MONUC, the UN remained actively involved in trying to resolve the conflict in North Kivu between the army and dissident forces. In 2007, the UN facilitated an agreement between the DRC and Rwanda to address the threat posed to the region by local and foreign armed groups that still remained in the eastern DRC, including the former Hutu militias ("Interahamwe") and Rwandan Armed Forces ("ex-FAR").

In October 2008, RCD forces seized a major military camp, strategically situated on the way to the city of Goma, for use as a base for attacks. Riots erupted around the UN compound in Goma as the national army retreated under pressure from the RCD. UN armoured vehicles were used to halt the advance of the rebels on the city. Peacekeepers were deployed from Goma to North Kivu. The United Nations took action to prevent further harm to the population and, in November, the Security Council unanimously decided to send an additional 3,085 peacekeepers to the area, citing "extreme concern at the deteriorating humanitarian situation and in particular the targeted attacks against the civilian population, sexual violence, recruitment of child soldiers and summary executions".

In late 2009, MONUC dispatched peacekeepers to the Sud-Ubangi Province, where a new conflict had erupted, to protect the population. In July 2010, MONUC became the **United Nations Organization Stabilization Mission in the Democratic Republic of the Congo (MONUSCO)**, reflecting the new phase reached in the country. The Council decided that MONUSCO would comprise, in addition to its civilian and judiciary components, a maximum of 19,815 military personnel, 760 military observers, 391 police personnel and 1,050 members of formed police units. Future reconfigurations of MONUSCO would be determined as the situation evolved, including: the completion of military operations in North and South Kivu as well as the Orientale provinces; improved government capacity to protect the population; and the consolidation of state authority throughout the DRC.

Central African Republic. The conflict in the Central African Republic began when soldiers staged a series of mutinies in the mid-1990s. In 1998, the UN established the **United Nations Mission in the Central African Republic (MINURCA)**— a peacekeeping operation with a mandate to help improve security in the capital, Bangui. Later, the UN also provided support for the 1999 presidential elections. The **United Nations Peacebuilding Support Office in the Central African Republic (BONUCA)** was created in February 2000, succeeding MINURCA.

An attempted coup was thwarted in May 2001. Two years later, in March 2003, a rebel military leadership seized power, ousting the elected president. The Security Council condemned the coup, stressing that the Bangui authorities had to elaborate a plan for national dialogue, including a timeframe for the holding of elections. A process of national dialogue led to two rounds of legislative and presidential elections in March and May 2005. In the final runoff, François Bozizé, who had led the coup, was elected with 64.6 per cent of the vote. The newly elected National Assembly held its first regular session in mid-2006.

The UN mission played a significant role in encouraging the signing in 2008 of the Global Peace Agreement between the government and three main rebel groups. It also facilitated the holding in December 2008 of the Inclusive Political Dialogue between the government, leaders of rebel groups, exiled political opponents, civil society and other stakeholders. The Dialogue called for the creation of a government of national unity; the holding of municipal, legislative and presidential elections; the creation of a truth and reconciliation commission; and the launch of a programme for the disarmament, demobilization and reintegration of former combatants.

The **United Nations Mission in Central African Republic and Chad (MINURCAT)** was established by the Security Council in September 2007 to contribute to the protection of civilians, and to promote human rights, the rule of law and regional peace. In January 2009, the Council authorized the deployment of a military component of MINURCAT to follow up the European Union military force (EUFOR), which was completing its mandate. (MINURCAT's mandate ended on 31 December 2010.) Also in 2009, the **United Nations Integrated Peacebuilding Office in the Central African Republic (BINUCA)** succeeded BONUCA. The new Peacebuilding Office focuses on promoting the implementation of the various agreements and commitments in the face of persistent challenges, including recurring flare-ups of violence in the northeastern part of the country.

International Conference on the Great Lakes Region. In view of the important regional dimension of the conflicts involving the Great Lakes countries, the Security Council, following the 1994 Rwanda genocide, called for the convening of an international conference on the region. At the end of the 1990s, the Office of the Special Representative of the Secretary-General for the Great Lakes Region was established. It played a key role in promoting dialogue and also served, with the African Union, as joint Secretariat for the conference. The first International Conference on the Great Lakes Region was held in Dar es Salaam, Tanzania, in November 2004.

Meeting again in 2006, the 11 regional heads of state and governments which had participated in that conference—Angola, Burundi, Central African Republic, Congo, the DRC, Kenya, Rwanda, the Sudan, Tanzania, Uganda and Zambia—signed a Pact on Security, Stability and Development in the Great Lakes Region, concluding a four-year diplomatic process. It provided a framework for the signatories to collectively identify problems facing the region and formulate plans for addressing them.

Upon resumption of large-scale hostilities between the government of the DRC and rebels in the region, the UN Secretary-General in 2008 appointed former President Olusegun Obasanjo of Nigeria as Special Envoy on the Great Lakes Region. His mandate was to help end the crisis in eastern DRC by pursuing talks with the region's governments, and in particular those of the DRC and Rwanda; restore mutual confidence, and assist Great Lakes countries in addressing the challenges to peace, security and development in the region. An office was created by the UN Department for Political Affairs (DPA) in Nairobi to support the special envoy and his 'co-facilitator', former Tanzanian President Benjamin Mkapa, who were tasked by the heads of state of the region to offer their 'good offices' for resolving the conflict on behalf of the region, the African Union and the UN. The co-facilitators worked closely with the UN peacekeeping mission in the DRC, MONUSCO, as well as with the Special Envoy for the Lord's Resistance Army-affected areas, former President Joaquim Chissano of Mozambique.

Under the auspices of the co-facilitators, peace agreements were signed in 2009 between the government of the DRC and the National Congress for the Defence of the People (CNDP), and the government and other armed groups of North and South Kivu. They provide for the transformation of the CNDP and other armed groups into political parties, the release of political prisoners, the promotion of national reconciliation, the creation of permanent local conciliation committees, the return of refugees and internally displaced persons, and the reform of the public service and security institutions. Many, but not all, of the provisions of the Agreements have been implemented. The implementation of the Agreements is being overseen by a National Follow-up Committee, working closely with representatives of DPA, the co-facilitators and MONUSCO.

Based on recommendations by the special envoy in his final report to the Secretary-General in March 2010, the Office of the Special Envoy in Nairobi closed in June 2010. MONUSCO and DPA continue to monitor implementation of the Agreements.

West Africa

A United Nations inter-agency mission visited 11 countries in West Africa in March 2001. It recommended that the interlinked political, economic and social problems faced by West African countries be addressed through an integrated subregional strategy involving the UN and its partners. In 2001, the Secretary-General decided to establish the **Office of the Special Representative of the Secretary-General for West Africa (UNOWA)** (*www.un.org/unowa*) to promote such an integrated approach. Based in Dakar, Senegal, it became operational in 2002.

UNOWA is the first UN regional peacebuilding office in the world. It carries out good offices roles and special assignments in West African countries, liaising with subregional organizations and reporting to UN Headquarters on key development issues. The special representative has been closely involved in international efforts aimed at resolving conflicts such as in Côte d'Ivoire and Liberia. UNOWA is involved in addressing such cross-border challenges as mercenaries; child soldiers; small arms proliferation; security sector reform; democratization; economic integration; youth unemployment; and transborder cooperation. It has organized regional meetings aimed at harmonizing programmes for the disarmament, demobilization and reintegration of former combatants.

The special representative is also chairperson of the Cameroon-Nigeria Mixed Commission, established by the Secretary-General at the request of the Presidents of Nigeria and Cameroon, to consider all aspects of the implementation of a ruling by the International Court of Justice on the boundary between the two countries. Relations between Cameroon and Nigeria have been strained over issues relating to their 1,600-kilometre land boundary, extending from Lake Chad to the Bakassi peninsula, with a maritime boundary in the Gulf of Guinea. Issues included rights over oil-rich land and sea reserves, and the fate of local populations. Tensions escalated into military confrontation at the end of 1993 with the deployment of Nigerian military personnel to the 1,000-square-kilometre Bakassi peninsula. In 1994, Cameroon brought the border dispute to the International Court of Justice. In October 2002, the Court issued its judgment, and the Mixed Commission held its first meeting in December, meeting every two months thereafter—alternating between Yaoundé, Cameroon, and Abuja, Nigeria. In 2006, the Presidents of both countries signed an agreement to end the border dispute over the Bakassi peninsula, following intense mediation by the Secretary-General. By mid-August, Nigeria had completely withdrawn its troops and formally transferred authority over the region to Cameroon. In 2007, the parties agreed on the delineation of the maritime boundary line between the two countries, and thereby resolved the four sections addressed by the Court's ruling. Progress continued to be made in marking their common land boundary, under the supervision of the Mixed Commission, and it was estimated that the boundary demarcation would be completed by 2012.

Côte d'Ivoire. In December 1999, General Robert Guei overthrew Côte d'Ivoire's government. New presidential elections were scheduled for October 2000. Realizing that he was losing in the polls to Laurent Gbagbo, leader of the Front populaire ivorien, Guei claimed victory in late October. Alassane Ouattara, leader of the Rassemblement démocratique des républicains, had been barred from contesting the elections under controversial new nationality laws and eligibility conditions. As thousands demonstrated against Guei's action in Abidjan, Gbagbo declared himself president, and Guei fled the city. Violent clashes ensued between Gbagbo's supporters, those backing Ouattara and security forces, causing hundreds of deaths.

An independent commission established by the Secretary-General later concluded that the security forces had been repressing the protests and were implicated in the killings. A national reconciliation process was launched under the chairmanship of former Prime Minister Seydou Diarra, and in August 2002, President Gbagbo formed a new, broad-based government. Despite this action, in September, some military personnel attempted a coup and occupied the northern part of the country. The attempted coup resulted in a de facto partition of the country, with the government controlling only the south. The fighting caused massive displacements.

The Economic Community of West African States (ECOWAS) established a peace-keeping force to monitor a ceasefire agreement between the government and one of the rebel groups. In January 2003, the government and the remaining rebel groups agreed to a ceasefire. A peace agreement was reached, providing for the establishment of a government of national reconciliation. President Gbagbo established the national reconciliation government in March, and two months later, the army and the Forces nouvelles—comprising the three rebel groups—signed a ceasefire agreement. Subsequently, the Security Council established the **United Nations Mission in Côte d'Ivoire (MINUCI)**, consisting of up to 76 military liaison officers and a civilian component, to facilitate implementation of the agreement. In September, however, the Forces nouvelles rejected President Gbagbo's appointment of defence and internal security ministers and pulled out of the government. It also protested that President Gbagbo had not delegated enough power to the Prime Minister and national reconciliation government.

Responding to this situation, the Security Council, in early 2004, established the **United Nations Operation in Côte d'Ivoire (UNOCI)**, asking the Secretary-General to transfer authority from MINUCI and the ECOWAS forces to UNOCI, and authorizing the French troops in the country to use all necessary means to support the new Mission, which had an authorized maximum strength of 6,240 military personnel and a wide-ranging mandate.

In April 2005, the government and the rebel Forces nouvelles began a withdrawal of weapons from the frontline—an area held by peacekeepers of UNOCI and the UN-authorized French forces. In June, the Security Council expanded UNOCI to prevent the situation from deteriorating. Towards the end of the year, President Gbagbo agreed to the appointment of a powerful interim Prime Minister, as proposed by the AU and endorsed by the Council. President Gbagbo and Forces nouvelles secretary-general Guillaume Soro signed the 'Ouagadougou Agreement' in March 2007. It called for the creation of a new transitional government; free and fair presidential elections; merging the Forces nouvelles with the national forces; dismantling the militias; and replacing the so-called zone of confidence separating the government-controlled south and rebel-controlled north with a 'green line' to be monitored by UNOCI.

Mr. Soro became Prime Minister, and the country's major political parties adopted a code of good conduct for the presidential elections. The Independent Electoral Commission, in November 2010, declared Alassane Ouattara the winner, with over 54 per cent of the vote. The President of the Constitutional Council, however, stated that the results were invalid, and declared Laurent Gbagbo the winner. Both Gbagbo and Ouattara claimed victory and took the presidential oath of office. The United Nations, AU, ECOWAS, EU and most states recognized Mr. Ouattara as President elect and called for Mr. Gbagbo to step down. Mr. Gbagbo refused, and ordered UN peacekeepers to leave the country. The Security Council extended UNOCI's mandate until the end of June 2011, and also decided to send 2,000 supplementary peacekeepers. The World Bank halted loans to the country and travel restrictions were placed on Mr. Gbagbo and his allies.

Liberia. After eight years of civil strife, a democratically elected government was installed in Liberia in 1997, and the **United Nations Peace-building Support Office in Liberia (UNOL)** was established. In 1999, however, fighting broke out between government forces and the Liberians United for Reconciliation and Democracy (LURD). In early 2003, a new armed group emerged in the west—the Movement for Democracy in Liberia (MODEL). By May, rebel forces controlled 60 per cent of the country. As the parties gathered in June in Accra, Ghana, for peace talks sponsored by ECOWAS, the UN-backed Special Court for Sierra Leone announced its indictment of Liberian President Charles Taylor for war crimes in Sierra Leone during its 10-year civil war. The President offered to remove himself from the peace process. Barely two weeks later, the government, LURD and MODEL signed a ceasefire accord, aiming to reach a comprehensive peace agreement within 30 days—and the formation of a transitional government without President Taylor. Despite that promising development, the fighting escalated, and, as a result, ECOWAS decided to send in a vanguard force of over 1,000 troops.

The UN and other relief agencies began rushing food and medical supplies to hundreds of thousands of desperate people crowding the streets of Monrovia. President Taylor resigned in mid-August, and his Vice-President, Moses Blah, succeeded him, heading an interim government. A few days after President Taylor's departure, the Secretary-General's special representative secured a signed agreement by the parties to ensure free and unimpeded access of humanitarian aid to all territories under their control, and to guarantee the security of aid workers. The parties also signed a comprehensive peace agreement.

In September 2003, the Security Council established the **United Nations Mission in Liberia (UNMIL)**—with up to 15,000 military personnel and over 1,000 civilian police officers—to take over from the ECOWAS force, and replace UNOL. Its mandate included: monitoring the ceasefire; assisting in the disarmament, demobilization, reintegration and repatriation (DDRR) of all armed parties; providing security at key government installations and vital infrastructure; protecting UN staff, facilities and civilians; and assisting in humanitarian aid and human rights. UNMIL was also mandated to help the transitional government develop a strategy to consolidate its institutions, with a view to holding free and fair elections by October 2005. As scheduled, 3,500 ECOWAS soldiers were 'rehatted' with the UN blue helmet. Within two weeks, the parties declared Monrovia a 'weapons-free zone'. In October, the national transitional government was installed, led by Chairman Gyude Bryant, and former President Blah turned over a large quantity of arms to UN peacekeepers, declaring: "We do not want to fight anymore."

The DDRR process was launched in December. Over the next 12 months, nearly 100,000 Liberians turned in guns, ammunition, rocket-propelled grenades and other weapons. In late 2004, Liberia's warring militias formally disbanded in a ceremony at UNMIL headquarters in Monrovia. By the end of February 2006, more than 300,000 internally displaced Liberians had been returned to their home villages.

After 15 years of conflict, the people of Liberia, with UN assistance, held their first post-war elections in October 2005. In a later run-off between the top two contenders, they elected Ellen Johnson-Sirleaf as President, with 59.4 per cent of the vote. She had previously occupied the post of director of the UNDP Regional Bureau for Africa. Soon after assuming office in 2006, President Johnson-Sirleaf set up a Truth and Reconciliation Commission to heal the country's wounds.

Although major challenges remain, Liberia has been making steady progress towards peaceful nationhood and reconstruction. The country became eligible to receive assistance from the UN Peacebuilding Fund in 2007. This funding has been allocated to projects that consolidate peace, address insecurity and catalyze the nation's broader development. Work on these projects commenced in 2009. UNMIL continues to work with the government and UN partners towards these ends and prepare for the presidential elections scheduled for 2011.

Guinea-Bissau. Following a period of conflict in Guinea-Bissau, a government of national unity was inaugurated in February 1999. In March, the UN established the **United Nations Peace-building Support Office in Guinea-Bissau (UNOGBIS)** to help create and promote democracy and the rule of law, and to facilitate the organization of free and transparent elections. In May, the peace accord broke down, and rebel troops ousted President João Bernardo Vieira. Following parliamentary and presidential elections in November 1999 and January 2000, the transitional government turned over power to the civilian government under the new President, Koumba Yala.

Although UNOGBIS continued to help the new government in the transitional period, the consolidation of peace and economic recovery was hampered by political instability, causing donors to limit their assistance, which led to mounting social tensions. In November 2002, President Yala dissolved the National Assembly, appointing a new caretaker government. Parliamentary elections scheduled for May 2003 were repeatedly postponed. In September, President Yala was ousted in a bloodless coup. Reporting to the Security Council the Secretary-General said that removal of the democratically elected president, however reprehensible, took place after constitutional norms had been repeatedly violated. Describing the military coup as "the culmination of an untenable situation", he called on the international community to recommend ways of preventing democratically elected governments in post-conflict countries from flouting the principles of basic governance.

In September 2003, a political transitional charter was signed by the military and 23 of the nation's 24 recognized parties. It provided for a civilian transitional government led by a civilian transitional president and prime minister; parliamentary elections to be held within six months; and presidential elections to be organized within one year of the swearing-in of the new parliamentarians. By early October, all transitional mechanisms were in place and Henrique Perreira Rosa was sworn in as transitional President.

Legislative elections in March 2004 were deemed to be free, fair and transparent by international observers. In June and September 2005, two rounds of peaceful voting elected João Bernardo Vieira as President. Though political tensions along party lines continued to pose a challenge to national reconciliation and the effective functioning of key government institutions, a national political stability pact signed by the three main political parties led, in April 2007, to the swearing-in of the government of Prime Minister Martinho Dafa Cabi.

On 2 March 2009, President Vieira was assassinated by a group of soldiers. The army pledged to respect the constitutional order of succession, and National Assembly Speaker Raimundo Pereira was appointed as interim president. Following the holding of presidential elections in June, Malam Bacai Sanhá was sworn in as the newly elected President on 8 September. Also in June, the UN established a **United Nations Integrated Peace-building Office in Guinea-Bissau (UNIOGBIS)** to succeed UNOGBIS, for an initial 12-month period from 1 January to 31 December 2010. Unrest occurred again in April 2010, when Prime Minister Carlos Gomes Junior was briefly detained by soldiers, along with the Army Chief of Staff. Secretary-General Ban Ki-moon deplored the military mutiny as "a major setback to the process of consolidating stability and implementing key reforms". He also expressed his concern over reports linking the April events to drug trafficking.

In such a critical context, UNIOGBIS has continued to work on assisting the UN Peacebuilding Commission in its multidimensional engagement with Guinea-Bissau; strengthening the capacity of national institutions to maintain constitutional order and respect for the rule of law; supporting the establishment of effective and efficient law enforcement and criminal justice systems; providing support in developing and coordinating the implementation of the security sector reform strategy; and promoting human rights in general and women's rights in particular. In doing so, UNIOGBIS cooperates with the AU, the Community of Portuguese Language Countries (CPLP), ECOWAS, the EU, and other partners.

Sierra Leone. In 1991, the Revolutionary United Front (RUF) launched a war to overthrow the government of Sierra Leone, but in 1992, the country's own army overthrew the government. In 1995, the Secretary-General appointed a special envoy who, working with the Organization of African Unity (OAU) and ECOWAS, negotiated a return to civilian rule. Following presidential elections in 1996, in which the RUF did not participate, the army relinquished power to the winner, Ahmad Tejan Kabbah. The special envoy then helped negotiate the 1996 Abidjan Peace Accord between the government and the RUF. Following a military coup in 1997, the army joined with the RUF to form a ruling junta. President Kabbah went into exile, and the Security Council imposed an oil and arms embargo—authorizing ECOWAS to ensure its implementation by using the troops of the Economic Community of West African States Monitoring Group (ECOMOG).

In February 1998, in response to an attack by rebel and junta forces, ECOMOG conducted military operations that led to the fall of the junta. President Kabbah returned to office, and the Council ended the embargo. In June, the Council established the **United Nations Observer Mission in Sierra Leone (UNOMSIL)** to monitor the security situation, the disarmament of combatants, and the restructuring of the security forces. Unarmed UNOMSIL teams, under ECOMOG protection, documented atrocities and human rights abuses.

The rebel alliance, however, soon gained control of more than half of the country, and in January 1999 overran the capital, Freetown. Later that month, ECOMOG troops retook Freetown and reinstalled the government. The fighting resulted in 700,000 internally displaced persons (IDPs) and 450,000 refugees. The special representative, in consultation with West African states, began diplomatic efforts to open up a dialogue with the rebels. These negotiations led in July to the Lomé Peace Agreement—to end the war and form a government of national unity.

The Security Council replaced UNOMSIL in October 1999 with the larger **United Nations Mission in Sierra Leone (UNAMSIL),** to help the parties put the agreement into effect and assist in disarming, demobilizing and reintegrating some 45,000 combatants. In February 2000, following the announced withdrawal of ECOMOG, UNAMSIL's strength was increased to 11,000 troops. In April, however, RUF attacked UN forces, killing four peacekeepers and taking hostage nearly 500 UN personnel. In May, British troops serving under a bilateral arrangement secured the capital and its airport, and assisted in capturing the RUF leader, Foday Sankoh. By the end of the month, around half of the UN hostages had been released. The Council increased UNAMSIL's strength to 13,000 troops to help restore peace, and in July UNAMSIL rescued the remaining hostages. In August, the Council began the process of setting up a special court to try those responsible for war crimes.

UNAMSIL completed its deployment to all areas of the country in November 2001, and the disarmament process was completed in January 2002. Following presidential and parliamentary elections in May 2002, the Mission focused on extending state authority throughout the country, reintegrating ex-combatants, and resettling IDPs and returnees. The IDP resettlement was completed in December, the repatriation of some 280,000 Sierra Leonean refugees in July 2004. A Truth and Reconciliation Commission and the Special Court for Sierra Leone began to function in mid-2002.

When UNAMSIL was withdrawn in December 2005, it left the country with a growing sense of stability and an improvement in basic services. It was replaced in January 2006 by the **UN Integrated Office in Sierra Leone (UNIOSIL),** the first integrated UN office established to support a peace-consolidation process.

In April 2006, former Liberian President Charles Taylor appeared before the Special Court for Sierra Leone to answer 11 counts of war crimes, crimes against humanity, and other violations. In June, the Security Council approved the Court's request to try him at The Hague, as his continued presence in the region represented "a threat to the peace of Liberia and of Sierra Leone". The trial began in June 2007, and oral arguments were concluded in March 2011. Also in June 2007, the UN-backed Special Court issued its first verdicts, finding three former rebel leaders guilty of multiple counts of war crimes and crimes against humanity—terrorism, murder, rape, enslavement and conscripting children into armed groups. They were sentenced to terms ranging from 45 to 50 years.

Sierra Leone's development efforts took a significant leap forward when the **UN Peacebuilding Commission** singled it out, along with Burundi, for its first activities. In March 2007, on the Commission's recommendation, Secretary-General Ban Ki-moon made $35 million available for Sierra Leone from the UN Peacebuilding Fund, set up the previous October to assist countries emerging from conflict to rebuild and avert a relapse into bloodshed.

In July 2007, campaigning began for Sierra Leone's presidential and parliamentary elections. UNIOSIL's participation included training 49 district officers on polling and counting procedures, to be passed on to 37,000 polling staff. The elections were held in August with high voter turnout. In a run-off election for the presidency, Ernest Bai Koroma of the All People's Congress was elected with 54.6 per cent of the vote. He was inaugurated on 15 November. President Koroma has since then focused on rebuilding the country with UN assistance.

In August 2008, the Security Council established the **United Nations Integrated Peacebuilding Office in Sierra Leone (UNIPSIL)**, which took over from UNIOSIL. With some 70 staff, UNIPSIL provides advice to foster peace, offering support and training to the national police and security forces. The Office also helps build democratic institutions in furtherance of good governance and the promotion of human rights.

Central and East Africa

The Sudan and Southern Sudan. The Sudan has endured civil conflict for years since it became independent on 1 January 1956. In the phase that began in 1983, the government and the Sudan People's Liberation Movement/Army (SPLM/A), the main rebel movement in the south, fought over resources, power, the role of religion in the state, and self-determination. A UN-supported initiative by the Intergovernmental Authority on Development (IGAD) in 2002 led to the signing of the 'Machakos Protocol' in Machakos, Kenya. In 2004, an African Union Mission in the Sudan (AMIS) was deployed as a monitoring mission, and a **United Nations Advance Mission in the Sudan (UNAMIS)** was established to prepare for a peace operation. Over 2 million people died, 4 million were uprooted and some 600,000 others fled the country until the signing of the Comprehensive Peace Agreement (CPA) in January 2005. The CPA covered security arrangements, power-sharing in the capital, some autonomy for the south, and more equitable distribution of economic resources, including oil. Under its terms, interim institutions would govern for six-and-a-half years, observed by international monitors. Then, in an internationally monitored referendum, the people would vote for Sudanese unity or secession.

In March 2005, the Security Council established the **United Nations Mission in the Sudan (UNMIS)**, with a mandate to support implementation of the CPA; facilitate and coordinate humanitarian assistance and the voluntary return of refugees and internally displaced persons; and assist the parties in mine action. It was also mandated to protect and promote human rights, and coordinate international efforts to protect civilians—with particular attention to vulnerable groups. In September 2005, a Government of National Unity was established. Although the parties were respecting the letter of the CPA on the whole, the spirit of cooperation, inclusiveness and transparency was less than had been hoped. The continuing crisis in Darfur was also having a negative effect on its implementation.

A referendum took place in Southern Sudan in January 2011, on whether the region should remain a part of Sudan or become independent. A simultaneous referendum to be held in the Abyei area on whether to become part of Southern Sudan was postponed, due to demarcation and residency issues. The Southern Sudan Referendum Commission (SSRC) organized the referendum process, while the United Nations provided technical and logistical assistance in preparation for the referendum. The AU and the IGAD observer missions commended the SSRC for the conduct of the referendum and declared the process free and fair. Meanwhile, the Office of the High Commissioner for Refugees (UNHCR) reported that it had enhanced its assistance to the tens of thousands of Southern Sudanese people returning home.

Darfur. Ethnic, economic and political tensions had long combined with competition over scarce resources to fuel violence in Darfur. In 2003, the government's decision to deploy its national armed forces and to mobilize local militias in response to attacks by the Sudan Liberation Movement/Army (SLM/A) and the Justice and Equality Movement (JEM) escalated the violence to unprecedented levels. Indiscriminate air bombardment by Sudan's armed forces, along with attacks by the Janjaweed and other militias, left villages across the region razed to the ground. Civilians were murdered, women and girls raped, children abducted, and food and water sources destroyed. In July 2004, the AU started sponsoring inter-Sudanese peace talks in Abuja, Nigeria, while deploying 60 military observers and 310 protection troops to Darfur to monitor compliance with a humanitarian cease-fire agreement that had been signed in April by the government, SLM/A and JEM. Meanwhile, the UN and NGOs launched a massive humanitarian operation.

In January 2005, a **Commission of Inquiry**, established at the request of the Security Council, reported that while the Sudanese government had not pursued a policy of genocide in Darfur, both its forces and allied Janjaweed militias had carried out "indiscriminate attacks, including killing of civilians, torture, enforced disappearances, destruction of villages, rape and other forms of sexual violence, pillaging and forced displacement". Stating that war crimes and crimes against humanity might be no less heinous than genocide, the Commission concluded that rebel forces in Darfur were responsible for possible war crimes, including pillaging and the murder of civilians. The Security Council referred the Commission's dossier on Darfur to the International Criminal Court (ICC) in The Hague.

After three years of intense conflict, AU efforts led, in May 2006, to the signing of the Darfur Peace Agreement, which addressed power-sharing, wealth-sharing, a comprehensive ceasefire and security arrangements. All parties to the conflict were present, but only the government and the SLM/A signed the Agreement. In August 2006, the Security Council authorized an expansion of the UNMIS mandate to enable its deployment to Darfur. The Sudanese government, however, objected to the deployment of UN peacekeepers in the region. It was only in November 2006 that the Sudanese government expressed support, in principle, for the establishment of a hybrid UN-AU Mission in Sudan. After months of negotiations, in July 2007, the Council established the **African Union-United Nations Hybrid Operation in Darfur (UNAMID)** to deal with the situation in Darfur in a comprehensive manner—the first hybrid force involving the United Nations, and the largest UN peacekeeping operation ever.

Meanwhile, in April 2007, the ICC issued arrest warrants against a former Minister of State for the Interior and a Janjaweed militia leader for crimes against humanity and war crimes. The Sudanese government's stance has been that the ICC has no jurisdiction to try Sudanese citizens and that it will not hand the two over to authorities in The Hague. In 2008, the ICC Prosecutor filed charges of war crimes and crimes against humanity against Sudan's President, and an arrest warrant was issued in March 2009. In July 2010, the President was further charged on three counts of genocide.

The Sudanese government and the rebel JEM group signed a ceasefire agreement in February 2010, with a tentative agreement to pursue further peace. Yet talks stalled amid accusations that the army had launched raids and air strikes against a village, in violation of the accord. JEM said they would boycott further negotiations.

The African Union-United Nations Hybrid Operation in Darfur (UNAMID)

The Security Council, on 31 July 2007, established the first-ever hybrid force involving the United Nations—the **African Union-United Nations Hybrid Operation in Darfur (UNAMID)**. Based in El Fasher, northern Darfur, UNAMID combines UN forces with those of the former African Union Mission in Sudan (AMIS) in a comprehensive operation aimed at bringing peace to that troubled part of the world.

At full authorization, UNAMID would be the largest peacekeeping operation ever. As of late 2010, UNAMID consisted of more than 22,000 uniformed personnel, 3,762 local and international civilian staff members and 454 UN Volunteers.

In 2010, UNAMID, in addition to protecting the civilian population, was also tasked with contributing to security for humanitarian assistance, monitoring and verifying implementation of agreements, assisting in fostering an inclusive political process, promoting human rights and the rule of law, and monitoring and reporting on the situation along the borders with Chad and the Central African Republic.

Full deployment of UNAMID has been marred by a lack of cooperation from the government and delays in the readiness of troop and police contributors to deploy, together with the immense logistical challenges inherent to the area. Late into 2010, UNAMID continued to face shortfalls in troops, transport and aviation assets. Nevertheless, despite its limited resources the mission continues to provide protection to civilians, facilitate the humanitarian aid operation, and help provide an environment in which peace can take root at last. In September 2010, the Under-Secretary-General for Field Support noted that a joint action plan had been developed among the parties to address all ongoing issues with monthly meetings. While acknowledging that there remained much work to do, she noted some improvements. Earlier in 2010, UN officials had warned that the humanitarian situation was worsening due to resumed clashes between government forces and rebels, as well as tribal fighting. The situation was aggravated by attacks on UN-AU peacekeepers and abductions and mistreatment of UN staff and aid workers.

Somalia. Somalia's 6.8 million people have been living with anarchy since the government of President Siad Barre was overthrown in 1991 and a civil war broke out, dividing the country into fiefdoms controlled by rival warlords, with arms, ammunition and explosives flowing freely across its borders in breach of a UN embargo. When talks organized by the Secretary-General led to a ceasefire in the capital, Mogadishu, the Security Council in April 1992 established the **United Nations Operation in Somalia (UNOSOM I)** to monitor the ceasefire; provide protection and security for UN personnel, equipment and supplies; and escort deliveries of humanitarian supplies. However, the deteriorating security situation led the Council in December to authorize member states to form a **Unified Task Force (UNITAF)** to ensure the safe delivery of humanitarian assistance. In March 1993, the Council established **UNOSOM II** to complete UNITAF's efforts to restore peace, but the escalation of inter-clan fighting led to the withdrawal of UNOSOM II in March 1995. The Secretary-General established the **United Nations Political Office for Somalia (UNPOS)** (*www.un-somalia.org*) in April 1995 to help him advance peace and reconciliation through contacts with Somali leaders, civic organizations, and concerned states and organizations. UNPOS supported a Djibouti initiative that led, in 2000, to the formation of a Transitional National Government, but its authority was subsequently challenged by Somali leaders in the south, and by regional administrations in 'Puntland' in the north-east, and 'Somaliland' in the north-west.

In 2002, a national reconciliation conference sponsored by the Intergovernmental Authority on Development (IGAD) led to agreement on a cessation of hostilities and on structures and principles to govern the national reconciliation process. That process bore fruit in 2004, when Somali leaders agreed on a Transitional Federal Government (TFG)—the internationally recognized federal government of Somalia—with a five-year term, and a Transitional Federal Parliament (TFP). The TFG and TFP were established as two of the Transitional Federal Institutions (TFIs) of government as defined in the Transitional Federal *Charter* adopted in 2004. The *Charter* outlines a five-year mandate leading toward the establishment of a new constitution and a transition to a representative government after the holding of national elections. The President of 'Puntland', Abdullahi Yusuf Ahmed, was elected President of TFG in October 2004, and all 25 presidential candidates promised to support him and to demobilize their militias. By May 2006, however, militias of the Alliance for the Restoration of Peace and Counter-Terrorism and of the Sharia Courts were battling each other in Mogadishu. In June, the TFG and the Union of Islamic Courts pledged mutual recognition, continued dialogue, and to refrain from actions that might increase tensions. Then, in July, forces loyal to the Islamic Courts advanced towards the city of Baidoa.

In December 2006, the Security Council authorized IGAD and AU member states to establish a protection and training mission in Somalia. Its mandate included: monitoring progress by the parties in implementing agreements; maintaining security in Baidoa; protecting members and infrastructure of the TFIs; and assisting in re-establishing Somalia's national forces. With hundreds of thousands fleeing heavy fighting in Mogadishu, the Council, in February 2007, authorized the AU to establish a wider operation, known as **AMISOM (African Union Mission in Somalia)**. Replacing the IGAD mission, it was authorized to take all necessary measures to fulfill its mandate of creating a safe and secure environment. The Council has extended AMISOM since, and approved continued contingency planning for a possible UN operation beginning in 2011. In 2009, the United Nations Support Office for AMISOM (UNSOA) was established in Nairobi to provide logistical and technical support to the AU operation. Up to late 2010, Secretary-General Ban Ki-moon maintained that deploying a UN mission was neither realistic nor viable given the security situation. For those reasons, the UN focused on encouraging dialogue between the TFG and opposition groups and on strengthening AMISOM.

In 2006, the Islamic Courts Union (ICU) had taken much of the south. The TFG, with the assistance of Ethiopian troops and AU peacekeepers, managed to drive out the ICU, which then splintered into factions. Radical elements, Al-Shabab included, regrouped to resume insurgency against the TFG and oppose Ethiopian military presence. By 2008, Al-Shabab had gained control of key areas, including Baidoa. In December 2008, President Abdullahi Yusuf Ahmed resigned. The following January, Sharif Ahmad was elected President, and Omar Abdirashid Ali Sharmarke was selected as Prime Minister. During that same month, the Ethiopian troops withdrew. The TFG, backed by AU troops, began a counteroffensive in February 2009 to retake control of the south. Conflict continued between TFG troops and extremists with links to Al Qaeda throughout 2010.

At the end of 2009, about 678,000 uprooted persons were under the responsibility of UNHCR, constituting the third largest refugee group in the world after Iraq and Afghanistan, respectively. Due to fighting in the southern half of the country, an estimated 132,000 people left in 2009, and another 300,000 were internally displaced. Meanwhile UNPOS continued to promote peace and reconciliation through contacts with Somali leaders, civic organizations and the states and organizations concerned.

A consequence of the conflict has been an upsurge of piracy off the coast of Somalia. The Security Council adopted resolutions to combat piracy and, in 2008, a multinational coalition established a Maritime Security Patrol Area within the Gulf of Aden. These efforts led in 2010 to a drop in piracy in the Gulf of Aden, even as it remains a serious threat to shipping in the area.

Ethiopia-Eritrea. With the collapse of the military government in Ethiopia in 1991, the Eritrean People's Liberation Front (EPLF) announced the formation of a provisional government and the holding of a referendum to determine the wishes of the Eritrean people regarding their status in relation to Ethiopia. In response to a request from its referendum commission, the General Assembly established the **United Nations Observer Mission to Verify the Referendum in Eritrea (UNOVER)**, to observe the organization and holding of the 1993 referendum. With 99 per cent of voters favouring independence, Eritrea declared independence shortly thereafter and joined the UN.

In May 1998, hostilities between Ethiopia and Eritrea erupted over disputed border areas. The Security Council demanded an end to the conflict and offered technical support for the delimitation and demarcation of the border. Two years later, following proximity talks under OAU auspices, a cessation of hostilities agreement was reached in Algiers. To assist in its implementation, the Council in July 2000 established the **United Nations Mission in Ethiopia and Eritrea (UNMEE)**, deploying liaison officers to each capital and military observers along the border. The Council authorized deployment of up to 4,200 military personnel to monitor the cessation of hostilities and help ensure observance of the security commitments agreed to by the parties.

With the arrival of the peacekeepers, the Ethiopian and Eritrean forces redeployed and a temporary security zone (TSZ) was created. UNMEE was mandated to patrol and monitor the zone. In December 2000 an agreement between the parties provided for a permanent end to military hostilities and the release of prisoners of war. It also required the establishment of an independent commission to delimit and demarcate the border. In April 2002, the neutral Boundary Commission reached its final and binding decision on delimitation of the border. The Security Council adjusted UNMEE's mandate to include demining in support of demarcation and support for the Commission's field offices. The ensuing military situation was generally stable, but the peace process remained at a critical stage, owing to Ethiopia's rejection of the Boundary Commission's recommendations. In the absence of progress in implementing the Commission's decision, Eritrea began what the Secretary-General described as "massive violations" of the TSZ, coupled with "impediments" to UNMEE's work, including a ban on UN helicopter flights. UNMEE's authorized troop strength was reduced—from 4,200 when it began, to 2,300 in 2006, and then to 1,700 at the beginning of 2007.

In November of that year, Secretary-General Ban Ki-moon expressed concern about military build-up and military exercises along the border, and the Security

Council urged both parties to implement the 2002 delimitation ruling immediately and without preconditions. The Council also called upon the parties to refrain from the use of force, to settle their differences by peaceful means, and to normalize their relations. In July 2008, the Council terminated UNMEE's mandate in response to restrictions imposed on the mission by Eritrea.

The Americas

The United Nations has been instrumental in bringing peace to the Central American region, in one of its most complex and successful peacemaking and peace-keeping efforts.

The UN became involved in Central America in 1989, when Costa Rica, El Salvador, Guatemala, Honduras and Nicaragua requested its assistance to end the conflicts that plagued the region, promote democratic elections and pursue democratization and dialogue. The Security Council established the **United Nations Observer Group in Central America (ONUCA)** to verify compliance with commitments to cease assistance to irregular and insurrectionist forces, and not allow the territory of any country to be used for attacks into other countries.

Nicaragua. The five countries also agreed to draw up a plan for demobilizing the Nicaraguan resistance, and the Nicaraguan government announced it would hold elections under international and UN monitoring. The **United Nations Observation Mission for the Verification of Elections in Nicaragua (ONUVEN)** observed the preparation and holding of the 1990 elections—the first to be observed by the UN in an independent country. Its success helped create conditions for the voluntary demobilization of the 'contras', which was overseen by ONUCA in 1990.

El Salvador. In El Salvador, negotiations brokered by the Secretary-General and his personal representative culminated in the 1992 peace accords, which put an end to a 12-year conflict that had claimed some 75,000 lives. The **United Nations Observer Mission in El Salvador (ONUSAL)** monitored the accords, including the demobilization of combatants and both parties' compliance with their human rights commitments. ONUSAL also assisted in bringing about reforms—such as judicial reforms and the establishment of a new civilian police force—needed to tackle the root causes of the civil war. At the request of the government, ONUSAL observed the 1994 elections, and its mandate ended in 1995.

Guatemala. At the request of the government and the Guatemalan National Revolutionary Unity (URNG), the United Nations in 1991 began to assist in talks aimed at ending that country's civil war, which had lasted over three decades and resulted in some 200,000 people killed or missing. In 1994, the parties concluded accords providing for the UN to verify all agreements reached and to establish a human rights mission. Accordingly, the General Assembly established the **United Nations Human Rights Verification Mission in Guatemala (MINUGUA)**. In December 1996, a ceasefire was reached and the parties signed a peace agreement—ending the last and longest of Central America's conflicts. For the first time in 36 years, the region was at peace. MINUGUA remained until November 2004 to verify compliance with the accords, while UN agencies continued to address the social and economic roots of conflict throughout the region.

Haiti. In 1990, following the departure of 'life president' Jean-Claude Duvalier and a series of short-lived governments, Haiti's provisional government asked the United Nations to observe that year's elections. The **United Nations Observer**

Group for the Verification of the Elections in Haiti (ONUVEH) monitored the preparation and holding of the elections, in which Jean-Bertrand Aristide was elected President. A military coup in 1991 ended democratic rule, however, and the newly elected President went into exile. A joint United Nations/Organization of American States (OAS) mission, the **International Civilian Mission in Haiti (MICIVIH)**, was deployed in 1993 to monitor the human rights situation and investigate violations. To encourage the restoration of constitutional rule, the Security Council imposed an oil and arms embargo in 1993 and a trade embargo in 1994. Subsequently, it authorized a multinational force to facilitate the return to democratic rule. As the force was about to intervene, the United States and the military rulers reached an agreement aimed at avoiding further violence, and the US-led multinational force deployed peacefully. President Aristide returned in October 1994, and the embargo was lifted. In 1995, a UN peacekeeping mission took over from the multinational force, to help the government maintain security and stability and create the first national civil police.

As Haiti celebrated its bicentennial in January 2004, a severe political deadlock threatened the country's stability. Clashes between pro- and anti-government militias led to a spiral of increasing violence, which forced President Aristide, who had been serving a second term since 2001, to resign and leave the country. The Security Council authorized the immediate deployment of a **Multinational Interim Force (MIF)**, following a request for assistance by newly sworn-in President Boniface Alexandre. A United States-led force immediately began its deployment. In April 2004, the Council established the **United Nations Stabilization Mission in Haiti (MINUSTAH)**, to support the continuation of a peaceful and constitutional political process in a secure and stable environment. In the following years, the mandate of MINUSTAH, its concept of operations and the authorized strength were adjusted by the Council on several occasions to adapt to the changing circumstances on the ground and to the evolving requirements as dictated by the prevailing political, security and socio-economic situation. In February 2006, Haitians elected former President René Préval as their new President.

Following the devastating January 2010 earthquake, the Council increased the overall force levels of MINUSTAH to support recovery, reconstruction and stability efforts. MINUSTAH, together with the UN Office for the Coordination of Humanitarian Affairs and the United Nations Country Team, provided humanitarian and recovery efforts throughout 2010. It assisted the government in its resettlement strategy for displaced persons. The UN also coordinated international electoral assistance to Haiti in cooperation with other international stakeholders including the OAS.

Asia and the Pacific

The Middle East

From its earliest days, the United Nations has been concerned with the question of the Middle East. It has formulated principles for a peaceful settlement and dispatched various peacekeeping operations, and continues to support efforts towards a just, lasting and comprehensive solution to the underlying political problems.

The question has its origin in the issue of the status of Palestine. In 1947, Palestine was a territory administered by the United Kingdom under a mandate from the League of Nations. It had a population of some 2 million—two thirds Arabs and one third Jews. The General Assembly in 1947 endorsed a plan, prepared by the **United Nations Special Committee on Palestine**, for the partition of the territory. It provided for creating an Arab and a Jewish state, with Jerusalem under international status. The plan was rejected by the Palestinian Arabs, the Arab states and other states.

On 14 May 1948, the United Kingdom relinquished its mandate, and the Jewish Agency proclaimed the state of Israel. The following day, the Palestinian Arabs, assisted by Arab states, opened hostilities against the new state. The military confrontation was halted through a truce called for by the Security Council and supervised by a mediator appointed by the General Assembly, assisted by a group of military observers which came to be known as the **United Nations Truce Supervision Organization (UNTSO)**—the first United Nations observer mission.

As a result of the conflict, some 750,000 Palestinian Arabs lost their homes and livelihoods and became refugees. To assist them, the General Assembly in 1949 established the **United Nations Relief and Works Agency for Palestine Refugees in the Near East (UNRWA)**, which has since been a major provider of assistance and a force for stability in the region.

The conflict remaining unresolved, Arab-Israeli warfare erupted again in 1956, 1967 and 1973, each time leading member states to call for United Nations mediation and peacekeeping missions. The 1956 conflict saw the deployment of the first full-fledged peacekeeping force—the **United Nations Emergency Force (UNEF I)**— which oversaw troop withdrawals and contributed to peace and stability.

The 1967 war involved fighting between Egypt and Israel, Jordan and Syria, during which Israel occupied the Sinai Peninsula, the Gaza Strip, the West Bank of the Jordan River, including East Jerusalem, and part of Syria's Golan Heights. The Security Council called for a ceasefire, and subsequently dispatched observers to supervise the ceasefire in the Egypt-Israel sector.

The Council, by resolution 242(1967), defined principles for a just and lasting peace, namely: "withdrawal of Israel armed forces from territories occupied in the recent conflict"; and "termination of all claims or states of belligerency and respect for and acknowledgement of the sovereignty, territorial integrity and political independence of every state in the area and their right to live in peace within secure and recognized boundaries, free from threats or acts of force". The resolution also affirmed the need for "a just settlement of the refugee problem".

After the 1973 war between Egypt and Israel and Syria, the Security Council adopted resolution 338(1973), which reaffirmed the principles of resolution 242(1967) and called for negotiations aimed at "a just and durable peace". These resolutions remain the basis for an overall settlement in the Middle East.

To monitor the 1973 ceasefire, the Security Council established two peacekeeping forces. One of them, the **United Nations Disengagement Observer Force (UNDOF)**, established to supervise the disengagement agreement between Israel and Syria, is still in place on the Golan Heights. The other operation was **UNEF II**, in the Sinai.

In the following years, the General Assembly called for an international peace conference on the Middle East, under United Nations auspices. In 1974, the Assembly invited the Palestine Liberation Organization (PLO) to participate in its work as an observer. The following year, it established the **Committee on the Exercise of the Inalienable Rights of the Palestinian People**, which continues to work as the General Assembly's subsidiary organ supporting the rights of the Palestinian people and a peaceful settlement of the question of Palestine.

Bilateral negotiations between Egypt and Israel, mediated by the United States, led to the Camp David accords (1978) and the Egypt-Israel peace treaty (1979). Israel withdrew from the Sinai, which was returned to Egypt. Israel and Jordan concluded a peace treaty in 1994.

Lebanon. From April 1975 through October 1990, Lebanon was torn by civil war. Early on, southern Lebanon became a theatre of hostilities between Palestinian groups, on one hand, and, on the other, Israeli forces and its local Lebanese auxiliary. After Israeli forces invaded southern Lebanon in 1978, following a Palestinian commando raid in Israel, the Security Council adopted resolutions 425(1978) and 426(1978), calling upon Israel to withdraw and establishing the **United Nations Interim Force in Lebanon (UNIFIL)**. The Force was set up to confirm the Israeli withdrawal, restore international peace and security, and assist Lebanon in re-establishing its authority in the area. In 1982, after intense exchanges of fire in southern Lebanon and across the Israel-Lebanon border, Israeli forces moved into Lebanon, reaching and surrounding Beirut. Israel withdrew from most of the country in 1985, but kept control of a strip of land in southern Lebanon, where Israeli forces and its local Lebanese auxiliary remained, and which partly overlapped UNIFIL's area of deployment. Hostilities between Lebanese groups and Israeli forces continued. In May 2000, Israeli forces withdrew in accordance with the 1978 Security Council resolutions. The Council endorsed the Secretary-General's plan to assist Lebanon in re-establishing its authority. Nevertheless, the situation along the 'blue line' marking Israel's withdrawal from southern Lebanon remained precarious.

Tensions escalated in February 2005, when former Lebanese Prime Minister Rafiq Hariri was assassinated. In November, the Security Council supported establishment of a special tribunal to try those allegedly responsible for the assassination. In April, the UN verified the withdrawal of Syrian troops, military assets and intelligence operations from Lebanon. In May and June, parliamentary elections were held with UN assistance. Violations of the 'blue line' continued through 2005 and 2006 with intermittent clashes between Israel and Hezbollah. When two Israeli soldiers were seized by Hezbollah in July 2006, Israel responded with air attacks, and Hezbollah retaliated with rocket attacks. The fighting ended in August, by the terms of Security Council resolution 1701(2006), which called for an immediate cessation of hostilities—to be followed by deployment of Lebanese troops; a significantly expanded UNIFIL peacekeeping presence across southern Lebanon; and the withdrawal of Israeli forces from the area. Massive amounts of UN aid as well as reinforcements of peacekeepers were sent to the area. A significant problem facing UNIFIL was the risk posed by up to 1 million pieces of unexploded ordnance left from the 34-day war. In April 2007, concerned at reported breaches of its arms embargo across the Lebanese-Syrian border, the Security Council invited the Secretary-General to send an independent mission to assess the monitoring of the border—which was found to be lacking. The Secretary-General proposed actions to help remedy the situation.

Fighting erupted in 2007 between militants and Lebanese forces at a Palestinian camp. A series of explosions rocked Beirut—including one which killed a Lebanese parliamentarian and nine others. An attack on UNIFIL killed six peacekeepers, and rockets were fired into Israel. In 2008, clashes erupted between pro- and anti-government forces. Hezbollah blocked Beirut's international airport and roads.

The United Nations called on all parties to engage in peaceful dialogue. In May, in Doha, Qatar, a six-point agreement was reached to end the crisis, though occasional clashes continued until the end of the year. Relations with Syria improved, and diplomatic relations were established between the two countries in October 2008.

The Secretary-General welcomed the peaceful conduct of parliamentary elections in June 2009, when the alliance led by Saad Hariri won majority in Parliament against the Hezbollah's coalition. The newly elected Prime Minister Hariri formed a national unity government in November. At the beginning of 2011, the unity government collapsed after Hezbollah and its allies resigned from the cabinet over arguments stemming from the investigation into the assassination of Rafiq Hariri and others in 2005. Five days later the prosecutor of the Special Tribunal for Lebanon filed a confidential indictment in connection with the attack on Mr. Hariri. The indictment was filed with the Tribunal's registrar, to be submitted to the pre-trial judge.

The Middle East peace process. In 1987, the Palestinian uprising (intifada) began in the occupied territories of the West Bank and Gaza Strip with a call for Palestinian independence and statehood. In 1988, the Palestine National Council proclaimed the state of Palestine, which the General Assembly acknowledged. The Assembly also decided to employ the designation 'Palestine' when referring to the Palestine Liberation Organization (PLO) within the UN system, without prejudice to its observer status. In September 1993, following talks in Madrid and subsequent Norwegian-mediated negotiations, Israel and the PLO established mutual recognition and signed the *Declaration of Principles on Interim Self-Government Arrangements*. The United Nations created a task force on the social and economic development of Gaza and Jericho. It also appointed a special coordinator for UN assistance, whose mandate was expanded in 1999 to include good offices assistance to the Middle East peace process.

The transfer of powers from Israel to the Palestinian Authority (PA) in the Gaza Strip and Jericho began in 1994. One year later, Israel and the PLO signed an agreement on Palestinian self-rule in the West Bank, providing for the withdrawal of Israeli troops and the handover of civil authority to an elected Palestinian Council. In 1996, Yasser Arafat was elected President of the PA. An interim agreement in 1999 led to further redeployment of Israeli troops from the West Bank, agreements on prisoners, the opening of safe passage between the West Bank and Gaza, and resumption of negotiations on permanent status issues. High-level peace talks held under United States mediation, however, ended inconclusively in the middle of 2000. Unresolved issues included the status of Jerusalem, the Palestinian refugee question, security, borders and Israeli settlements.

In September of that year, a new wave of violence flared up. The Security Council repeatedly called for an end to the violence and affirmed the vision of two states, Israel and Palestine, living side by side within secure and recognized borders. International efforts to bring the two parties back to the negotiating table were increasingly carried out through the mechanism of the 'Quartet'—composed of the European Union, the Russian Federation, the United States and the United Nations. In April 2003, the Quartet presented its 'road map' to a permanent two-state solution—a plan with distinct phases and benchmarks, calling for parallel and reciprocal steps by the two parties, to resolve the conflict by 2005. It also envisaged a comprehensive settlement of the Middle East conflict, including the Syrian-Israeli and Lebanese-Israeli tracks. The Council endorsed the road map in resolution 1515(2003) and both parties accepted it. Nevertheless, the last half of 2003 saw a sharp escalation of violence. The UN special coordinator for the Middle East peace process said neither side had addressed the other's concerns: for Israel, security and freedom from terrorist attack; for Palestinians, a viable and independent state based on pre-1967-war borders. Palestinian suicide bombings continued, and Israel constructed a 'separation barrier' in the West Bank—later held to be contrary to international law under an advisory opinion of the International Court of Justice requested by the General Assembly.

In early 2004, Israeli Prime Minister Ariel Sharon announced that Israel would withdraw its military and settlements from the Gaza Strip. In November, PA President Yasser Arafat died, and was replaced in January 2005 by Mahmoud Abbas in elections conducted with UN technical and logistic support. In February, Prime Minister Sharon and President Abbas met in Egypt, and announced steps to halt the violence. They met again in June, and by September Israel's withdrawal was complete. At last, genuine progress towards a negotiated solution seemed possible. Despite that optimism, two significant events took place in January 2006 that changed the political landscape: Prime Minister Sharon suffered a stroke and fell into a coma, and in legislative elections, the Palestinians voted the militant Hamas faction into power. Despite appeals from the Quartet and others, Hamas did not formally recognize Israel's right to exist. The Israeli government, now led by Ehud Olmert, took the position that the entire PA had become a terrorist entity, and imposed a freeze on Palestinian tax revenues. Violence escalated, including the launching of rockets from Gaza into Israel, along with major Israeli counter-operations. International aid donors balked at funding the Hamas-led government as long as it did not renounce violence, recognize Israel's right to exist, and abide by signed agreements. The humanitarian situation in the West Bank and Gaza deteriorated.

In May 2007, intra-Palestinian clashes left 68 dead and more than 200 wounded, as Hamas militants and Executive Force members clashed with PA security forces and Fatah armed groups. As a result, the PA ended up controlling the West Bank and Hamas controlling the Gaza strip. Rocket attacks from Gaza into southern Israel escalated, followed by Israeli strikes aimed at militants and their facilities. Towards the end of 2008, following a spate of rocket attacks from Gaza, Israel launched a military operation against the territory, which culminated in a ground invasion. In early 2009, the Security Council adopted resolution 1860(2009), calling for an immediate ceasefire leading to the withdrawal of Israeli forces from Gaza and condemning violence and acts of terrorism. The Secretary-General began a mission to the Middle East to obtain a ceasefire. Following intense diplomatic efforts, Israel announced a unilateral ceasefire in mid-January, followed by a unilateral ceasefire declaration by Hamas.

That same month, the UN Human Rights Council approved an investigation into the conflict and, shortly afterwards, appointed Richard Goldstone as the head of the investigative team. A September report recommended, among other things, that the Security Council monitor investigations by both Israel and Gaza authorities. The report concluded that both sides had committed violations of the laws of war. Two months later, the General Assembly in resolution 64/10 endorsed the Goldstone report and requested the Secretary-General to report on implementation of the resolution "with a view to considering further action ... including [by] the Security Council".

The Quartet reiterated that negotiations should resolve all final status issues and lead to a settlement. In March 2010, it urged Israel to freeze all settlement activity, reaffirmed that unilateral action would not be recognized by the international community, and underscored that the status of Jerusalem was an issue that remained to be resolved. In September, the United States launched direct Israeli-Palestinian negotiations in Washington D.C. with a one-year time limit. The talks ended, however, when an Israeli partial moratorium on settlement construction in the West Bank expired. The Palestinians refused to negotiate if Israel did not extend the freeze.

Afghanistan

The most recent chapter in United Nations involvement in Afghanistan dates back to September 1995, when the Taliban faction in Afghanistan's civil war, having seized most of the country, took Kabul, its capital. President Burhannudin Rabbani fled, joining the 'Northern Alliance', which held territory in the northern part of the country. Over the years, the Security Council repeatedly voiced its concern that the Afghan conflict provided fertile ground for terrorism and drug trafficking. In August 1998, terrorist bomb attacks on United States embassies in Nairobi, Kenya, and Dar-es-Salaam, Tanzania, claimed hundreds of lives. By resolution 1193(1998), the Council repeated its concern at the continuing presence of terrorists in Afghanistan, and in December, by resolution 1214(1998), it demanded that the Taliban stop providing sanctuary and training for international terrorists and their organizations.

Citing the Taliban's failure to respond to this demand, the Council, in October 1999, applied broad sanctions under the enforcement provisions of the UN *Charter*. It noted, in resolution 1267(1999), that Osama bin Laden had been indicted by the United States for the embassy bombings and demanded that the Taliban faction— never recognized as Afghanistan's legitimate government—turn him over to the appropriate authorities to be brought to justice. Also in October, the Council expressed distress over reports that thousands of non-Afghans were involved in the fighting on the Taliban side. It also noted with concern the forced displacements of civilian populations, summary executions, abuse and arbitrary detention of civilians, violence against women and girls, and indiscriminate bombing. The Taliban's religious intolerance aroused widespread condemnation. In early 2001, they blew up two statues of the Buddha carved out of the sandstone cliff-face in the Bamiyan Valley some 1,300 years ago, including the largest statue of the Buddha in the world. Later that year, an edict required Hindu women to veil themselves like their Muslim counterparts, and all non-Muslims were required to wear identity labels.

On 11 September 2001, members of Osama bin Laden's Al Qaeda organization hijacked four commercial jets in the United States, crashing two into the World Trade Center in New York City, one into the Pentagon in the US capital, and the fourth into a field in Pennsylvania when passengers tried to stop them. Nearly 3,000 people were killed in the attacks. In the days that followed, the US administration issued an ultimatum to the Taliban: turn over bin Laden and close the terrorist operations in Afghanistan or risk a massive military assault. The Taliban refused. In October, forces of the United States and United Kingdom unleashed missile attacks against Taliban military targets and bin Laden's training camps in Afghanistan. Two weeks of bombings were followed by the deployment of US ground forces. In December, Afghan militiamen, supported by American bombers, began an offensive strike on a suspected mountaintop stronghold of Al Qaeda forces in Tora Bora, in eastern Afghanistan near the Pakistan border. Also in the weeks following 11 September, the Security Council supported efforts of the Afghan people to replace the Taliban regime, as the United Nations continued to promote dialogue among Afghan parties aimed at establishing a broad-based, inclusive government. A UN-organized meeting of Afghan political leaders in Bonn, Germany, concluded in early December with agreement on a provisional arrangement, pending re-establishment of permanent government institutions. As a first step, the Afghan Interim Authority was established.

In December 2001, the Security Council authorized the establishment of an **International Security Assistance Force (ISAF)** to help the Authority maintain security in Kabul and its surrounding areas. Later that month, the internationally recognized administration of President Rabbani handed power to the new Afghan Interim Authority headed by Chairman Hamid Karzai, and the first ISAF troops were deployed. In January 2002, an International Conference on Reconstruction Assistance to Afghanistan garnered pledges of over $4.5 billion. It was announced that an Emergency Loya Jirga (Pashto for 'Grand Council')—a traditional forum in which tribal elders come together and settle affairs—would be constituted to elect a head of state for the transitional administration and determine its structure and key personnel. The Security Council, welcoming the positive changes in Afghanistan as a result of the collapse of the Taliban, adjusted its sanctions to reflect the new realities, targeting Al Qaeda and its supporters. In March, the Council established the **United Nations Assistance Mission in Afghanistan (UNAMA)** to fulfil the tasks entrusted to the UN under the Bonn Agreement in such areas as human rights, the rule of law and gender issues. Headed by the Secretary-General's special representative, it would also promote national reconciliation, while managing all UN humanitarian activities in coordination with the Interim Authority and its successors. UNAMA's mandate has been extended every year since then.

A few months later, the process of electing members to the Emergency Loya Jirga began. The nine-day council was opened in June by Zahir Shah, the former King of Afghanistan, who nominated Hamid Karzai to lead the nation. Subsequently, Mr. Karzai was elected as Afghanistan's head of state, to lead the transitional government for the next two years. In January 2004, the Constitutional Loya Jirga reached agreement on a text which was adopted as Afghanistan's Constitution. In October of that year, more than 8 million Afghans went to the polls, choosing Hamid Karzai as the country's first-ever elected President. In September 2005, the Afghan people voted for the members of their National Assembly and Provisional Councils, despite a series of deadly attacks during the campaign. Parliament was inaugurated at the end of December.

Drug control, reconstruction and development. By the late 1990s, Afghanistan had become notorious as the source of nearly 80 per cent of the world's illicit opium, the source of heroin. By 2007, the country's $3 billion opium trade accounted for more than 90 per cent of the world's illegal output, according to a UN Office on Drugs and Crime report. Cultivation was mainly in the south, where the Taliban was profiting from the drug trade. In 2008 and 2009, however, opium cultivation was reported to have declined by 36 per cent.

In January 2006, a high-level group meeting in London launched the Afghanistan Compact—a five-year agenda to consolidate democratic institutions, curb insecurity, control the illegal drug trade, stimulate the economy, enforce the law, provide basic services to the Afghan people, and protect their human rights. The next month, the Security Council unanimously endorsed the Compact as providing a framework for partnership between the Afghan government and the international community. In June 2008, the International Conference in support of Afghanistan, co-chaired by Afghanistan, France and the United Nations brought together delegations from 67 countries and 17 international organizations. About $20 billion were pledged to finance the Compact's implementation, including support for the preparation of elections in 2009 and 2010, which saw the re-election of President Karzai. During the run-up to the elections of September 2010, the Taliban intimidated villagers in certain areas from voting, and turn-out was low as a result. Only 4 million Afghans actually went to the polls in a climate of exacerbated tension.

Lack of security remained a major impediment to development. The UNDP found that 6.6 million Afghans— one third of the population— did not have enough to eat, while the mortality rate for children under five years and the proportion of mothers dying in childbirth was among the highest in the world.

Security. In September 2007, the Security Council voiced concern about the increased violence and terrorism as it approved the extension of ISAF. Addressing this situation, the Secretary-General said that the key to sustaining gains in the long term lay in increasing the capability, autonomy and integrity of the National Security Forces, and especially the National Police. The difficulty in achieving those goals was made evident by the recurrence and escalation of violence throughout 2008 and 2009. In a Taliban attack on a UN guesthouse in Kabul in October 2009, five foreign UN employees and three Afghans were killed. In January 2010, the Secretary-General, the Afghan President and the British Prime Minister co-hosted an international conference on Afghanistan that highlighted the need to transfer responsibility for security matters to the Afghan authorities by 2011. In July, a conference co-hosted by the UN and the Afghan government discussed the transition of Afghan provinces from ISAF control to the National Security Forces by 2014. The conference also considered issues of good governance, fairness of the judicial system and human rights, as well as the continued problem posed by drug trafficking. The Council renewed ISAF's mandate for another year in October 2010.

Iraq

The United Nations' response to Iraq's invasion of Kuwait in 1990, and the situation following the collapse of Saddam Hussein's regime in 2003, illustrate the scope of the challenges the UN faces in seeking to restore international peace and security. The Security Council, by its resolutions 660(1990) and 661(1990), immediately condemned the invasion of Kuwait, demanded Iraq's withdrawal and imposed sanctions against Iraq, including a trade and oil embargo. In November, the Council set 15 January 1991 as the deadline for Iraq's compliance with resolution 660(1990), and authorized member states to use "all necessary means" to restore international peace and security. On 16 January 1991, multinational forces authorized by the Council, but not under UN direction or control launched military operations against Iraq. Hostilities were suspended in February after the Iraqi forces withdrew from Kuwait. On 8 April, by resolution 687(1991) the Council set the terms of the ceasefire.

Deciding that Iraq's weapons of mass destruction should be eliminated, the Council established the **United Nations Special Commission (UNSCOM)** on the disarmament of Iraq, with powers of no-notice inspection, and entrusted the **International Atomic Energy Agency (IAEA)** with similar verification tasks in the nuclear sphere, with UNSCOM assistance. It also established a demilitarized zone along the Iraq-Kuwait border. Resolution 689(1991) set up the **United Nations Iraq-**

Kuwait Observation Mission (UNIKOM) to monitor it. In addition, the Council established an Iraq-Kuwait Boundary Demarcation Commission, whose boundary decisions were accepted by Iraq in 1994. It also established a **United Nations Compensation Commission** to process claims and compensate governments, nationals or corporations for any loss or damage resulting from Iraq's invasion of Kuwait, out of a percentage of the proceeds from sales of Iraqi oil. Thus far, the Commission has approved a total of $52.4 billion in claims, of which $30.7 billion had been paid out by the end of 2010. It is still processing payments, as Iraq continues to pay 5 per cent of its oil revenue to the Compensation Fund.

Concerned about the severe humanitarian impact of economic sanctions on the Iraqi people, the Council, in December 1995, created an 'oil-for-food' programme to offer them a degree of relief. Established by resolution 986(1995), it monitored sales of oil by the government of Iraq to purchase food and humanitarian supplies, and managed the distribution of food in the country. It served as the sole source of sustenance for 60 per cent of Iraq's estimated 27 million people, until it ended in November 2003.

Responding to allegations about the programme that began to surface afterwards, an Independent Investigation Committee appointed by the Secretary-General and chaired by Paul Volcker (former Chairman of the United States Federal Reserve Board) found there had been mismanagement by the head of the Office of the Iraq Programme Oil-for-Food. The Secretary-General immediately lifted his immunity from prosecution. The UN also implemented several management reform initiatives to strengthen ethical conduct, internal oversight and accountability, as well as transparency, financial disclosure and 'whistleblower' protection.

In the course of their inspections during the 1990s, UNSCOM and the IAEA uncovered and eliminated large quantities of Iraq's banned weapons programmes and capabilities in the nuclear, chemical and biological field. In 1998, Iraq called on the Council to lift its oil embargo, declaring that there were no more proscribed weapons. UNSCOM declared it lacked evidence of Iraq's full compliance with resolution 687(1991). In October, Iraq suspended cooperation with UNSCOM, which conducted its final mission in December. In the same month, the United States and the United Kingdom launched air strikes on Iraq.

In December 1999, by its resolution 1284, the Security Council established the **United Nations Monitoring, Verification and Inspection Commission (UNMOVIC)** to replace UNSCOM, expressing its intention to lift economic sanctions, contingent upon Iraq's cooperation with UNMOVIC and the IAEA. In November 2002, the Council adopted resolution 1441, providing for an enhanced inspection regime and offering Iraq a final opportunity to comply with its resolutions. UN inspectors returned to Iraq and the Council was repeatedly briefed by the Executive Chairman of UNMOVIC and the Director-General of the IAEA, but it remained divided about how to ensure the fulfilment of Iraq's obligations. In the midst of negotiations, and outside the framework of the Security Council, Spain, the United Kingdom and the United States presented Iraq with a 17 March 2003 deadline to disarm completely. With military action imminent, the Secretary-General ordered the withdrawal of UN international staff on 17 March and the suspension of all operations. Military action by a coalition headed by the United Kingdom and the United States began three days later. Following the collapse of Saddam Hussein's regime, the Security Council, in May, adopted resolution 1483(2003), stressing the right of the Iraqi people to freely determine their political future. It recognized the authorities, responsibilities and obligations of the Coalition (the 'Authority') until the swearing in of an internationally recognized government. It also lifted international sanctions and provided a legal basis for the UN to resume operations in Iraq.

In August 2003, by resolution 1500, the Security Council established the **United Nations Assistance Mission for Iraq (UNAMI)**, with a mandate to coordinate humanitarian and reconstruction aid and assist with the political process towards establishment of an internationally recognized sovereign Iraqi government. It welcomed the creation of the Iraqi Governing Council as an important step in that direction. On 19 August 2003, the UN headquarters in Baghdad was the target of a terrorist attack that resulted in 22 deaths, and more than 150 injured. Fifteen of the dead were UN staff. Among them was the head of mission, Sergio Vieira de Mello. Following the attack, the Secretary-General withdrew most UN international personnel from Baghdad, maintaining only a small team, principally Iraqis, to provide essential humanitarian assistance—including the delivery of food, water and health care country-wide. In October, the Council authorized a multinational force under unified command to take all necessary measures to contribute to the maintenance of security and stability in Iraq, and to the security of UNAMI and institutions of the Iraqi Interim Administration. In November, the Iraqi Governing Council and the Coalition Provisional Authority (CPA) reached agreement on the restoration of sovereignty by the end of June 2004.

Following requests from the Iraqi Governing Council and the CPA for UN help with the transition to sovereignty, the Secretary-General sent an electoral assistance team to assess what was needed to hold credible elections in January 2005. He also asked his special adviser on Iraq, who arrived there in April 2004, to work with the Iraqis on these arrangements. In May, the Iraqi Governing Council named Iyad Allawi as Iraq's Prime Minister-designate, and the following month, the Security Council endorsed the formation of the new interim government. On 28 June 2004, sovereignty was officially transferred from the CPA to the new Iraqi interim government.

The Independent Electoral Commission of Iraq, established in June 2004, conducted in just over 18 months, with UN support, two national elections and a constitutional referendum, despite an extremely serious security situation on the ground. At the beginning of 2005, millions participated in elections for a provisional national assembly responsible for the drafting of a constitution. The Transitional National Assembly held its first meeting in March 2005. Its President requested UN support in drafting and building consensus around the country's new constitution. In October, Iraq's draft constitution was adopted in a nation-wide referendum. Parliamentary elections were held in December, with the participation of millions of voters of all communities, and hundreds of thousands of observers, agents and poll workers. By June 2006, the new government had been formed. The UN pledged assistance to the people and government of Iraq in promoting national dialogue and reconciliation. Despite the successful political transition, however, the security situation worsened, as waves of sectarian violence and revenge swept the country. By late 2007, some 2.2 million Iraqis had fled the country, and there were nearly 2.4 million internally displaced persons (IDPs). The United Nations took on a lead role in relation to the refugee and IDP situation.

Nonetheless, there were some positive developments. In March 2007, the International Compact with Iraq was launched, with world leaders pledging billions of dollars to Iraq's five-year plan for peace and development. In June, the

Security Council, expressing its gratitude for the "comprehensive contributions" made by UNMOVIC and the IAEA, formally terminated their respective mandates in Iraq. In August, the Council renewed and expanded the mandate of UNAMI, paving the way for the UN to enhance its role in such key areas as national reconciliation, regional dialogue, humanitarian assistance and human rights. In August 2008, the United Nations and the Iraqi government signed the United Nations Assistance Strategy for Iraq 2008–2010, which defined UN support for Iraq's reconstruction, development and humanitarian needs over three years.

Assisted by UNAMI, parliamentary elections were held in March 2010, with an estimated turnout of 62 per cent of the eligible voting population. Iraq's Supreme Court validated the results in June, and the Security Council called on all political actors to engage in an inclusive process to form a representative government. In November, Iraq's main political parties agreed to form a government after months of deadlock, and in December, the parliament unanimously approved Nouri al-Maliki's new government. The coalition includes Kurds, Shias and Sunnis.

Iraq and UNAMI in May 2010 launched a UN Development Assistance Framework for 2011–2014 to support the country's five-year National Development Plan. In August, the Security Council extended the mandate of UNAMI for another year.

India-Pakistan

The United Nations is actively committed to promoting harmonious relations between India and Pakistan, for these have been troubled by a decades-old dispute over Kashmir. The issue dates back to the 1940s, when the princely state of Jammu and Kashmir became free to accede to India or Pakistan under the partition plan and the India Independence Act of 1947. The Hindu Maharaja of mostly Muslim Jammu and Kashmir signed his state's instrument of accession to India.

The Security Council first discussed the issue in 1948, following India's complaint that tribesmen and others, with Pakistan's support and participation, were invading Jammu and Kashmir and fighting was taking place. Pakistan denied the charges and declared Jammu and Kashmir's accession to India illegal. The Council recommended measures to stop the fighting, including the use of UN military observers. It established a UN Commission for India and Pakistan, which made proposals for a ceasefire, troop withdrawals and a plebiscite to decide the issue. Both sides accepted, but could not agree on the modalities for the plebiscite. Since 1949, based on a ceasefire signed by the parties, the **United Nations Military Observer Group in India and Pakistan (UNMOGIP)** has monitored the ceasefire line in Jammu and Kashmir. Following a 1972 agreement, the parties undertook to settle their differences peacefully, but tensions remained. In 2003, India's Prime Minister and the President of Pakistan began a series of reciprocal steps to improve bilateral relations. The Secretary-General expressed hope that the normalization of diplomatic relations, the restoration of rail, road and air links, and other confidence-building measures being introduced would lead to resumption of a sustained dialogue. In November, Pakistan offered to implement a unilateral ceasefire along the Line of Control in Jammu and Kashmir. India responded positively. Eventually, all these efforts led to a summit meeting at the beginning of 2004 in Islamabad, Pakistan, between Prime Minister Atal Bihari Vajpayee of India, and Pakistan's President Pervez Musharraf and its Prime Minister Zafarullah Khan Jamali. As a powerful gesture of peace, and an opportunity to reunite families divided for nearly

60 years, a landmark bus service across the ceasefire line was inaugurated in 2005. An attack on the Delhi-Lahore 'Friendship Express' in February 2007, however, left 67 people dead and nearly 20 injured. The Secretary-General, in a statement echoed by the Security Council, strongly condemned the terrorist bombing and called for its perpetrators to be brought to justice. He also expressed satisfaction that the leaders of India and Pakistan had reaffirmed their determination, in the wake of the bombing, to continue on the path of dialogue.

A wave of coordinated terrorist attacks took place in November 2008 across Mumbai, India's financial hub, by Lashkar-e-Taiba extremists, a terrorist group based in Pakistan. The attacks, which drew global condemnation, lasted three days, killing at least 173 people and wounding more than 300. An operation by India's armed forces resulted in the death of the attackers at the Taj Mahal hotel, with one captured alive. Although Pakistan condemned the attacks, the atrocities committed by the terrorists sharply strained relations between the two neighbours once again. The Security Council and the Secretary-General condemned the attacks and urged all states to cooperate with India to bring the perpetrators, organizers, financiers and sponsors of these acts of terrorism to justice.

In September 2010, the Secretary-General called for an immediate end to violence in Kashmir after reports indicated that dozens of people had been killed there since June. The following month he stated that the United Nations will "stand with Pakistan in facing the challenge of violent extremism and in furthering the democratic transformation of the country".

Tajikistan

Following the break-up of the Soviet Union, Tajikistan became independent in 1991. Soon facing a social and economic crisis, regional and political tensions, and differences between secularists and pro-Islamic traditionalists, the country plunged into a civil war that killed more than 50,000 people. In 1994, talks under the auspices of the Secretary-General's special representative led to a ceasefire agreement; the Security Council established the **United Nations Mission of Observers in Tajikistan (UNMOT)** to assist in monitoring it. In 1997, UN-sponsored negotiations led to a peace agreement. UNMOT assisted in its implementation, in close cooperation with a peacekeeping force of the Commonwealth of Independent States (CIS) and a mission of the Organization for Security and Co-operation in Europe (OSCE). The country's first multiparty parliamentary elections were held in February 2000. UNMOT withdrew in May, and was replaced by the much smaller **UN Tajikistan Office of Peacebuilding (UNTOP)**, with a mandate to help consolidate peace and promote democracy. UNTOP completed its work in July 2007.

Even as the closure of UNTOP ended one chapter in UN political assistance to Central Asia, a new one began in December 2007 with the inauguration of the **United Nations Regional Centre for Preventive Diplomacy for Central Asia**. Based in Ashgabat, Turkmenistan, the Centre was established to help the governments of the region to peacefully and cooperatively manage an array of common challenges and threats—including terrorism, drug trafficking, organized crime and environmental degradation. The Centre offers governments assistance in a number of areas, including: building capacity to prevent conflict; facilitating dialogue; and catalysing international support for specific projects and initiatives. The Centre cooperates closely with the UN programmes and agencies in Central Asia, as well as with regional organizations. Among its priorities in 2009–2011 were cross-border threats from illicit activities—terrorism, organized crime and drug trafficking—environmental degradation, management of common resources such as water and energy, and implications stemming from the precarious situation in Afghanistan.

Cambodia

Prior to implementation of the UN-brokered 1991 Paris Peace Agreements, Cambodia was in a state of deep internal conflict and relative isolation. Since its emergence from French colonialism in the 1950s, the country had suffered the spillover of the Viet Nam war in the 1960s and 1970s, followed by devastating civil conflicts and the genocidal totalitarian rule of Pol Pot. Under his 'Khmer Rouge' regime, from 1975 to 1979, nearly 2 million people perished of murder, disease or starvation, many on Cambodia's infamous 'killing fields'. In 1993, with help from the **United Nations Transitional Authority in Cambodia (UNTAC)**, the country held its first democratic elections. Since then, UN agencies and programmes have assisted the government in strengthening reconciliation and development. The Office of the High Commissioner for Human Rights and the Secretary-General's special representative have helped it promote and protect those rights—cornerstones of the rule of law and democratic development.

In 2003, agreement was reached with the government for the UN to help it set up and run a special court to prosecute crimes committed under the Khmer Rouge. Established in 2005, its judges and prosecutors were sworn in the next year. Twelve months later, they had agreed on its internal rules. In July 2007 the **Extraordinary Chambers in the Courts of Cambodia** issued its first charges for crimes against humanity, taking several persons charged into provisional detention. In 2008, the Cambodians who suffered under the Khmer Rouge participated for the first time in the court through their lawyers. This was described by the tribunal's Victims Unit as "a historic day in international criminal law". Ieng Sary, Ieng Thirith, Khieu Samphan and Nuon Chea—the four most senior members of the Democratic Kampuchea regime—were indicted in 2010 and are being tried for crimes against humanity, including murder, enslavement, torture and rape. They are also charged with the genocide of the Cham and Vietnamese ethnic groups, grave breaches of the *Geneva Conventions*, and violations of the 1956 Cambodian criminal code, including murder, torture and religious persecution.

Myanmar

Since Myanmar's military leadership voided the results of democratic elections in 1990, the UN has sought to help bring about a return to democracy and improvements in the human rights situation there though an all-inclusive process of national reconciliation. In 1993, the General Assembly urged an accelerated return to democracy, asking the Secretary-General to assist the government in that process. In using his good offices to that end, the Secretary-General designated successive special envoys to engage in dialogue with all parties.

The Assembly has renewed the Secretary-General's good offices mandate annually since 1993. Through this mandate, the UN seeks to promote progress in four key areas: the release of political prisoners, a more inclusive political process, a halt to hostilities in the border areas, and a more enabling environment for the provision of humanitarian assistance. Following a period during 2004–2006 when there was no high-level dialogue between the UN and the government, the Secretary-

General's good offices mission resumed in 2006 with two visits to Myanmar by the Under-Secretary-General for Political Affairs, later designated by Secretary-General Ban Ki-moon as his special adviser on Myanmar. The special adviser made another two trips to the country in 2007 and met with Myanmar's senior leadership, as well as with detained opposition leader Daw Aung San Suu Kyi and her party—the National League for Democracy. The special adviser also engaged in a series of high-level consultations with key interested member states, including in Europe and Asia. The Security Council issued a presidential statement expressing "strong and unwavering support" for the Secretary-General's good offices mission.

While the Security Council in 2008 underlined the need for the government to "establish the conditions and create an atmosphere conducive to an inclusive and credible process", a referendum that year on a new constitution written under military guidance which approved the draft constitution has been criticized by the international community. The Secretary-General visited the country in 2009, at the invitation of the government. He argued for the release of all political prisoners, including Aung San Suu Kyi, the resumption of substantive dialogue between the government and the opposition, and the creation of conditions conducive to credible and legitimate elections. In August of that year, however, Aung San Suu Kyi was sentenced to three years of hard labour, which was commuted to 18 months of house arrest—a verdict criticized by the Secretary-General. At the invitation of the government, the UN special rapporteur designated to monitor and report on the situation of human rights in Myanmar, whose mandate was established in 1992, last visited the country in February 2010.

In March 2010, the government approved new laws relating to elections. The political-parties registration law prohibited persons serving a prison term from voting or being a member of a political party, which effectively prevented Aung San Suu Kyi from participating in the elections, unless she was freed from house arrest. The Secretary-General said that the new election laws did not meet "international expectations of what is required for an inclusive political process".

Then, in May, a cyclone devastated the Irrawaddy delta and left tens of thousands dead and missing. It was estimated that between 1.2 million to 1.9 million had been affected, left homeless, and exposed to the risk of disease and possible starvation. UN agencies offered assistance, but the government only allowed in limited aid and restricted the access of foreign aid workers. The Secretary-General expressed his "deep concern and immense frustration at the unacceptably slow response to the grave humanitarian crisis" and went to Myanmar to persuade the government to accept international aid. After the talks, the government accepted humanitarian personnel, who began to arrive in early June. It was also agreed that the aid effort should be led by the Association of Southeast Asian Nations (ASEAN), which resulted in the formation of an ASEAN-UN-Myanmar tripartite mechanism.

Later that year, the General Assembly president called for continued engagement to "promote national reconciliation, democracy and respect for human rights in Myanmar as mandated by the General Assembly" after he was briefed on the special adviser's August visit to Myanmar. The Secretary-General said that "Myanmar's lack of engagement is deeply frustrating" and "contradicts its stated policy of cooperation with the United Nations". In November 2010, the Secretary-General described the elections of that month—Myanmar's first in 20 years and only the third multi-party poll in more than 60 years since independence—as "insufficiently inclusive, participatory and transparent", and called for the release of all political prisoners.

Nepal

Ten years of armed conflict came to an end in Nepal in 2006 under the terms of the Comprehensive Peace Agreement signed between a governing alliance of political parties and the Maoist insurgents who had waged an armed struggle in the South Asian country since 1996. The agreement came six months after a popular movement, loosely coordinated with the Maoists, brought an end to Nepal's authoritarian monarchy. Amid these sweeping changes and their aftermath, the UN has played an important role, at Nepal's request, in helping the country to improve its human rights situation and consolidate peace. The United Nations work in Nepal gained visibility in 2005 when the United Nations High Commissioner for Human Rights established a sizeable office in the country. The office has played a key role in monitoring human rights commitments contained in the code of conduct of the ceasefire, as well as all the human rights provisions of the peace agreement. Through its reports and statements, the office is active in persuading Nepali security forces and Maoists to exercise restraint and stop deliberately targeting civilians.

The UN had been engaged for several years in political efforts to end the hostilities and encourage a negotiated political solution. In 2006, following a government request the for UN assistance, the Secretary-General dispatched a pre-assessment mission to the country. Afterwards, the government and the Maoists sent identical letters to the Secretary-General requesting UN assistance in monitoring the ceasefire code of conduct; observing elections for the constituent assembly; deploying civilian personnel to monitor and verify the confinement of Maoist combatants and their weapons in designated cantonment areas; and monitoring the Nepal Army to ensure that it remained within its barracks and that its weapons were not used. That same year, the personal representative of the Secretary-General in Nepal was instrumental in helping the parties find common ground on key elements, including organization of the elections for the constituent assembly, the management of arms and armies, and reaching consensus on the UN role in the peace process.

When the government reiterated the two sides' request for UN assistance, the Security Council, by resolution 1740(2007), established the **United Nations Mission in Nepal (UNMIN)**. UNMIN was active on various fronts. Its arms monitors supervised the registration of Maoist weapons and combatants. UNMIN electoral experts assisted Nepal's Election Commission by providing technical support for the planning, preparation and conduct of the election of the constituent assembly. A small team of UN electoral monitors independent from UNMIN were involved in reviewing all technical aspects of the electoral process and reporting on the conduct of the election. Meanwhile, UNMIN civil affairs officers provided the Mission with the ability to engage communities outside Kathmandu, and to help create a climate conducive to a peaceful election.

The Council congratulated the people of Nepal for the largely peaceful 2008 elections, and urged all parties to respect the will of the people and the rule of law. After the Constituent Assembly convened for the first time and proclaimed Nepal a republic, and a government incorporating the two sides formed, the Secretary-General approved $10 million in assistance to Nepal from the UN Peacebuilding Fund. The Secretary-General in 2009, however, following a visit to Nepal, assessed the situation as fragile—which it proved to be. Political deadlock ensued. Following the discharge, however, of some 3,000 former Maoist combatants who had been identified as children—a key component of an action plan signed by the government, the Maoists and the UN in 2009—the country's opposing political groups reached a so-called Four-Point Agreement in September 2010 on completing the remaining tasks of the peace process by 14 January 2011. They agreed to complete the integration and rehabilitation of the ex-Maoist combatants by that date. In turn, the Council, by resolution 1939(2010), extended UNMIN's mandate until 15 January 2011, after which the mandate was terminated.

Bougainville/Papua New Guinea

In early 1998, following a decade of armed conflict over the issue of independence for the island of Bougainville, the government of Papua New Guinea and Bougainville leaders concluded the Lincoln Agreement, which established the framework for a peace process. Under the Agreement, a regional truce-monitoring team, with monitors from Australia, Fiji, New Zealand and Vanuatu, was transformed into a Peace Monitoring Group. In accordance with the Lincoln Agreement, the government of Papua New Guinea sought and obtained the Security Council's endorsement of the Agreement, as well as of the appointment of a small UN observer mission. The **United Nations Political Office in Bougainville (UNPOB)**, the first UN political mission in the South Pacific, became operational that same year.

In 2001, after more than two years of talks facilitated and chaired by UNPOB, the parties signed the Bougainville Peace Agreement—providing for a weapons disposal plan, autonomy and a referendum. UNPOB took the lead in supervising the weapons disposal plan. Completion of the second stage of the plan, as certified by UNPOB, opened the way for the drafting of a Bougainville Constitution, as well as for preparations for the election of an autonomous Bougainville government. In 2004, responding to increased stability in Bougainville, the UN replaced UNPOB with a smaller mission, the **United Nations Observer Mission in Bougainville (UNOMB)**. Elections for the first autonomous government in the Papua New Guinea province of Bougainville were held the next year. In June 2005, the new autonomous provincial government of the island, including its President and House of Representatives, was sworn in. UNOMB's work was complete.

The war in Bougainville had been little noticed but brutal, costing some 15,000 lives during the 1980s and 1990s. UN efforts leading to a successful outcome included its involvement in negotiating, mediating and facilitating the resolution of the conflict. The United Nations also undertook the collection and destruction of some 2,000 weapons, encouraged the parties to meet agreed upon pre-election deadlines, and facilitated the election.

Timor-Leste

In 2002, the formerly dependent Territory of East Timor declared its independence as Timor-Leste, following engagement by the United Nations over many years in its struggle for self-determination. Its constituent assembly was subsequently transformed into a national parliament, and in September of that year, Timor-Leste became the 191st member state of the UN. Following the declaration of independence, the Security Council established a **United Nations Mission of Support in East Timor (UNMISET)** to assist the nascent state in developing core administrative structures, providing interim law enforcement and security, developing a police service, and contributing to the maintenance of internal and external security.

Upon completing its work in 2005, UNMISET was replaced by a **United Nations Office in Timor-Leste (UNOTIL)**, which worked to support the development of critical state institutions, the police and the border patrol unit, and to provide training in democratic governance and the observance of human rights.

The dismissal of nearly 600 members of the armed forces in 2006, however, triggered a violent crisis that peaked in May, resulting in casualties. The government requested, and the Security Council endorsed, the deployment of international police and military assistance to secure critical locations and facilities. The Secretary-General sent his special envoy to help diffuse the crisis and to find a political solution. Following extensive negotiations among the political actors, a new government was formed in July. The next month, the Council, established a new and expanded operation, the **United Nations Integrated Mission in Timor-Leste (UNMIT)**, to support the government in "consolidating stability, enhancing a culture of democratic governance, and facilitating dialogue among Timorese stakeholders". Since then, stability in the country has been largely maintained, and presidential and parliamentary elections were held in a generally calm security environment in 2007.

In early 2008, a group led by a former military officer attacked both the President and the Prime Minister of Timor-Leste. The Security Council condemned the attacks and urged full cooperation of all parties to bring to justice those responsible. The Council welcomed the Secretary-General's intention to send an expert mission, which in March conducted an assessment of the requirements of the national police and adjustments to UNMIT's police skill sets. According to the ensuing report, UNMIT faced problems of deployment, capacity, conflicting training standards, resources and limited timeframe for its mandate. A further UN team visited Timor-Leste to begin implementation of the recommendations made in the report, including the phased handover of UNMIT policing responsibilities to the Timorese police. Later that year the Council adopted a presidential statement which commended the Timorese leaders and institutions for the "rapid, firm and responsible manner" in which they responded to the attacks. It also reaffirmed the importance of the review and reform of the security sector and the need for sustained support from the international community in helping Timor-Leste develop its institutions.

In 2009, on the anniversary of the UN-organized referendum that led to the country's independence, the Council commended the people and government of Timor-Leste on their efforts towards peace, stability and development. The next year, in February, the Council extended UNMIT's mandate for a year while endorsing the Secretary-General's intention to reconfigure its police component in line with the phased resumption of policing responsibilities by the national police.

Europe

Cyprus

The **United Nations Peacekeeping Force in Cyprus (UNFICYP)** was established in 1964 to prevent a recurrence of fighting between the Greek Cypriot and Turkish Cypriot communities and to contribute to the maintenance and restoration of law and order and a return to normal conditions. In 1974, a coup d'état by Greek Cypriot and Greek elements favouring union of the country with Greece was followed by military intervention by Turkey and the de facto division of the island.

Since that year, UNFICYP has supervised a de facto ceasefire which came into effect on 16 August 1974, and maintained a buffer zone between the lines of the Cyprus National Guard and of the Turkish and Turkish Cypriot forces. In the absence of a political settlement, UNFICYP continues its presence on the island.

The Secretary-General used his good offices in search of a comprehensive settlement, hosting proximity talks between the two Cyprus leaders in 1999 and 2000, followed by intensive direct talks beginning in 2002. He also submitted a comprehensive proposal aimed at bridging the gaps between them, but agreement could not be reached on submitting it to referendums on each side in time to allow a reunited Cyprus to sign the *Treaty of Accession* to the European Union. The talks were suspended in 2003. In April of that year, the Turkish Cypriot authorities began to open crossing points for public travel by Greek Cypriots to the north and Turkish Cypriots to the south for the first time in nearly three decades. As UN engineers worked to improve the roads, the Security Council authorized an increase in UNFICYP's police component to ensure the safe and orderly passage of people and vehicles. Seven months later, there had been some 2 million crossings.

The Secretary-General welcomed the new initiative, but stressed that it could not substitute for a comprehensive settlement. In 2004, the Greek Cypriot and Turkish Cypriot leaders—along with the guarantor nations of Greece, Turkey and the United Kingdom—resumed negotiations in New York on the basis of the Secretary-General's detailed proposals. After six weeks of negotiations, with agreement just out of reach, the Secretary-General stepped in to complete the "Comprehensive Settlement of the Cyprus Problem", calling for creation of a United Cyprus Republic—composed of a Greek Cypriot constituent state and a Turkish Cypriot constituent state linked by a federal government. Seventy-six per cent of voters in the Greek Cypriot referendum opposed the plan, while 65 per cent of voters in the Turkish Cypriot referendum supported it. Without the approval of both communities, the plan was defeated, and so Cyprus entered the European Union as a divided and militarized island.

In 2006, the Greek Cypriot and Turkish Cypriot leaders met face-to-face, together with the UN Under-Secretary-General for Political Affairs. In a resulting "set of principles" and "decision by the two leaders", they committed to the unification of Cyprus based on a bi-zonal, bi-communal federation and political equality, as set out in Security Council resolutions, and to a process to achieve that end. They also met in 2007, at the official residence of the Secretary-General's special representative in Cyprus, where they agreed on the need for the earliest start of that process.

The last round of negotiations was initiated following the agreement in 2008 between the Greek Cypriot and the Turkish Cypriot leaders, who also decided to open a crossing at Ledra Street in the centre of old town Nicosia, which had for many years been a symbol of the division of Cyprus. Negotiations began later that year, and joint papers were produced by the leaders, their representatives and experts, setting out the positions of the two sides on different issues and indicating areas of convergence and divergence. Those negotiations were continuing in 2011.

Georgia

Relations between the Abkhaz and the Georgians have been tense for decades. Renewed attempts in 1990 by the local authorities in Abkhazia (north-western region of Georgia) to separate from Georgia, which became independent in 1991, escalated in 1992 into a series of armed confrontations. Hundreds died and some 30,000 fled to the Russian Federation. An envoy of the Secretary-General, appointed in 1993, began mediation among the parties, and a ceasefire agreement was reached later that year. The Security Council established the **United Nations Observer Mission in Georgia (UNOMIG)** to verify compliance. Fighting resumed, however, turning into civil war. In 1994, the parties, meeting in Moscow, agreed on a new ceasefire to be monitored by a peacekeeping force of the Commonwealth of Independent States (CIS). UNOMIG monitored implementation of the agreement and observed the operation of the force.

Over the years, successive special representatives of the Secretary-General conducted negotiations, and the Security Council stressed the need for a comprehensive settlement. Tensions between Georgia and Russia continued to rise, however, and in 2008 escalated into a full scale war over South Ossetia, which was followed by the annulment of the 1994 ceasefire agreement and later by the termination of the CIS mission. The dramatic escalation of hostilities profoundly affected the situation in the Georgian-Abkhaz zone of conflict and the overall conflict-settlement process. Abkhazia's separatist forces opened a second front and seized territory in western Georgia in August. The Russian president immediately announced the intent to halt military operations in Georgia, but the troops remained in South Ossetia and Abkhazia—recognized by Russia as "independent", but considered by Georgia to be territories under Russian occupation. According to UNHCR estimates, some 192,000 people were forced to flee their homes during the August 2008 conflict. UNOMIG came to an end in June 2009 due to a lack of consensus among Security Council members on mandate extension. UN agencies, however, have continued to assist those displaced by the conflicts.

The Balkans

Former Yugoslavia. The Federal Republic of Yugoslavia was a founding member of the United Nations. In 1991, two republics of the federation, Croatia and Slovenia, declared independence. Croatian Serbs, supported by the national army, opposed the move, and war broke out between Croatia and Serbia. The Security Council imposed an arms embargo on Yugoslavia, and the Secretary-General appointed a personal envoy to support peace efforts by the European Community. To create conditions for a settlement, the Security Council in 1992 established the **United Nations Protection Force (UNPROFOR)**, initially in Croatia. The war extended to Bosnia and Herzegovina, however, which had also declared independence—a move supported by Bosnian Croats and Muslims but opposed by Bosnian Serbs. The Croatian and Serb armies intervened, and the Council imposed economic sanctions on the Federal Republic of Yugoslavia, consisting by then of Serbia and Montenegro.

The war intensified, generating the largest refugee crisis in Europe since the Second World War. Faced with widespread reports of 'ethnic cleansing', the Security Council in 1993 created, for the first time, an international court to prosecute war crimes. It also declared certain places as 'safe areas', in an attempt to insulate them from the fighting. UNPROFOR sought to protect the delivery of humanitarian aid in Bosnia and to protect Sarajevo, its capital, as well as other 'safe areas'. Peacekeeping commanders requested 35,000 troops, but the Council authorized only 7,600. To deter continuing attacks against Sarajevo, the North Atlantic Treaty Organization (NATO) in 1994 authorized air strikes at the Secretary-General's request. Bosnian Serb forces detained some 400 UNPROFOR observers, using some as 'human shields'.

Fighting intensified in 1995. Croatia launched major offensives against its Serb-populated areas. NATO responded to Bosnian Serb shelling of Sarajevo with massive air strikes. Bosnian Serb forces took over the 'safe areas' of Srebrenica and Zepa. They killed some 7,000 unarmed men and boys in Srebrenica in the worst massacre in Europe since the Second World War. In a 1999 report, the Secretary-General acknowledged the errors of the UN and member states in their response to the ethnic cleansing campaign that culminated in Srebrenica. The tragedy, he said, "will haunt our history forever".

In 1995, agreement was reached between Bosnia and Herzegovina, Croatia and Yugoslavia to end the 42-month war. To ensure compliance, the Security Council authorized a multinational, NATO-led, 60,000-strong Implementation Force. The Council also established a UN International Police Task Force. It later became part of a larger **United Nations Mission in Bosnia and Herzegovina (UNMIBH)**, which facilitated the return of refugees and displaced persons, fostered peace and security, and helped build up state institutions. In 1996, the Council established the **United Nations Mission of Observers in Prevlaka (UNMOP)**, to monitor the demilitarization of the Prevlaka peninsula, a strategic area in Croatia contested by Yugoslavia. UNMIBH and UNMOP completed their work at the end of 2002.

In May 2006, the people of Montenegro voted for independence in a referendum, and the next month the country declared its independence. Montenegro became the 192nd member of the United Nations. The same month, in the wake of the referendum in Montenegro, the Serbian parliament declared the Republic of Serbia to be the legal successor to the State Union of Serbia and Montenegro—which was already a member of the UN.

Kosovo. In 1989, the Federal Republic of Yugoslavia revoked local autonomy in Kosovo, a province in southern Yugoslavia historically important to Serbs which was more than 90 per cent ethnically Albanian. Kosovo Albanians dissented, boycotting Serbian state institutions and authority in a quest for self-rule. Tensions increased, and the Kosovo Liberation Army (KLA) surfaced in 1996, seeking independence through armed rebellion. It launched attacks against Serb officials and Albanians who collaborated with them, and Serb authorities responded with mass arrests. Fighting erupted in March 1998 as Serbian police swept the Drenica region, ostensibly looking for KLA members. The Security Council imposed an arms embargo against Yugoslavia, including Kosovo, but the situation deteriorated into open warfare.

Then, in 1999, following warnings to Yugoslavia, and against the backdrop of a Serbian offensive in Kosovo, NATO began air strikes against Yugoslavia. The Secretary-General said it was tragic that diplomacy had failed. Although there were times when "the use of force may be legitimate in the pursuit of peace", he said, the Security Council should be involved in any such decisions. Yugoslavia launched a major offensive against the KLA and began mass deportations of ethnic Albanians from Kosovo, causing an unprecedented outflow of 850,000 refugees. UNHCR and other humanitarian agencies rushed to assist them in Albania and The former Yugoslav Republic of Macedonia. Yugoslavia accepted a peace plan proposed by the Group of Eight (the seven Western industrialized nations and Russia). The Security Council endorsed it and authorized member states to establish a security presence to deter hostilities, demilitarize the KLA and facilitate the return of refugees.

It also asked the Secretary-General to establish an interim international civilian administration, under which the people could enjoy substantial autonomy and self-government. Yugoslav forces withdrew, NATO suspended its bombings, and a 50,000-strong multinational **Kosovo Force (KFOR)** arrived to provide security.

The **United Nations Interim Administration Mission in Kosovo (UNMIK)** immediately established a presence on the ground. Its task was unprecedented in complexity and scope. The Security Council vested UNMIK with authority over the territory and people of Kosovo, including all legislative and executive powers and administration of the judiciary. At least 841,000 refugees of the approximately 850,000 who fled during the war returned, and the first priority was to equip them for the rigours of the coming winter. That accomplished, UNMIK made significant progress towards re-establishing normal life and ensuring long-term economic reconstruction. The KLA was completely demilitarized before the end of 1999 and its members reintegrated in civil society. In the following months, as some 210,000 non-Albanian Kosovars left Kosovo for Serbia and Montenegro, a joint committee facilitated their safe return. Remaining non-Albanian minorities lived in isolated enclaves guarded by KFOR.

In 2001, the International Criminal Tribunal for the former Yugoslavia indicted former Yugoslav President Slobodan Milosevic and four others for crimes against humanity during a "systematic attack directed against the Kosovo Albanian civilian population of Kosovo". When the defence had nearly completed its case, Milosevic died in 2006 of natural causes while in detention. He was facing 66 counts of genocide, crimes against humanity and war crimes in Bosnia and Herzegovina, Croatia, and Kosovo.

Also in 2001, the Security Council lifted its arms embargo. In November, a 120-member Kosovo Assembly was elected which, in 2002, elected the province's first President and Prime Minister. In December, UNMIK completed the transfer of responsibilities to local provisional institutions, though it retained control over security, foreign relations, protection of minority rights, and energy—pending determination of the province's final status.

During 2006, the Secretary-General's special envoy conducted four rounds of direct negotiations between the parties and the first high-level meeting between top Serbian and Kosovar leaders, but Kosovo's ethnic Albanian government and Serbia remained at odds. In February 2007, he presented his final status plan as "a compromise proposal", but the parties were unmoved. He subsequently reported that the only viable option for Kosovo was independence—which has been consistently opposed by Serbia. Later that year, the Secretary-General welcomed an agreement to have a troika composed of the European Union, Russia and the United States lead further negotiations on Kosovo's future status; however, the parties have not been able to reach an agreement (see *www.unmikonline.org*).

In 2008, the Assembly of Kosovo adopted a declaration of independence. In 2010, the International Court of Justice issued an advisory opinion on the declaration that stated it did not violate international law. By September, Kosovo had been recognized as an independent state by 70 of the 192 UN member states, while Serbia considers it as part of its territory. At the same time, the Secretary-General reaffirmed the readiness of the UN to contribute to the process of dialogue between Belgrade and Pristina in close coordination with the EU.

Disarmament

Since the birth of the United Nations, the goals of multilateral disarmament and arms limitation have been central to its efforts to maintain international peace and security (*www.un.org/disarmament*). The UN has given highest priority to reducing and eventually eliminating nuclear weapons, destroying chemical weapons and strengthening the prohibition against biological weapons—all of which pose the most dire threats to humankind. While these objectives have remained constant over the years, the scope of deliberations and negotiations has changed as political realities and the international situation evolved. The international community is now considering more closely the excessive and destabilizing proliferation of small arms and light weapons and has mobilized to combat the massive deployment of landmines—phenomena that threaten the economic and social fabric of societies and kill and maim civilians, all too many of whom are women and children. Consideration is also being given to the need for multilaterally negotiated norms against the spread of ballistic missile technology, the explosive remnants of war, and the impact of new information and telecommunications technologies on international security.

The tragic events of 11 September 2001 in the United States, and subsequent terrorist attacks in a number of countries, have underlined the potential danger of weapons of mass destruction falling into the hands of non-state actors. Such attacks could have had even more devastating consequences had the terrorists been able to acquire and use chemical, biological or nuclear weapons. Reflecting these concerns, the General Assembly adopted in 2002, for the first time, a resolution (57/83) on measures to prevent terrorists from acquiring weapons of mass destruction and their means of delivery.

In 2004, the Security Council took its first formal decision on the danger of the proliferation of weapons of mass destruction, particularly to non-state actors. Acting under the enforcement provisions of the UN *Charter*, the Council unanimously adopted resolution 1540(2004), obliging states to refrain from any support for non-state actors in the development, acquisition, manufacture, possession, transport, transfer or use of nuclear, chemical and biological weapons and their means of delivery. The resolution imposes far-reaching obligations on states to establish domestic measures to prevent the proliferation of nuclear, chemical and biological weapons, and their means of delivery, including the establishment of appropriate controls over related materials. Subsequently, the General Assembly adopted the *International Convention for the Suppression of Acts of Nuclear Terrorism*, which entered into force in 2007.

In addition to its role in the actual disarmament of weapons and in verifying compliance, the UN plays an essential role in multilateral disarmament by assisting member states in establishing new norms and in strengthening and consolidating existing agreements. One of the most effective means of deterring the use or threatened use of weapons of mass destruction by terrorists is to strengthen multilateral regimes already developed to ban those weapons and prevent their proliferation.

Disarmament machinery

The *Charter of the United Nations* gives the **General Assembly** the chief responsibility for considering "the general principles of cooperation in the maintenance of international peace and security, including the principles governing disarmament and the regulation of armaments" (Article 11). The Assembly has two subsidiary bodies dealing with disarmament issues: the First (Disarmament and International Security) Committee, which meets during the Assembly's regular session and deals with all disarmament issues on its agenda; and the Disarmament Commission, a specialized deliberative body that focuses on specific issues and meets for three weeks every year.

The **Conference on Disarmament** is the international community's sole multilateral negotiating forum for disarmament agreements. The Conference negotiated both the *Chemical Weapons Convention* and the *Comprehensive Nuclear-Test-Ban Treaty*. Since it addresses matters that touch upon the national security interests of states, it works strictly on the basis of consensus. It has a limited membership of 65 states and a unique relationship with the General Assembly. While the Conference defines its own rules and develops its own agenda, it takes into account the recommendations of the Assembly and reports to it annually. Since 1997, the Conference has been unable to adopt and carry out a programme of work due to lack of consensus among its members on disarmament priorities.

The **United Nations Office for Disarmament Affairs (UNODA)** implements the decisions of the Assembly on disarmament matters. The **United Nations Institute for Disarmament Research (UNIDIR)** undertakes independent research on disarmament and related problems, particularly international security issues. The **Advisory Board on Disarmament Matters** advises the Secretary-General on matters relating to arms limitation and disarmament, and serves as the Board of Trustees of UNIDIR. It also advises on implementation of the recommendations of the **United Nations Disarmament Information Programme**.

Weapons of mass destruction

Nuclear weapons

Through sustained efforts, the world community has achieved numerous multilateral agreements aimed at reducing nuclear arsenals, excluding their deployment from certain regions and environments (such as outer space and the ocean floor), limiting their proliferation and ending testing. Despite these achievements, nuclear weapons and their proliferation remain a major threat to peace and a major challenge to the international community. Issues of concern in this area include the need for reductions in nuclear weapons, upholding the viability of the nuclear non-proliferation regime, and preventing the development and proliferation of ballistic missiles and missile defence systems.

Bilateral agreements on nuclear weapons. While international efforts to contain nuclear weapons continue in different forums, it has been generally understood that the nuclear-weapon powers hold special responsibility for maintaining a stable international security environment. During and after the cold war, the two major powers arrived at agreements that have significantly reduced the threat of nuclear war.

Multilateral agreements on nuclear weapons and non-proliferation. The *Treaty on the Non-Proliferation of Nuclear Weapons (NPT)*, the most universal of all multilateral disarmament treaties, was opened for signature in 1968 and came into force in 1970. The NPT is the cornerstone of the global nuclear non-proliferation regime and the foundation for the pursuit of nuclear disarmament. The 2000 Review Conference of the Parties to the NPT adopted a final document in which

Multilateral disarmament and arms regulation agreements

A chronology of important international disarmament and arms regulation measures concluded through negotiations in multilateral and regional forums includes:

- 1925 *Geneva Protocol*: prohibits the first use of chemical and biological weapons.
- 1959 *Antarctic Treaty*: demilitarizes the continent and bans the testing of any kind of weapon on the continent.
- 1963 *Treaty Banning Nuclear Weapon Tests in the Atmosphere, in Outer Space and under Water (Partial Test-Ban Treaty)*: restricts nuclear testing to underground sites only.
- 1967 *Treaty for the Prohibition of Nuclear Weapons in Latin America and the Caribbean (Treaty of Tlatelolco)*: prohibits testing, use, manufacture, storage, or acquisition of nuclear weapons by the countries of the region.
- 1967 *Treaty on Principles Governing the Activities of States in the Exploration and Use of Outer Space, including the Moon and Other Celestial Bodies (Outer Space Treaty)*: mandates that outer space be used for peaceful purposes only and that nuclear weapons not be placed or tested in outer space.
- 1968 *Treaty on the Non-Proliferation of Nuclear Weapons (NPT)*: establishes that the non-nuclear-weapon states agree never to acquire nuclear weapons and, in exchange, are promised access to and assistance in the peaceful uses of nuclear energy. Nuclear-weapon states pledge to carry out negotiations relating to the cessation of the nuclear arms race and to nuclear disarmament, and not to assist in any way in the transfer of nuclear weapons to non-nuclear-weapon states.
- 1971 *Treaty on the Prohibition of the Emplacement of Nuclear Weapons on the Sea-bed and the Ocean Floor and in the Subsoil Thereof (Sea-bed Treaty)*: bans the emplacement of nuclear weapons, or any weapon of mass destruction, on the sea-bed or ocean floor.
- 1972 *Convention on Bacteriological (Biological) Weapons (BWC)*: bans the development, production and stockpiling of biological and toxin agents, and provides for the destruction of such weapons and their means of delivery.
- 1980 *Convention on Certain Conventional Weapons (CCW)*: prohibits certain conventional weapons deemed excessively injurious or having indiscriminate effects. Protocol I bans weapons which explode fragments that are undetectable by X-ray within the human body. Amended Protocol II (1995) limits the use of certain types of mines, booby-traps and other devices. Protocol III bans incendiary weapons. Protocol IV bans the use of blinding laser weapons.
- 1985 *South Pacific Nuclear Free Zone Treaty (Treaty of Rarotonga)*: bans the stationing, acquisition or testing of nuclear explosive devices and the dumping of nuclear waste within the zone.
- 1990 *Treaty on Conventional Armed Forces in Europe (CFE Treaty)*: limits the numbers of various conventional armaments in a zone stretching from the Atlantic Ocean to the Urals.
- 1992 *Open Skies Treaty*: enables states parties to overfly and observe the territory of one another, based on principles of cooperation and openness. Has been used for the verification of several arms control agreements and for other monitoring mechanisms.
- 1993 *Chemical Weapons Convention (CWC)*: prohibits the development, production, stockpiling and use of chemical weapons and requires their destruction.
- 1995 *Southeast Asia Nuclear-Weapon-Free Zone Treaty (Treaty of Bangkok)*: bans the development or stationing of nuclear weapons on the territories of the states parties.

- 1996 *African Nuclear-Weapon-Free Zone Treaty (Treaty of Pelindaba)*: bans the development or stationing of nuclear weapons on the African continent.
- 1996 *Comprehensive Nuclear-Test-Ban Treaty (CTBT)*: places a worldwide ban on nuclear test explosions of any kind and in any environment.
- 1997 *Mine-Ban Convention*: prohibits the use, stockpiling, production and transfer of antipersonnel mines and provides for their destruction.
- 2005 *International Convention for the Suppression of Acts of Nuclear Terrorism (Nuclear Terrorism Convention)*: outlines specific acts of nuclear terrorism, aims to protect a broad range of possible targets, bring perpetrators to justice and promote cooperation among countries.
- 2006 *Central Asia Nuclear-Weapon-Free Zone Treaty*: establishes this zone, comprising the five central Asian states—Kazakhstan, Kyrgyzstan, Tajikistan, Turkmenistan and Uzbekistan.
- 2008 *Convention on Cluster Munitions (CCM)*: prohibits the use, development, production, acquisition, stockpiling, retention or transfer of such munitions.
- 2010 *Central African Convention for the Control of Small Arms and Light Weapons (Kinshasha Convention)*: restricts the manufacture, transfer between States, and possession by civilians of small arms and light weapons; requires arms to be marked, brokering activities and brokers to be regulated and States to limit the number of entry points of weapons on their national territory.

(For status of ratification of these agreements, see *http://unhq-appspub-01.un.org/ UNODA/TreatyStatus.nsf.http://disarmament.un.org/TreatyStatus.nsf.*)

---

the nuclear-weapon states made "an unequivocal undertaking … to accomplish the total elimination of their nuclear arsenals".

The Conference agreed on the need for increased transparency about nuclear-weapon capabilities, and a diminishing role for nuclear weapons in security policies. The decision by the Democratic People's Republic of Korea to withdraw from the *Treaty* in January 2003—the first such decision since the *Treaty's* entry into force 33 years earlier—was of great concern to the international community. Participants in the 2005 Review Conference, however, were unable to reach agreement on a substantive outcome.

To verify obligations assumed under the NPT, states parties are required to accept the nuclear safeguards of the International Atomic Energy Agency (IAEA). At the end of 2010, there were safeguards agreements in force with over 170 states. In addition to the NPT, the *Treaties of Bangkok, Pelindaba, Rarotonga and Tlatelolco* require non-nuclear-weapon states to apply IAEA safeguards.

In 1996, an overwhelming majority of General Assembly members adopted the *Comprehensive Nuclear-Test-Ban Treaty (CTBT)*, proscribing any nuclear-test explosions anywhere. Originally proposed in 1954, it had taken four decades to adopt the *Treaty*, which extended the 1963 partial test ban to all environments. The CTBT has not yet entered into force. The *Treaty* opened for signature in New York in 1996, when it was signed by 71 States, including five of the eight then nuclear-capable countries. At the end of 2010, 153 states had ratified the CTBT and another 29 states had signed but not ratified it. The *Treaty* will enter into force 180 days after the 44 states listed in its Annex 2 have ratified it. These 'Annex 2' states are countries that participated in the negotiations for the CTBT between 1994 and 1996 and possessed nuclear power reactors or research reactors at that time. As of 2010, nine 'Annex 2' states remained outside of the treaty: China, the Democratic Peo-

Bilateral disarmament agreements

The 1972 *Treaty on the Limitation of Anti-Ballistic Missile Systems (ABM Treaty)* limited the number of anti-ballistic missile systems of the United States and the Soviet Union to one each. A 1997 'demarcation' agreement between the United States and the Russian Federation distinguished between 'strategic', or long-range ABMs, which were prohibited, and 'non-strategic', or shorter-range ABMs, which were not. The Treaty ceased to be in effect as of 13 June 2002, when the United States withdrew from it.

The 1987 *United States-Soviet Union Intermediate- and Shorter-Range Nuclear Forces Treaty (INF Treaty)* eliminated an entire class of nuclear weapons, which includes all land-based ballistic and cruise missiles with a range of 500 to 5,500 km. By the end of 1996, all the weapons slated for destruction under the provisions of the *Treaty* had been eliminated.

The 1991 *United States-Soviet Union Strategic Arms Limitation and Reduction Treaty (START I)* placed a ceiling of 6,000 warheads on 1,600 deployed long-range nuclear missiles for each side by 2001, thereby reducing the 1991 stockpile levels by about 30 per cent.

The 1992 *Lisbon Protocol to START I* committed Belarus, Kazakhstan, the Russian Federation and Ukraine, as successor states to the Soviet Union, to abide by the *START I Treaty*; Belarus, Kazakhstan and Ukraine were to adhere to the NPT as non-nuclear-weapon states. By 1996, these three states had removed all nuclear weapons from their territories.

The 1993 *Strategic Arms Limitation and Reduction Treaty II (START II)* committed both parties to reduce the number of warheads on long-range nuclear missiles to 3,500 on each side by 2003, and eliminated ICBMs (intercontinental ballistic missiles) equipped with MIRVs (multiple independently targetable re-entry vehicles). A 1997 agreement extended the deadline for destruction of the launching systems—missile silos, bombers and submarines—to the end of 2007.

In 2002, the Presidents of the Russian Federation and the United States signed the *Strategic Offensive Reductions Treaty (SORT)*, also known as the *Moscow Treaty*, agreeing to limit the level of their deployed strategic nuclear warheads to between 1,700 and 2,200. The *Treaty* will remain in force until December 2012, and may be extended or superseded by agreement of the parties.

In February 2011, the Russian Federation and the United States ratified a new *START* treaty, which commits them to reduce their deployed strategic warheads to no more than 1,550 in seven years—up to 30 per cent lower than in the 2002 *Moscow Treaty*. It limits each side to 700 deployed strategic missiles and bombers and establishes verification rules, absent since *START I* expired in 2009, enabling them to keep tabs on each other's arsenals.

---

ple's Republic of Korea, Egypt, India, Indonesia, Iran, Israel, Pakistan and the United States. The UN Secretary-General, in his capacity as the Depositary of the *Treaty*, has convened a series of Conferences on Facilitating the Entry into Force of the CTBT—in 1999, 2001, 2003, 2005, 2007 and 2009. At the latest conference, states agreed to "spare no effort and use all avenues ... to encourage further signature and ratification of the Treaty".

With 182 signatory states participating in the Vienna-based Preparatory Commission for the Comprehensive Nuclear-Test-Ban-Treaty Organization (CTBTO PrepCom), work is under way in the Provisional Technical Secretariat, established in 1997, to ensure that an international monitoring system is operational by the time the *Treaty* enters into force. The Agreement to Regulate the Relationship between the United Nations and the Preparatory Commission for the Comprehensive Nuclear-Test-Ban Treaty Organization was signed in 2000.

Nuclear-weapon-free zones. In a development that was to herald a new movement in regional arms control, the signing of the 1967 *Treaty for the Prohibition of Nuclear Weapons in Latin America and the Caribbean (Treaty of Tlatelolco)* established for the first time a nuclear-weapon-free zone in a populated area of the world. With the deposit of Cuba's instrument of ratification in 2002, the nuclear-weapon-free zone in Latin America and the Caribbean was consolidated to include all states in the region. Subsequently, four additional zones were established—in the South Pacific *(Treaty of Rarotonga,* 1985), South-East Asia *(Treaty of Bangkok,* 1995), Africa *(Treaty of Pelindaba,* 1996), and Central Asia *(Central Asia Nuclear-Weapon-Free Zone Treaty,* 2006). Proposals have been made for establishing nuclear-weapon-free zones in Central Europe and South Asia, as well as for a zone free of weapons of mass destruction in the Middle East. The concept of an individual country as a nuclear-weapon-free zone was acknowledged by the international community in 1998, when the General Assembly supported Mongolia's self-declaration of its nuclear-weapon-free status.

Preventing nuclear proliferation. The International Atomic Energy Agency (IAEA) *(www.iaea.org)* plays a prominent role in international efforts to prevent the proliferation of nuclear weapons—serving as the world's inspectorate for the application of nuclear safeguards and verification measures covering civilian nuclear programmes. Under agreements concluded with states, IAEA inspectors regularly visit nuclear facilities to verify records on the whereabouts of nuclear material, check IAEA-installed instruments and surveillance equipment and confirm inventories of nuclear material. Taken together, these and other safeguards provide independent, international verification that governments are abiding by their commitment to peaceful uses of nuclear energy.

To verify the implementation of the safeguards agreements in force in some 170 states, IAEA experts conduct hundreds of inspections every year. Their aim is to ensure that the nuclear material held in some 900 nuclear installations in dozens of countries is not diverted away from legitimate peaceful uses to military purposes. Through such annual inspections, IAEA contributes to international security and reinforces efforts to halt the spread of arms and move towards a world free of nuclear weapons.

Various types of safeguards agreements can be concluded with IAEA. Those in connection with the NPT, the *Model Protocol Additional to Existing Safeguards Agreements,* as well as those relating to the *Treaty of Tlatelolco,* the *Treaty of Pelindaba* and the *Treaty of Rarotonga* require non-nuclear-weapon states to submit their entire nuclear-fuel-cycle activities to IAEA safeguards. Other agreements cover safeguards at single facilities. IAEA safeguards under the NPT are an integral part of the international regime for non-proliferation and play an indispensable role in ensuring the implementation of the *Treaty.*

In 2010, the Security Council imposed yet more sanctions on Iran for failing to comply with its previous resolutions on ensuring the peaceful nature of its nuclear programme. The Council expanded an arms embargo and tightened restrictions on financial and shipping enterprises related to "proliferation-sensitive activities". The Council also requested the Secretary-General to create a panel of experts to monitor implementation of the sanctions. In 2009, the Security Council had imposed similar sanctions against the Democratic People's Republic of Korea for having conducted an underground nuclear test and ballistic tests. Two sanctions committees have been established to oversee the sanctions.

Chemical and biological weapons

The entry into force of the *Chemical Weapons Convention* (CWC) in 1997 completed a process that began in 1925, when the *Geneva Protocol* prohibited the use of poison gas weapons. The *Convention* created, for the first time in the history of international arms control, a stringent international verification regime (involving collection of information on chemical facilities and routine global inspections) to oversee compliance with treaty obligations by states parties to the *Convention*. Established for that purpose at The Hague, the **Organisation for the Prohibition of Chemical Weapons (OPCW)** (*www.opcw.org*) is very active. By the end of 2010, 188 nations, representing 98 per cent of the global population, had joined OPCW. During that year OPCW reported that some 43,131 metric tonnes—or 60.58 per cent—of the world's declared stockpile of 71,194 metric tonnes of chemical agent had been destroyed, and 3.95 million—45.56 per cent—of the 8.67 million chemical munitions and containers had been destroyed. Also, some 4,166 inspections had taken place at 195 chemical weapon-related and 1,103 industrial sites in 81 countries since April 1997. Worldwide, 4,918 industrial facilities were liable to inspection by the end of 2010. The Agreement Concerning the Relationship between the United Nations and OPCW was signed in 2000.

Unlike the CWC, the 1972 *Biological and Toxin Weapons Convention* (BTWC or BWC) (*www.opbw.org*), which entered into force in 1975, does not provide for a verification mechanism. States parties exchange, as a confidence-building measure, detailed information each year on such items as their high-risk biological research facilities. In 2006, the Sixth Review Conference of the States Parties to the Biological and Toxin Weapons Convention decided to establish an **Implementation Support Unit** to help states parties bolster implementation of the *Convention*. Unlike the nuclear non-proliferation and chemical weapons treaties—which are supported by IAEA and OPCW, respectively—there was no such institutional support with respect to biological weapons. The Unit was launched in 2007 in Geneva, as part of the UN Office for Disarmament Affairs. It is funded by states parties to the *Convention*. Meetings of the states parties to the *Convention* take place at the UN on a regular basis .

Universalizing and fully implementing the BWC and the CWC, and preventing the proliferation of biological and chemical weapons, represent a major task for the international community. In addition, a panel of governmental experts established by the General Assembly has addressed the issue of missiles in all its aspects.

Conventional weapons, confidence-building and transparency

Small arms, light weapons and practical disarmament. Following the end of the cold war, the international community was confronted with the eruption of intrastate conflicts in many parts of the world in which small arms and light weapons were the weapons of choice. Though not the root cause of conflict, these weapons exacerbate violence, facilitate the use of child combatants, hinder humanitarian assistance and delay post-conflict reconstruction and development.

There are hundreds of millions of licensed firearms in the world. Of these, roughly two thirds are in the hands of civil society, while the rest belong to state militaries and law enforcement agencies. Estimates of most other types of small arms and light weapons remain elusive. The legal trade in these arms and weapons exceeds several billion dollars a year, while the illicit trade is believed to be worth over $1 billion annually. Controlling the proliferation of illicit weapons is a necessary step towards better international, regional or national control over all aspects of the issue of small arms.

In 2001, an international **Conference on the Illicit Trade in Small Arms and Light Weapons in All Its Aspects** was held at the United Nations. Under its resulting programme of action, member states agreed to ensure that licensed manufacturers apply a reliable marking on each small arm and light weapon in the production process; to keep comprehensive and accurate records on the manufacture, holding and transfer of such weapons; to improve their ability to cooperate in identifying and tracing the illicit trade of such weapons; and to guarantee that all small arms and light weapons thus confiscated, seized or collected are destroyed. The result was a huge increase in government anti-trafficking activities. In the five years following adoption of the programme, nearly 140 countries had reported on illegal gun trafficking, while a third of all states had made efforts to collect weapons from those not legally entitled to hold them. There was also increased cooperation among and within regions to stem the flow of illicit weapons across borders. In 2006, more than 2,000 representatives from governments, international and regional organizations and civil society took part in a two-week event at UN Headquarters to review implementation of the programme of action. Another review conference of the programme of action is scheduled for 2012.

Since the uncontrolled spread of illicit small arms impacts many aspects of the United Nations' work—from children to health to refugees to development—a mechanism called 'Coordinating Action on Small Arms' was put in place in 1998 to guarantee that the UN system addressed the many sides of small arms control in a coordinated manner. A comprehensive global effort to address the small arms scourge was also launched and sustained by civil society—through research, the promotion of coordinated national action, and global lobbying for an international convention on the arms trade.

Anti-personnel mines. The growing proliferation and indiscriminate use of anti-personnel landmines around the world has been a particular focus of the UN's attention. In 1995, a review of the *Convention on Certain Conventional Weapons (CCW)*—also known as the *Inhumane Weapons Convention*—produced the *Amended Protocol II*, which entered into force in 1998, strengthening restrictions on certain uses, transfers and types (self-destroying and detectable) of landmines. As of 2010, 96 states were bound by this *Protocol*. The *Convention* has five protocols that, besides banning landmines and booby-traps, also ban non-detectable fragments; incendiary weapons; blinding lasers; and explosive remnants of war.

Not satisfied with what they considered an inadequate response to a serious humanitarian crisis, a group of like-minded states negotiated an agreement on a total ban on all anti-personnel landmines—the *Convention on the Prohibition of the Use, Stockpiling, Production and Transfer of Anti-personnel Mines and on Their Destruction (Mine-Ban Convention)*, which was opened for signature in 1997 and entered into force in 1999. In 2010, 156 states had become parties to it.

The fight against landmines

The United Nations is addressing the problems posed by millions of landmines scattered in over 70 countries. Every year, they kill hundreds of people—most of them children, women and the elderly—and those who are not killed are often severely maimed. Years, and even decades after conflicts have ended, landmines continue to wreak havoc on civilian populations. Yet landmines continue to be used as weapons of war.

The UN–sponsored *Inhumane Weapons Convention* (1980) was strengthened in 1996 to include mine use in internal conflicts and to require that all mines be detectable. The 1997 landmark *Convention on the Prohibition of the Use, Stockpiling, Production and Transfer of Anti-personnel Mines and on Their Destruction* (*Mine-Ban Convention*) banned the production, use and export of these weapons.

On the ground, 14 UN agencies, programmes, departments and funds are active in mine-related service. They find and destroy landmines and explosive remnants of war; assist victims; teach people how to remain safe in mine-affected areas; destroy stockpiles; and promote international agreements such as the *Mine-Ban Convention*.

The **United Nations Mine Action Service (UNMAS)** (*www.mineaction.org*) coordinates all mine-related activities of the UN system. It develops policies and standards, conducts assessment and monitoring of the threat posed by mines and unexploded ordnance, collects and disseminates information, mobilizes resources, and engages in advocacy in support of the global ban on antipersonnel landmines. It also provides mine-action assistance in humanitarian emergencies and for peacekeeping operations.

Implementation of both instruments has led to the destruction of stockpiles, mine clearance in affected countries, and fewer victims. While there were still some 3,956 casualties caused by mines in 2009, this continued a downward trend of the last few years (see *www.icbl.org*).

Explosive Remnants of War (ERW) and Mines Other than Anti-Personnel Landmines (MOTAPM). While significant steps have been taken to address anti-personnel landmines, many civilians are killed or injured by other explosive munitions. They pose a potential hazard to populations through inadvertent contact or deliberate tampering, especially if the danger is not well understood. They can cause severe damage even in small numbers; when placed in strategic locations, a single mine can cause entire roads to be closed and can disrupt normal activities. Combined with other possible characteristics of MOTAPM, such as anti-handling devices and minimum metal content, their humanitarian impact can be quite serious.

Under *Protocol V* to the *CCW*, states parties to armed conflict are required to take action to clear, remove or destroy ERW, and record, retain and transmit information related to the use or abandonment of explosive ordnance. They are also obligated to take all feasible precautions for the protection of civilians and humanitarian missions and organizations. States parties in a position to do so should provide cooperation and assistance for marking, clearance, removal, destruction, and victim assistance. *Protocol V* entered into force in 2006.

Register of Conventional Arms. In order to contribute to building confidence and security among states, the General Assembly in 1991 established the *United Nations Register of Conventional Arms* (*http://disarmament.un.org/un_register.nsf*). The *Register* is run and maintained by the United Nations Office for Disarmament

Affairs (UNODA). This voluntary reporting arrangement enables participating governments to provide information on the export and import of seven categories of major conventional weapons systems: warships, including submarines; battle tanks; armoured combat vehicles; combat aircraft; attack helicopters; large-calibre artillery; and missiles and missile-launchers, including short-range man-portable air-defence systems. Member states are also invited to provide data on transfers of small arms and light weapons, procurement through national production, and military holdings. Such data are compiled and published annually by the UN as official documents available to the general public, as well as through the United Nations website. By 2010, 173 states had reported to the *Register* one or more times since the opening of the *Register* in 1991. In 2010, UNODA received 69 national reports. It is estimated that the *Register* captures more than 95 per cent of the global trade in major conventional weapons.

Transparency of military expenditures. Another global mechanism designed to promote transparency in military matters is the United Nations Standardized Instrument for Reporting Military Expenditures (*www.unclef.com/disarmament/ convarms/Milex/html/MilexIndex.shtml*), a system for standardized reporting introduced in 1980. This voluntary instrument covers national expenditures on military personnel, operations and maintenance, procurement and construction, and research and development. The UN collects this information and makes it public. As 2010 drew to a close, some 124 countries had reported to this instrument at least once since its inception.

Prevention of an arms race in outer space. Matters related to outer space have been pursued in international forums along two separate lines: those related to peaceful applications of space technology, and those related to the prevention of an arms race in that environment. These issues have been discussed in the General Assembly, the Committee on the Peaceful Uses of Outer Space and its subsidiary bodies, and the Conference on Disarmament. These discussions have contributed to the conclusion of a number of international agreements concerning both peaceful and military aspects of the use of outer space. Reflecting the importance of preventing the militarization of outer space, the General Assembly's first special session on disarmament (1978) called for international negotiations on the issue. Since 1982, the Conference on Disarmament has had on its agenda an item entitled "Prevention of an arms race in outer space", but little progress has been made to date in negotiating a multilateral agreement, owing to continuing differences among its members.

Relationship between disarmament and development. The question of promoting economic and social progress, especially for less developed nations, by using the resources released through general disarmament under a system of effective international control has long been debated among member states. Eventually, an international conference on the relationship between disarmament and development was held in 1987. The General Assembly has urged the international community to devote part of the resources made available through disarmament and arms limitation agreements to economic and social development, with a view to reducing the gap between developed and developing countries.

Regional approaches to disarmament. The United Nations supports both regional and subregional initiatives towards disarmament, promoting security and confidence-building measures among states within a region. It also assists them in implementing the guidelines and recommendations for regional approaches to disarmament adopted by the Disarmament Commission in 1993. To foster regional disarmament, the UN works with governmental organizations and arrangements—such as the African Union, the European Union, the Euro-Atlantic Partnership Council, the League of Arab States, the Organization of American States, the Organization of the Islamic Conference, the Organization for Security and Co-operation in Europe, and the Stability Pact for South Eastern Europe—as well as with international, regional and local non-governmental organizations.

Disarmament information and education activities. The United Nations undertakes information and education activities on multilateral disarmament in the framework of its Disarmament Information Programme—through publications, special events, meetings, seminars, panel discussions, exhibits and a comprehensive website on disarmament issues. The United Nations Programme of Fellowship on Disarmament, launched by the General Assembly in 1978, has trained over 600 public officials from about 150 countries—many of whom are now in positions of responsibility in the field of disarmament within their own governments. (For further UN involvement in disarmament information and the dissemination of educational resources, see *www.un.org/disarmament/education* and *http://cyberschoolbus.un.org*.)

Gender perspective in disarmament. The face of warfare has changed in recent years as women and girls have increasingly been affected by conflicts, both as victims and perpetrators. The UN promotes understanding of the importance of gender perspectives in all aspects of disarmament—whether collecting and destroying weapons, demining, conducting fact-finding missions, or participating in decision-making and peace processes. A gender perspective on small arms, for example, would consider how their spread affects women in particular and what might be done about their negative effects.

Peaceful uses of outer space

The United Nations works to ensure that outer space is used for peaceful purposes and that the benefits from space activities are shared by all nations. This concern with the peaceful uses of outer space began soon after the launch of Sputnik—the first artificial satellite—by the Soviet Union in 1957, and has kept pace with advances in space technology. The United Nations has played an important role by developing international space law and by promoting international cooperation in space science and technology.

The main intergovernmental body in this field is the **United Nations Committee on the Peaceful Uses of Outer Space** (*www.unoosa.org*). It reviews the scope of international cooperation in peaceful uses of outer space, devises programmes and directs United Nations technical cooperation, encourages research and dissemination of information, and contributes to the development of international space law. Set up by the General Assembly in 1959, it is made up of 69 member states. A number of international organizations, both intergovernmental and non-governmental, have observer status with the Committee. It has two subcommittees: the **Scientific and Technical Subcommittee** is the focal point of international cooperation in space technology and research, and the **Legal Subcommittee** works to develop a legal framework concomitant with the rapid technological advances of space activities. The Committee and its subcommittees meet annually to consider questions put before them by the General Assembly, reports submitted to them and issues raised by member states. Working on the basis of consensus, the Committee makes recommendations to the General Assembly.

Legal instruments

The work of the Committee and its Legal Subcommittee has resulted in the adoption by the General Assembly of five legal instruments, all of which are in force:

- The 1966 *Treaty on Principles Governing the Activities of States in the Exploration and Use of Outer Space, including the Moon and Other Celestial Bodies (Outer Space Treaty)* provides that space exploration shall be carried out for the benefit of all countries, irrespective of their degree of development. It seeks to maintain outer space as the province of all humankind, free for exploration and use by all states, solely for peaceful purposes, and not subject to national appropriation.
- The 1967 *Agreement on the Rescue of Astronauts, the Return of Astronauts and the Return of Objects Launched into Outer Space (Rescue Agreement)* provides for aiding the crews of spacecraft in case of accident or emergency landing, and establishes procedures for returning to the launching authority a space object found beyond the territory of that authority.
- The 1971 *Convention on International Liability for Damage Caused by Space Objects (Liability Convention)* provides that the launching state is liable for damage caused by its space objects on the earth's surface, to aircraft in flight, and to space objects of another state or persons or property on board such objects.
- The 1974 *Convention on Registration of Objects Launched into Outer Space (Registration Convention)* provides that launching states maintain registries of space objects and provide information to the United Nations on objects launched. Under the *Convention*, the Office for Outer Space Affairs maintains a United Nations Registry on objects launched into outer space. Information has been provided by all launching states and organizations. A searchable on-line index of objects launched into outer space is maintained by that Office on its website (*www.oosa.unvienna.org*).
- The 1979 *Agreement Governing Activities of States on the Moon and Other Celestial Bodies (Moon Agreement)* elaborates the principles relating to the moon and other celestial bodies set out in the 1966 *Treaty*, and sets up the basis to regulate the future exploration and exploitation of natural resources on those bodies.

On the basis of the work of the Committee and its Legal Subcommittee, the General Assembly has adopted sets of principles, including the following, on the conduct of space activities:

- The *Principles Governing the Use by States of Artificial Earth Satellites for International Direct Television Broadcasting* (1982) recognize that such use has international political, economic, social and cultural implications. Such activities should promote the dissemination and exchange of information and knowledge, foster development, and respect the sovereign rights of states, including the principle of non-intervention.
- The *Principles Relating to Remote Sensing of the Earth from Outer Space* (1986) state that such activities are to be conducted for the benefit of all countries, respecting the sovereignty of all states and peoples over their natural re-

sources, and for the rights and interests of other states. Remote sensing is to be used to preserve the environment and to reduce the impact of natural disasters.

- The *Principles Relevant to the Use of Nuclear Power Sources in Outer Space* (1992) recognize that such sources are essential for some space missions, but that their use should be based on a thorough safety assessment. The *Principles* provide guidelines for the safe use of nuclear power sources and for notification of a malfunction of a space object where there is a risk of re-entry of radioactive material to the earth.

- The *Declaration on International Cooperation in the Exploration and Use of Outer Space for the Benefit and in the Interest of All States, Taking into Particular Account the Needs of Developing Countries* (1996) provides that states are free to determine all aspects of their participation in international space cooperation on an equitable and mutually acceptable basis, and that such cooperation should be conducted in ways that are considered most effective and appropriate by the countries concerned.

Office for Outer Space Affairs

The Vienna-based **United Nations Office for Outer Space Affairs** (*www.oosa. unvienna.org*) serves as the secretariat for the Committee on the Peaceful Uses of Outer Space and its subcommittees, and assists developing countries in using space technology for development. The Office disseminates space-related information to member states through its International Space Information System, and maintains the United Nations Register on Objects Launched into Outer Space. Through its United Nations Programme on Space Applications, the Office works to improve the use of space science and technology for the economic and social development of all nations, in particular developing countries. Under this programme, it also provides technical advisory services to member states in conducting pilot projects, and undertakes training and fellowship programmes in such areas as remote sensing, satellite communication, satellite meteorology, satellite navigation, basic space science and space law.

The Office is a cooperating body of the *International Charter 'Space and Major Disasters'*—a mechanism through which UN agencies can request satellite imagery to support their response to disasters. The Office also serves as secretariat to the International Committee on Global Navigation Satellite Systems—an informal body that promotes cooperation on civil satellite-based positioning, navigation, timing and value-added services, as well as on the compatibility and interoperability of global navigation satellite systems, while increasing their use to support sustainable development, particularly in developing countries.

The Office for Outer Space Affairs manages the **United Nations Platform for Space-based Information for Disaster Management and Emergency Response (UN-SPIDER)**. Established by the General Assembly in December 2006, UN-SPIDER aims to provide all countries and relevant international and regional organizations with universal access to all types of space-based information and services supporting the full disaster-management cycle. It helps to increase the number of countries that receive assistance with respect to disaster-management planning, risk reduction and emergency response using space-based information, and devises policies on the use of space-based technologies.

UNISPACE: Using space for development and relief

The United Nations has organized three major conferences on the exploration and peaceful uses of outer space, all held in Vienna. The first conference, held in 1968, examined the practical benefits deriving from space research and exploration, and the extent to which non-space countries, especially developing countries, might enjoy them. The second conference (UNISPACE '82) reflected the growing involvement of all nations in outer space activities. It assessed the state of space science and technology, considered the applications of space technology for development, and discussed international space cooperation. The third conference (UNISPACE III), held in 1999, outlined a wide variety of actions to protect the global environment and manage natural resources; increase use of space applications for human security, development and welfare; protect the space environment; increase developing countries' access to space science and its benefits; and enhance training and education opportunities, especially for young people. UNISPACE III also called for a global system to manage natural disaster mitigation, relief and prevention; the improvement of educational programmes and satellite-related infrastructure to promote literacy; and international coordination of activities related to near earth objects.

In 2004, the General Assembly conducted a five-year review of progress made in implementing the recommendations of UNISPACE III. A plan of action endorsed by the Assembly calls for further action in the use of space to support global agendas for sustainable development.

UNISPACE III recommendations are implemented by various mechanisms. The results of their efforts have included the establishment of the UN Platform for Space-based Information for Disaster Management and Emergency Response (UN-SPIDER) and the International Committee on Global Navigation Satellite Systems.

The Office provides technical assistance to the regional centres for space science and technology education and to the network of space science and technology education affiliated with the United Nations. The centres work with member states to enhance their capability in space science and technology. They also help scientists and researchers develop skills and knowledge in using space science and technology for sustainable development. There are four regional centres: two African regional centres in Morocco and Nigeria; the Asia and the Pacific regional centre in India; and the joint Latin America and Caribbean centre in Mexico and Brazil.

Space technology and its applications are increasingly utilized throughout the UN system. The Office for Outer Space Affairs also serves as secretariat to the **Inter-Agency Meeting on Outer Space Activities**, which has met annually since 1975 to increase space-related cooperation among UN bodies, coordinate activities, build synergies, and consider new initiatives. The Meeting produces the Secretary-General's report on the coordination of space-related activities of the UN system and publishes outreach materials, such as the brochure on "Space Solutions for the World's Problems: How the United Nations family is using space technology for sustainable development" (*www.oosa.unvienna.org/pdf/publications/IAM2006E.pdf*).

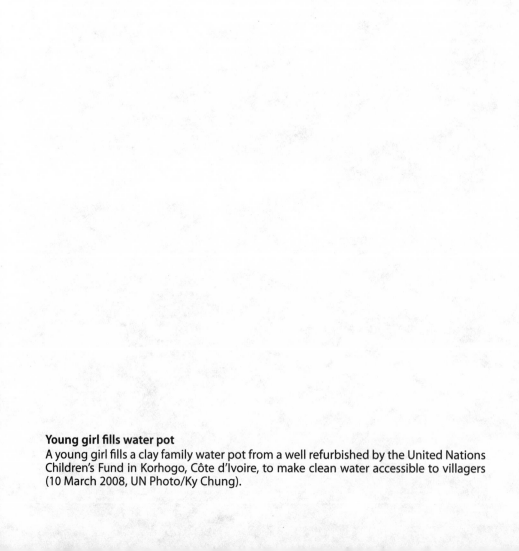

Young girl fills water pot
A young girl fills a clay family water pot from a well refurbished by the United Nations Children's Fund in Korhogo, Côte d'Ivoire, to make clean water accessible to villagers (10 March 2008, UN Photo/Ky Chung).

III. ECONOMIC AND SOCIAL DEVELOPMENT

Although most people associate the United Nations with the issues of peace and security, the vast majority of the Organization's resources are in fact devoted to advancing the *Charter's* pledge to "promote higher standards of living, full employment, and conditions of economic and social progress and development". United Nations development efforts have profoundly affected the lives and well-being of millions of people throughout the world. Guiding the UN endeavours is the conviction that lasting international peace and security are possible only if the economic and social well-being of people everywhere is assured.

Many of the economic and social transformations that have taken place globally since 1945 have been significantly affected in their direction and shape by the work of the United Nations. As the global centre for consensus-building, the UN has set priorities and goals for international cooperation to assist countries in their development efforts and to foster a supportive global economic environment.

Since the 1990s, the UN has provided a platform for formulating and promoting key new developmental objectives on the international agenda through a series of global conferences. It has articulated the need for incorporating issues such as the advancement of women, human rights, sustainable development, environmental protection and good governance into the development paradigm. This global consensus was also expressed through a series of international development decades, the first beginning in 1961. These broad statements of policy and goals, while emphasizing certain issues of particular concern in each decade, consistently stressed the need for progress on all aspects of development, social as well as economic, and the importance of narrowing the disparities between industrialized and developing countries. As the twentieth century drew to a close, the focus shifted to implementing these commitments in an integrated and coordinated manner.

At their **Millennium Summit** in 2000, member states adopted the *Millennium Declaration*, which contained a set of wide-ranging goals for the future course of the UN. The *Declaration* was translated into a roadmap that included eight time-bound and measurable goals to be reached by 2015, known as the **Millennium Development Goals (MDGs)**. The MDGs aim to eradicate extreme poverty and hunger; achieve universal primary education; promote gender equality and the empowerment of women; reduce child mortality; improve maternal health; combat HIV/AIDS, malaria and other diseases; ensure environmental sustainability; and develop a global partnership for development. The international community recommitted itself to those goals during the World Summit in 2005.

In September 2010, the UN Summit on the MDGs (formally known as the High-Level Plenary Meeting on the MDGs) concluded with the adoption of a global action plan to achieve the eight anti-poverty goals by their 2015 target date and the announcement of major new commitments for the health of women and children and other initiatives against poverty, hunger and disease. Secretary-General Ban Ki-moon called on the richer donor countries to continue to provide aid to the poor despite budgetary problems.

Making globalization work for all

In their *Millennium Declaration* of September 2000, world leaders highlighted the central challenge before the international community: ensuring that globalization becomes a positive force for all. For globalization to succeed, however, as the Secretary-General said in his report to the Millennium Summit, entitled *We the Peoples: The Role of the United Nations in the 21st century*, people must feel included. The benefits of globalization—including faster growth, higher living standards, and new opportunities for countries and individuals—are obvious, he added. However, such benefits are unequally distributed.

Global companies should be guided by the concept of global 'corporate citizenship', and apply good practices wherever they operate, promoting equitable labour standards, respect for human rights and protection of the environment.

The Millennium Summit was followed up in 2005 and 2010 by summits that reaffirmed the 2000 *Declaration*.

The UN endeavours to forge coalitions for change by ensuring participation of the many actors involved in globalization—civil society, the private sector, parliamentarians, local authorities, scientific associations and educational institutions. The United Nations strives to ensure that globalization provides benefits for all and that opportunity exists not merely for the privileged, but for every human being.

International debate on economic and social issues has increasingly reflected the commonality of interests between rich and poor countries in solving the many problems that transcend national boundaries. Issues such as refugee populations, organized crime, drug trafficking, AIDS and climate change are seen as global challenges requiring coordinated action. The impact of persistent poverty and unemployment in one region can be quickly felt in others, not least through migration, social disruption and conflict. Similarly, in the age of a global economy, financial instability in one country is immediately felt in the markets of others.

There is also growing consensus on the role played by democracy, human rights, popular participation, good governance and the empowerment of women in fostering economic and social development.

Coordinating development activities

Despite advances on many fronts, gross disparities in wealth and well-being continue to characterize the world's economic and social structure. Reducing poverty and redressing inequalities, both within and between countries, remain fundamental goals of the United Nations.

The UN system works in a variety of ways to promote its economic and social goals: by providing policy analysis and addressing ongoing and emerging global challenges, advising governments on their development plans and strategies, setting international norms and standards, and mobilizing funds for development programmes. Through the work of its various funds and programmes and its family of specialized agencies in areas as diverse as education, air safety, environmental protection and labour conditions, the UN touches the lives of people everywhere.

In 2008, the UN system spent $18.3 billion on operational activities for development, with 62 per cent development-related and 38 per cent with a humanitarian focus. The World Bank, the International Monetary Fund (IMF) and the International Fund for Agricultural Development (IFAD) also provide billions annually in grants and loans that help to eradicate poverty, foster development and stabilize the world economy.

The **Economic and Social Council (ECOSOC)** (*www.un.org/en/ecosoc*) is the principal body coordinating the economic and social work of the United Nations and its operational arms. It is also the central forum for discussing international economic and social issues and for formulating policy recommendations. The Council's responsibilities include: promoting higher standards of living, full employment, and economic and social progress; identifying solutions to economic, social and health problems; facilitating cultural and educational cooperation; and encouraging universal respect for human rights and fundamental freedoms.

Under ECOSOC, the **Committee for Development Policy**, made up of 24 experts working in their personal capacity, acts as an advisory body on emerging economic, social and environmental issues. It also sets the criteria for the designation of least developed countries (LDCs) and reviews the list of countries belonging to that category.

The **United Nations Development Group** (*www.undg.org*) unites the 32 UN funds, programmes, agencies, departments and offices that play a role in the management and coordination of development work within the Organization. This executive body works to enhance cooperation between policy-making entities and the distinct operational programmes.

The **Executive Committee on Economic and Social Affairs** (*www.un.org/esa/ ecesa*), comprised of Secretariat bodies and including the regional commissions, is also an instrument for policy development and management. It aims to bring coherence and common approaches among UN entities engaged in normative, analytical and technical work in the economic and social field.

Within the United Nations Secretariat, the **Department of Economic and Social Affairs (DESA)** (*www.un.org/esa/desa*) helps countries to address their economic, social and environmental challenges. It operates within a framework of internationally agreed goals known as the UN development agenda. Within this framework, DESA provides analytical support, carries out policy analysis and coordination, and provides substantive and technical support to member states in the social, economic and environmental spheres. It provides support to member states in setting norms and standards and in agreeing on common courses of action in response to global challenges. DESA provides a crucial interface between global policies and national action, and among research, policy and operational activities.

The five **regional commissions** facilitate similar exchanges of economic and social information and policy analysis in the regions of Africa (ECA) (*www.uneca. org*), Asia and the Pacific (ESCAP) (*www.unescap.org*), Europe (ECE) (*www.unece.org*), Latin America and the Caribbean (ECLAC) (*www.eclac.org*), and Western Asia (ESCWA) (*www.escwa.org*). Many United Nations funds and programmes deal with operational activities for development in programme countries and several UN specialized agencies provide support and assistance for countries' development efforts. At a time of increasingly limited resources, both human and financial, enhanced coordination and cooperation among the various arms of the UN system are vital if development goals are to be realized.

The United Nations' competitive advantage

The United Nations system has unique strengths in promoting development:

- *universality* ensuring that all countries have a voice when policy decisions are made;
- *impartiality* entailing that it does not represent any particular national or commercial interest, and can thus develop special relations of trust with countries and their people to provide aid with no strings attached;
- *global presence* reflecting the fact that it has the world's largest network of country offices for delivering assistance for development;
- *comprehensive mandate* encompassing development, security, humanitarian assistance, human rights and the environment;
- *commitment* to "the peoples of the United Nations".

Economic development

The world has witnessed enormous economic development in recent decades, but the generation of wealth and prosperity has been very uneven—so uneven that economic imbalances are seen to exacerbate social problems and political instability in virtually every region of the world. The end of the cold war and the accelerating integration of the global economy have not solved persistent problems of extreme poverty, indebtedness, underdevelopment and trade imbalance.

One of the founding principles of the United Nations is the conviction that economic development for all peoples is the surest way to achieve political, economic and social security. It is a central preoccupation of the Organization that half the world's population—mostly in Africa, Asia, and Latin America and the Caribbean—must live on less than $2 per day. In 2009, it was estimated that some 212 million workers were unemployed worldwide, while the 'working poor'—those who earn less than $2 a day—stood at 2.1 billion. The number of undernourished people in developing countries was estimated at approximately one billion in 2009, and decreased slightly to 925 million in 2010.

The UN continues to be the sole institution dedicated to finding ways to ensure that economic expansion and globalization are guided by policies aimed at ensuring human welfare, sustainable development, the eradication of poverty, fair trade and the reduction of immobilizing foreign debt.

The UN urges the adoption of macroeconomic policies that address current imbalances—particularly the growing gap between the North and South—as well as the persistent problems of the LDCs and the unprecedented needs of countries in transition from centralized to market economies. All over the world, UN programmes of assistance promote poverty reduction, child survival, environmental protection, women's progress and human rights. For millions of people in poor countries, these programmes *are* the United Nations.

Official development assistance

Through their policies and loans, the lending institutions of the UN system have, collectively, a strong influence on the economies of developing countries. This is especially true for the LDCs, which include 49 nations whose extreme poverty and indebtedness have marginalized them from global growth and development. These nations, 33 of which are in Africa, are given priority attention in several UN assistance programmes.

Small island developing states, landlocked developing countries and countries with economies in transition also suffer from critical problems requiring special attention from the international community. These, too, are given priority in the assistance programmes of the UN system, as well as through official development assistance (ODA) from member states. Of the world's 33 landlocked developing countries, 16 are LDCs. Of the 38 small island developing states, 12 are LDCs.

In 1970, the General Assembly set an ODA target of 0.7 per cent of gross national product (GNP)—now referred to as gross national income (GNI). (GDP is the market value of all final goods and services made within the borders of a nation annually; GNI is GDP plus net receipts of primary income from other countries.) For years, the collective effort of members of the Development Assistance Committee (DAC) of the Organization for Economic Co-operation and Development (OECD), now comprising 33 industrialized countries, hovered at around half that level.

In the 1990s, ODA fell sharply. However, within the reduced total, more assistance went to basic social services—from 4 per cent of ODA in 1995 to 14 per cent (nearly $4 billion) by 2000. More than four fifths of aid was no longer tied to the procurement of goods and services in the donor country.

ODA levels began to recover during the new century. Among DAC members, total ODA was up to 0.31 per cent of combined GNI in 2009, at $119.6 billion. To date, only five countries—Denmark, Luxembourg, the Netherlands, Norway and Sweden—have met and maintained the 0.7 per cent target for ODA. In 2010, the largest donor nations by volume, on the other hand, were the United States, France, Germany, the United Kingdom and Japan.

The International Conference on Financing for Development, held at Monterrey, Mexico, in 2002, stimulated commitments from major donors to increase ODA as a first step towards reversing its decline in the 1990s. It also sought to shift the focus of such assistance more towards poverty reduction, education and health.

United Nations ODA is derived from two sources: grant assistance from UN specialized agencies, funds and programmes; and support from lending institutions of the UN system, such as the World Bank and IFAD.

The World Bank committed $58.8 billion in fiscal year 2009, a 54 per cent increase compared to 2008 and a record high for the organization. Between 1978 and 2010, IFAD invested $11.5 billion in projects and programmes, reaching some 350 million rural people. Governments and other financing sources in recipient countries contributed $10.1 billion, and multilateral, bilateral and other donors provided approximately another $8.2 billion in co-financing.

In 2009, total contributions to UN operational activities for development, including for humanitarian assistance, were estimated at between $21.5 billion and $22 billion. Some 65 per cent of those contributions were estimated to have been development-related, with 35 per cent having a humanitarian assistance focus. ODA from UN agencies, funds and programmes is widely distributed among the many countries in need.

International Conference on Financing for Development

The International Conference on Financing for Development (*www.un.org/esa/ffd*) was held in 2002 in Monterrey, Mexico. This UN-hosted Conference on key financial and development issues attracted 50 heads of state or government and over 200 ministers, as well as leaders from the private sector, civil society and all the major intergovernmental financial, trade, economic and monetary organizations.

The Conference marked the first quadripartite exchange of views between governments, civil society, the business community and institutional stakeholders on global economic issues. These global discussions involved over 800 participants in 12 separate roundtables co-chaired by heads of governments, the heads of the World Bank, the International Monetary Fund (IMF), the World Trade Organization (WTO) and the regional development banks, as well as ministers of finance, trade and foreign affairs. The Conference outcome, known as the *Monterrey Consensus*, provided a picture of the new global approach to financing development.

Subsequently, the General Assembly decided to hold the follow-up on the Conference during odd-numbered years beginning in 2003. It includes a policy dialogue on implementation of the Conference results, as well as on the coherence and consistency of the international monetary, financial and trading systems in support of development.

The Follow-up International Conference on Financing for Development was held in 2008 in Doha, Qatar and resulted in the *Doha Declaration*. In March 2010, the Assembly held its fourth High-level Dialogue on Financing for Development. In September, the Assembly reaffirmed the *Monterrey Consensus* and the *Doha Declaration*, and called upon developed countries to deliver on their commitments towards achieving the MDGs.

Promoting development worldwide

The **United Nations Development Programme (UNDP)** (*www.undp.org*) is committed to making a pivotal contribution to halving world poverty by 2015. UNDP provides sound policy advice and helps build institutional capacity that generates equitable economic growth.

With a global network of over 160 country offices, UNDP works on the ground to help people help themselves. It focuses on helping countries build and share solutions to challenges such as poverty reduction and the achievement of the MDGs; democratic governance, including the governance of HIV/AIDS responses; crisis prevention and recovery; and environment and sustainable development. In each of these areas, UNDP advocates for the protection of human rights and the empowerment of women.

Most of UNDP's core programme funds go to those countries that are home to the world's extreme poor. Globally, the number of people living below the international poverty line fell from 1.8 billion in 1990 to 1.4 billion in 2005. However, progress was uneven across regions. Estimates of the 2009 increase in the number of people living in poverty due to the economic crisis range from 53 million people (under $1.25 a day) to 64 million people (under $2 a day). Food prices, which continued to be high in most domestic markets in 2009–2010, combined with the effects of the economic crisis, were estimated to have increased the number of hungry people in the world to 1.02 billion in 2010.

In 2009, UNDP spent an estimated $4.1 billion on development activities. Contributions to UNDP are voluntary, and come from nearly every government in the world. Countries that receive UNDP-administered assistance contribute to project costs through personnel, facilities, equipment and supplies.

To ensure maximum impact from global development resources, UNDP coordinates its activities with other UN funds and programmes and international financial institutions, including the World Bank and the IMF. In addition, UNDP's country and regional programmes draw on the expertise of developing country nationals and NGOs. Seventy-five per cent of all UNDP-supported projects are implemented by local organizations.

At the country level, UNDP promotes an integrated approach to the provision of UN development assistance. In several developing countries, it has established a **United Nations Development Assistance Framework (UNDAF)** made up of UN teams under the leadership of the local United Nations resident coordinator, who is in many instances the resident representative of UNDP. The frameworks articulate a coordinated response to the main development challenges identified for the United Nations by governments. Resident coordinators serve as coordinators of humanitarian assistance in cases of human disasters, natural disasters and complex emergency situations.

In addition to its regular programmes, UNDP administers various special-purpose funds. The **UN Capital Development Fund (UNCDF)** offers a combination of investment capital, capacity-building and technical advisory services to promote microfinance and local development in the least developed countries. The **United Nations Volunteers (UNV) programme** (*www.unv.org*) is the UN focal point for promoting and harnessing volunteerism for effective development. More than 7,700 UNVs from over 150 countries were deployed worldwide in 2008. The mandate of the UN Development Fund for Women (UNIFEM), which empowers women and works for gender equality at all levels of development planning and practice, was subsumed in 2010 by the newly created entity, **UN-Women** (*www.unwomen.org*).

UNDP, together with the World Bank and the United Nations Environment Programme (UNEP), is one of the managing partners of the Global Environment Facility. UNDP is also one of the sponsors of the Joint United Nations Programme on HIV/AIDS (UNAIDS).

Lending for development

The **World Bank** (*www.worldbank.org*) comprises two unique institutions—the International Bank for Reconstruction and Development and the International Development Association—and works in more than 100 developing countries, bringing finance and/or technical expertise to help them reduce poverty. Its portfolio of projects covers Latin America and the Caribbean, the Middle East and North Africa, Europe and Central Asia, East Asia and the Pacific, Africa, and South Asia.

The Bank is currently involved in more than 1,800 projects in virtually every sector and developing country. One of the world's largest sources of development assistance, the Bank supports the efforts of developing country governments to build schools and health centres, provide water and electricity, fight disease and protect the environment. It does this through the provision of loans, which are repaid. In 2009, the Bank provided $46.9 billion for 303 projects in developing

Africa: a United Nations priority

The United Nations, reflecting the concern of the international community, has made the critical socio-economic conditions in Africa a priority concern. In affirming its commitment to supporting the region's development, it has devised special programmes to find durable solutions to external debt and debt-service problems; to increase foreign direct investment; to enhance national capacity-building; to deal with the shortage of domestic resources for development; to facilitate the integration of the African countries into international trade; and to tackle HIV/AIDS.

In 1996, the General Assembly launched the United Nations System-wide Special Initiative on Africa, a multi-billion dollar programme of concrete actions, springing from development priorities identified by Africa's leadership. The Initiative was brought to a close in 2002 following a review by the Assembly, which then adopted the New Partnership for Africa's Development (NEPAD) (*www.nepad.org*)—an African-owned and -led initiative launched by the Organization of African Unity (now the African Union) in 2001 as the framework of international efforts for Africa's development. In 2008, the Assembly adopted a political declaration on the occasion of the High-level meeting on Africa's development needs, whereby the participants reaffirmed their support for NEPAD, as well as the implementation of various commitments on Africa's development.

The UN participates at the country, regional and global levels through such efforts as the United Nations Development Assistance Framework, as well as programmes led by the Economic Commission for Africa, which provide a framework for increased coordination and collaboration at the subregional and regional levels. The Office of the Special Adviser on Africa (OSAA) (*www.un.org/africa/osaa*) reports on support provided by the UN system and the international community and coordinates global advocacy in support of NEPAD. OSAA, NEPAD and the OECD work together in close partnership.

The Joint United Nations Programme on HIV/AIDS (UNAIDS) has intensified its campaign against HIV/AIDS in Africa. Seeking as broad a base as possible for its campaign, UNAIDS has brought together governments, regional bodies, development agencies, NGOs and the corporate sector, including pharmaceutical corporations, under an umbrella group known as the International Partnership Against AIDS in Africa.

The Secretary-General and UN agencies have called on industrialized countries to ease Africa's economic hurdles by arranging greater debt relief, lowering tariffs that penalize African exports and increasing official development assistance. UN efforts are also linked with other development undertakings, such as the Tokyo International Conference on African Development, the Heavily Indebted Poor Countries Debt Initiative and the Alliance for African Industrialization.

---

countries worldwide. It also helped Haiti to rebuild in the wake of the devastating earthquake that ravaged the country in January 2010.

There are two types of World Bank lending. The first type is for higher-income developing countries that are able to pay near-market interest rates or can borrow from commercial sources. These countries receive loans from the **International Bank for Reconstruction and Development (IBRD)**, which aims to reduce poverty in middle-income and creditworthy poorer countries by promoting sustainable development through loans, guarantees, risk management products, and analytical and advisory services. IBRD loans allow countries more time to repay than if they borrowed from a commercial bank: 15 to 20 years with a three-to-five-year grace period before the repayment of principal begins. Funds are borrowed for specific programmes in support of poverty reduction, delivery of social services, environmental protection and economic growth. In fiscal year 2009, the IBRD committed a record $32.9 billion for 126 projects in middle-income and creditworthy low-income countries—a 144 per cent increase compared to $13.5 billion in 2008—and was on target to deliver another record $44 billion in fiscal year 2010. The IBRD, with its AAA credit rating, raises nearly all its money through the sale of its bonds in the world's financial markets.

The second type of loan goes to the poorest countries, which are usually not creditworthy in the international financial markets and are unable to pay near-market interest rates on the money they borrow. The **International Development Association (IDA)** is the part of the World Bank that makes loans to the world's poorest countries and aims to reduce poverty by providing grant financing and credits for programmes that boost economic growth, reduce inequalities and improve people's living conditions. The 'credits' are actually interest-free loans with a 10-year grace period and maturities of 35 to 40 years. IDA assistance is largely funded by contributions from 40 rich member countries. In 2009, IDA commitments rose to nearly $15 billion for development activities in the 79 least developed countries. As part of the reconstruction efforts following the January 2010 earthquake in Haiti, some 210,000 children received daily meals through the IDA.

Under its regulations, the Bank can lend only to governments, but it works closely with local communities, NGOs and private enterprise. Its projects are designed to assist the poorest sectors of the population. Successful development requires that governments and communities 'own' their development projects. The Bank encourages governments to work closely with NGOs and civil society to strengthen participation by people affected by Bank-financed projects. NGOs based in borrowing countries collaborate in about half of these projects.

The Bank encourages the private sector by advocating stable economic policies, sound government finances, and open, honest and accountable governance. It supports many areas in which private-sector development is making rapid inroads—finance, power, telecommunications, information technology, oil and gas, and industry. The Bank's regulations prohibit it from lending directly to the private sector, but a Bank affiliate—the International Finance Corporation (IFC)—exists expressly to promote private sector investment by supporting high-risk sectors and countries. Another affiliate, the Multilateral Investment Guarantee Agency (MIGA), provides political risk insurance (guarantees) to those who invest in or lend to developing countries.

The World Bank does much more than lend money. It also routinely includes technical assistance in the projects it finances. This may include advice on such issues as the overall size of a country's budget and where the money should be allocated, or how to set up village health clinics, or what sort of equipment is needed to build a road. The Bank funds a few projects each year devoted exclusively to providing expert advice and training. It also trains people from borrowing countries on how to create and carry out development programmes. Over the past decade, the IDA trained more than 3 million teachers and provided more than 105 million children with new or rehabilitated classrooms.

The IBRD supports sustainable development projects in such areas as reforestation, pollution control and land management; water, sanitation and agriculture;

and conservation of natural resources. It is the main funder of the **Global Environment Facility (GEF)**, which is the largest funder of projects to improve the global environment. The IBRD and the IDA also support the **Heavily Indebted Poor Countries (HIPC) Initiative**, which aims to reduce the external debt of the world's poorest, most heavily indebted countries. In fiscal year 2009, $76 million of development credits and $10 million of charges were written off as debt relief under the partial forgiveness of the IDA debt service as it came due. At their July 2005 summit, the leaders of the 'Group of Eight' developed nations proposed 100 per cent cancellation of debt owed to the IDA, the IMF and the African Development Fund by some of the world's poorest countries, mostly in Africa and Latin America. Debt relief under the resulting **Multilateral Debt Relief Initiative (MDRI)** amounted to $1.1 billion of development credits being written off in fiscal year 2010 as four countries reached their HIPC completion points. As at June 2010, on a cumulative basis, $34.5 billion of development credits had been written off under the MDRI.

Lending for stability

Many countries turn to the **International Monetary Fund (IMF)** (*www.imf.org*), a UN specialized agency, when internal or external factors seriously undermine their balance-of-payments position, fiscal stability or capacity to meet debt service commitments. The IMF offers advice and policy recommendations to overcome these problems, and often makes financial resources available to member countries in support of economic reform programmes.

Members with balance-of-payments problems generally avail themselves of the IMF's financial resources by purchasing reserve assets—in the form of other members' currencies and Special Drawing Rights (SDRs)—with an equivalent amount of their own currencies. The IMF levies charges on these loans and requires that members repay the loans by repurchasing their own currencies from the IMF over a specified time.

In 2010, the IMF upgraded its support for low-income countries (LICs) to reflect the changing nature of economic conditions in those countries and their increased vulnerability due to the effects of the global economic crisis. It would more than double the resources available to LICs to up to $17 billion in 2014. As part of a broader reform to make the Fund's financial support more flexible and better tailored to the needs of LICs, the IMF established the **Poverty Reduction and Growth Trust**, with three new concessional lending windows—extended, standby and rapid credit facilities—that became effective in January 2010.

The main IMF financing facilities are:

- Stand-By Arrangements, designed to provide medium-term balance-of-payments assistance for deficits of a temporary, short-term or cyclical nature and must be repaid within 3¼–5 years after disbursement;
- Flexible Credit Line (FCL), a flexible instrument in the credit tranches designed to address all balance-of-payments needs, potential or actual, and must be repaid within 3¼–5 years after disbursement;
- Precautionary Credit Line (PCL), a dedicated credit line for crisis-prevention designed to meet the needs of countries that have sound economic fundamentals and institutional policy frameworks, yet have some remaining vulnerabilities that preclude them from using the FCL. PCLs must be repaid within 3¼–5 years after disbursement;

- Extended Fund Facility (EFF), designed to provide longer-term assistance for balance-of-payments difficulties of a long-term character or stemming from macroeconomic and structural problems. EFFs must be repaid within 4½–10 years after disbursement;
- Extended Credit Facility, a new concessional facility designed to provide longer-term assistance to LICs with deep-seated balance-of-payments difficulties of a structural nature, with the goal of sustained poverty reduction. Members qualifying for funding may borrow up to 100 per cent of their quota (and up to 300 per cent cumulative) under a three-year arrangement. Financing carries a zero interest rate and repayments are made beginning 5½ years and ending 10 years after disbursement;
- Standby Credit Facility, a new concessional facility providing flexible support to LICs with short-term financing and adjustment needs caused by domestic or external shocks or policy slippages. Financing carries a zero interest rate and repayments are made beginning 4 years and ending 8 years after disbursement;
- Rapid Credit Facility (RCF), a new concessional facility that provides rapid financial support with limited conditionality in a single, up-front payout for LICs facing urgent balance of payment needs arising from such shocks as natural disasters, commodity price changes or crises in neighbouring countries. The RCF offers successive drawings for countries in post-conflict or other fragile situations. Financing carries a zero interest rate, and repayments are made beginning 5½ years and ending 10 years after disbursement;
- Emergency assistance, which provides assistance for balance of payment difficulties related to natural disasters or post-conflict situations, such as the aftermath of civil unrest, political turmoil or international armed conflict. Emergency loans are subject to the basic rate of charge (interest subsidies are available for some countries, subject to resource availability) and must be repaid within 3¼–5 years after disbursement.

To provide debt relief to heavily indebted poor countries following sound policies, the IMF and the World Bank jointly provide, under the Heavily Indebted Poor Countries (HIPC) Initiative, exceptional assistance to eligible countries to reduce their external debt burdens to sustainable levels. They have now also joined in supporting the Multilateral Debt Relief Initiative developed to supplement the HIPC Initiative.

Surveillance is the process by which the IMF appraises its members' exchange rate policies through a comprehensive analysis of the general economic situation and policies of each member. The IMF carries out surveillance through annual consultations with individual countries; multilateral surveillance twice a year; regional surveillance through discussion with regional groupings; and precautionary arrangements, enhanced surveillance, and programme monitoring, which provide a member with close IMF monitoring in the absence of the use of the IMF resources.

The IMF provides technical assistance to its members in several broad areas: the design and implementation of fiscal and monetary policy; institution-building; and the collection and refinement of statistical data. The IMF also provides training to member country officials at its principal training locations: IMF Headquarters in Washington, D.C. and its regional centres in Abu Dhabi (United Arab Emirates), Brasilia, Dalian (China), Pune (India), Singapore, Tunis and Vienna.

Investment and development

As foreign direct investment (FDI) has continued to expand dramatically, developing countries have increasingly opened up their economies to such investment. At the same time, they also are investing more in other developing countries. Various parts of the UN system, such as the Food and Agriculture Organization of the United Nations (FAO), UNDP and the United Nations Industrial Development Organization (UNIDO), monitor and assess developments and assist developing country governments in attracting investment.

Two affiliates of the World Bank—the International Finance Corporation and the Multilateral Investment Guarantee Agency—help promote investment in developing countries. Through its advisory work, the **International Finance Corporation (IFC)** (*www.ifc.org*) helps governments create conditions that stimulate the flow of both domestic and foreign private savings and investment. It also mobilizes private investment in the developing world by demonstrating that investments there can be profitable. The IFC invested a record $18 billion in fiscal year 2010 in 528 projects in 103 countries. As of fiscal year 2010, the IFC had committed more than $75 million of its own funds and had arranged more than $30 billion in syndications for over 4,000 companies in 142 countries since its founding in 1956.

The **Multilateral Investment Guarantee Agency (MIGA)** is an investment insurance affiliate of the Bank. Its goal is to facilitate the flow of private investment for productive purposes to developing member countries, by offering investors long-term political risk insurance—coverage against the risks of expropriation, currency transfer, war and civil disturbance—and by providing advisory services. MIGA carries out promotional programmes, disseminates information on investment opportunities, and provides technical assistance that enhances the investment promotion capabilities of countries. In fiscal year 2010, MIGA issued $1.5 billion in investment guarantees (insurance) for 19 projects in developing countries. Since its inception in 1988, MIGA has issued 980 guarantees amounting to $22.4 billion for projects in more than 100 countries.

The United Nations Conference on Trade and Development (UNCTAD) assists developing countries and economies in transition to promote foreign direct investment and improve their investment climate. It also helps governments understand the policy implications of FDI and to formulate and implement policies accordingly.

UNCTAD promotes understanding of the linkages between investment, trade, enterprise development and technological capacity-building, and conducts research on global FDI trends. These are presented in its annual *World Investment Report, Investment Policy Reviews, World Investment Directory* and other studies.

Trade and development

The **United Nations Conference on Trade and Development (UNCTAD)** (*www.unctad.org*) is tasked with ensuring the integration of all countries in global trade. As the UN focal point for dealing with development-related issues in the areas of trade, finance, technology, investment and sustainable development, UNCTAD works to maximize the trade, investment and development opportunities of developing countries. It helps them face the challenges arising from globalization and integrate into the world economy on an equitable basis. UNCTAD pursues

Foreign direct investment and development

Foreign direct investment (FDI) continues to be a driving force in the world economy, and the expansion of investment flows underscores the central role played by transnational corporations (TNCs) in both industrialized and developing countries. According to UNCTAD's *World Investment Report 2010*:

- FDI inflows fell 37 per cent from 2008 to 2009 to $1.1 trillion, yet had a modest recovery in the first half of 2010. Global inflows were expected to reach $1.2 trillion in 2010, $1.3–1.5 trillion in 2011, and $1.6–2 trillion in 2012.

- Developing and transition economies, which were leading the FDI recovery, took in half of global FDI inflows, invested one quarter of global FDI outflows and remained favourable destinations for FDI in 2010.

- As TNCs are both major carbon emitters and low-carbon investors, they are both the problem and the solution to climate change. Forty per cent of low-carbon emission FDI projects by value were in developing countries during 2003–2009, and there was potential for more 'green' FDI to flow into developing countries.

- Low-carbon FDI was estimated to have reached a significant level, with flows of $90 billion in 2009. Established TNCs were major investors, but new players were emerging, including from the South and TNCs from other industries.

- Developing and transition economies hosted the majority of foreign affiliates' labour force and accounted for 28 per cent of the 82,000 TNCs worldwide in 2008. TNCs foreign employment increased in 2009 to 80 million workers.

- A dichotomy in investment policy trends was emerging and was characterized by moves to further investment liberalization and promotion on one hand, and investment regulation in pursuit of public policy objections on the other.

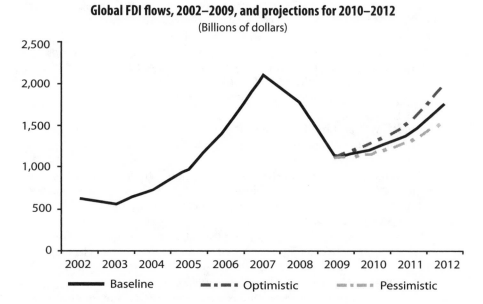

Global FDI flows, 2002–2009, and projections for 2010–2012
(Billions of dollars)

Source: UNCTAD, *World Investment Report, 2010*.

these goals through research and policy analysis, intergovernmental deliberations, technical cooperation and interaction with civil society and the business
sector. In particular, UNCTAD:

- examines trends in the global economy and evaluates their impact on development;
- helps developing countries—particularly the least developed ones—to become part of the international trading system and actively involved in international trade negotiations;
- examines global trends in FDI flows and their impact on trade, technology and
  development;
- helps developing countries attract investment;
- assists developing countries in establishing enterprises and entrepreneurship;
  and
- helps developing countries and countries with economies in transition
  improve the efficiency of their trade-supporting services.

UNCTAD's work helps clarify trends and shape thinking and policies on the trade-
development nexus in the context of globalization. It also enables developing
countries to participate effectively in international trade in goods, services and
commodities. It was one of the main authors of the notion of special and differen-
tial treatment for developing countries, and a key actor in its incorporation into the
General Agreement on Tariffs and Trade and the World Trade Organization. UNCTAD
is also the UN system focal point on trade logistics. By providing institutional, legal
and operational solutions to reduce transaction costs and increase transport con-
nectivity, it improves developing countries' access to world markets.

UNCTAD promotes enterprise development, particularly for small and medium-
sized enterprises, through regular intergovernmental discussions and through
technical cooperation. UNCTAD's technical cooperation activities involve approximately 300 projects in close to 100 countries. These activities include:

- The Automated System for Customs Data (*www.asycuda.org*), using state-of-
  the-art technology, helps governments modernize customs procedures and
  management. Used by 89 countries in 2010, the System is fast becoming the
  internationally accepted standard for customs automation. It is also an instrument for improving economic governance.
- The EMPRETEC Programme (*www.unctadxi.org/templates/Startpage____7428.aspx*)
  promotes small and medium-sized enterprise development. An information
  network provides entrepreneurs with access to business databases.

The **International Trade Centre UNCTAD/WTO (ITC)** (*www.intracen.org*) is the
focal point in the UN system for technical cooperation with developing countries
in trade promotion. It works with developing countries and countries with economies in transition in setting up trade promotion programmes to expand their exports and improve their import operations.

The ITC has been successful in addressing the MDGs as integral components of
its programmes. The MDGs serve as critical benchmarks for the ITC in its efforts to
reduce poverty and enhance the competitiveness of enterprises in poor communities by promoting their integration into the global value chain.

The Centre conducts programmes in six areas: product and market development; development of trade support services; trade information; human resource

Promoting equitable trade for inclusive development

Intergovernmental negotiations, research and technical assistance under UNCTAD auspices have resulted in the following:

- Agreement on a Generalized System of Preferences, adopted by UNCTAD in 1968, whereby developed economies grant improved market access to exports from developing countries;
- Agreement on a Global System of Trade Preferences among developing countries, effective in 1989, which grants tariff and non-tariff preferences among its members;
- International commodity agreements that aim to stabilize the prices of export products crucial to developing countries, including cocoa, coffee, sugar, natural rubber, jute and jute products, tropical timber, tin, olive oil and wheat;
- The Common Fund for Commodities, an intergovernmental financial institution that supports developing countries that are commodity dependent to improve and diversify commodities production and trade;
- The General Assembly's 1980 adoption of the only universally applicable, voluntary code on competition—the UN Set of Multilaterally Agreed Equitable Principles and Rules for the Control of Restrictive Business Practices—also known as the 'UN Set of Principles and Rules on Competition (UN Set)', which is reviewed every five years;
- The 2007 creation of the East African Organic Standard, which became the second regional organic standard in the world following the one developed by the European Union;
- The Trade Analysis and Information System, an international database on trade, tariffs and non-tariff measures available through the World Integrated Trade Solution (WITS) website (*http://wits.worldbank.org/wits*).

---

development; international purchasing and supply management; and assessment of needs and programme design for trade promotion.

Technical cooperation projects in trade promotion are carried out by ITC specialists working in close liaison with local trade officials. National projects often take the form of a broad-based package of services to expand country exports and improve import operations.

Agricultural development

The majority of people on the planet continue to live in rural areas and derive their livelihood, directly or indirectly, mostly from agriculture. In recent decades, rural poverty has spread and deepened and, in the rush to industrialization, insufficient investment has been made in the agricultural sector. The UN has addressed this imbalance in a variety of ways.

The **Food and Agriculture Organization of the United Nations (FAO)** (*www.fao. org*) is the lead agency for agriculture, forestry, fisheries and rural development. It gives practical help to developing countries through a wide range of technical assistance projects. A specific priority is to encourage rural development and sustainable agriculture—a long-term strategy for increasing food production and food security while conserving and managing natural resources.

In promoting sustainable agricultural development, the FAO encourages an integrated approach, with environmental, social and economic considerations included in the formulation of development projects. In some areas, for example, particular combinations of crops can improve agricultural productivity, provide a source of fuel wood for local villagers, improve soil fertility and reduce the impact of erosion.

The FAO has more than 1,000 field projects operating worldwide at any given time, ranging from integrated land management projects and emergency response to policy and planning advice to governments in areas as diverse as forestry and marketing strategies. The FAO usually takes one of three roles: implementing its own programme; executing a programme on behalf of other agencies and donors; or providing advice and management assistance to national projects.

The FAO Investment Centre assists developing and in-transition countries in formulating investment operations in agricultural and rural development, in partnership with international financing institutions (IFIs). Each year, the Centre carries out more than 700 field missions around the world. Since 1964, the Centre and its IFI partners have facilitated more than $89 billion in agriculture and rural development investment. Of that amount, IFIs have financed over $53 billion.

The FAO is active in land and water development; plant and animal production; forestry; fisheries; economic, social and food security policy; investment; nutrition; food standards and food safety; and commodities and trade. For example:

- In 2010, the FAO and the Haitian Ministry of Agriculture distributed agricultural aid to 72,000 farming families in earthquake-hit and rural areas in time for the critical spring planting season, which accounts for 60 per cent of Haiti's agricultural production. This assistance enabled over 360,000 people to produce and consume their own locally produced food, selling the surplus to cover health and education expenses.
- "Njaa Marufuku Kenya", a 10-year programme of the government of Kenya that the FAO helped to formulate, aims to increase food availability and reduce chronic hunger. Its initial focus is on community capacity-building, school feeding programmes, and food-for-work activities in support of natural resource conservation. Grants of $89.3 million were disbursed to 2,593 community groups comprising 77,140 small-scale farmers from June 2005 to December 2010. In addition, 854 community groups facilitators were trained and attached to the benefiting groups to build their technical capacity.
- Since its creation in 1976, the FAO Technical Cooperation Programme (TCP) has funded some 8,800 projects valued at more than $1.1 billion. It also manages the Edouard Saouma Award, which honours national or regional institutions for particularly effective implementation of a TCP-funded project.

The **International Fund for Agricultural Development (IFAD)** (*www.ifad.org*) finances agricultural development programmes and projects that enable rural people to overcome poverty. The IFAD provides loans and grants for programmes and projects that promote the economic advancement and food security of poor rural people. IFAD-supported initiatives enable these people to access the land, water, financial resources and agricultural technologies and services they need to farm productively, and to access markets and opportunities for enterprise that could help them increase their incomes. It also works to build the knowledge, skills and organizations of poor rural people.

IFAD-supported programmes and projects benefit the poorest of the world's people: small farmers, landless labourers, nomadic pastoralists, artisanal fishing communities, indigenous peoples and, across all groups, poor rural women. Most of IFAD's resources are made available to poor countries on highly concessional terms, repayable over 40 years, including a grace period of 10 years, and a 0.75 per cent service charge per annum. The Fund is particularly committed to achieving the Millennium Development Goal of halving the proportion of hungry and extremely poor people by 2015.

Since starting operations in 1978, the IFAD has invested $11.5 billion in 838 projects and programmes, reaching some 350 million poor rural people in over 100 countries and territories. Governments and other financing sources in recipient countries, including project participants, contributed $10.1 billion, while multilateral, bilateral and other donors provided an additional $8.2 billion in co-financing. This represents a total investment of some $29.8 billion, and means that for every dollar IFAD invested, the Fund was able to mobilize nearly two dollars in additional resources. In December 2010, the IFAD released its *Rural Poverty Report, 2011*, which provides a comprehensive look at rural poverty, its global consequences and the prospects for its eradication.

Industrial development

The globalization of industry has created unprecedented industrial challenges and opportunities for developing countries and countries with economies in transition. The **United Nations Industrial Development Organization (UNIDO)** (*www.unido.org*) is the specialized agency helping these countries pursue sustainable industrial development in the new global environment. UNIDO has assumed an enhanced role in the global development agenda by focusing its activities on poverty reduction, inclusive globalization and environmental sustainability. Its services are based on two core functions: as a global forum, it generates and disseminates industry-related knowledge; and as a technical cooperation agency, it provides technical support and implements projects. UNIDO's technical cooperation programmes focus on the following three thematic priorities, which directly respond to global development priorities:

- Poverty reduction through productive activities—by providing a range of services, from industrial policy advice to entrepreneurship and small and medium enterprise development, and from technology diffusion to sustainable production and the provision of rural energy for productive uses;

- Trade capacity-building—by providing trade-related development services and advice and integrated technical assistance in the areas of competitiveness, trade policies, industrial modernization and upgrading, and compliance with trade standards, testing methods and metrology; and

- Environment and energy—by promoting sustainable patterns of industrial consumption and production and assisting clients in implementing multilateral environmental agreements, while simultaneously reaching their economic and environmental goals.

UNIDO assists governments, business associations and the private industrial sector with services which translate its core functions and thematic priorities into action. UNIDO's 13 investment and technology promotion offices, financed by the countries in which they are located, promote business contacts between industrialized countries and developing countries and countries with economies in transition.

Labour

Concerned with both the economic and social aspects of development, the **International Labour Organization (ILO)** (*www.ilo.org*) is one of the few specialized agencies that predates the UN, as it was established in 1919. It is responsible for drawing up and overseeing international labour standards and is the only tripartite UN agency that brings together representatives of governments, employers and workers to shape policies and programmes promoting decent work for all. The main goals of ILO are to promote rights at work, encourage decent employment opportunities, enhance social protection and strengthen dialogue on work-related issues. The ILO has provided a framework of labour standards and guidelines which have been adopted in national legislation by virtually all countries.

The ILO is guided by the principle that social stability and integration can be sustained only if they are based on social justice—particularly the right to employment with fair compensation in a healthy workplace. Over the decades, the ILO has helped create such hallmarks as the eight-hour work day, maternity protection, child-labour laws, and a wide range of policies that promote safety in the workplace and peaceful industrial relations. Specifically, the ILO engages in:

- the formulation of international policies and programmes to promote basic human rights, improve working and living conditions and enhance employment opportunities;
- the creation of international labour standards to serve as guidelines for national authorities in putting sound labour policies into practice;
- an extensive programme of technical cooperation, formulated and carried out in partnership with beneficiaries, to help countries make these policies effective; and
- training, education, research and information activities to help advance all these efforts.

The central purpose of the ILO is to promote opportunities for decent work for all people. The organization has four strategic objectives that converge on that primary goal:

- to promote and realize standards and fundamental principles and rights at work;
- to create greater opportunities for women and men to secure decent employment and income;
- to enhance the coverage and effectiveness of social protection for all; and
- to strengthen dialogue among governments, labour and business.

To implement those objectives, the ILO focuses on areas such as the progressive abolition of child labour; safety and health at work; socio-economic security; promoting small and medium-sized enterprises; developing skills, knowledge and employability; eliminating discrimination and gender inequality; and promoting the *ILO Declaration on Fundamental Principles and Rights at Work,* adopted by the International Labour Conference in 1998.

The ILO's technical cooperation focuses on support for democratization, poverty alleviation through employment creation, and the protection of workers. It helps countries develop their legislation and take practical steps towards putting the ILO standards into effect—for instance, by developing occupational health and safety departments, social security systems and worker education programmes. Projects are carried out through close cooperation between recipient countries, donors and the ILO, which maintains a network of area and regional offices worldwide. The ILO conducts more than 1,000 technical cooperation programmes in over 80 countries. In the last decade, the ILO spent an average of $130 million annually on technical cooperation projects.

The ILO **International Training Centre** (*www.itcilo.org/en*), located in Turin, Italy, carries out training for senior and mid-level managers in private and public enterprises, leaders of workers' and employers' organizations, government officials and policy makers. It runs more than 450 programmes and projects each year for some 11,000 people from over 180 countries.

The ILO **International Institute for Labour Studies** (*www.ilo.org/public/english/bureau/inst*), located in Geneva, promotes policy research and public discussion of emerging issues of concern to the ILO. The organizing theme is the relationship between labour institutions, economic growth and social equity. The Institute acts as a global forum on social policy, maintains international research networks and carries out educational programmes.

International civil aviation

In 2009, an estimated 2.3 billion passengers flew on some 25 million flights, and 38 million tonnes of freight were shipped by air. The **International Civil Aviation Organization (ICAO)** (*www.icao.int*) is a UN specialized agency that serves as the global forum for cooperation among its member States and with the world aviation community. The ICAO's ongoing mission is to foster a global civil aviation system that consistently and uniformly operates at peak efficiency and provides optimum safety, security and sustainability. ICAO activities are guided by its strategic objectives for 2011–2013, which focus on three main areas, namely safety, security, and environmental protection and sustainable development of air transport. To meet those objectives, the ICAO:

- adopts international standards and recommendations applied to the design and performance of aircraft and much of their equipment; the performance of airline pilots, flight crews, air traffic controllers and ground and maintenance crews; and the security requirements and procedures at international airports;
- formulates visual and instrument flight rules, as well as the aeronautical charts used for international navigation, and is responsible for aircraft telecommunications systems, radio frequencies and security procedures;
- works towards minimizing the impact of aviation on the environment through reductions in aircraft emissions and through noise limits; and
- facilitates the movement of aircraft, passengers, crews, baggage, cargo and mail across borders by standardizing customs, immigration, public health and other formalities.

As acts of unlawful interference continue to pose a serious threat to the safety and security of international civil aviation, such as the terrorist attacks of 11 September 2001 in the United States, the ICAO continues to pursue policies and programmes designed to prevent them. The ICAO developed an aviation security plan of action, including a universal audit programme to evaluate the implementation of security standards and recommend remedial action where necessary in response to those attacks.

During its thirty-seventh Assembly, held in the fall of 2010, the ICAO produced new agreements and declarations on air transport's challenges and priorities. The meeting participants endorsed the ICAO's approach for addressing runway safety and adopted an historic resolution on reducing the impact of aviation emissions on climate change that will guide the activities of its 190 member States on that issue through 2050.

The ICAO meets requests from developing countries for assistance in improving air transport systems and training for aviation personnel. It has helped to establish regional training centres in several developing countries. The criteria for ICAO assistance are based on what countries need to make civil aviation safe and efficient, in accordance with the ICAO's Standards and Recommended Practices.

The ICAO works in close cooperation with other UN specialized agencies such as the IMO, the ITU and the WMO. The International Air Transport Association, the Airports Council International, the International Federation of Air Line Pilots' Associations and other organizations also participate in many ICAO meetings.

International shipping

When the **International Maritime Organization (IMO)** (*www.imo.org*) held its first Assembly in 1959, it had less than 40 member states. Today it has 169 members (168 UN member states plus the Cook Islands) and three associate members. Over 98 per cent of the world's merchant fleets (by tonnage) adhere to the key international shipping conventions developed by the IMO.

The adoption of maritime legislation is the IMO's best known responsibility. The IMO has adopted around 40 conventions and protocols—mostly related to changes in world shipping—and some 1,000 codes and recommendations concerning maritime safety, the prevention of pollution and related matters. Maritime security has been added to the IMO's objectives of improving the safety of international shipping and preventing marine pollution from ships. Key environmental concerns being addressed include the transfer of harmful aquatic organisms in ballast water and sediments, the emission of greenhouse gases from ships, and ship recycling.

Initially, the IMO focused on developing international treaties and other legislation concerning ship safety and marine pollution prevention. Today, the main focus is on implementation of international standards, while continuing to amend and update existing legislation and to fill in any gaps in the regulatory framework. During 2010, key issues on the IMO agenda included responding to the scourge of modern-day piracy, particularly in the waters off Somalia and in the Gulf of Aden; addressing the reduction of greenhouse gas emissions from ships; and keeping the safety of life at sea, and the human element, especially the seafarer, at the heart of its work.

The main IMO treaties on maritime safety and prevention of marine pollution by ships that are in force worldwide include: the *International Convention on Load Lines*, 1966; the *International Regulations for Preventing Collisions at Sea*, 1972; the

International Convention for Safe Containers, 1972; the *International Convention for the Prevention of Pollution from Ships, 1973 as modified by the Protocol of 1978 relating thereto*; the *International Convention for the Safety of Life at Sea* (SOLAS), 1974; the *International Convention on Standards of Training, Certification and Watchkeeping for Seafarers* (STCW), 1978; and the *International Convention on Maritime Search and Rescue*, 1979.

Numerous codes, some of which have been made mandatory, address specific issues, such as carriage of dangerous goods and high-speed craft. The International Safety Management Code, made mandatory by means of SOLAS amendments adopted in 1994, addresses the people who operate and run ships. Special attention has been paid to crew standards, including the complete revision in 1995 of the 1978 STCW, which for the first time gave the IMO the task of monitoring compliance with the *Convention*.

Safety of life at sea remains one of the key objectives of the IMO. In 1999, the Global Maritime Distress and Safety System became fully operational, guaranteeing assistance to a ship in distress virtually anywhere in the world; even if its crew does not have time to radio for help, the message is transmitted automatically.

Various IMO conventions address liability and compensation issues. The most significant include the 1992 *Protocol of the International Convention on Civil Liability for Oil Pollution Damage* (1969) and the 1992 *Protocol of the International Convention on the Establishment of an International Fund for Compensation for Oil Pollution Damage* (IOPC Fund, 1971), which together provide compensation to victims of oil pollution damage. The *Athens Convention relating to the Carriage of Passengers and their Luggage by Sea* (1974) sets compensation limits for passengers on ships.

In 2002, the IMO adopted an International Ship and Port Facility Security Code that requires compliance with new measures aimed at protecting shipping against terrorist attacks. Adopted under amendments to SOLAS, the Code became mandatory in 2004. The next year, the IMO adopted amendments to the *Convention for the Suppression of Unlawful Acts Against the Safety of Maritime Navigation*, 1988 and its related *Protocol* introducing the right of a state party to board a ship flying the flag of another state party when the requesting party has reasonable grounds to suspect that the ship or a person on board the ship is, has been, or is about to be involved in the commission of an offence under the *Convention*.

The IMO's technical cooperation programme aims to support the implementation of its international standards and regulations, particularly in developing countries, and to assist governments in operating a shipping industry successfully. The emphasis is on training, and the IMO has under its auspices the World Maritime University in Malmö, Sweden, the International Maritime Law Institute in Malta, and the International Maritime Academy in Trieste, Italy.

Telecommunications

Telecommunications have become a key to the global delivery of services. Banking, tourism, transportation and the information industry all depend on quick and reliable global telecommunications. The sector is being revolutionized by powerful trends such as globalization, deregulation, restructuring, value-added network services, intelligent networks and regional arrangements. Such developments have transformed telecommunications from its earlier status as a public utility to one having strong links with commerce and trade. It was projected that the global telecommunications market would grow to some $3 trillion in 2010.

The **International Telecommunication Union (ITU)** (*www.itu.int*) is the world's oldest intergovernmental organization, dating back to 1865. The ITU's mission is to enable the growth and sustained development of telecommunications and information networks, and to facilitate universal access so that people everywhere can participate in, and benefit from, the information society and global economy. A key priority lies in bridging the digital divide—the gap between people with effective access to digital and information technology and those with very limited or no access. The ITU also concentrates on strengthening emergency communications for disaster prevention and mitigation. In order to achieve its goals, the ITU coordinates the public and private sectors to provide global telecommunications networks and services. Specifically, the ITU:

- develops standards which foster the interconnection of national communications infrastructures into global networks, allowing the seamless exchange of information—be it data, faxes or phone calls—around the world;

- works to integrate new technologies into the global telecommunications network, allowing for the development of new applications, such as the Internet, electronic mail, multimedia and electronic commerce;

- adopts international regulations and treaties governing the sharing of the radio frequency spectrum and satellite orbital positions—finite natural resources which are used by a wide range of equipment, including television and radio broadcasting, mobile telephones, satellite-based communications systems, aircraft and maritime navigation and safety systems, and wireless computer systems;

- strives to expand and improve telecommunications in the developing world by providing policy advice, technical assistance, project management and training, and by fostering partnerships between telecommunications administrations, funding agencies and private organizations.

As the UN specialized agency for information and communication technology (ICT), the ITU had the leading managerial role for the **World Summit on the Information Society (WSIS)** held in Geneva in 2003 and in Tunis in 2005. The Summit adopted a *Declaration of Principles* and *Plan of Action* aimed at building a people-centred, inclusive and development-oriented information society, where everyone can create, access, use and share information and knowledge.

Taking the lead in implementing the Summit goals, the ITU organized the Connect Africa Summit in Kigali, Rwanda in 2007, bringing together governments, the private sector and funding agencies to invest in the ICT infrastructure in Africa. Participants committed $55 billion towards the target of connecting all African cities by 2012. The ITU also maintains the WSIS Stocktaking Database, a publicly accessible system providing information on ICT-related initiatives and projects with reference to the 11 WSIS action lines. The WSIS Stocktaking Platform is a unique portal that highlights ICT-related projects and initiatives in line with WSIS implementation.

Membership in the ITU gives governments and private organizations a unique opportunity to contribute to the developments rapidly reshaping the world. ITU membership represents a cross-section of the telecommunications and information technology industry—from the world's largest manufacturers and carriers to small, innovative players working in fields like Internet Protocol (IP) networking.

In addition to its 192 member states (191 UN member states and the Holy See), the ITU has over 700 sector members and associates, representing scientific and industrial companies, public and private operators and broadcasters, and regional and international organizations. Founded on the principle of international co-operation between government and the private sector, the ITU is a global forum through which government and industry can work towards consensus on a wide range of issues affecting the future of this increasingly important industry.

International postal service

More than 5 million postal employees worldwide process and deliver 435 billion letter-posts every year, as well as 6 billion parcels, international and domestic, and offer a range of electronic and financial services. There are also more than 665,000 points of access for postal services worldwide. The **Universal Postal Union (UPU)** (*www.upu.int*) is the UN specialized agency regulating the international postal service.

The UPU forms a single postal territory of countries for the reciprocal exchange of letter-post items. Every member state agrees to transmit the mail of all other members by the best means used for its own mail. As the primary vehicle of coop-eration between national postal services, the UPU works to improve international postal services, provide postal customers in every country with harmonized and simplified procedures for their international mail, and make available a universal network of up-to-date products and services.

The UPU sets indicative rates, maximum and minimum weight and size lim-its, and the conditions of acceptance of letter-post items, including priority and non-priority items, letters, aerogrammes, postcards, printed matter and small packets. It prescribes the methods for calculating and collecting transit charges (for letter-post items passing through one or more countries) and terminal dues (for imbalance of mails). It also establishes regulations for registered and air mail, and for items requiring special precautions, such as infectious and radioactive substances.

Thanks to the UPU, new products and services are integrated into the interna-tional postal network. In this way, such services as registered letters, postal money orders, international reply coupons, small packets, postal parcels and expedited mail services have been made available to most of the world's inhabitants.

The agency has taken a leadership role in certain activities, such as the appli-cation of electronic data interchange technology by the postal administrations of member countries and the monitoring of the quality of postal services worldwide.

The UPU provides technical assistance through multi-year projects aimed at optimizing national postal services. It also conducts short-term projects which may include study cycles, training fellowships, and the expertise of development consultants who carry out on-the-spot studies on training, management or postal operations. The UPU has also made international financial institutions increasingly aware of the need for investment in the postal sector.

Around the world, postal services are making a determined effort to revitalize the postal business. As part of a communications market that is experiencing explosive growth, they have to adapt to a rapidly changing environment, becoming more independent, self-financing enterprises and providing a wider range of services. The UPU takes the lead in promoting this revitalization.

Intellectual property

Intellectual property in various forms—books, feature films, artistic performance media and computer software—has become a central issue in international trade relations. Millions of patent, trademark and industrial design registrations are currently in force worldwide. In today's knowledge-based economy, intellectual property is a tool for promoting wealth creation as well as economic, social and cultural development.

A specialized UN agency, the **World Intellectual Property Organization (WIPO)** (*www.wipo.int*), is responsible for promoting the protection of intellectual property (IP) all over the world through cooperation among states, and for administering various international treaties dealing with the legal and administrative aspects of intellectual property. IP comprises two main branches: industrial property, which primarily means inventions, trademarks, industrial designs and appellations of origin; and copyright, covering chiefly literary, musical, artistic, photographic and audiovisual works.

WIPO administers 24 treaties covering all aspects of intellectual property, some dating back to the 1880s. The two pillars of the international IP system are the *Paris Convention for the Protection of Industrial Property* (1883) and the *Berne Convention for the Protection of Literary and Artistic Works* (1886). WIPO member states concluded the *Singapore Treaty on the Law of Trademarks* (2006). WIPO's policy of adopting recommendations on such themes as the protection of well-known marks (1999), trademark licenses (2000) and marks on the Internet (2001) complements the treaty-based approach to international legal standard-setting.

Its **Arbitration and Media Centre** helps individuals and companies from around the world resolve their disputes, particularly those relating to technology, entertainment and other issues involving intellectual property. It is also the leading dispute resolution service for challenges relating to abuses in the registration and use of Internet domain names—known as 'cybersquatting'. It provides this service both for the generic top-level domains, such as .com, .net, .org, and .info, and for certain country-code domains. WIPO's dispute resolution mechanism is much faster and cheaper than litigation in the courts; a domain name case is normally concluded within two months using online procedures.

WIPO helps countries strengthen their intellectual property infrastructure, institutions and human resources while promoting the development of international IP law. It provides a forum for formulating policies, and hosts international discussions on IP with respect to traditional knowledge, folklore, biodiversity and biotechnology.

In addition, WIPO offers expert advice to developing countries to strengthen their capacity for the strategic use of intellectual property to promote economic, social and cultural development. It provides legal and technical advice and expertise in drafting and revising national legislation. Training programmes are organized for policy makers, officials and students. The organization's focal point for training is the WIPO Worldwide Academy (*www.wipo.int/academy/en*).

WIPO also provides services to industry and the private sector to facilitate the process of obtaining IP rights in multiple countries in a simple, efficient and cost-effective manner. These include services offered under the *Patent Cooperation Treaty*, the *Madrid System for the International Registration of Trademarks*, the *Hague System for the International Registration of Industrial Designs*, the *Lisbon Agreement for the International Registration of Geographical Indications* and the *Budapest Treaty for the International Deposit of Micro-organisms*. The revenues from these services generate some 95 per cent of WIPO's income.

Global statistics

Governments, public institutions and the private sector rely heavily on relevant, accurate, comparable and timely statistics at national and global levels, and the United Nations has served as a global focal point for statistics since its founding.

The United Nations **Statistical Commission**, an intergovernmental body composed of 24 member states, is the highest decision-making body for international statistical activities. It oversees the work of the **UN Statistics Division** (*http://unstats.un.org/unsd*), which compiles and disseminates global statistical information, develops standards and norms for statistical activities, and supports countries' efforts to strengthen their national statistical systems. The Division also facilitates the coordination of international statistical activities and supports the functioning of the Commission.

The Statistics Division offers a broad range of services for producers and users of statistics, including the following: the UN-data portal (*http://data.un.org*), the *Statistical Yearbook*, the *Monthly Bulletin of Statistics*, the *World Statistics Pocketbook*, the official *Millennium Development Goals Indicators* database, the *Demographic Yearbook* and *UN Comtrade*. Its specialized publications cover such matters as demographic, social and housing statistics, national accounts, economic and social classifications, energy, international trade, the environment and geospatial information.

The Division also aims to strengthen national capabilities in developing countries by providing technical advisory services, training programmes and workshops organized throughout the world on various topics.

Public administration

A country's public sector is arguably the most important component in the successful implementation of its national development programmes. The new opportunities created by globalization, the information revolution and democratization have dramatically affected the state and how it functions. Managing the public sector in an environment of unremitting change has become a demanding challenge for national decision-makers, policy developers and public administrators.

The UN, through its **Programme on Public Administration and Finance** (*www.unpan.org/dpadm*), assists governments in their efforts to strengthen and improve their governance systems and administrative institutions and to address emerging issues of a globalized world. Managed by DESA's Division for Public Administration and Development Management, the Programme helps governments ensure that they function in an effective, responsive, pro-poor and democratic manner. Assistance is provided to governments in three focus areas: institutional and human resource capacity development; e-government and mobile-government development; and development management through citizen engagement. The

Programme carries out analytical research; advisory services and technical assistance; training and tools such as the UNPAN Training Centre; and advocacy, including such stakeholder dialogue and knowledge sharing platforms as the UN Public Service Day Awards and Forum and the UN Public Administration Network (UNPAN) (*www.unpan.org*).

Science and technology for development

The United Nations has been promoting the application of science and technology for the development of its member states since the 1960s. The 43-member **Commission on Science and Technology for Development** (*www.unctad.org/cstd*) was established in 1992 to examine science and technology questions and their implications for development; promote the understanding of science and technology policies in respect of developing countries; and formulate recommendations on science and technology matters within the UN system.

The Commission also serves as a focal point for the Economic and Social Council, its parent body, in the system-wide follow-up to the World Summit on the Information Society (WSIS). At its 2010 session, the Commission undertook a five-year review of the progress made in the implementation of WSIS. It also considered two priority themes, "Improvements and innovations in existing financial mechanisms" and "New and emerging technologies". Substantive and secretariat support for the Commission is provided by UNCTAD.

UNCTAD also promotes policies favouring technological capacity-building, innovation and technology flows to developing countries. It helps these countries review their science and technology policies, promotes South-South scientific networking, and provides technical assistance on information technologies.

The FAO, IAEA, ILO, UNDP, UNIDO and WMO all address scientific and technological issues within their specific mandates. Science for development is also an important element in the work of UNESCO.

Social development

Inextricably linked to economic development, social development has been a cornerstone of UN work from its inception. Over the decades, the United Nations has emphasized the social aspects of development to ensure that the aim of better lives for all people remains at the centre of development efforts.

In its early years, the United Nations arranged for groundbreaking research and data collection in the areas of demographics, education and health, compiling—often for the first time—reliable data on global social indicators. In addition, the UN undertook efforts to protect cultural heritage, from architectural monuments to languages, reflecting concern for those societies particularly vulnerable to the rapid processes of change.

The Organization has been in the forefront of supporting government efforts to extend social services relating to health, education, family planning, housing and sanitation to all people. In addition to developing models for social programmes, the UN has helped integrate economic and social aspects of development. Its evolving policies and programmes have always stressed that the components of development—social, economic, environmental and cultural—are interconnected and cannot be pursued in isolation.

Major world conferences since 2000

- Millennium Summit, 2000 (New York)
- World Education Forum, 2000 (Dakar)
- Third United Nations Conference on the Least Developed Countries, 2001 (Brussels)
- World Conference against Racism, 2001 (Durban) and 2009 (Geneva)
- World Food Summit: five years after, 2002 (Rome)
- International Conference on Financing for Development, 2002 (Monterrey) and 2008 (Doha, Qatar)
- Second World Assembly on Ageing, 2002 (Madrid)
- World Summit on Sustainable Development, 2002 (Johannesburg)
- International Ministerial Conference of Landlocked and Transit Developing Countries and Donor Countries and Representatives of International Financial and Development Institutions on Transit Transport Cooperation, 2003 (Almaty, Kazakhstan)
- World Conference on Disaster Reduction, 2005 (Kobe, Japan)
- World Summit on the Information Society, 2003 (Geneva) and 2005 (Tunis)
- World Summit, 2005 (New York)
- World Conference on Dialogue, 2008 (Madrid)
- Conference on World Food Security: the Challenges of Climate Change and Bioenergy, 2008 (Rome)
- World Conference on Education for Sustainable Development: Moving into the Second Half of the UN Decade, 2009 (Bonn, Germany)
- Summit on Millennium Development Goals and 10-Year Review, 2010 (New York)

Special sessions of the General Assembly have reviewed progress made five years after the United Nations Conferences on Women (2000), Social Development (2000), Human Settlements (2001), Children (2002), the *Millennium Declaration* (2005 and 2010), and Small Arms (2006). Another special session addressing the problems of HIV/AIDS (2001) was reviewed in 2006.

Globalization and liberalization are posing new challenges to social development. There is a growing desire to see a more equitable sharing of the benefits of globalization. The UN takes a people-centred approach in the social area, placing individuals, families and communities at the centre of development strategies. It places great emphasis on social development and addressing such social issues as health, education and population, or the situation of vulnerable groups such as women, children and older persons.

The UN strives to strengthen international cooperation for social development, particularly in the areas of poverty eradication, full and productive employment, and the social inclusion of older persons, youth, families, persons with disabilities, indigenous peoples and others marginalized from society and development. Many UN global conferences have focused on these issues, including the 1995 World Summit for Social Development, which marked the first time the international community came together to advance the struggle against poverty, unemployment and social disintegration. The resulting *Copenhagen Declaration for Social Development* and its 10 commitments represent a social contract at the global level.

The diverse issues of social development represent a challenge for developing and developed countries alike. To differing degrees, all societies are confronted by the problems of unemployment, social fragmentation and persistent poverty. A growing number of social problems—from forced migration to drug abuse, organized crime and the spread of diseases—can be successfully tackled only through concerted international action.

The United Nations addresses the issues of social development through the General Assembly and the Economic and Social Council (ECOSOC), where system-wide policies and priorities are set and programmes endorsed. One of the Assembly's six main committees, the **Social, Humanitarian and Cultural Committee**, takes up agenda items relating to the social sector. Under ECOSOC, the main intergovernmental body dealing with social development concerns is the **Commission for Social Development** (*www.un.org/esa/socdev/csd*). Composed of 46 member states, the Commission advises ECOSOC and governments on social policies and on the social aspects of development. The priority theme for the Commission's 2011 session was "Poverty Eradication".

Within the Secretariat, the **Division for Social Policy and Development** (*www.un.org/esa/socdev*) of the Department of Economic and Social Affairs services these intergovernmental bodies, providing research, analysis and expert guidance. Throughout the UN system, there are also many specialized agencies, funds, programmes and offices that address different aspects of social development.

Progress in attaining the Millennium Development Goals

At the UN Millennium Summit held in September 2000 in New York, 189 world leaders endorsed the *Millennium Declaration*, a commitment to a new global partnership to reduce extreme poverty and build a safer, more prosperous and equitable world. The *Declaration* was translated into a roadmap setting out eight time-bound goals to be reached by 2015, known as the **Millennium Development Goals (MDGs)** (*www.un.org/millenniumgoals*). The 2010 Summit on the MDGs concluded with the adoption of a global action plan, entitled "Keeping the promise: united to achieve the Millennium Development Goals", to achieve the eight anti-poverty goals by their 2015 target date. New commitments for women's and children's health and other initiatives against poverty, hunger and disease were also announced.

Extreme poverty and hunger. In 1990, more than 1.8 billion people lived in extreme poverty on less than $1.25 a day. By 2005, the proportion had decreased to 1.4 billion, according to *The Millennium Development Goals Report, 2010*, yet progress was uneven. While robust growth in the first half of the decade reduced the number of very poor people in developing regions from 46 per cent to 27 per cent, the global economic and financial crisis, which began in the advanced economies of North America and Western Europe in 2008, sparked abrupt declines in exports and commodity prices and reduced trade and investment, slowing growth in developing countries. Despite those setbacks, the overall poverty rate was expected to fall to 15 per cent by 2015, indicating that the MDG target to halve the world's number of poor between 2000 and 2015 could indeed be met. It was estimated that by 2015, around 920 million people—half the number in 2000—would live under the poverty line, but that the effects of the crisis were likely to linger on well after 2015. The sharpest reductions in poverty continued to be recorded

World Summit for Social Development

The landmark 1995 World Summit for Social Development was part of a series of global conferences convened by the United Nations to raise awareness of major issues through cooperation by member states and the participation of other development actors. Some 117 heads of state or government, supported by ministers representing another 69 countries, adopted the *Copenhagen Declaration on Social Development* and *Programme of Action.*

Governments pledged to confront the profound social problems of the world by addressing three core issues common to all countries: eradication of poverty, promotion of full employment, and promotion of social integration, particularly of disadvantaged groups. The Summit signaled the emergence of a collective determination to treat social development as one of the highest priorities of national and international policies, and to place the human person at the centre of development.

Five years later, a special session of the General Assembly (Geneva, 2000) reaffirmed the centrality of these principles and agreed on new initiatives to advance them, including a coordinated international strategy on employment, and the development of innovative sources of public and private funding for social development and poverty eradication. For the first time, a global target was set for halving the proportion of people living in extreme poverty by 2015—a theme later picked up by the Millennium Development Goals.

---

in Eastern Asia. Developing regions such as sub-Saharan Africa, Western Asia and parts of Eastern Europe and Central Asia remained a concern.

Since 1990, developing regions have made some progress towards the MDG target to halve the proportion of people suffering from hunger. The share of undernourished populations decreased from 20 per cent in 1990–1992 to 16 per cent in 2005–2007. Progress stalled in the latter part of the decade, as food prices spiked in 2008. The number of undernourished people exceeded 1 billion in 2009, yet fell back to 925 million in 2010.

Universal primary education. By 2008, primary school enrolment had increased to 89 per cent in the developing world, up from 82 per cent in 1999, and gains had been accomplished in many regions. Although enrolment in sub-Saharan Africa remained the lowest of all regions, it still increased from 58 per cent to 76 per cent between 1999 and 2008. Progress was also reported in Southern Asia and Northern Africa, where enrolment increased by 11 and 8 percentage points, respectively, over the last decade.

Gender equality and empowering women. The gender gap in the out-of-school population narrowed, with the share of girls in that group decreasing from 57 per cent to 53 per cent globally between 1999 and 2008. However, the share was much larger in some regions, such as Northern Africa, where 66 per cent of out-of-school children are girls.

HIV/AIDS, malaria and other diseases. The spread of HIV has stabilized in most regions and more people are surviving longer. Globally, the spread of HIV peaked in 1996, when 3.5 million people were newly infected. By 2008, that number had dropped to an estimated 2.7 million. While AIDS-related mortality reached 2.2 million deaths in 2004, it had dropped to 2 million by 2008. The epidemic has stabilized in most regions, although prevalence continues to rise in Eastern Europe,

Central Asia and other parts of Asia, due to high rates of new infections. Sub-Saharan Africa remains the most heavily affected region with 72 per cent of all new HIV infections in 2008. Although the number of new infections has peaked, the number of people living with the virus continues to rise, mainly because of the life-sustaining impact of antiretroviral therapy. In 2008, an estimated 33.4 million people lived with HIV, of whom 22.4 million were in sub-Saharan Africa.

Understanding how to prevent transmission of HIV is a key to avoiding infection. This is extremely important for adolescents and young people, aged 15 to 24, who accounted for 40 per cent of new HIV infections worldwide in 2008. In sub-Saharan Africa and other regions, knowledge of HIV increases with wealth and living in urban areas. Similarly, condom use increases dramatically with wealth and among those living in urban areas.

Major progress has been achieved in the fight against malaria and other major diseases, which remains high on the UN agenda. Major increases in funding and a stronger commitment to control malaria have accelerated delivery of malaria interventions. Across Africa, more communities are benefiting from bed net protection, and more children are being treated with effective drugs. Global production of mosquito nets has increased fivefold since 2004, saving many lives. Tuberculosis remains the second leading killer after HIV. In 2008, some 1.8 million people died from the disease, half of whom were living with HIV. Many of these deaths resulted from the lack of antiretroviral therapy resulting from poverty. The global burden of tuberculosis is falling slowly. Incidence fell to 139 cases per 100,000 people in 2008, after peaking in 2004 at 143 cases per 100,000.

Environmental sustainability. Deforestation is continuing at an alarming rate (some 13 million hectares of land per year over the last decade, compared to 16 million hectares per year in the 1990s). However, the net loss of forest area is slowing down. Tree-planting programmes in several countries, combined with the natural expansion of forests in some regions, have added more than 7 million hectares of new forest annually. As a result, the net loss of forest area over 2000–2010 was reduced to 5.2 million hectares per year, down from 8.3 million hectares per year in 1990–2000.

Energy use has become more efficient in most regions, but CO_2 emissions continue to rise globally, reaching 30 billion metric tonnes in 2007. The *Montreal Protocol*, which provides for internationally coordinated control of ozone-depleting substances (ODSs) in order to protect public health and the environment from the adverse effects of the depletion of stratospheric ozone, is the first treaty of any kind to achieve universal ratification. Consequently, all states are now legally bound to phase out ODSs, and 2010 marked the start of a world virtually free of the most widely used ODSs.

Although 1.6 billion more people gained access to safe drinking water between 1990 and 2010, some 2.5 billion people—nearly half of developing-country populations—still lacked adequate sanitation at the turn of the decade. In 2010, for the first time in history, the majority of the world's people were living in urban areas, resulting in larger slum populations (an estimated 1 billion people) and challenges such as extreme health threats, child mortality, gender inequity and overall illiteracy. Slum improvements, though considerable, are failing to keep pace with the growing ranks of the urban. The share of the urban population living in slums in the developing world declined from 39 per cent in 2000 to 33 per cent in

Millennium Development Goals and targets for poverty, disease, the environment and development

Goal 1: Eradicate extreme poverty and hunger

Reduce by half, between 1990 and 2015, the proportion of people with income less than $1 a day and the proportion of people who suffer from hunger; achieve full and productive employment and decent work for all, including women and young people.

Goal 2: Achieve universal primary education

Ensure that by 2015, children everywhere—boys and girls alike—will be able to complete a full course of primary schooling.

Goal 3: Promote gender equality and empower women

Eliminate gender disparity in primary and secondary education, preferably by 2005, and in all levels of education no later than 2015.

Goal 4: Reduce child mortality

Reduce by two thirds, between 1990 and 2015, the under-five mortality rate.

Goal 5: Improve maternal health

Reduce by three quarters, between 1990 and 2015, the maternal mortality ratio; achieve universal access to reproductive health by 2015.

Goal 6: Combat HIV/AIDS, malaria and other diseases

Halt and reverse the spread of HIV/AIDS by 2015; achieve universal access to treatment for HIV/AIDS for all those who need it by 2010; halt and reverse the incidence of malaria and other major diseases by 2015.

Goal 7: Ensure environmental sustainability

Integrate sustainable development principles into country policies and programmes and reverse the loss of environmental resources; reduce biodiversity loss, achieving a significant reduction in the rate of loss by 2010; reduce by half, by 2015, the proportion of the population without sustainable access to safe drinking water and basic sanitation; achieve, by 2020, a significant improvement in the lives of at least 100 million slum dwellers.

Goal 8: Develop a global partnership for development

Develop further an open, rule-based, predictable, non-discriminatory trading and financial system; address the special needs of LDCs, landlocked countries and small island developing states; deal with developing countries' debt problems; in cooperation with pharmaceutical companies, provide access to affordable essential drugs in developing countries; in cooperation with the private sector, make available the benefits of new technologies, especially in information and communications.

2010. However, the number of slum dwellers in the developing world is growing. The number of urban residents living in slum conditions in 2010 was estimated at some 828 million, compared to 657 million in 1990 and 767 million in 2000.

Global partnership for development. Over the last decade, developing countries and LDCs have gained greater access to the markets of developed countries. The proportion of imports (except arms and oil) by developed countries from all developing countries admitted free of duty reached almost 80 per cent in 2008—up from 54 per cent in 1998. LDCs continue to benefit from larger tariff reductions, especially for their agricultural products. In addition, debt burdens have eased for developing countries, and remain well below historical levels.

In 2009, net disbursements of official development assistance amounted to $119.6 billion, a slight increase from 2008 in real terms. Although aid continues to rise, Africa is short-changed. Only five donor countries have reached the UN target of 0.7 per cent of gross national income. It was estimated that Africa will receive only about $11 billion of the $25 billion increase envisaged in 2005, mainly due to the underperformance of European donors. Moreover, the economic slowdown has put pressure on government budgets in the developed countries.

Mobile telephony continues to expand in the developing world and is increasingly being used for mobile banking, disaster management and other non-voice applications for development. By the end of 2009, cellular subscriptions per 100 people had reached the 50 per cent mark.

The international financial institutions of the UN system play a central role in funding numerous programmes that focus on the social aspects of poverty eradication and support for the MDGs. For example, in September 2010, the World Bank pledged to focus on 35 countries that were facing challenges in achieving their MDGs because of high fertility, poor child and maternal nutrition, and disease.

At the 2010 UN Summit on the MDGs (*www/un.org/en/mdg/summit2010*), the **Global Strategy for Women's and Children's Health** was launched. With pledges of more than $40 billion over a five-year period, the Strategy has the potential of saving the lives of more than 16 million women and children; preventing 33 million unwanted pregnancies; protecting 120 million children from pneumonia and 88 million children from stunting; advancing the control of deadly diseases such as malaria and HIV/AIDS; and ensuring access for women and children to quality facilities and skilled health workers.

Reducing poverty

The UN system put poverty reduction at the top of the international agenda when it proclaimed 1997–2006 as the International Decade for the Eradication of Poverty. In December 2007, the General Assembly proclaimed 2008–2017 as the **Second UN Decade for the Eradication of Poverty**, reiterating that eradicating poverty was the greatest global challenge facing the world and a core requirement for sustainable development, especially for developing countries. The theme for the UN system-wide plan of action for the Second Decade is "Full Employment and Decent Work for All".

At the 2010 UN Summit on the MDGs, world leaders renewed their commitment to implement the goals by 2015, including to reduce by half the number of people living on less than $1 a day, and to reach the targets set in the fight against poverty and disease. A key player in this effort is the **United Nations Development Programme (UNDP)**, which has made poverty alleviation its chief priority. UNDP works to strengthen the capacity of governments and civil society organizations to address the whole range of factors that contribute to poverty. These include increasing food security; generating employment opportunities; increasing people's access to land, credit, technology, training and markets; improving the availability of shelter and basic services; and enabling people to participate in the political processes that shape their lives. The heart of UNDP's anti-poverty work lies in empowering the poor.

Fighting hunger

Food production has increased at an unprecedented rate since the United Nations was founded in 1945, and during the period 1990–1997, the number of hungry people worldwide fell dramatically, from 959 million to 791 million. However, today that number has risen again, and approximately 1 billion people do not have enough to eat. This is despite the fact that there is enough food in the world today for every man, woman and child to lead a healthy and productive life.

Most of the UN bodies fighting hunger have important social programmes to advance food security for the poorer sectors of the population, particularly in rural areas. Since its establishment, the **Food and Agriculture Organization of the United Nations (FAO)** (*www.fao.org*) has been working to alleviate poverty and hunger by promoting agricultural development, improved nutrition and the pursuit of food security—physical and economic access by all people at all times to sufficient, safe and nutritious food to meet their dietary needs and food preferences for an active and healthy life.

In 2009, the number of hungry people worldwide increased to 1 billion, partly due to soaring food prices and the financial crisis. The FAO launched a campaign to reflect the moral outrage of the situation. The "1 billion hungry project" reaches out to people through online social media to invite them to sign the anti-hunger petition (*www.1billionhungry.org*).

The FAO's Committee on World Food Security is responsible for monitoring, evaluating and consulting on the international food security situation. It analyses the underlying causes of hunger and food shortages, assesses availability and stock levels, and monitors policies aimed at food security. The FAO, through its Global Information and Early Warning System, uses meteorological and other satellites to monitor conditions affecting food production and alert governments and donors to any potential threat to food supplies.

The FAO's Special Programme for Food Security is its flagship initiative for reaching the MDG target to reduce by half the proportion of hungry people in the world by 2015. Through projects in over 100 countries, it promotes effective solutions for the elimination of hunger, undernourishment and poverty. It seeks to achieve food security in two ways: by assisting governments to run focused national food security programmes, and by working with regional economic organizations to optimize regional conditions for attaining food security in such areas as trade policy.

At the 1996 World Food Summit, hosted by the FAO, 186 countries approved a *Declaration and Plan of Action on World Food Security*, which aims to halve hunger by 2015 and outlines ways to achieve universal food security. Participants at the 2002 World Food Summit renewed their commitment to reduce the number of hungry by half—to about 400 million—by 2015. The Summit asked the FAO to elaborate guidelines in support of the progressive realization of the right to adequate food in the context of national food security. Those voluntary guidelines, also known as the "Right to Food Guidelines", were adopted by the FAO Council in 2004.

In 2009, the World Summit on Food Security adopted a declaration committing all nations to eradicate hunger at the earliest possible date. It pledged to substantially increase aid for agriculture in developing countries, confirmed the target of 2015 for reducing hunger by half, and agreed to face up to the challenges that climate change poses to food security.

The **International Fund for Agricultural Development (IFAD)** (*www.ifad.org*) provides development funding to combat rural poverty and hunger in the poorest regions of the world. The majority of the world's poorest people—those living on less than $1 a day—live in rural areas of developing countries and depend on agriculture and related activities for their livelihoods. To ensure that development aid reaches those who need it most, IFAD involves poor rural men and women in their own development, working with them and their organizations to develop opportunities that enable them to thrive economically in their own communities.

IFAD-supported initiatives enable the rural poor to access the land, water, financial resources and agricultural technologies and services needed to farm productively. These initiatives also allow them to access markets and enterprise opportunities. In addition, IFAD helps them advance their knowledge, skills and organization so they can take the lead in their own development and influence the decisions and policies that affect their lives.

Since starting operations in 1978, IFAD has invested $11.5 billion in 838 projects and programmes, reaching some 350 million poor rural people in over 100 countries and territories, with its partners contributing $18.3 billion in co-financing.

The **World Food Programme (WFP)** (*www.wfp.org*) is the UN front-line agency in the fight against global hunger. In 2010, the WFP food assistance reached more than 100 million people in over 70 countries. With around half of its received donations in cash, the agency is able to purchase three quarters of the food in developing countries. With the aim of reinforcing local economies, the WFP buys more goods and services from developing countries than any other UN agency or programme. The WFP also provides passenger air transport to the entire humanitarian community through the **UN Humanitarian Air Service**, which flies to more than 200 locations worldwide.

Serving the world's hungry since 1962, the WFP's efforts to combat hunger focus on emergency assistance, relief and rehabilitation, development aid and special operations. In emergencies, the WFP is often first on the scene, delivering food aid to the victims of war, civil conflict, drought, floods, earthquakes, hurricanes, crop failures and natural disasters. When the emergency subsides, the WFP uses food aid to help communities rebuild shattered lives and livelihoods. In 2010, some 60 per cent of the WFP expenditures were for protracted crises. This demonstrates the WFP's continuing commitment to helping break the cycle of hunger in these countries, with humanitarian assistance not only saving lives, but also serving as critical investment for longer-term food security and development.

Food and food-related assistance are among the most effective weapons in the struggle to break the perpetual cycle of hunger and poverty that entraps so many in the developing world. WFP development projects focus on nutrition, especially for mothers and children, through programmes such as school feeding. In 2008, 22.6 million girls and boys were fed under the school feeding programme on all continents. Some 2.7 million girls and 1.6 million boys were also given added take-home rations as an incentive for their families to send them to the classroom and not work in the fields. The WFP also builds in-country capacity and infrastructure to help governments and their people in a number of areas, including disaster mitigation.

Breaking the hunger cycle requires that humanitarian responses include long-lasting measures that address the root causes of crises. To meet these challenges, the WFP has developed programmes that focus on selected vulnerable sectors of society. These include food and nutrition programmes such as school feeding; livelihood support programmes such as food-for-training and food-for-work; programmes to address the generational hunger cycle such as mother-and-child nutrition; and nutritional support to HIV/AIDS victims.

The WFP relies entirely on voluntary contributions to finance its humanitarian and development projects. Governments are its principal source of funding, but the WFP's corporate partners are making an increasingly vital contribution to its mission. As of December 2010, the WFP had received $3.6 billion from 78 funding sources, including 71 government donors. Funding levels from 44 donor governments were above their recent averages, demonstrating continued support and increased commitment to the WFP operations. The WFP also works with some 2,840 NGOs, whose grass-roots and technical knowledge are invaluable in assessing how to deliver its food aid to the right people.

Health

In most parts of the world, people are living longer, infant mortality is decreasing and illnesses are being kept in check as more people have access to basic health services, immunization, clean water and sanitation. The United Nations has been deeply involved in many of these advances, particularly in developing countries, by supporting health services, delivering essential drugs, making cities healthier, providing health assistance in emergencies and fighting infectious diseases. The *Millennium Declaration* includes measurable targets to be achieved by countries in nutrition, access to safe water, maternal and child health, infectious disease control, and access to essential medicines by 2015.

Illness, disability and death caused by infectious diseases have a massive social and economic impact. New diseases, including avian influenza and SARS (severe acute respiratory syndrome), add to the urgency of the need to control epidemics. The causes and the solutions for most infectious diseases are known, however, and illness and death can in most cases be avoided at an affordable cost. The major infectious diseases are HIV/AIDS, malaria and tuberculosis. Stopping and reversing their transmission is a key Millennium Development Goal.

For decades, the UN system has been in the forefront of the fight against disease through the creation of policies and systems that address the social dimensions of health problems. The **United Nations Children's Fund (UNICEF)** focuses on child and maternal health, and the **United Nations Population Fund (UNFPA)** focuses on reproductive health and family planning. The specialized agency coordinating global action against disease is the **World Health Organization (WHO)** (*www. who.int*). The WHO has set ambitious goals for achieving health for all, making reproductive health available, building partnerships and promoting healthy lifestyles and environments.

The WHO was the driving force behind various historic achievements, including the global eradication of smallpox in 1979, achieved after a 10-year campaign. Together with its partners, the WHO eliminated poliomyelitis from the Americas in 1994, and remains engaged in the effort to eliminate this disease entirely. Another UN entity, the FAO, was the driving force behind the eradication of rinderpest in October 2010. The disease, which has remained undetected in the field since 2001, will be the first animal disease ever to be eliminated. The elimination of rinderpest

On the verge of a polio-free world

When the Global Polio Eradication Initiative (*www.polioeradication.org*) was launched in 1988, there were 350,000 cases of the disease worldwide, paralysing more than 1,000 children in more than 125 countries on five continents every day. After a concerted campaign, including National Immunization Days to immunize millions of children under five, that figure dropped to 1,951, then to 1,606 and finally to 767 cases reported in 2005, 2009, and 2010, respectively. Only four countries remained endemic for the disease: Afghanistan, India, Nigeria and Pakistan.

More than 5 million people in the developing world who would otherwise have been paralysed are walking today because they have been immunized against polio. Tens of thousands of public health workers and millions of volunteers have been trained. Transport and communications systems for immunization have been strengthened. Since the launch of the Initiative some 22 years ago, more than 2.5 billion children worldwide have been immunized.

This success has been possible through an unprecedented partnership for health spearheaded by the WHO, UNICEF, the United States Centers for Disease Control and Prevention, and Rotary International. As the largest private sector donors, Rotary and the Bill and Melinda Gates Foundation have contributed hundreds of millions of dollars to the effort. Health ministries, donor governments, foundations, corporations, celebrities, philanthropists, health workers and volunteers have also been engaged. The public health savings resulting from polio eradication, once immunization stops, are estimated to be $1.5 billion a year.

---

is only the second time that a disease has been eradicated worldwide, after smallpox in humans.

The adoption of a ground-breaking public health treaty to control tobacco supply and consumption was another major achievement. The *WHO Framework Convention on Tobacco Control* covers tobacco taxation, smoking prevention and treatment, illicit trade, advertising, sponsorship and promotion, and product regulation. It was adopted unanimously by the WHO's member states in 2003 and became binding international law in 2005. The *Convention* is a key part of the global strategy to reduce the worldwide epidemic of tobacco use, which kills nearly 5 million people every year. The WHO also takes a leading role in action to combat obesity, a worldwide health concern affecting an increasing number of people every year. In 2008, there were 500 million obese people. The WHO projects that by 2015, approximately 2.3 billion adults will be overweight and more than 700 million will be obese.

Between 1980 and 1995, a joint UNICEF-WHO effort raised global immunization coverage against six killer diseases—polio, tetanus, measles, whooping cough, diphtheria and tuberculosis—from 5 to 80 per cent, saving the lives of some 2.5 million children a year. A similar initiative is the Global Alliance for Vaccines and Immunization (GAVI) (*www.gavialliance.org*). By the end of 2009, GAVI had helped prevent 5.4 million future deaths through routine immunization against hepatitis B, *Haemophilus influenzae* type b (Hib) and pertussis (whooping cough), and through one-off investments in immunization against measles, polio and yellow fever. Launched in 1999 with initial funds from the Bill and Melinda Gates Foundation, the Alliance incorporates the WHO, UNICEF, the World Bank and private sector partners.

UN stands against HIV/AIDS

The number of people dying from AIDS-related illnesses has fallen by 19 per cent since 2004, due to the life-prolonging effects of antiretroviral therapy and also to HIV prevention campaigns and measures, according to the *UNAIDS Report on the Global AIDS Epidemic, 2010.*

While an estimated 33.3 million people worldwide were infected with the HIV virus, the epidemic had slowed down and even reversed. Encouragingly, the Joint United Nations Programme on HIV/AIDS (UNAIDS) (*www.unaids.org*) reported that nearly 60 countries had either stabilized or achieved significant declines in rates of new HIV infections. In 2009, some 1.2 million people received HIV antiretroviral therapy for the first time—which was also a 30 per cent increase in the number of people receiving treatment in a single year. Among young people in 15 of the most severely affected countries, rates of HIV had fallen by more than 25 per cent, as the young adopted safer sexual practices.

Yet while more than 5 million people needing life-saving AIDS drugs in poorer countries received them, another 10 million people still had no access to them. Marginalized groups like drug users and sex workers were far less likely to get help than others. Stigma, discrimination and bad laws continued to place roadblocks for people living with HIV and people on the margins. Meanwhile, one in four AIDS deaths was caused by tuberculosis, a preventable and curable disease. In sub-Saharan Africa, the region worst hit by HIV and AIDS, there were 1.3 million AIDS-related deaths in 2009, and 1.8 million people became newly infected with HIV.

UNAIDS—the leading advocate for a worldwide response to AIDS—is a combined effort of 10 UN agencies: the ILO, UNDP, UNESCO, UNFPA, UNHCR, UNICEF, UNODC, the WHO, the WFP and the World Bank. Its priorities include: leadership and advocacy; developing information; evaluating the effectiveness of policy commitments and national responses; mobilizing resources; and promoting global, regional and national partnerships among people living with HIV, civil society and high-risk groups. It has negotiated with pharmaceutical companies to reduce drug prices in developing countries, and works closely with those countries to help them achieve universal access to HIV prevention, care and treatment.

UNAIDS played a key role in the General Assembly's 2001 special session on HIV/AIDS, which produced the *Declaration of Commitment on HIV/AIDS.* It manages the World AIDS Campaign (*worldaidscampaign.info*) and initiated the Global Coalition on Women and AIDS (*womanandaids.unaids.org*).

In their 2000 *Millennium Declaration,* world leaders resolved to halt and reverse the spread of HIV/AIDS by 2015, and to provide assistance to children orphaned by the disease. Since the beginning of the epidemic in the early 1980s, more than 60 million people have been infected with HIV and nearly 30 million have died of HIV-related causes.

The incidence of guinea-worm disease has been dramatically reduced, owing to new and better methods of treatment, and leprosy is also being overcome, with the help of free supplies of multi-drug therapies. River blindness has been virtually eliminated from the 11 West African countries once affected—an achievement benefiting millions. The WHO is now targeting elephantiasis for elimination as a public health problem.

The WHO's priorities in the area of communicable diseases are: to reduce the impact of malaria and tuberculosis through global partnership; to strengthen surveillance, monitoring and response to communicable diseases; to reduce the

Malaria and tuberculosis

The Roll Back Malaria (RBM) Initiative (*www.rollbackmalaria.org*), sponsored by the WHO, was launched in 1998 with the declared objective of halving the global burden of malaria by 2010. Its founding partners—UNDP, UNICEF, the World Bank and the WHO—are working to bring about a world in which malaria is no longer a major cause of mortality or a barrier to social and economic development. The RBM Partnership has expanded exponentially to include malaria-endemic countries, bilateral and multilateral development partners, the private sector, non-governmental and community-based organizations, foundations, and research and academic institutions.

Almost two million people die every year from tuberculosis (TB), a disease that is treatable. The Global "Stop TB" Partnership (*www.stoptb.org*), a WHO initiative, comprises more than 1,200 partners, including international organizations, countries, public and private-sector donors and non-governmental and governmental organizations. It gave rise, in 2001, to the Global Plan to Stop TB, a five-year plan based on a health strategy known as DOTS ('Directly Observed Treatment, Short-course').

In the 15 years from 1995 to 2009, some 49 million TB patients were treated according to the DOTS strategy—41 million successfully. The TB incidence rate (per 100,000 population) peaked in 2004, and has since fallen each year. By 2009, the global mortality rate had fallen by 35 per cent compared to the 1990 baseline. Building on the achievements of the last 15 years, the DOTS component of the Global Plan to Stop TB, 2011–2015, sets out how TB control can be further improved, reaching more people with TB and achieving higher rates of treatment success.

The Global Plan to Stop TB aims to halve TB prevalence and deaths by 2015, as compared with 1990 levels. The Global Fund to Fight AIDS, Tuberculosis and Malaria (*www.theglobalfund.org*) is a major contributor to all these efforts.

impact of diseases through intensified and routine prevention and control; and to generate new knowledge, intervention methods, implementation strategies and research capabilities for use in developing countries. The WHO is also a key player in promoting primary health care, delivering essential drugs, making cities healthier, promoting healthy lifestyles and environments, and in tackling health emergencies such as outbreaks of Ebola haemorrhagic fever.

The WHO-UNICEF Global Immunization Vision and Strategy, 2006–2015, aims to reduce global measles deaths by 90 per cent and 95 per cent, respectively, by the end of 2010 and 2015. Since 1999, some 686 million children have been vaccinated under the programme, and the lives of 4.3 million children have been saved. The WHO has been fighting malaria for decades. By the end of 2010, the Organization aimed to provide more than 700 million insecticide-treated bednets—half of those in Africa; more than 200 million doses of effective treatment; indoor spraying for around 200 million homes annually; and approximately 1.5 billion diagnostic tests annually.

A motor for health research. Working with its partners in health research, the WHO gathers data on current conditions and needs, particularly in developing countries. These range from epidemiological research in remote tropical forests to monitoring the progress of genetic research. The WHO's tropical disease research programme has focused on the resistance of the malaria parasite to the most commonly used drugs, and on fostering the development of new drugs and diagnostics against tropical infectious diseases. Its research also helps to improve national and international surveillance of epidemics, and to develop preventive strategies for new and emerging diseases.

Standard-setting. The WHO establishes international standards on biological and pharmaceutical substances. It has developed the concept of 'essential drugs' as a basic element of primary health care.

The WHO works with countries to ensure the equitable supply of safe and effective drugs at the lowest possible cost and with the most effective use. To this end, it has developed a 'model list' of several hundred drugs and vaccines considered essential to help prevent or treat over 80 per cent of all health problems. Some 160 countries have adapted the list to their own requirements, and the list is updated every two years. The WHO also cooperates with member states, civil society and the pharmaceutical industry to develop new essential drugs for priority health problems in poor and middle-income countries, and to continue production of established essential drugs.

Through the international access afforded to the United Nations, the WHO oversees the global collection of information on communicable diseases, compiles comparable health and disease statistics, and sets international standards for safe food, as well as for biological and pharmaceutical products. It also provides unmatched evaluation of the cancer-producing risks of pollutants, and has put into place the universally accepted guidance for global control of HIV/AIDS.

Human settlements

In 1950, New York City was the only metropolitan area with a population of over 10 million, and only 30 per cent of the global population was urban. By 2010, there were 25 'megacities'—all but six in developing or in-transition countries—and more than half of the world's 6.9 billion people lived in towns and cities. Nearly 1 billion people lived in slums; indeed, in developing countries, more than one third of the urban population lived in slums.

The **United Nations Human Settlements Programme (UN-HABITAT)** (*www. unhabitat.org*) is the lead agency within the United Nations system for addressing this situation. It is mandated by the General Assembly to promote socially and environmentally sustainable towns and cities, with the goal of providing adequate shelter for all. To that end, it implements dozens of technical programmes and projects in a wide range of countries, most of them in the least developed world. In 1996 the Second United Nations Conference on Human Settlements, known as Habitat II, adopted the *Habitat Agenda*, a global plan of action in which governments committed themselves to the goals of adequate shelter for all and sustainable urban development. UN-HABITAT is the focal point for implementing the Agenda, assessing its implementation, and monitoring global trends and conditions.

UN-HABITAT runs two major worldwide campaigns—the Global Campaign on Urban Governance and the Global Campaign for Secure Tenure:

- *Global Campaign on Urban Governance.* In many cities, poor governance and inappropriate policies have led to environmental degradation, increased poverty, low economic growth and social exclusion. This campaign aims to increase local capacity for good urban governance—the efficient, effective response to urban problems by democratically elected and accountable local governments, working in partnership with civil society.

- *Global Campaign for Secure Tenure.* This campaign identifies the provision of secure tenure as vital for a sustainable shelter strategy and the promotion of housing rights. It spearheads a shelter strategy that promotes the rights and interests of the poor, particularly the rights of women and their role in success-ful shelter policy.

Through various means, UN-HABITAT focuses on a range of issues and spe-cial projects which it helps implement. Together with the World Bank, it began a slum upgrading initiative called the Cities Alliance (*www.citiesalliance.org*). Other initiatives over the years have addressed post-conflict land management and re-construction in countries devastated by war or natural disasters, and ensure that women's rights and gender issues are brought into urban development and man-agement policies. The agency also helps strengthen rural-urban linkages, as well as infrastructure development and public service delivery.

UN-HABITAT programmes include:

- Best Practices and Local Leadership Programme—a global network of gov-ernment agencies, local authorities and civil society organizations dedi-cated to identifying and disseminating best practices to improve the living environment and apply lessons learned to policy development and capacity-building;
- Housing Rights Programme—a joint UN-HABITAT/Office of the United Nations High Commissioner for Human Rights initiative to assist states and other stake-holders to implement their commitments in the Habitat Agenda to ensure the full and progressive realization of the right to adequate housing, as provided for in international instruments;
- Global Urban Observatory—monitors global progress in implementing the Habitat Agenda, and monitors and evaluates urban conditions and trends. The programme aims to improve the worldwide urban knowledge base by sup-porting governments, local authorities and civil society in the development and application of policy-oriented urban indicators, statistics and other urban information;
- Sustainable Cities Programme—a joint UN-HABITAT/UNEP initiative that builds capacities in urban environmental planning and management. With its sister programme, Localizing Agenda 21, it currently operates in over 30 cities world-wide;
- Localizing Agenda 21 Programme—promotes the global plan of action for sustainable development adopted at the 1992 'Earth Summit' (*Agenda 21*) by translating its human settlements components into action at the local level and stimulating joint initiatives in selected medium-sized cities;
- Safer Cities Programme—launched in 1996 at the request of African mayors, it promotes the development of strategies at the city level to adequately address and ultimately prevent urban crime and violence;
- Urban Management Programme—a joint effort by UN-HABITAT, UNDP and ex-ternal support agencies. This network of over 40 anchor and partner institu-tions, covering 140 cities in 58 countries, works to strengthen the contribution made by cities and towns in developing countries towards economic growth, social development and poverty alleviation;

- Water and Sanitation Programme—aims to improve access to safe water, help provide adequate sanitation to millions of low-income urban dwellers and measure the impact of those efforts. It supports the Millennium Development Goal target to halve, by 2015, the proportion of people without sustainable access to safe drinking water and basic sanitation, as well as the related target of the 2002 World Summit on Sustainable Development.

Education

Great strides have been made in education in recent years, marked by a significant increase in the number of children in schools. Nevertheless, in 2010, some 67.4 million children had no access to primary education, and many who started attending school were forced to leave because of poverty, family and social pressures or tradition. In some countries, civil strife, acts of terrorism and insurgency also prevented school attendance. Despite enormous efforts to increase literacy, 796 million adults lacked minimum literacy skills, two thirds of them women. The United Nations Literacy Decade (2003–2012) seeks to draw greater attention to this pressing issue.

Research has shown that access to education is closely related to improved social indicators. Schooling has a multiplier effect for women. An educated woman will typically be healthier, and have fewer children and more opportunities to increase household income. Her children, in turn, will experience lower mortality rates, better nutrition and better overall health. For this reason, girls and women are the focus of the education programmes of numerous UN agencies. Because of the multiplicity of factors involved in education, many parts of the UN system are involved in the funding and development of a variety of education and training programmes. These range from traditional basic schooling, to technical training for human resources development in areas such as public administration, agriculture and health services, to public awareness campaigns to educate people about HIV/AIDS, drug abuse, human rights, family planning, and other issues. UNICEF, for example, devotes more than 20 per cent of its annual programme expenditure to education, paying special attention to girls' education.

The lead agency in the area of education is the **United Nations Educational, Scientific and Cultural Organization (UNESCO)** (*www.unesco.org*). Together with other partners, it works to ensure that all children are enrolled in child-friendly schools with trained teachers providing quality education. UNESCO provides the secretariat for the campaign to achieve universal, quality primary education by 2015, the most ambitious UN inter-agency campaign ever launched. The campaign's goal was based on a framework for action adopted by more than 160 nations at the World Education Forum in Dakar, Senegal, in 2000, and was reconfirmed by world leaders in their *Millennium Declaration*, adopted in September of that year. At the Forum, governments committed themselves to the achievement of quality education for all, with particular emphasis on girls and such groups as working children and children affected by war. Donor countries and institutions pledged that no nation committed to basic education would be thwarted by lack of resources. The Forum drew from the results of six high-level regional conferences and the largest, most comprehensive and statistically rigorous stocktaking of education in history: the two-year "Education for All Assessment".

Youth and schools

In addition to declaring universal primary education the second Millennium Development Goal, the UN has launched numerous initiatives in the area of education.

The **UN Cyberschoolbus** (*cyberschoolbus.un.org*) is an award-winning UN website where students from primary to secondary schools can:

- learn the origins, purpose and organization of the United Nations;
- gain information about member states;
- discover what global issues are on the agenda and why, from human rights to peace and security to climate change;
- participate in finding solutions to global problems;
- interact with UN diplomats or experts on a wide range of issues trough live video chats;
- enter artistic competitions;
- follow events at UN Headquarters that appeal to children and youth.

Teachers can find lesson plans on the entire range of global issues for teaching children in this age group and collaborate with other classrooms around the world on educational projects dealing with issues on the UN agenda. Cyberschoolbus reaches over 200 countries and territories around the world and is available in English, Spanish, French and Russian.

Youth represent a top priority for the United Nations and a new generation of support for the work of the Organization. Several hundred Model UN conferences are organized each year at all educational levels from primary school to university in a variety of configurations, including the **Global Model United Nations Conference** (*un.org/gmun*). Many of today's leaders in law, government, business and the arts participated in Model UN programmes during their youth. Model UN programmes provide an understanding of the work of the United Nations and an opportunity to build skills in diplomacy and conflict resolution, as youth from around the world are exposed to the intricacies of international affairs. Students act as foreign diplomats and participate in simulated sessions of the United Nations General Assembly and other multilateral bodies in the UN system. Preparing for these conferences helps students develop skills in leadership, research, writing, public speaking and problem-solving that they will use throughout their lives.

Each year, **videoconferences** are held for middle and high school students to mark four UN observances: the International Day of Remembrance of the Victims of Slavery and the Transatlantic Slave Trade (25 March), World Environment Day (5 June), the International Day of Peace (21 September), and Human Rights Day (10 December). During events for these observances, students from around the world participate via videoconference and connect with youth audiences and the UN community in New York. All the events are webcast live, and students have the additional opportunity to send questions and comments in real time through the UN Cyberschoolbus website.

UNESCO's education sector focuses on: providing educational access to all, at all levels; the success of special-needs and marginalized populations; teacher training; developing competencies for work forces; success through education; ensuring opportunities for non-formal and lifelong learning; and using technology to enhance teaching and learning, and to expand educational opportunities. UNESCO undertakes these actions in the context of the *Dakar Framework for Action*; the UN Literacy Decade, 2003–2012; the UN Decade of Education for Sustainable

Academic Impact

United Nations Academic Impact (*academicimpact.org/engpage.php*) is a global initiative that aligns institutions of higher education with the United Nations in supporting ten universally accepted principles in the areas of human rights, literacy, sustainability and conflict resolution. It taps into the recognized potential of higher education to foster world peace as well as economic and social development. By formally endorsing the ten principles of the Academic Impact Programme, institutions make commitments to:

- the principles inherent in the *Charter of the United Nations* as values that education seeks to promote and help fulfil;
- human rights, among them freedom of inquiry, opinion and speech;
- educational opportunity for all people regardless of gender, race, religion or ethnicity;
- the opportunity for every interested individual to acquire the skills and knowledge necessary for the pursuit of higher education;
- building capacity in higher education systems across the world;
- encouraging global citizenship through education;
- advancing peace and conflict resolution through education;
- addressing issues of poverty through education;
- promoting sustainability through education;
- promoting intercultural dialogue and understanding, and the 'unlearning' of intolerance, through education.

Academic Impact asks each participating college or university to demonstrate support of at least one of these commitments each year.

Development, 2005–2014; and the Global Initiative on Education and HIV/AIDS. It is also working towards the MDG targets to ensure that all boys and girls complete primary school; and eliminate disparities in primary and secondary education at all levels by 2015.

Towards the end of 2010, more than 8,500 schools in 180 countries were involved in UNESCO's Associated Schools Project Network (ASPnet), an international network that elaborates ways and means to enhance the role of education in learning to live together in a world community. Some 3,700 UNESCO clubs, centres and associations in more than 100 countries, mainly comprising teachers and students, carry out a wide range of educational and cultural activities.

Research and training

Academic work in the form of research and training is carried out by a number of specialized UN organizations. This work is aimed at enhancing understanding of the global problems we face, as well as fostering the human resources required for the more technical aspects of economic and social development and the maintenance of peace and security.

The **United Nations University (UNU)** (*www.unu.edu*) contributes, through research and capacity-building, to efforts to resolve the pressing global problems that are the concern of the United Nations, its peoples and member states. UNU is a bridge between the United Nations and the international academic community, acting as a think-tank for the UN system; a builder of capacities, particularly in developing countries; and a platform for dialogue and new creative ideas. UNU partners with over 40 UN entities and hundreds of cooperating research institutions around the world.

In contributing to global sustainable development, UNU focuses on five areas: peace, security and human rights; human and socio-economic development and good governance; global health, population and sustainable livelihoods; global change and sustainable development; and science, technology, innovation and society. Academic activities are carried out at the UNU Centre in Tokyo, and at training centres and programmes located in various parts of the world. These include:

- UNU BIOLAC (Programme for Biotechnology in Latin America and the Caribbean), Caracas, Venezuela—biotechnology and society;
- UNU-CRIS (Institute on Comparative Regional Integration Studies), Bruges, Belgium—local and global governance, regional integration;
- UNU-EHS (Institute for Environment and Human Security), Bonn, Germany—environment and human security;
- UNU-FNP (Food and Nutrition Programme for Human and Social Development), Ithaca, New York, United States—food and nutrition capacity-building;
- UNU-FTP (Fisheries Training Programme), Reykjavík, Iceland—postgraduate fisheries research and development;
- UNU-GTP (Geothermal Training Programme), Reykjavík, Iceland—geothermal research, exploration and development;
- UNU-IAS (Institute of Advanced Studies), Yokohama, Japan—strategic approaches to sustainable development;
- UNU-IIGH (International Institute for Global Health), Kuala Lumpur, Malaysia—efficiency of health care systems, newly emerging and re-emerging diseases, non-communicable diseases and control policy, information technology in health, and climate change and health;
- UNU-IIST (International Institute for Software Technology), Macau, China—software technologies for development;
- UNU-INRA (Institute for Natural Resources in Africa), Accra, Ghana—natural resources management;
- UNU-INWEH (International Network on Water, Environment and Health), Hamilton, Ontario, Canada—water, environment and human health;
- UNU-ISP (Institute for Sustainability and Peace), Tokyo, Japan—sustainability, peace and international cooperation;
- UNU-LRT (Land Restoration Training Programme), Reykjavík, Iceland—sustainable land management and restoration of degraded land;
- UNU-MERIT (Maastricht Economic and Social Research and Training Centre on Innovation and Technology), Maastricht, The Netherlands—social and economic impact of new technologies;
- UNU-WIDER (World Institute for Development Economics Research), Helsinki, Finland—economic and social development;
- UN-WDPC (Water Decade Programme on Capacity Development), Bonn, Germany—UN organizations and programmes cooperating within the UN-Water interagency mechanism.

The Geneva-based **United Nations Institute for Training and Research (UNITAR)** (*www.unitar.org*) works to enhance the effectiveness of the United Nations through appropriate training and research. It conducts training and capacity development programmes in multilateral diplomacy and international cooperation for diplomats accredited to the UN, as well as for national officials working on international issues. UNITAR also carries out a wide range of training programmes in the fields of social and economic development, and the maintenance of peace and security. Each year, UNITAR conducts research on training methodologies and knowledge systems, encompassing capacity development, e-learning and adult training. It also develops pedagogical materials, including distance learning training packages, workbooks, software and video training packs. UNITAR is supported entirely from voluntary contributions, principally from governments, intergovernmental organizations and foundations.

The **United Nations System Staff College (UNSSC)** (*www.unssc.org*), located in Turin, Italy, assists the staff of UN organizations in developing the skills and competencies needed to meet the global challenges faced by the United Nations. It does so by strengthening inter-agency collaboration; promoting a cohesive management culture; supporting continuous learning and staff development; and fostering strategic leadership. Thematic areas of its work include: leadership; UN coherence at the country level; monitoring and evaluation; social and economic development; conflict prevention and peacebuilding; staff safety and security; staff orientation; learning methods and knowledge management; and communities of practice.

The **United Nations Research Institute for Social Development (UNRISD)** (*www.unrisd.org*), located in Geneva, engages in multidisciplinary research on the social dimensions of contemporary development issues. Working through a global network of researchers and institutes, UNRISD provides governments, development agencies, civil society organizations and scholars with a better understanding of how development policies and processes affect different social groups. Recent research themes have included gender equality, social policy, poverty reduction, governance and politics, and corporate social responsibility.

Population and development

The United Nations estimates that despite significant reductions in fertility as contraceptive use has increased in most countries, world population has continued to increase globally by about 1.18 per cent per year over the past five years. More significantly, world population is expected to increase from 6.9 billion in 2010 to over 9 billion by 2050, with most of the additional people enlarging the population of developing countries. Rapid population growth weighs heavily on the earth's resources and environment, often outstripping development efforts. The UN has addressed the relationship between population and development in many ways, placing special emphasis on advancing the rights and status of women, which is seen as key to social and economic progress.

Shifting demographic patterns are creating new needs. For example, the global number of persons aged 60 or over—the fastest growing segment of the population—is expected to increase from 737 million in 2009 to over 2 billion in 2050, when the number of older persons will exceed the number of children for the first time in history. The population of developing countries, however, is still young.

Hence, whereas in the more developed regions the population in the main working ages of 25 to 59 is expected to peak over the next decade and decline thereafter, reaching 528 million in 2050, in the less developed regions it will continue to rise, reaching 3.6 billion in 2050. Already, and again for the first time in history, more than half of the world's people are now living in cities.

The United Nations has been at work in many developing countries in response to population trends. Various parts of the Organization have worked together to build national statistical offices, take censuses, make projections and disseminate reliable data. The pioneering quantitative and methodological work of the United Nations, particularly its authoritative estimates and projections of population size and change, has led to a significant increase in the capacities of nations to plan ahead, incorporate population policies into development planning, and take sound economic and social decisions.

The **Commission on Population and Development**, composed of 47 member states, is charged with studying and advising ECOSOC on population changes and their effects on economic and social conditions. It holds primary responsibility for reviewing the implementation of the programme of action of the 1994 International Conference on Population and Development.

The **Population Division** of the United Nations Department of Economic and Social Affairs (*www.un.org/esa/population*) serves as the secretariat of the Commission. It also provides the international community with up-to-date, scientifically objective information on population and development. It undertakes studies on population levels, trends, estimates and projections, as well as on population policies and the link between population and development. The Division maintains major databases, among them the *Population, Resources, Environment and Development Databank; World Population Prospects; World Population Policies;* and *World Urbanization Prospects.* In addition, it coordinates the Population Information Network (POPIN), which promotes the use of the Internet to facilitate global sharing of population information.

The **United Nations Population Fund (UNFPA)** (*www.unfpa.org*) leads the operational activities of the UN system in this field, helping developing countries and those with economies in transition find solutions to their population problems. It assists states in improving reproductive health and family planning services on the basis of individual choice, and in formulating population policies in support of sustainable development. It also promotes awareness of population problems, and helps governments deal with them in ways best suited to each country's needs. In line with its mission statement, UNFPA "promotes the right of every woman, man and child to enjoy a life of health and equal opportunity. UNFPA supports countries in using population data for policies and programmes to reduce poverty and to ensure that every pregnancy is wanted, every birth is safe, every young person is free of HIV/AIDS, and every girl and woman is treated with dignity and respect." Its primary role in fulfilling this mission is as a funding organization for population projects and programmes carried out by governments, UN agencies and NGOs.

Its core programme areas are:
- reproductive health, assisting governments in delivering sexual and reproductive health care throughout the life cycle of women, with a particular focus on improving maternal health;

- gender equality, which is intimately linked to improving maternal and new-born health and reducing the spread of HIV; critical factors include girls' education, women's economic empowerment, women's political participation and the balancing of reproductive and productive roles;
- population and development strategies, which help countries gather adequate information about population dynamics and trends in order to create and manage sound policies and generate the political will to address both current and future needs, especially with regard to migration, ageing, climate change and urbanization.

UNFPA does not provide any support for abortion services. Rather, it seeks to prevent abortion by helping to increase access to family planning. It also addresses the reproductive health needs of adolescents, with programmes to prevent teenage pregnancy, prevent and treat fistulas, prevent HIV/AIDS and other sexually transmitted infections, reduce recourse to abortion, and improve access to reproductive health services and information.

The ability of parents to choose the number and spacing of their children is an essential component of reproductive health and an internationally recognized basic human right. It is estimated that at least 200 million women want to use safe and effective family planning methods, but are unable to do so because they lack access to information and services or the support of their husbands and communities. UNFPA works with governments, the private sector and NGOs to meet family planning needs.

Gender equality and empowerment of women

Promotion of equality between women and men and the empowerment of women are central to the work of the United Nations. Gender equality is not only a goal in its own right, but is also recognized as a critical means for achieving all other development goals, including the Millennium Development Goals. Eradicating poverty and hunger, achieving universal primary education and health for all, combating HIV/AIDS and facilitating sustainable development all require systematic attention to the needs, priorities and contributions of women as well as men. The Organization actively promotes women's human rights and works to eradicate the scourge of violence against women, including in armed conflict and through trafficking. The UN also adopts global norms and standards and supports follow-up and implementation at the national level, including through its development assistance activities.

Under the Economic and Social Council (ECOSOC), the **Commission on the Status of Women** monitors progress towards gender equality throughout the world by reviewing implementation of the platform for action that emerged from the Fourth World Conference on Women, held in 1995. The Commission makes recommendations for further action to promote women's rights, and to address discrimination and inequality in all fields. Major accomplishments of the 45-member Commission over its more than 60 years of activity include the preparation of, and follow-up to, four world conferences on women and development of the treaty on women's human rights: the 1979 *Convention on the Elimination of All Forms of Discrimination against Women*.

World conferences on women

Building on the energy of national women's movements, United Nations conferences in Mexico City (1975), Copenhagen (1980), Nairobi (1985) and Beijing (1995) have galvanized understanding, commitment and action concerning gender equality and the empowerment of women around the world. At the Fourth (1995) World Conference on Women, representatives of 189 governments adopted the *Beijing Declaration* and *Platform for Action* to address discrimination and inequality and ensure the empowerment of women in all spheres of public and private life. The *Platform* identifies 12 critical areas of concern:

- the persistent and increasing burden of poverty on women;
- inadequate educational opportunities and unequal access to education;
- inequalities in health status, inadequate health-care service, and unequal access to health care;
- violence against women;
- the effects of conflict on women;
- inequality of women's participation in the definition of economic structures and policies, and in the production process;
- inequality in the sharing of power and decision-making;
- insufficient mechanisms to promote the advancement of women;
- lack of awareness of, and commitment to, internationally and nationally recognized women's human rights;
- insufficient mobilization of mass media to promote women's contribution to society;
- lack of adequate recognition and support for women's contribution to managing natural resources and safeguarding the environment;
- the girl child.

In 2010, the Beijing+15 review welcomed progress made towards achieving gender equality, while emphasizing the necessity of the implementation of the *Declaration* and *Platform for Action* for achieving internationally agreed development goals, including those contained in the *Millennium Declaration*.

The **Committee on the Elimination of Discrimination against Women (CEDAW)** monitors adherence to the *Convention*. The 23-member Committee holds constructive dialogue with states parties on their implementation of the *Convention*, based on reports they submit. Its recommendations have contributed to a better understanding of women's rights, and of the means to ensure the enjoyment of those rights and the elimination of discrimination against women.

UN-Women (*www.unwomen.org*) is the **United Nations Entity for Gender Equality and the Empowerment of Women**, which resulted from a merger in 2010 of the Office of the Special Adviser on Gender Issues and Advancement of Women; the Division for the Advancement of Women in the Department of Economic and Social Affairs; the International Research and Training Institute for the Advancement of Women; and the United Nations Development Fund for Women. UN-Women works towards eliminating discrimination against women and girls, empowering women and achieving equality between women and men as partners and beneficiaries of development, human rights, humanitarian action, and peace and security. UN-Women supports intergovernmental bodies, such as the Commission on the Status of Women, in their formulation of policies, global standards and norms; helps member states implement these standards by providing suitable technical and financial support to those countries that request it and forging effective partnerships with civil society; and holds the UN system accountable for its own commitments on gender equality, including regular monitoring of system-wide progress.

Beyond the Secretariat, all the organizations of the UN family address issues relating to women and gender in their policies and programmes; and empowering women is central to the MDGs.

Promoting the rights of children

Up to 10 million children die every year before their fifth birthday due to preventable diseases, and tens of millions more are left physically or mentally disabled because they lack what is needed to survive and flourish. Whether due to outright illness or to the pernicious effects of poverty, ignorance, discrimination and violence, this represents a terrible loss to families, communities, nations and the world. Beyond infancy, the young still confront forces that threaten their lives and well-being. They are made more vulnerable because their rights are often denied them, including their right to education, participation and protection from harm.

The **United Nations Children's Fund (UNICEF)** (*www.unicef.org*) acts to protect children's rights to survival, development and protection. It advocates for full implementation of the *Convention on the Rights of the Child* along with the *Convention on the Elimination of All Forms of Discrimination against Women*. In 191 countries, UNICEF works in partnership with governments, international organizations, civil society and young people to overcome obstacles faced by children, including poverty, violence, disease and discrimination. UNICEF's major areas of focus are child survival and development; basic education and gender equality; HIV/AIDS and children; child protection; and policy advocacy and partnerships. These aims are congruent with the MDGs and with the objectives expressed in *A World Fit for Children*, the outcome document of the 2002 special session of the General Assembly on children.

The Fund is widely engaged in every facet of child health, from before birth through adolescence. It acts to ensure that pregnant women have access to proper prenatal and delivery care, strengthens the ability of families to manage childhood illnesses at home, and offers guidance to communities in achieving the best health care possible. UNICEF works to reduce the risks of HIV/AIDS to young people by sharing information that will keep them safe. It makes special efforts to see that children who lose their parents to HIV/AIDS receive the same kind of care as their peers. It also helps women and children afflicted with AIDS to live their lives with dignity.

UNICEF is also involved in worldwide immunization efforts, from the purchase and distribution of vaccines to safe inoculation. It is a global leader in vaccine supply, reaching 40 per cent of the world's children. Together with the WHO, UNICEF has worked to achieve Universal Childhood Immunization with the six vaccines of the Expanded Programme on Immunization: BCG, OPV, diphtheria, tetanus, pertussis and measles. A record 106 million children were vaccinated in 2008; and global immunization rates are at their highest level ever (82 per cent that same year). The Fund uses the opportunity of immunization to deliver other life-saving

A World Fit for Children

In 2002, a special session of the United Nations General Assembly convened to review progress made since the 1990 World Summit for Children and re-energize global commitment to children's rights. The special session was a landmark—the first one devoted exclusively to children and the first to include them as official delegates.

The special session culminated in the adoption, by some 180 nations, of *A World Fit for Children*. This new agenda for the world's children comprised 21 specific goals and targets for the next decade, with a focus on four key priority areas: promoting healthy lives; providing quality education for all; protecting children against abuse, exploitation and violence; and combating HIV/AIDS.

An attendant *Declaration* committed leaders to completing the unfinished agenda of the 1990 Summit and to achieving other goals and objectives, in particular those of the UN *Millennium Declaration*. It also reaffirmed leaders' obligation to promote and protect the rights of each child, acknowledging the legal standards set by the 1989 *Convention on the Rights of the Child* and its *Optional Protocols*.

The *Plan of Action* set out three necessary outcomes: the best possible start in life for children; access to a quality basic education, including free and compulsory primary education; and ample opportunity for children and adolescents to develop their individual capacities. To achieve those goals, the *Plan* supported the global target for industrialized countries to allocate 0.7 per cent of their gross national product (GNP) for official development assistance (ODA).

In 2007, the General Assembly re-convened to consider the progress that had been made. Noting that failure to achieve the original goals would undermine efforts towards realizing the aspirations of the *United Nations Millennium Declaration* and the Millennium Development Goals, its report called for scaled-up efforts by governments to maximize their capacities, and for enhanced support by the international community.

The Secretary-General, in his 2010 follow-up report on the 2002 special session, stated that the global economic crisis in 2009 threatened to halt or reverse progress in achieving the goals set out in *A World Fit for Children*. However, partnerships with foundations, NGOs and global programmes had expanded, providing opportunities to leverage more funding for children worldwide.

---

services, including providing regular vitamin A supplements, insecticide-treated mosquito nets to help protect families from malaria, and other locally appropriate interventions.

In its support of various initiatives that educate children from pre-school age through adolescence, UNICEF mobilizes teachers, registers children, prepares school facilities and organizes curricula, sometimes rebuilding educational systems from the ground up. It makes sure that children have the chance to play and learn, even in times of conflict, because sports and recreation are equally important to a child's progress. It encourages proper nutrition for pregnant mothers and breastfeeding after birth. It improves water and sanitation facilities at kindergartens and child-care centres. The Fund also helps create protective environments for the young. It encourages legislation that bans child labour, condemns female genital mutilation, and acts to make it more difficult to exploit children for sexual and economic ends. UNICEF also designs landmine awareness campaigns and helps demobilize child soldiers.

Social integration

The United Nations has come to recognize several social groups as deserving special attention, including youth, older persons, the impoverished, persons with disabilities, minorities and indigenous populations. Their concerns are addressed by the General Assembly, ECOSOC and the Commission for Social Development. Specific programmes for these groups are carried out within the United Nations Department of Economic and Social Affairs (*www.un.org/esa/socdev*). The UN has been instrumental in defining and defending the human rights of such vulnerable groups. It has helped formulate international norms, standards and recommendations for policies and practices regarding these groups, and strives to highlight their concerns through research and data gathering, as well as through the declaration of special years and decades aimed at encouraging awareness and international action.

Families

The United Nations recognizes the family as the basic unit of society. Families have been substantially transformed over the past 60 years as a result of changes in their structure (smaller-sized households, delayed marriage and childbearing, increased divorce rates and single parenthood); global trends in migration; the phenomenon of demographic ageing; the HIV/AIDS pandemic; and the impact of globalization. These dynamic social forces have had a manifest impact on the capacities of families to perform such functions as socializing children and care giving for younger and older family members. The **International Day of Families** on 15 May of each year is aimed at increasing awareness of issues relating to the family and encouraging appropriate action.

The UN **Programme on the Family** (*www.un.org/esa/socdev/family*) provides substantive servicing to UN intergovernmental bodies in the areas of family and family policy; promotes the realization of the objectives of the International Year of the Family (1994), along with the integration of a family perspective into national, regional and international policy-making; acts as an exchange for expertise and experiences, disseminating information and supporting networking on family issues; supports family research and diagnostic studies; encourages and supports coordination on family policies and programmes within governments and the UN system; provides technical assistance and capacity-building support to developing country governments; and liaises with governments, civil society and the private sector on family issues.

Youth

The General Assembly has adopted several resolutions and campaigns specific to youth—defined as those between 15 and 24 years of age—and the Secretariat has overseen related programmes and information campaigns. The UN **Programme on Youth** (*www.un.org/youth*) is the focal point on youth within the United Nations. It aims to build an awareness of the global situation of young people; promote their rights and aspirations; and increase participation of young people in decision-making as a means of achieving peace and development. Governments regularly include youth delegates in their official delegations to the Assembly and other UN meetings.

In 1999, the General Assembly declared that **International Youth Day** be commemorated each year on 12 August. It recommended that public information activities be organized to support the Day as a way to enhance awareness of the World Programme of Action for Youth, adopted in 1995 as a policy framework and set of practical guidelines for national action and international support to improve the situation of young people around the world. In promotion of the ideals of peace, freedom, progress and solidarity for youth development and the achievement of the Millennium Development Goals, the Assembly proclaimed the year commencing on 12 August 2010 as the **International Year of Youth: Dialogue and Mutual Understanding**.

The **Youth Employment Network** (*www.ilo.org/yen*) is a joint initiative of the United Nations, the ILO and the World Bank to translate into action the commitments of the 2000 Millennium Summit to "develop and implement strategies that give young people everywhere a real chance to find decent and productive work".

Older persons

The world is in the midst of an historically unique and irreversible process of demographic transition due to falling birth and death rates, which will result in older populations everywhere. By 2050, one out of five persons will be 60 years or older. The world community has come to recognize the need to integrate the emerging process of global ageing into the larger context of development, and to design policies within a broader 'life-course' and a society-wide perspective. Creating a new 'architecture' for ageing and transmitting it to the world stage and into policy is the focus of the UN **Programme on Ageing** (*www.un.org/esa/socdev/ageing*).

In response to the challenges and opportunities of global ageing, the United Nations has taken several initiatives:

*   The first World Assembly on Ageing (Vienna, 1982) adopted the *Vienna International Plan of Action on Ageing*, which recommended measures in such areas as employment and income security, health and nutrition, housing, education and social welfare. It saw older persons as a diverse and active population group with wide-ranging capabilities and, at times, particular health-care needs.
*   The *United Nations Principles for Older Persons,* adopted by the General Assembly in 1991, established universal standards pertaining to the status of older persons in five areas: independence, participation, care, self-fulfilment and dignity.
*   The Second World Assembly on Ageing (Madrid, 2002) designed international policy on ageing for the 21st century. It adopted the *Madrid International Plan of Action on Ageing*, by which member states committed themselves to action in three priority areas: older persons and development; advancing health and well-being into old age; and ensuring the existence of enabling and supportive environments.

Indigenous issues

There are more than 370 million indigenous people living in some 70 countries worldwide, where they often face discrimination and exclusion from political and economic power. Indigenous people are overrepresented among the poorest, the illiterate and the destitute of the world. They have often been displaced by wars and environmental disasters, removed from their ancestral lands, and deprived of resources needed for physical and cultural survival. Indigenous people have also seen their traditional knowledge marketed and patented without their consent or participation.

The **Permanent Forum on Indigenous Issues** (*www.un.org/esa/socdev/unpfii*), established by the Economic and Social Council in 2000, considers indigenous issues relating to economic and social development, culture, education, environment, health and human rights. It provides expert advice and recommendations to the Council and, through it, to the programmes, funds and agencies of the United Nations. The aim is to raise awareness, promote the integration and coordination of activities relating to indigenous issues within the UN system, and disseminate information on indigenous issues. The Forum also addresses ways in which indigenous issues may best be pursued in meeting the Millennium Development Goals, given the fact that, in many countries, attention to indigenous communities will directly contribute to the goal of halving extreme poverty by 2015.

The General Assembly has declared 2005–2015 as the **Second International Decade on the World's Indigenous People**. Its main objectives are:

* promoting non-discrimination and the inclusion of indigenous people in the design, implementation and evaluation of laws, policies, resources, programmes and projects;
* promoting the full and effective participation of indigenous people in decisions that affect their lifestyles, traditional lands and territories, cultural integrity, collective rights, and any other aspect of their lives;
* re-evaluating development policies that depart from a vision of equity, including respect for the cultural and linguistic diversity of indigenous people;
* adopting targeted policies, programmes, projects and budgets for the development of indigenous people, including concrete benchmarks, with particular emphasis on indigenous women, children and youth; and
* developing strong monitoring mechanisms and enhancing accountability at all levels in the implementation of legal, policy and operational frameworks for the protection of indigenous people and the improvement of their lives.

In 2007, the General Assembly adopted the *United Nations Declaration on the Rights of Indigenous Peoples*, setting out the individual and collective rights of indigenous people, including their rights to culture, identity, language, employment, health and education. The *Declaration* emphasizes the rights of indigenous people to maintain and strengthen their own institutions, cultures and traditions, and to pursue their development in keeping with their own needs and aspirations. It prohibits discrimination against them, and promotes their full and effective participation in all matters that concern them, as well as their right to remain distinct and to pursue their own visions of economic and social development.

Persons with disabilities

Persons with disabilities are often excluded from the mainstream of society. Discrimination takes various forms, ranging from invidious discrimination, such as the denial of educational opportunities, to more subtle forms of discrimination, such as segregation and isolation because of the imposition of physical and social barriers. Society also suffers, since the loss of the enormous potential of persons with disabilities impoverishes humankind. Changes in the perception and concepts of disability involve both changes in values and increased understanding at all levels of society. Since its inception, the United Nations has sought to advance the status of persons with disabilities and to improve their lives. The Organization's concern for the well-being and rights of such persons is rooted in its founding principles, which are based on human rights, fundamental freedoms and the equality of all human beings.

Following three decades of advocacy and standard-setting for equal treatment and access to services for disabled persons, the General Assembly, in 2006, adopted the *Convention on the Rights of Persons with Disabilities* and its *Optional Protocol.* A human rights instrument with an explicit social development dimension, the *Convention*—which entered into force in 2008—codified all categories of human rights and fundamental freedoms to be applied to all persons with disabilities. It is based on the following principles: respect for inherent dignity and individual autonomy; non-discrimination; full and effective participation and inclusion in society; respect for differences and acceptance of persons with disabilities as part of human diversity; equal opportunity; accessibility; equality of men and women; and respect for the evolving capacities of children with disabilities and their right to preserve their identities. The *Convention* focuses particularly on areas where rights have been violated, where protections must be reinforced, and where adaptations are needed to enable such persons to exercise their rights. It requires states to monitor its implementation by setting up national focal points within their governments, as well as independent monitoring mechanisms, usually in the form of an independent human rights institution.

The **Committee on the Rights of Persons with Disabilities**, composed of 18 expert members, monitors implementation of the *Convention*. Under the *Convention*'s *Optional Protocol*, states parties recognize the Committee's competence to examine individual complaints with regard to alleged violations of the *Convention* by parties to the *Protocol*.

Uncivil society: crime, illicit drugs and terrorism

Transnational organized crime, illicit drug trafficking and terrorism have become social, political and economic forces capable of altering the destinies of entire countries and regions. Such practices as the large-scale bribery of public officials, the growth of 'criminal multinationals', trafficking in human beings, and the use of terrorism to intimidate communities large and small and to sabotage economic development are threats that require effective international cooperation. The United Nations is addressing these threats to good governance, social equity and justice for all, and is orchestrating a global response.

The Vienna-based **United Nations Office on Drugs and Crime (UNODC)** (*www. unodc.org*) leads the international effort to combat drug trafficking and abuse, organized crime and international terrorism—what have been called the 'uncivil' elements of society. The Office is composed of a crime programme, which also addresses terrorism and its prevention, and a drug programme. It has 21 field offices, and liaison offices in New York.

Drug control

Up to 250 million people a year worldwide use illicit drugs, and between 16 and 38 million persons are addicts or 'problem users'. Drug abuse is responsible for lost wages, soaring health-care costs, broken families and deteriorating communities. In particular, drug use by injection is fuelling the spread of HIV/AIDS and hepatitis in many parts of the world. There is a direct link between drugs and an increase in crime and violence. Drug cartels undermine governments and corrupt legitimate businesses. Revenues from illicit drugs fund some of the deadliest armed conflicts. The financial toll is staggering. Enormous sums are spent to strengthen police forces, judicial systems and treatment and rehabilitation programmes. The social costs are equally high: street violence, gang warfare, fear, urban decay and shattered lives.

The United Nations is tackling the global drug problem on many levels. The **Commission on Narcotic Drugs**, a functional commission of ECOSOC, is the main intergovernmental policy-making and coordination body on international drug control. Made up of 53 member states, it analyses the world drug abuse and trafficking problem and develops proposals to strengthen drug control. It monitors implementation of international drug control treaties, as well as the guiding principles and measures adopted by the General Assembly.

The **International Narcotics Control Board (INCB)** (*www.incb.org*) is a 13-member, independent, quasi-judicial body that monitors and assists in governments' compliance with international drug control treaties. It strives to ensure that drugs are available for medical and scientific purposes and to prevent their diversion into illegal channels. The Board sends investigative missions and makes technical visits to drug-affected countries. It also conducts training programmes for drug control administrators, particularly those from developing countries.

A series of treaties, adopted under UN auspices, require that governments exercise control over the production and distribution of narcotic and psychotropic substances; combat drug abuse and illicit trafficking; and report to international organs on their actions.

- The *Single Convention on Narcotic Drugs* (1961) seeks to limit the production, distribution, possession, use and trade in drugs exclusively to medical and scientific purposes, and obliges states parties to take special measures for particular drugs, such as heroin. Its 1972 *Protocol* stresses the need for treatment and rehabilitation of drug addicts.

- The *Convention on Psychotropic Substances* (1971) establishes an international control system for psychotropic substances. It stands as a response to the diversification and expansion of the drug spectrum, and introduces controls over a number of synthetic drugs.

- The *United Nations Convention against Illicit Traffic in Narcotic Drugs and Psychotropic Substances* (1988) provides comprehensive measures against drug trafficking, including provisions against money laundering and the diversion of precursor chemicals. As the main instrument for international cooperation against drug trafficking, it provides for the tracing, freezing and confiscation of proceeds and property derived from drug trafficking; the extradition of drug traffickers; and the transfer of criminal prosecution proceedings. States parties commit themselves to eliminating or reducing drug demand.

Providing leadership for all UN drug control activities, UNODC takes a multifaceted approach to the global drug problem by working with NGOs and civil society, including through community-based programmes in prevention, treatment and rehabilitation, and the provision of new economic opportunities to economies dependent on illicit crops. Better training and technology to curb drug trafficking make law enforcement agencies more effective—as does improving judicial cooperation among countries—while assistance to businesses and NGOs helps them create programmes to curtail illicit production and consumption.

Crime prevention

Crime is increasing in scope, intensity and sophistication. It threatens the safety of citizens around the world and hampers the social and economic development of countries. Globalization has opened up new forms of transnational crime. Multinational criminal syndicates have expanded the range of their operations from drug and arms trafficking to money laundering. Traffickers move millions of illegal migrants each year, generating billions in profits. A country plagued by corruption is likely to attract less investment than a relatively uncorrupt country, and lose economic growth as a result.

The **Commission on Crime Prevention and Criminal Justice**, made up of 40 member states, is a functional body of ECOSOC. It formulates international policies and coordinates activities in crime prevention and criminal justice. Through its crime programme, UNODC carries out the mandates established by the Commission, and is the UN office responsible for crime prevention, criminal justice and criminal law reform. It pays special attention to combating transnational organized crime, corruption, terrorism and trafficking in human beings. The UNODC strategy is based on international cooperation and the provision of assistance for those efforts. It fosters a culture based on integrity and respect for the law, and promotes the participation of civil society in combating crime and corruption.

UNODC supports the development of international legal instruments on global crime, including the *United Nations Convention against Transnational Organized Crime* and its three *Protocols*, which entered into force in 2003; and the *United Nations Convention against Corruption*, which entered into force in 2005. It also helps states put those instruments into effect. The Office provides technical cooperation to strengthen the capacity of governments to modernize their criminal justice systems. Its Anti-Organized Crime and Law Enforcement Unit assists states in taking effective, practical steps, in line with the *Convention against Corruption*, to fight organized crime.

UNODC advances the application of UN standards and norms in crime prevention and criminal justice as cornerstones of humane and effective criminal justice systems—basic requisites for fighting national and international crime. More than 100 countries have relied on these standards for elaborating national legislation and policies. The Office also analyses emerging trends in crime and justice; develops databases; issues global surveys; gathers and disseminates information; and undertakes country-specific needs assessments and early warning measures with regard to such issues as the escalation of terrorism.

In 2003, UNODC expanded its technical cooperation activities to strengthen the legal regime against terrorism, providing legal technical assistance to countries for becoming party to and implementing the universal anti-terrorism instruments.

UNODC also collaborates with the **Counter-Terrorism Implementation Task Force**, established by the Secretary-General in 2005 to enhance coordination and coherence of the UN system's counter-terrorism efforts. The working groups of this task force consist of 30 international entities that, by virtue of their work, have a stake in counter-terrorism efforts. They deal with preventing and resolving conflict; supporting victims of terrorism; preventing and responding to terrorist attacks involving weapons of mass destruction; tackling the financing of terrorism; countering the use of the Internet for terrorist purposes; strengthening the protection of vulnerable targets; and protecting human rights while countering terrorism.

The **Global Programme against Money Laundering** assists governments in confronting criminals who launder the proceeds of crime through the international financial system. In close cooperation with international anti-money laundering organizations, the Programme provides governments, law enforcement and financial intelligence units with anti-money laundering schemes; advises on improved banking and financial policies; and assists national financial investigation services.

In 2007, UNODC launched the Global Initiative to Fight Human Trafficking (UN.GIFT) (*www.ungift.org*), aimed at producing a turning point in the worldwide movement against this crime.

The **United Nations Interregional Crime and Justice Research Institute (UNICRI)** (*www.unicri.it*), the interregional research body that works in close association with UNODC's crime programme, undertakes and promotes research aimed at preventing crime, treating offenders and formulating improved policies. As decided by the General Assembly, a United Nations Congress on the Prevention of Crime and the Treatment of Offenders is held every five years as a forum to exchange policies and stimulate progress in the fight against crime. Participants include criminologists, penologists and senior police officers, as well as experts in criminal law, human rights and rehabilitation. The Twelfth Crime Congress met in Salvador, Brazil, in April 2010 on the theme "Comprehensive strategies for global challenges: crime prevention and criminal justice systems and their development in a changing world".

Science, culture and communication

The United Nations sees cultural and scientific exchanges, as well as communication, as instrumental to the advancement of international peace and development. Several UN entities concern themselves with work in these areas. In addition to its central work on education, for example, the **United Nations Educational, Scientific and Cultural Organization (UNESCO)** (*www.unesco.org*) carries out activities in the fields of science and culture, fostering the advancement, transfer and sharing of knowledge.

Natural and social and human sciences

UNESCO's international and intergovernmental programmes in the natural sciences include the Man and the Biosphere Programme; the Intergovernmental Oceanographic Commission; the Management of Social Transformations Programme; the International Hydrological Programme; the International Basic Sciences Programme; and the International Geoscience Programme. Through science education and capacity-building initiatives, UNESCO also helps increase the scientific capacity of developing countries for sustainable development.

In the wake of the 1997 *Universal Declaration on the Human Genome and Human Rights*—the first international text on the ethics of genetic research and practice—UNESCO's General Conference adopted the *International Declaration on Human Genetic Data* in 2003, and the *Universal Declaration on Bioethics and Human Rights* in 2005.

In its efforts to facilitate social transformations conducive to the universal values of justice, freedom and human dignity, UNESCO focuses on philosophy and social sciences research, including the ethics of science and technology; promoting and teaching human rights and democracy; combating all forms of discrimination, including those related to illnesses such as HIV/AIDS; and improving the status of women. Central to the work of UNESCO on these issues is its intergovernmental programme on the Management of Social Transformations. In 2005, the UNESCO General Conference adopted *International Convention against Doping in Sport*, which seeks the elimination of doping in sport to the benefit of its potential as a means to promote education, health, development and peace.

Culture and development

UNESCO's cultural activities are concentrated on promoting tangible and intangible heritage, to help achieve sustainable development and social cohesion; protecting and promoting the diversity of cultural expressions and the dialogue of cultures, to foster a culture of peace; and building upon cultural factors for reconciliation and reconstruction in post-conflict and post-natural disaster countries.

In 2003, the UNESCO General Conference adopted the *UNESCO Declaration concerning the Intentional Destruction of Cultural Heritage*, mainly in response to the tragic destruction of the Buddhas of Bamiyan in Afghanistan in 2001. The 2003 *Convention for the Safeguarding of the Intangible Cultural Heritage* covers oral traditions, customs, languages, performing arts, social practices, rituals, festive events, traditional knowledge, traditional crafts, endangered languages and the promotion of linguistic diversity. The 2005 *Convention on the Protection and Promotion of the Diversity of Cultural Expressions*, recognizing cultural goods and services as vehicles of identity and values, seeks to strengthen their creation, production, distribution and enjoyment, particularly by supporting related industries in developing countries.

Sport for development and peace

The **United Nations Office on Sport for Development and Peace (UNOSDP)** (*www. un.org/wcm/content/site/sport/*), based in Geneva, assists the Special Adviser to the United Nations Secretary-General on Sport for Development and Peace in his worldwide activities as an advocate, facilitator and representative of the social purposes of sport. The Office brings the worlds of sport and development together, in particular through the engagement of sport organizations, civil society, athletes and the private sector. Through dialogue, knowledge-sharing and partnerships, UNOSDP encourages cross-cutting and interdisciplinary exchanges between all stakeholders interested in using sport as a tool for education and health. The Office and the Special Adviser also raise awareness about the use of physical activity to advance development and peace, including through the Millennium Development Goals, the promotion of gender equality and the fight against HIV/AIDS. In the lead-up to and during major global sports events such as the FIFA World Cup and the Olympic Games, UNOSDP fosters UN-wide coordination and representation.

Communication and information

UNESCO promotes press freedom and pluralistic, independent media. It works in favour of the free flow of ideas, especially strengthening the communication capacities of developing countries and their access to information and knowledge. It assists member states in adapting their media laws to democratic standards, and in pursuing editorial independence in public and private media. When violations of press freedom occur, UNESCO's Director-General intervenes through diplomatic channels or public statements.

An Alliance of Civilizations

In 2005, Secretary-General Kofi Annan announced a new initiative—the **Alliance of Civilizations** (*www.unaoc.org*). Originally proposed by Spanish Prime Minister José Luis Rodriguez Zapatero and co-sponsored by Turkish Prime Minister Recep Tayyip Erdogan, the Alliance was launched in response to concerns that extremists were exploiting the perception of a widening gap between Islamic and Western societies. It was established as a coalition to advance mutual respect for religious beliefs and traditions, and to reaffirm humanity's increasing interdependence in all areas. The Alliance represents a committed international effort to bridge divides and overcome prejudice, misconceptions, misperceptions and polarization, which threaten world peace.

A high-level group of eminent persons was established to guide the Alliance, including such renowned theologians as Archbishop Desmond Tutu of South Africa, author Karen Armstrong of the United Kingdom, Rabbi Arthur Schneier of the United States, and Prof. Mehmet Aydin of Turkey, as well as administrators of cultural institutions, such as Ismail Serageldin of Egypt's Biblioteca Alexandrina. It is co-chaired by Mr. Aydin and former UNESCO Director-General Federico Mayor.

The group's first report, issued in 2006, analyzed the state of relations between Muslim and Western societies and put forward a range of proposals in the areas of education, media, youth and migration, to build bridges and promote a culture of respect. It also recommended the appointment of a high representative to help defuse crises that arise at the intersection of culture and politics, take steps to restart the Middle East peace process, and encourage political pluralism in Muslim countries.

In 2007, Secretary-General Ban Ki-moon appointed former Portuguese President Jorge Sampaio as the first UN High Representative for the Alliance of Civilizations. In 2010, the Alliance held its third Annual Forum in Rio de Janeiro, aimed at developing partnerships to promote cross-cultural understanding at the global level.

At UNESCO's initiative, 3 May is observed annually as **World Press Freedom Day**. **World Telecommunication and Information Society Day** is celebrated each year on 17 May, on the initiative of the ITU, to promote the vision of a people-centred, inclusive and development-oriented information society.

With the aim of reinforcing developing countries' communication infrastructures and human resources, UNESCO provides training and technical expertise and helps develop national and regional media projects—especially through its International Programme for the Development of Communication.

New information and communication technologies (ICTs) are extending the principle of the free flow of ideas by multiplying the possibilities for producing, disseminating and receiving information on an unprecedented scale. UNESCO seeks to ensure that as many people as possible benefit from these opportunities. Additional issues being addressed by UNESCO include the social and cultural impact of ICTs, and policy approaches to legal and ethical issues relating to cyberspace.

In 2006, the United Nations launched the **Global Alliance for Information and Communication Technologies and Development** (*www.un-gaid.org*). As a network of governments, the private sector, civil society, the technical and Internet communities and academia, the Alliance is a direct response to the demand for an inclusive global forum and platform for cross-sectoral policy dialogue on the use of ICT for achieving internationally agreed development goals, notably the reduction of poverty.

Objectives of the Global Alliance include: incorporating the global ICT agenda into the broader UN development agenda; bringing together key organizations involved in ICT for development (ICT4D) to enhance their collaboration and effectiveness; raising awareness of policy makers on ICT4D policy issues; facilitating identification of technological solutions for specific development goals and pertinent partnerships; creating an enabling environment and innovative business models for pro-poor investment and growth, and for empowering people living in poverty; and acting as a 'think-tank' on ICT4D-related issues and as an advisory group to the Secretary-General.

The **Internet Governance Forum** (*www.intgovforum.org*) brings together governments, the private sector, NGOs and the technical and academic community to discuss Internet governance issues.

Sustainable development

In the first decades of the United Nations, environmental concerns rarely appeared on the international agenda. The related work of the Organization emphasized the exploration and use of natural resources, while seeking to ensure that developing countries in particular would maintain control over their own resources. During the 1960s, agreements were made concerning marine pollution, especially oil spills. Since then, there has been increasing evidence of the deterioration of the environment on a global scale, and the international community has shown increasing alarm over the impact of development on the ecology of the planet and on human well-being. The United Nations has been a leading advocate for environmental concerns, and a leading proponent of 'sustainable development'.

The relationship between economic development and environmental degradation was first placed on the international agenda in 1972, at the United Nations Conference on the Human Environment, held in Stockholm, Sweden. After the Conference, governments set up the **United Nations Environment Programme (UNEP)** (*www.unep.org*), which has become the world's leading environmental agency.

In 1973, the United Nations Sudano-Sahelian Office—now the **Drylands Development Centre** of the United Nations Development Programme (UNDP)—was set up to spearhead efforts to reverse the spread of desertification in West Africa. The Centre later took on a global mandate. In 1996, the entry into force of the *United Nations Convention to Combat Desertification in those Countries Experiencing Serious Drought and/or Desertification, Particularly in Africa* gave added impetus to the Centre's work.

The 1980s witnessed landmark negotiations among member states on environmental issues, including treaties protecting the ozone layer and controlling the movement of toxic wastes. The World Commission on Environment and Development, established in 1983 by the General Assembly, brought a new understanding and sense of urgency to the need for a new kind of development that would ensure economic well-being for present and future generations, while protecting the environmental resources on which all development depends. The Commission's 1987 report to the General Assembly put forward the concept of sustainable development as an alternative to development based simply on unconstrained economic growth. After considering the report, the Assembly called for the United Nations Conference on Environment and Development—the Earth Summit, held in Rio de Janeiro, Brazil, in 1992. Unprecedented in its size, scope and influence, the Earth Summit linked sustainable development with issues of human rights, population, social development and human settlements.

Today, awareness of the need to support and sustain the environment is reflected in virtually all areas of UN work. Dynamic partnerships between the United Nations and governments, NGOs, the scientific community and the private sector are bringing new knowledge and specific action to global environmental problems. For the United Nations, economic and social development are inextricably linked to protection of the environment. Achieving sustainable development requires integrating economic, environmental and social concerns at all levels.

Agenda 21

Governments took an historic step towards ensuring the future of the planet when the Earth Summit adopted *Agenda 21,* a comprehensive plan for global action in all areas of sustainable development. Its implementation and related commitments were reaffirmed at the World Summit on Sustainable Development held in Johannesburg, South Africa, in 2002. In *Agenda 21,* governments outlined actions that could move the world away from an unsustainable model of economic growth towards activities that will protect and renew the environmental resources on which growth and development depend. Areas for action include: protecting the atmosphere; combating deforestation, soil loss and desertification; preventing air and water pollution; halting the depletion of fish stocks; and promoting the safe management of toxic wastes.

Agenda 21 also addresses patterns of development which cause stress to the environment, including: poverty and external debt in developing countries; unsustainable patterns of production and consumption; demographic stress; and the structure of the international economy. The action programme also recommends ways to strengthen the part played by major groups—women, trade unions, farmers, children and young people, indigenous peoples, the scientific community, local authorities, business, industry and NGOs—in achieving sustainable development.

The United Nations has acted to integrate the concept of sustainable development in all relevant policies and programmes. Income-generating projects increasingly take environmental consequences into account. Development assistance programmes are more than ever directed towards women, in view of their roles as producers of goods, services and food, and as caretakers of the environment. The moral and social imperatives for alleviating poverty are given additional urgency by the recognition that poverty eradication and environmental quality go hand-in-hand.

To ensure full support for *Agenda 21,* the General Assembly, in 1992, established the **Commission on Sustainable Development**. A functional commission of ECOSOC, the 53-member body monitors the implementation of *Agenda 21* and the other Earth Summit agreements, as well as the 2002 World Summit on Sustainable Development. It also addresses cross-cutting issues in the context of sustainable development, including those related to poverty eradication; changing patterns of consumption and production; protecting and managing the natural resource

Sustainable development summits

At the United Nations Conference on Environment and Development (UNCED) (Rio de Janeiro, 1992), also known as the Earth Summit, it was agreed that environmental protection and social and economic development are fundamental to *sustainable development*, based on the 'Rio Principles'. To achieve such development, world leaders adopted a global programme entitled *Agenda 21*—a blueprint for action to move the world away from an unsustainable model of economic growth towards one based on the protection and renewal of environmental resources.

In 1997, the General Assembly held a special session (Earth Summit+5) on the implementation of *Agenda 21*. While emphasizing the urgency of putting the *Agenda* into practice, states differed on how to finance sustainable development. The session's final document recommended adopting legally binding targets to reduce emission of greenhouse gases that lead to climate change; moving more forcefully towards sustainable patterns of energy production, distribution and use; and focusing on poverty eradication as a prerequisite for sustainable development.

The World Summit on Sustainable Development (Johannesburg, 2002) reviewed progress since the Earth Summit. Its *Johannesburg Declaration* and 54-page *Plan of Implementation* included commitments on specific time-bound goals relating to sanitation; chemical use and production; the maintenance and restoration of fish stocks; and reducing the loss of biodiversity. The special needs of Africa and of small island developing states were addressed, as were such new issues as sustainable production and consumption patterns, energy and mining.

In 2012, the UN Conference on Sustainable Development, or 'Rio+20', will take place in Rio de Janeiro.

---

base of economic and social development; globalization; health; small island developing states; Africa; gender equality; and education.

The **Division for Sustainable Development** of the UN Department of Economic and Social Affairs (*www.un.org/esa/dsd*)—the secretariat for the Commission—provides technical services for capacity-building in sustainable development, as well as other analytical and information services.

World Summit on Sustainable Development

The 2002 World Summit on Sustainable Development—held in Johannesburg, South Africa, to take stock of achievements, challenges and new issues since the 1992 Earth Summit—was an 'implementation summit' designed to turn the goals, promises and commitments of *Agenda 21* into tangible action. The Summit brought together a wide range of interests. Over 22,000 people participated, including 100 heads of state, more than 8,000 representatives from NGOs, businesses and other major groups, and 4,000 members of the press. At least as many people attended related parallel events.

Member states agreed to the *Johannesburg Declaration on Sustainable Development* and a 54-page *Plan of Implementation* detailing the priorities for action. The Summit reaffirmed sustainable development as a central element of the international agenda. Paving the way for measures addressing some of the world's most pressing challenges, it emphasized the links between economic and social development and the conservation of natural resources. The Summit's internationally agreed commitments were complemented by a range of voluntary partnership initiatives for sustainable development.

Financing sustainable development

At the 1992 Earth Summit, it was agreed that most financing for *Agenda 21* would come from each country's public and private sectors. However, new and additional external funds were deemed necessary to support developing countries' efforts to implement sustainable development practices and protect the global environment.

The **Global Environment Facility (GEF)** (*www.thegef.org/gef*), established in 1991, helps developing countries fund projects that protect the global environment and promote sustainable livelihoods in local communities. Over the years, it has provided more than $9.2 billion in grants and generated over $40 billion in cofinancing from recipient governments, international development agencies, private industry and NGOs to support 2,700 projects in 165 developing countries and economies in transition. GEF funds are the primary means for achieving the goals of the conventions on biological diversity, climate change, desertification and persistent organic pollutants. In line with those goals, GEF projects—principally carried out by UNDP, UNEP and the World Bank—are aimed at conserving and making sustainable use of biological diversity; addressing global climate change; reversing the degradation of international waters; phasing out substances that deplete the ozone layer; combating land degradation and drought; and reducing and eliminating the production and use of certain persistent organic pollutants.

The following agencies also contribute to the management and execution of GEF projects: the African Development Bank (*www.afdb.org*), the Asian Development Bank (*www.adb.org*), the European Bank for Reconstruction and Development (*www.ebrd.org*), the FAO (*www.fao.org*), the Inter-American Development Bank (*www.iadb.org*), the International Fund for Agricultural Development (*www.ifad.org*) and the United Nations Industrial Development Organization (*www.unido.org*)

Action for the environment

The entire United Nations system is engaged in environmental protection in diverse ways. Its lead agency in this area is the **United Nations Environment Programme (UNEP)** (*www.unep.org*). As the environmental conscience of the UN system, UNEP assesses the state of the world's environment and identifies issues requiring international cooperation. It helps formulate international environmental law, and integrate environmental considerations in the social and economic policies and programmes of the UN system. UNEP—with its motto "Environment for Development"—helps solve problems that cannot be handled by countries acting alone. It provides a forum for building consensus and forging international agreements. In doing so, it strives to enhance the participation of business and industry, the scientific and academic communities, NGOs, community groups and others in achieving sustainable development. UNEP's six priority areas are: climate change, disasters and conflicts, ecosystem management, environmental governance, harmful substances, and resource efficiency.

Scientific research promoted and coordinated by UNEP has generated a variety of reports on the state of the environment. Reports such as the *Global Environ-*

Changing human behaviour

Achieving sustainable development worldwide entails changing patterns of production and consumption—what we produce, how it is produced and how much we consume. The United Nations works to support the requisite efforts, in both developed and developing countries, to create and implement relevant policies; to promote cleaner production; to increase awareness; and to enhance corporate and individual responsibility. Discussions on these issues must involve business and industry, governments, consumer organizations, international bodies, the academic community and NGOs.

Using fewer resources and reducing waste is also better business. It saves money and generates higher profits while protecting the environment. It promotes good health by conserving natural resources and creating less pollution, thus sustaining the planet for future generations.

---

ment Outlook (*www.unep.org/geo*) have created worldwide awareness of emerging environmental problems and even triggered international negotiations on environmental conventions. UNEP has a growing network of centres of excellence, including the UNEP World Conservation Monitoring Centre; the Global Resource Information Database; the UNEP Risø Centre on Energy, Climate and Sustainable Development; the UNEP Collaborating Centre on Water and Environment; the Global Reporting Initiative; and the Basel Agency for Sustainable Energy.

UNEP's **Division of Technology, Industry and Economics** (*www.unep.org/ resources/business/DTIE*) is active in UN efforts aimed at encouraging decision makers in government, industry and business to adopt policies, strategies and practices that are cleaner and safer, use natural resources more efficiently, and reduce pollution risks to people and the environment. The Division facilitates the transfer of safer, cleaner and environmentally sound technologies, especially those that deal with urban and freshwater management; helps countries to build capacities for the sound management of chemicals and the improvement of chemical safety worldwide; supports the phase-out of ozone-depleting substances in developing countries and countries with economies in transition; assists decision makers to make better, more informed energy choices; and works with governments and the private sector to integrate environmental considerations into activities, practices, products and services.

UNEP Chemicals (*www.chem.unep.ch*)—the Division's chemicals branch—provides countries with access to information about toxic chemicals; assists countries in building their capacities to produce, use and dispose of chemicals safely; and supports international and regional actions for reducing or eliminating chemical risks. In 2001, UNEP facilitated the completion of the *Stockholm Convention on Persistent Organic Pollutants*, a treaty to reduce and eliminate releases of certain chemicals that remain intact in the environment for long periods, become widely distributed geographically, collect in the fatty tissue of living organisms and are toxic to humans and wildlife. These include pesticides and industrial chemicals and by-products that are highly mobile and accumulate in the food chain.

Over the years, UNEP has been the catalyst for the negotiation of other international agreements that form the cornerstone of UN efforts to halt and reverse damage to the planet. The historic 1987 *Montreal Protocol* and its subsequent amendments seek to preserve the ozone layer in the upper atmosphere. The 1989 *Basel Convention on the Control of Hazardous Wastes and their Disposal* has reduced the danger of pollution from toxic waste. In collaboration with the FAO, UNEP facilitated the negotiation of the 1998 *Rotterdam Convention on the Prior Informed Consent Procedure for Certain Hazardous Chemicals and Pesticides in International Trade*, which gives importing countries the power to decide which chemicals they want to receive and to exclude those they cannot manage safely.

The 1973 *Convention on International Trade in Endangered Species* is universally recognized for its contribution to controlling trade in wildlife products. UNEP assisted African governments in developing the 1994 *Lusaka Agreement on Cooperative Enforcement Operations Directed at Illegal Trade in Wild Fauna and Flora*. The 1992 *Convention on Biological Diversity* and the 2000 *Cartagena Protocol on Biosafety* seek to conserve and encourage the sustainable and equitable use of the planet's wide variety of plants, animals and micro-organisms. UNEP has also helped negotiate and implement conventions on desertification and climate change.

Climate change and global warming

Since the dawn of the industrial age, there has been a steady, and now dangerously increasing build-up of 'greenhouse gases' in the earth's atmosphere, leading to a continuing rise in global temperatures. When fossil fuels are burned to generate energy, or when forests are cut down and burned, carbon dioxide is released. Greenhouse gases—including methane, nitrous oxide and others—have accumulated in the atmosphere to such an extent that the planet now faces the prospect of massive and potentially destructive consequences. The UN system is meeting this challenge head-on through its work on climate change (see *www.un.org/climatechange*).

In 1988, at a time when the best research available was beginning to indicate the possible severity of the problem, two UN bodies—UNEP and the World Meteorological Organization (WMO)—came together to establish the **Intergovernmental Panel on Climate Change (IPCC)** (*www.ipcc.ch*) to assemble the current knowledge on climate change and its potential environmental and socio-economic impact, and to point the way forward. The Panel, a worldwide network of thousands of leading scientists and experts contributing on a voluntary basis, reviews scientific research on the issue, with a view to developing a legally binding and coordinated approach to the problem. In recognition of its work, the Panel was awarded the 2007 Nobel Peace Prize, together with former United States Vice President Albert Arnold (Al) Gore, Jr.

Heeding the warnings of scientists worldwide, the nations of the world came together in Rio de Janeiro in 1992 to sign the *United Nations Framework Convention on Climate Change* (UNFCCC) (*www.unfccc.int*). To date, 194 countries have joined in this international treaty, by which developed countries agreed to reduce to 1990 levels emissions of carbon dioxide and other greenhouse gases they release into the atmosphere. They also agreed to transfer to developing countries the technology and information needed to help them respond to the challenges of climate change.

In 1995, evidence presented by IPCC scientists made it clear that the 1992 target would not be enough to prevent global warming and its associated problems. Therefore, in 1997, countries that had ratified the *Convention* met in Kyoto, Japan, and agreed on a protocol under which developed countries were to reduce their

Synthesis Report on Climate Change

Climate Change 2007: Synthesis Report, issued by the Intergovernmental Panel on Climate Change (IPCC), set out a number of important findings on this issue of vital global concern, including the following:

- "Warming of the climate system is unequivocal, as is now evident from observations of increases in global average air and ocean temperatures, widespread melting of snow and ice, and rising global average sea level ... The temperature increase is widespread over the globe, and is greater at higher northern latitudes."

- "Global GHG [greenhouse gas] emissions due to human activities have grown since pre-industrial times, with an increase of 70 per cent between 1970 and 2004 ... There is *high agreement* and *much evidence* that with the current climate change mitigation policies and related sustainable development practices, global GHG emissions will continue to grow over the next few decades."

- "Continued GHG emissions at or above current rates would cause further warming and induce many changes in the global climate system during the 21st century ... Anthropogenic warming could lead to some impacts that are abrupt or irreversible."

- "There is new and stronger evidence of observed impacts of climate change on unique and vulnerable systems (such as polar and high mountain communities and ecosystems), with increasing levels of adverse impacts as temperatures increase further."

- "There is now higher confidence in the projected increases in droughts, heat waves, and floods as well as their adverse impacts."

- "There is increasing evidence of greater vulnerability of specific groups such as the poor and elderly in not only developing but also developed countries. Moreover, there is increased evidence that low-latitude and less-developed areas generally face greater risk, for example in dry areas and mega-deltas ... Sea level rise under warming is inevitable."

- "A wide variety of policies and instruments are available to governments to create the incentives for mitigation action ... There is *high agreement* and *much evidence* that notable achievements of the UNFCCC and its *Kyoto Protocol* are the establishment of a global response to climate change, stimulation of an array of national policies, and the creation of an international carbon market and new institutional mechanisms that may provide the foundation for future mitigation efforts."

---

collective emissions of six greenhouse gases by 5.2 per cent between 2008 and 2012, taking 1990 levels as the baseline. To date, 192 states have become party to the *Kyoto Protocol,* which also establishes several innovative 'mechanisms' aimed at reducing the costs of curbing emission levels.

The *Protocol* entered into force in 2005. Of the six gases it seeks to control, carbon dioxide, methane and nitrous oxide occur naturally in the atmosphere, but human activities have increased their levels dramatically. Sulfur hexafluoride is a synthetic gas with devastating impact on the atmosphere (1 kg is equal to 22,200 kg of carbon dioxide). As for hydrofluorocarbons (HFCs) and perfluorocarbons (PFCs), which are also synthetic, 1 kg of each is equivalent to many tonnes of carbon dioxide in terms of greenhouse warming. Through the *Protocol*'s Clean Development Mechanism (*www.cdmbazaar.net*), projects that reduce greenhouse gas emissions in developing countries and contribute to sustainable development can earn certified emission reduction credits, which can be bought by industrialized countries to cover a portion of their emission reduction commitments.

When the United Nations first began to mobilize world public opinion to address the threat posed by climate change, there were many who still considered it a mere theory that was unproven. Differences in scientific opinion, though minimal, were vocal, and the means required to make predictive models were still being perfected. In early 2007, however, the Panel, making use of major advances in climate modelling and the collection and analysis of data, and based on a review of the most up-to-date, peer-reviewed scientific literature, reported with 90 per cent certainty that significant global warming was in process and increasing, to a degree that was directly attributable to human activity and that would worsen unless major corrective actions were taken. The Panel's report—*Climate Change 2007*—represents a consensus agreement of climate scientists and experts from 40 countries and has been endorsed by 113 governments. It indicates that the world faces an average temperature rise of around 3 degrees Celsius by the end of this century if greenhouse gas emissions continue to rise at their current pace. The results of such an increase would include more extreme temperatures; heat waves; new wind patterns; worsening drought in some regions and heavier precipitation in others; melting glaciers and Arctic ice; and rising sea levels worldwide. While the number of tropical cyclones (typhoons and hurricanes) is projected to decline, their intensity is expected to increase, with higher peak wind speeds and more intense precipitation due to warmer ocean waters.

The *Hyogo Framework for Action, 2005–2015*, adopted by 168 nations at the 2005 UN World Conference on Disaster Reduction in Kobe, Japan, includes recommendations that can be effective in reducing the disaster risks caused by climate-related hazards. Ultimately, however, the only effective course is to turn back the tide of global warming by restoring the sustainability of the atmosphere. Fortunately, the means to do so have been outlined, and the goal can be accomplished if the people of the world come together to make it happen. In addition to action contemplated in such international agreements as the *Framework Convention on Climate Change* and its *Kyoto Protocol*, the United Nations recognizes that individuals, municipalities, NGOs and other bodies all have a part to play. For example, the UNEP Plant for the Planet: Billion Tree Campaign, a worldwide tree-planting initiative launched in 2006 to help mitigate the build-up of carbon dioxide, resulted in more than 7.4 billion trees planted by the end of 2009.

In 2007, the UN Foundation and Sigma Xi, the Scientific Research Society, published a report entitled *Confronting Climate Change: Avoiding the Unmanageable and Managing the Unavoidable*. It concluded that the world community could significantly slow and then reduce global emissions of greenhouse gases over the next several decades by exploiting cost-effective policies and current and emerging technologies. Its policy recommendations dealt with vehicle efficiency standards, fuel taxes, and support for the purchase of efficient and alternative fuel vehicles; improved design and efficiency of commercial and residential buildings; and incentives and financing for energy-efficiency investments. It also called on the international community, through the UN and related multilateral institutions, to help countries in need to finance and deploy new, energy-efficient technologies.

Also in 2007, in an unprecedented move highlighting the urgent need for concerted international action to deal with the problem of climate change, the UN Security Council held an open debate on energy, security and climate. Addressing that debate, Secretary-General Ban Ki-moon called for "a long-term global response, in line with the latest scientific findings, and compatible with economic and social development." Describing climate change as "a defining issue of our era," he identified it as one of his top priorities, and named a number of special envoys to discuss the issue with the world's national leaders.

Ozone depletion

The ozone layer is a thin layer of gas in the stratosphere, more than 10 kilometres (6 miles) above the ground, that shields the earth's surface from the sun's damaging ultraviolet rays. In the mid-1970s, it was discovered that certain man-made chemicals, including the chlorofluorocarbons (CFCs) used for refrigeration, air conditioning and industrial cleaning, were destroying atmospheric ozone and depleting the ozone layer. This became a matter of increasing international concern, since greater exposure to ultraviolet radiation results in skin cancer, eye cataracts and suppression of the human immune system; it also causes unpredictable damage to the global ecosystem.

In response to this challenge, UNEP helped negotiate the historic 1985 *Vienna Convention for the Protection of the Ozone Layer*, along with the 1987 *Montreal Protocol* and its amendments. Under these agreements, which UNEP now administers, developed countries banned the production and sale of chlorofluorocarbons, and developing countries are required to stop their production by 2010. Schedules were also put in place to phase out other ozone-depleting substances. UNEP's **Ozone Secretariat** (*ozone.unep.org*) has documented clear evidence of a recent decrease in the atmospheric burden of ozone-depleting substances in the lower atmosphere and in the stratosphere, as well as early signs of the expected ozone recovery of the stratosphere. In its view, continued elimination of all emissions of ozone-depleting substances should help restore the global ozone layer to pre-1980 levels by 2035.

Small islands

Small islands share specific disadvantages and vulnerabilities. Their ecological fragility, small size, limited resources and isolation from markets limit their ability to take advantage of globalization, posing a major obstacle to their socio-economic development. This makes sustainable development a unique challenge for them (see *www.un.org/ohrlls*). At present, 51 small island developing states and territories are included in the list used by the UN Department of Economic and Social Affairs in monitoring progress towards the implementation of the *Barbados Programme of Action*, adopted in 1994 at the Global Conference on the Sustainable Development of Small Island Developing States. The *Programme of Action* sets forth policies, actions and measures at all levels to promote sustainable development in these states.

In 2005, the international community, meeting at Mauritius to conduct a 10-year review of the *Programme of Action*, approved a wide-ranging set of further recommendations, known as the *Mauritius Strategy*. The *Strategy* addresses such issues as climate change and rising sea levels; natural and environmental disasters; waste management; coastal, marine, freshwater, land, energy, tourism and biodiversity resources; transportation and communication; science and technology; globalization and trade liberalization; sustainable production and consumption, capacity-building, and education for sustainable development; health; culture; and knowledge management and information for decision-making.

Sustainable forest management

With international trade in forest products generating hundreds of billions of dollars annually, more than 1.6 billion people around the world depend to varying degrees on forests for their livelihoods. As the foundation for indigenous knowledge, forests provide profound socio-cultural benefits. As ecosystems, they play a critical role in mitigating the effects of climate change and protecting biodiversity. While the rate of net forest loss is slowing down, thanks to new planting and natural expansion of existing forests, every year, some 13 million hectares of the world's forests are lost to deforestation, which in turn accounts for up to 20 per cent of the global greenhouse gas emissions that contribute to global warming. The world's forests and forest soils store more than one trillion tons of carbon—twice the amount found in the atmosphere.

The most common causes of deforestation are unsustainable timber harvesting, the conversion of forests to agricultural land, unsound land management practices, and the creation of human settlements. The UN has been at the forefront of the movement towards sustainable forest management since the 1992 Earth Summit, which adopted a non-binding statement of forest principles.

From 1995 to 2000, the Intergovernmental Panel on Forests and the Intergovernmental Forum on Forests, acting under the UN Commission on Sustainable Development, were the main intergovernmental forums for the development of forest policy. In 2000, the Economic and Social Council established the **United Nations Forum on Forests** (*www.un.org/esa/forests*), a high-level intergovernmental body charged with strengthening long-term political commitment for sustainable forest management.

In 2007, the Forum adopted a landmark agreement on international forest policy and cooperation: the *Non-Legally Binding Instrument on All Types of Forests*, adopted by the General Assembly the same year. Although the agreement is non-binding and includes a voluntary global financing mechanism, it nevertheless sets a standard in forest management aimed at reducing deforestation, preventing forest degradation, promoting sustainable livelihoods and reducing poverty for all forest-dependent peoples.

At the invitation of ECOSOC, the heads of relevant international organizations have also formed a 14-member **Collaborative Partnership on Forests**, which fosters cooperation and coordination in support of the goals of the UN Forum on Forests and the implementation of sustainable forest management worldwide. To bolster efforts towards the achievement of those goals, the General Assembly, in 2006, proclaimed 2011 as the International Year of Forests.

Desertification

Deserts are harsh, dry environments where few people live. Drylands, which cover about 41 per cent of the earth's land area, are characterized by low rainfall and high rates of evaporation. They are home to more than 2 billion people, including half of all those living in poverty worldwide. Some 1.8 billion of these people live in developing countries, and lag far behind the rest of the world in terms of development indicators.

Desertification is land degradation in arid, semi-arid and dry, sub-humid areas resulting from various factors, including climatic variations and human activities. Land degradation in drylands is the reduction or loss of biological or economic productivity in such areas. Its main human causes are overcultivation, overgrazing, deforestation and poor irrigation. UNEP has estimated that it affects one third of the earth's surface and more than 1 billion people in more than 110 countries. Sub-Saharan Africa, where two thirds of the land is either desert or dryland, is particularly at risk.

The consequences of desertification and drought include food insecurity, famine and poverty. Ensuing social, economic and political tensions can create conflicts, cause more impoverishment and further increase land degradation. Growing desertification worldwide threatens to increase by millions the number of poor people forced to seek new homes and livelihoods.

The 1994 *United Nations Convention to Combat Desertification in those Countries Experiencing Serious Drought and/or Desertification, Particularly in Africa* (*www.unccd.int*) seeks to address this problem. It focuses on rehabilitation of land, improving productivity, and the conservation and management of land and water resources. The *Convention* emphasizes the establishment of an enabling environment for local people to help reverse land degradation. It also sets out criteria for the preparation by affected countries of national action programmes and gives an unprecedented role to NGOs in preparing and carrying out such programmes. The *Convention*, which entered into force in 1996, has 193 states parties.

Many UN bodies provide assistance to combat desertification. UNDP funds anti-desertification activities through its Nairobi-based Drylands Development Centre (*www.undp.org/drylands*). The IFAD has committed more than $3.5 billion over the last three decades to support dryland development. The World Bank organizes and funds programmes aimed at protecting fragile drylands and increasing their agricultural productivity. The FAO provides practical help to governments for sustainable agricultural development. UNEP supports regional action programmes, data assessment, capacity-building and public awareness of the problem.

Biodiversity, pollution and overfishing

Biodiversity—the world's resplendent variety of plant and animal species—is essential for human survival. The protection and conservation of the diverse species of animal and plant life and their habitats is the aim of the 1992 *United Nations Convention on Biological Diversity* (*www.cbd.int*), to which 193 states are party. The *Convention* obligates states to conserve biodiversity, ensure its sustainable development, and provide for the fair and equitable sharing of benefits from the use of genetic resources. Its *Cartagena Protocol on Biosafety*, which entered into force in 2003, aims to ensure the safe use of genetically modified organisms. It has 143 states parties.

Protection of endangered species is also enforced under the 1973 *Convention on International Trade in Endangered Species* (*www.cites.org*), administered by UNEP.

The 175 states parties to the *Convention* meet periodically to update the list of plant and animal species or products, such as ivory, that should be protected by quotas or outright bans. The 1979 *Bonn Convention on the Conservation of Migratory Species of Wild Animals (www.cms.int)*, along with a series of associated agreements, aims to conserve terrestrial, marine and avian migratory species and their habitats, especially those threatened with extinction; the treaty has 114 states parties. UNESCO's **Man and the Biosphere Programme** (*www.unesco.org/mab*) concerns itself with the sustainable use and conservation of biological diversity, as well as the improvement of the relationship between people and their environment worldwide. The Programme combines natural and social sciences, economics and education to improve livelihoods and safeguard natural ecosystems, and so promote innovative approaches to economic development that are socially and culturally appropriate, as well as environmentally sustainable.

Caused by emissions of sulphur dioxide from industrial manufacturing processes, **acid rain** has been significantly reduced in much of Europe and North America, thanks to the 1979 *Convention on Long-Range Transboundary Air Pollution (www.unece.org/env/lrtap)*. The *Convention*, to which 51 states are party, is administered by the United Nations Economic Commission for Europe. Its scope has been extended by eight specific protocols, addressing such issues as ground-level ozone, persistent organic pollutants, heavy metals, further reduction of sulphur emissions, volatile organic compounds and nitrogen oxides.

Hazardous wastes and chemicals. To regulate the millions of tons of toxic waste that cross national borders each year, member states negotiated, in 1989, the *Basel Convention on the Control of Transboundary Movements of Hazardous Wastes and their Disposal (www.basel.int)*, administered by UNEP. The *Convention*, to which 175 states are party, was strengthened in 1995 to ban the export of toxic waste to developing countries, which often do not have the technology for safe disposal. In 1999, governments adopted the *Basel Protocol on Liability and Compensation* to deal with the question of financial responsiblity in the event of the illegal dumping or accidental spills of hazardous wastes.

High-seas fishing. Overfishing and the near exhaustion of many species of commercially valuable fish, along with the increasing incidence of illegal, unregulated and unreported fishing on the high seas, have led governments to call for measures to conserve and sustainably manage fish resources—especially those that migrate across broad areas of the ocean or move through the economic zone of more than one country. The 1995 *Agreement for the Implementation of the Provisions of the United Nations Convention on the Law of the Sea of 10 December 1982 relating to the Conservation and Management of Straddling Fish Stocks and Highly Migratory Fish Stocks,* which entered into force in 2001, provides a regime for the conservation and management of these stocks, with a view to ensuring their long-term conservation and sustainable use. It has 78 states parties, including the European Union.

Protecting the marine environment

Coastal and marine areas cover some 70 per cent of the earth's surface and are vital to the planet's life support system. Protecting the marine environment has become a primary concern of the United Nations, and UNEP has worked hard to focus the world's attention on oceans and seas.

Most water pollution comes from industrial wastes, mining, agricultural activities and emissions from motor vehicles; some of these forms of pollution occur thousands of miles inland. The **Global Programme of Action for the Protection of the Marine Environment from Land-based Activities** (*www.gpa.unep.org*), adopted in 1995 under UNEP auspices, is considered a milestone in international efforts to protect oceans, estuaries and coastal waters from such pollution.

Under its **Regional Seas Programme** (*www.unep.org/regionalseas*), which now covers more than 140 countries, UNEP addresses the accelerating degradation of the world's oceans and coastal areas through the sustainable management and use of the marine and coastal environment. The Programme works to protect shared marine and water resources through 13 conventions or action plans. Regional programmes, established under the auspices of UNEP, cover the Black Sea, East Asian Seas, Eastern Africa, the Regional Organization for the Protection of the Marine Environment (ROPME) Sea Area, the Mediterranean, the North-East Pacific, the North-West Pacific, the Red Sea and the Gulf of Aden, the South Asian Seas, the Pacific, the South-East Pacific, Western Africa and the Wider Caribbean.

Despite the dramatic expansion of world shipping, oil pollution from ships was reduced by around 60 per cent during the 1980s, and has continued to decline since then. This has been due partly to the introduction of better methods of controlling the disposal of wastes and partly to the tightening of controls through international conventions (*http://oils.gpa.unep.org*). The **International Maritime Organization (IMO)** (*www.imo.org*) is the UN specialized agency responsible for measures to help prevent marine pollution from ships and improve the safety of international shipping. The pioneering *International Convention for the Prevention of Pollution of the Sea by Oil* was adopted in 1954, and the IMO took over responsibility for it five years later. In the late 1960s, a number of major tanker accidents led to further action. Since then, the IMO has developed many measures to help prevent accidents at sea and oil spills; minimize the consequences of accidents and spills; and combat marine pollution, including that caused by the dumping of wastes generated by land-based activities.

Among the main international treaties in this area are: the 1969 *International Convention Relating to Intervention on the High Seas in Cases of Oil Pollution Casualties*; the 1972 *Convention on the Prevention of Marine Pollution by Dumping of Wastes and Other Matter*; and the 1990 *International Convention on Oil Pollution Preparedness, Response and Cooperation*.

The IMO has also tackled environmental threats caused by such routine operations as the cleaning of oil cargo tanks and the disposal of engine-room wastes, which, in terms of tonnage, constitute a bigger menace than accidents. The most important of related measures is the *International Convention for the Prevention of Marine Pollution from Ships, 1973, as modified by the Protocol of 1978 relating thereto.* It covers not only accidental and operational oil pollution, but also pollution by chemicals, packaged goods, sewage and garbage; a 1997 Annex addresses the prevention of air pollution from ships. Amendments to the *Convention* adopted in 1992 oblige all new oil tankers to be fitted with double hulls, or a design that provides equivalent cargo protection in the event of a collision or grounding, phasing out existing single-hull tankers by 2010, with certain exceptions.

Two IMO treaties—the 1969 *International Convention on Civil Liability for Oil Pollution Damage* and the 1971 *International Convention on the Establishment of an International Fund for Oil Pollution Damage*—established a system for providing compensation to those who have suffered financially as a result of pollution. The treaties, revised in 1992, enable victims of oil pollution to obtain compensation much more simply and quickly than had been possible before.

Weather, climate and water

From weather prediction to climate-change research and early warning on natural hazards, the **World Meteorological Organization (WMO)** (*www.wmo.int*) coordinates global scientific efforts to provide timely and accurate information on the state and behaviour of the Earth's atmosphere, its interaction with the oceans, the climate it produces and the resulting distribution of water resources. In the UN system, the WMO organizes and facilitates international cooperation in establishing and operating networks of stations for making meteorological, hydrological and related observations. It promotes the rapid exchange of meteorological information, standardization of meteorological observations, and uniform publication of observations and statistics. It also extends the application of meteorology to aviation, shipping, agriculture and other weather-sensitive socio-economic activities; promotes water resources development; and encourages research and training.

The World Weather Watch is the backbone of WMO activities. It offers up-to-the-minute worldwide weather information through observation systems and telecommunication links operated by member states and territories, employing satellites, aircraft, land observation stations, ship stations, moored buoys and drifting buoys carrying automatic weather stations. The resulting data, analysis and forecasts are exchanged every day, freely and without restriction, between WMO centres and weather offices in every country. As a result, a five-day weather forecast today is as reliable as a two-day forecast was 20 years ago.

The WMO makes it possible for complex international agreements on weather standards, codes, measurements and communications to be established. The Tropical Cyclone Programme helps countries vulnerable to cyclones minimize destruction and loss of life by improving forecasting and warning systems and disaster preparedness. The WMO Natural Disaster Prevention and Mitigation Programme ensures the integration of various WMO programme activities in this area and coordinates them with related activities of international, regional and national organizations, including civil defence bodies, particularly with respect to risk assessment, early warning systems, and capacity-building. It also provides scientific and technical support for the WMO's response to disaster situations.

The **World Climate Programme** collects and preserves climate data, helping governments plan for climate change. Such information can improve economic and social planning. The Programme can also warn governments of impending climate variations (such as the El Niño and La Niña phenomena) and their impact several months ahead of time, as well as of changes—natural or man-made—that could affect critical human activities. To assess all available information on climate change, the WMO and UNEP established in 1988 the Intergovernmental Panel on Climate Change (IPCC) (*www.ipcc.ch*).

The **Atmospheric Research and Environment Programme** coordinates research on the structure and composition of the atmosphere, the physics and chemistry of clouds, weather modification, tropical meteorology, and weather forecasting. It helps member states conduct research projects, disseminate scientific information, and incorporate the results of research into forecasting and other techniques. Under the Global Atmosphere Watch, a network of global and regional monitoring stations and satellites assesses the levels of greenhouse gases, ozone, radionuclides and other traces of gases and particles in the atmosphere.

The **Applications of Meteorology Programme** helps countries apply meteorology to the protection of life and property and to social and economic development. It seeks to improve public weather services; increase the safety of sea and air travel; reduce the impact of desertification; and improve agriculture and the management of water, energy and other resources. In agriculture, for instance, prompt meteorological advice can mean a substantial reduction in losses caused by droughts, pests and disease.

The **Hydrology and Water Resources Programme** helps assess, manage and conserve global water resources. It promotes global cooperation in evaluating water resources and developing hydrological networks and services, including data collection and processing, hydrological forecasting and warning, and the supply of meteorological and hydrological data for design purposes. It facilitates cooperation with respect to water basins shared between countries, and provides specialized forecasting in flood-prone areas, thus helping preserve life and property.

The WMO Space Programme contributes to the Global Observing System of the World Weather Watch and other WMO-supported programmes and associated observing systems. The Education and Training Programme and the Technical Cooperation Programme encourage the exchange of scientific knowledge, the development of technical expertise and the transfer of technology.

Natural resources and energy

The United Nations has long assisted countries in managing their natural resources. As early as 1952, the General Assembly declared that developing countries had "the right to determine freely the use of their natural resources" and that they should use such resources towards realizing economic development plans in accordance with their national interests.

Water resources. It has been estimated that around 1 billion people lack basic access to a sufficient water supply, defined as a source likely to provide 20 litres per person per day at a distance no greater than 1 kilometre (a 30-minute round-trip journey). Such sources would include household connections, public standpipes, boreholes, protected dug wells, protected springs and rainwater collections. The United Nations has long been addressing the global crisis caused by growing demands on the world's water resources to meet human, commercial and agricultural needs, as well as the need for basic sanitation. The United Nations Water Conference (1977), the International Drinking Water Supply and Sanitation Decade (1981–1990), the International Conference on Water and the Environment (1992) and the Earth Summit (1992) all focused on this vital resource. The Decade, in particular, helped some 1.3 billion people in developing countries gain access to safe drinking water.

Causes of inadequate water supply include inefficient use, degradation of water by pollution, and over-exploitation of groundwater reserves. Corrective action aims at achieving better management of scarce freshwater resources, with a particular focus on supply and demand, quantity and quality. UN system activities focus on the sustainable development of fragile and finite freshwater resources,

UN-Water

In the UN *Millennium Declaration* of 2000, the international community pledged to halve the total number of people who do not have access to clean water and stop the unsustainable exploitation of water resources by developing water management strategies at the local, regional and national levels by 2015. Launched in the wake of the World Summit on Sustainable Development, UN-Water has served as a mechanism of the United Nations to monitor and track progress relating to all freshwater and sanitation issues. The attainment of the Millennium Development Goals is strongly contingent upon universal access to safe, clean water.

The UN-Water flagship publication—the *United Nations World Water Development Report*—is released every three years as a comprehensive analysis on the state of the world's freshwater resources. It offers recommendations on ways to implement a sustainable use of water.

The first report, issued in 2003, established 11 challenges as a basis for monitoring future action, including meeting basic needs for safe and sufficient water and sanitation, protecting ecosystems, and effective water governance to promote the long-term viability of sustainable water use. The second report assessed freshwater resources throughout the globe, while addressing the effects of external sociopolitical factors such as increasing urbanization, population growth and food production. The third report addressed the demands of the Millennium Development Goals in relation to biodiversity, climate change, groundwater and biofuels, among other topics.

---

which are under increasing stress from population growth, pollution and the demands of agricultural and industrial uses. The crucial importance of water to so many aspects of health, development and well-being also led to specific water-related targets in support of every one of the Millennium Development Goals.

To help raise public awareness of the importance of intelligent development of freshwater resources, the General Assembly declared 2003 the UN International Year of Freshwater. Also that year, the United Nations System Chief Executives Board for Coordination (CEB) established **UN-Water** (*www.unwater.org*)—an interagency mechanism to coordinate UN system actions to achieve the water-related goals of the *Millennium Declaration* and the 2002 World Summit on Sustainable Development. To further strengthen global action to meet the water-related MDG targets, the Assembly proclaimed the period 2005–2015 the **International Decade for Action "Water for Life"**; the Decade began on 22 March 2005, observed annually as **World Water Day**. In 2009, UNESCO published the third edition of the triennial *United Nations World Water Development Report*. According to the report, global efforts were on track to halve, by 2015, the proportion of people without sustainable access to safe drinking water, part of the MDG target that also aimed to halve the proportion of people without access to basic sanitation.

Sanitation. The 2009 *World Water Development Report* estimated that while all regions were on track to meet the MDG target on water and sanitation as it pertained to access to safe drinking water, 2.4 billion people would still lack access to basic sanitation, defined as connection to a public sewer or septic system, a pour-flush latrine, a simple pit latrine, or a ventilated and improved pit latrine. Beyond the immediate short-term health benefits, investment in safe drinking water and sanitation makes good economic sense. For each $1 invested, the WHO estimates returns of $3–$34, depending on the region and technology. The overall economic loss in Africa alone due to lack of access to safe water and basic sanitation is estimated at $28.4 billion a year, or around 5 per cent of GDP.

Energy. About one quarter of the world's population lives without electricity, and even more people lack access to modern fuels for cooking and heating. Yet while an adequate supply of energy is essential to economic advancement and poverty eradication, the environmental and health effects of conventional energy systems are a matter of concern. Moreover, the increasing demand for energy per capita, coupled with the rising global population, is resulting in consumption levels that cannot be sustained using current energy systems.

UN system activities on energy help developing countries in many ways, including through education, training and capacity-building, assistance in policy reforms, and the provision of energy services. However, while efforts are being made to move towards renewable sources of energy that are significantly less polluting, additional demand still outpaces the introduction of new capacity. Further effort is needed to improve energy efficiency and move towards cleaner fossil fuel technologies in the transition towards sustainable development.

In 2004, the CEB established **UN-Energy** (*esa.un.org/un-energy*) as the principal inter-agency mechanism in the field of energy. Its task is to help ensure coherence in the UN system's response to the 2002 World Summit on Sustainable Development, as well as the engagement of major actors from the private sector and the NGO community for implementing the Summit's energy-related decisions.

Nuclear safety

Today, 439 nuclear power reactors produce approximately 16 per cent of the world's electricity. In nine countries, over 40 per cent of energy production comes from nuclear power. The **International Atomic Energy Agency (IAEA)** (*www.iaea.org*), a member of the United Nations family, fosters the development of the safe, secure and peaceful uses of atomic energy, playing a prominent role in international efforts to ensure the use of nuclear technology for sustainable development. In the current debate on energy options to curb carbon dioxide emissions, which contribute to global warming, the IAEA has stressed the benefits of nuclear power as an energy source free of greenhouse and other toxic gas emissions. The IAEA serves as the world's central intergovernmental forum for scientific and technical cooperation in the nuclear field. It is a focal point for the exchange of information and the formulation of guidelines and norms in the area of nuclear safety, as well as for the provision of advice to governments, at their request, on ways to improve the safety of reactors and avoid the risk of accidents.

The Agency's responsibility in the area of nuclear safety has increased as nuclear-power programmes have grown and the public has focused its attention on safety aspects. The IAEA formulates basic standards for radiation protection and issues, regulations and codes of practice on specific types of operations, including the safe transport of radioactive materials. Acting under the *Convention on Assistance in the Case of a Nuclear Accident or Radiological Emergency* and the *Convention on Early Notification of a Nuclear Accident*, both adopted in 1986, the Agency facilitates emergency assistance to member states in the event of a radiation accident.

Other international treaties for which the IAEA is the depositary include the 1987 *Convention on the Physical Protection of Nuclear Material*, the 1963 *Vienna Convention on Civil Liability for Nuclear Damage*, the 1994 *Convention on Nuclear Safety*, and the 1997 *Joint Convention on the Safety of Spent Fuel Management and on the Safety of Radioactive Waste Management*.

The IAEA's technical cooperation programme provides assistance in the form of in-country projects, experts, and training in the application of peaceful nuclear techniques. These help countries in such critical areas as water, health, nutrition, medicine and food production. Examples include work related to mutation breeding, through which beneficial varieties of crops have been developed using radiation-based technology, thereby improving food production. Another is the use of isotope hydrology to map underground aquifers, manage ground and surface water, detect and control pollution, and monitor dam leakage and safety, thus improving access to safe drinking water. Still another example concerns medical treatment, in which the Agency supplies radiotherapy equipment and trains staff to safely treat cancer patients in developing and middle-income countries.

The IAEA collects and disseminates information on virtually every aspect of nuclear science and technology through its International Nuclear Information System, based in Vienna. With UNESCO, it operates the International Centre for Theoretical Physics in Trieste, Italy (*www.ictp.trieste.it*), and maintains several laboratories. The IAEA works with the FAO in research on atomic energy in food and agriculture, and with the WHO on radiation in medicine and biology. Its Marine Environment Laboratory in Monaco carries out worldwide marine pollution studies with UNEP and UNESCO.

The **United Nations Scientific Committee on the Effects of Atomic Radiation (UNSCEAR)** (*www.unscear.org*), established in 1955, assesses and reports on the levels and effects of exposure to ionizing radiation. Governments and organizations worldwide rely on its estimates as the scientific basis for evaluating radiation risk, establishing radiation protection and safety standards, and regulating radiation sources.

South Africa holds first all-race elections
Nelson Mandela, President of the African National Congress, casting the ballot in his country's first all-race elections, at Ohlange High School near Durban (1 April 1994, UN Photo/Chris Sattlberger).

IV. HUMAN RIGHTS

One of the great achievements of the United Nations is the creation of a comprehensive body of human rights law—a universal and internationally protected code to which all nations can subscribe and all people aspire (see *www.un.org/rights*). The United Nations has defined a broad range of internationally accepted rights, including civil, cultural, economic, political and social rights. It has also established mechanisms to promote and protect these rights and to assist states in carrying out their responsibilities.

The foundations of this body of law are the *Charter of the United Nations* and the *Universal Declaration of Human Rights*, adopted by the General Assembly in 1945 and 1948, respectively. Since then, the United Nations has gradually expanded human rights law to encompass specific standards for women, children, persons with disabilities, minorities and other vulnerable groups, who now possess rights that protect them from discrimination that had long been common in many societies.

Rights have been extended through groundbreaking General Assembly decisions that have gradually established their universality, indivisibility and interrelatedness with development and democracy. Education campaigns have informed the world's public of their inalienable rights, while numerous national judicial and penal systems have been enhanced through UN training programmes and technical advice. The UN machinery for monitoring compliance with human rights treaties has acquired a remarkable cohesiveness and weight among member states.

The United Nations High Commissioner for Human Rights works to strengthen and coordinate UN efforts for the protection and promotion of the human rights of all persons around the world. Human rights, however, is a central theme that unifies the Organization's work in the key areas of peace and security, development, humanitarian assistance, and economic and social affairs. As a result, virtually every UN body and specialized agency is involved to some degree in the protection of human rights.

Human rights instruments

At the San Francisco Conference in 1945 that established the United Nations, some 40 non-governmental organizations (NGOs) representing women, trade unions, ethnic organizations and religious groups joined forces with government delegations, mostly from smaller countries, and pressed for more specific language on human rights than had been proposed by other states. Their determined lobbying resulted in the inclusion of some provisions on human rights in the **United Nations Charter**, laying the foundation for the post-1945 era of international lawmaking.

Thus, the Preamble to the Charter explicitly reaffirms "faith in fundamental human rights, in the dignity and worth of the human person, in the equal rights of men and women and of nations large and small". Article 1 establishes that one of the four principal tasks of the United Nations is to promote and encourage "respect for human rights and for fundamental freedoms for all without distinction as to race, sex, language, or religion". Other provisions commit states to take action in cooperation with the United Nations to achieve universal respect for human rights.

International Bill of Human Rights

Three years after the United Nations was created, the General Assembly laid the cornerstone of contemporary human rights law: the *Universal Declaration of Human Rights*, intended as a "common standard of achievement for all peoples". It was adopted on 10 December 1948, the day now observed worldwide as **International Human Rights Day**. Its 30 articles spell out basic civil, cultural, economic, political and social rights that all human beings in every country must enjoy.

The provisions of the *Universal Declaration* are considered by scholars to have the weight of customary international law because they are so widely accepted and used to measure the conduct of states. Many newly independent countries have cited the *Universal Declaration* or included its provisions in their basic laws or constitutions.

The broadest legally binding human rights agreements negotiated under UN auspices are the *International Covenant on Economic, Social and Cultural Rights* and the *International Covenant on Civil and Political Rights*. These agreements, adopted by the General Assembly in 1966, take the provisions of the *Universal Declaration* a step further by translating these rights into legally binding commitments, while committees of experts (Treaty Bodies) monitor compliance of states parties.

Together, the *Universal Declaration*, the *International Covenants* and the *First* and *Second Optional Protocols to the International Covenant on Civil and Political Rights* constitute the *International Bill of Human Rights*.

Economic, social and cultural rights

The *International Covenant on Economic, Social and Cultural Rights* entered into force in 1976, and had 160 states parties by the end of 2010. The human rights that the *Covenant* seeks to promote and protect include:

- the right to work in just and favourable conditions;
- the right to social protection, to an adequate standard of living and to the highest attainable standards of physical and mental well-being;
- the right to education and the enjoyment of benefits of cultural freedom and scientific progress.

The *Covenant* provides for the realization of these rights without discrimination of any kind. The **Committee on Economic, Social and Cultural Rights** (*www2. ohchr.org/english/bodies/cescr*) was established in 1985 by the Economic and Social Council (ECOSOC) to monitor implementation of the *Covenant* by states parties. This 18-member body of experts studies reports periodically submitted by states parties in accordance with Article 16 of the *Covenant* and discusses them with representatives of the states concerned. The Committee makes recommendations to states based on its review of their reports. It also adopts general comments which seek to outline the meaning of human rights or cross-cutting themes.

After much campaigning, a major new development occurred in 2008 with regard to individual complaints. That year the General Assembly unanimously adopted an *Optional Protocol* to the *Covenant* which provides the Committee on Economic, Social and Cultural Rights competence to receive and consider communications. The *Optional Protocol* was opened for signature in 2009, and had 35 signatories and 3 states parties by the end of 2010. It will enter into force when ratified by 10 states parties.

Defining universal rights

The *Universal Declaration of Human Rights* is the cornerstone of the wide-ranging body of human rights law created over the decades since the end of World War II.

Articles 1 and 2 state that "all human beings are born equal in dignity and rights" and are entitled to all the rights and freedoms set forth in the *Declaration* "without distinction of any kind such as race, colour, sex, language, religion, political or other opinion, national or social origin, property, birth or other status".

Articles 3 to 21 set forth the civil and political rights to which all human beings are entitled, including:

- the right to life, liberty and security;
- freedom from slavery and servitude;
- freedom from torture or cruel, inhuman or degrading treatment or punishment;
- the right to recognition as a person before the law; the right to judicial remedy; freedom from arbitrary arrest, detention or exile; the right to a fair trial and public hearing by an independent and impartial tribunal; the right to be presumed innocent until proved guilty;
- freedom from arbitrary interference with privacy, family, home or correspondence; freedom from attacks upon honour and reputation; the right to protection of the law against such attacks;
- freedom of movement; the right to seek asylum; the right to a nationality;
- the right to marry and to found a family; the right to own property;
- freedom of thought, conscience and religion; freedom of opinion and expression;
- the right to peaceful assembly and association;
- the right to take part in government and to equal access to public service.

Articles 22 to 27 set forth the economic, social and cultural rights to which all human beings are entitled, including:

- the right to social security;
- the right to work; the right to equal pay for equal work; the right to form and join trade unions;
- the right to rest and leisure;
- the right to a standard of living adequate for health and well-being;
- the right to education;
- the right to participate in the cultural life of the community.

Finally, Articles 28 to 30 recognize that everyone is entitled to a social and international order in which the human rights set forth in the *Declaration* may be fully realized; that these rights may only be limited for the sole purpose of securing recognition and respect of the rights and freedoms of others and of meeting the requirements of morality, public order and the general welfare in a democratic society; and that each person has duties to the community in which she or he lives.

Civil and political rights

The *International Covenant on Civil and Political Rights* and its *First Optional Protocol* entered into force in 1976. The *Covenant* had 167 states parties by the end of 2010. The *Second Optional Protocol* was adopted in 1989.

- The *Covenant* deals with such rights as freedom of movement; equality before the law; the right to a fair trial and presumption of innocence; freedom of thought, conscience and religion; freedom of opinion and expression; peaceful assembly; freedom of association; participation in public affairs and elections; and protection of minority rights.

- It prohibits arbitrary deprivation of life; torture, cruel or degrading treatment or punishment; slavery and forced labour; arbitrary arrest or detention; arbitrary interference with privacy; war propaganda; discrimination; and advocacy of racial or religious hatred.

The *Covenant* has two optional protocols. The *First Optional Protocol* (1966) provides the right of petition to individuals who claim to be victims of a violation of a right contained in the *Covenant*; it had 113 states parties at the end of 2010. The *Second Optional Protocol* (1989) establishes substantive obligations towards abolition of the death penalty; it had 72 states parties at the end of 2010.

The *Covenant* established an 18-member **Human Rights Committee** *(www2. ohchr.org/english/bodies/hrc/index.htm)* which considers reports submitted periodically by states parties on measures taken in their countries to implement the provisions of the *Covenant*. For states parties to the *First Optional Protocol*, the Committee also considers communications from individuals who claim to be victims of violations of any of the rights set forth in the *Covenant*. The Committee considers such communications in closed meetings; all related communications and documents remain confidential. The findings of the Committee, however, are made public and are reproduced in its annual report to the General Assembly. The Committee also publishes its interpretation of the content of human rights provisions, known as 'general comments', on thematic issues or its methods of work.

Other conventions

The *Universal Declaration* *(www2.ohchr.org/english/law/index.htm#instruments)* has served as the inspiration for some 80 conventions and declarations that have been concluded within the United Nations on a wide range of issues. Among the earliest of these were conventions on the crime of genocide and on the status of refugees called for at the time, as the world had just emerged from the horrors of the Second World War, the Holocaust and the uprooting of millions of people. They have remained just as pertinent in the new century.

- The *Convention on the Prevention and Punishment of the Crime of Genocide* (1948), a direct response to the atrocities of the Second World War, defines the crime of genocide as the commission of certain acts with intent to destroy a national, ethnic, racial or religious group, and commits states to bringing to justice alleged perpetrators. It has 141 states parties.

- The *Convention relating to the Status of Refugees* (1951), also a direct response to the Second World War, defines the rights of refugees, especially their right not to be forcibly returned to countries where they are at risk. It also provides for their everyday lives, including their right to work, education, public assistance and

The United Nations Democracy Fund

The *Charter of the United Nations* highlights the importance of democracy and democratic values. The *Universal Declaration of Human Rights* and many subsequent UN declarations, conventions and covenants express the UN vision and commitment to these values. In the *International Covenant on Civil and Political Rights*, states parties take on binding obligations with respect to elections, the freedoms of expression, association and assembly, and other democratic principles.

Fundamental changes in various parts of the world made democracy a key theme of the 1990s. The UN system increased its operational activities in support of democratization, and in 1992 the Electoral Assistance Division was established. In 2000, UNDP placed democratic governance at the heart of its development cooperation programme.

Continuing this process, Secretary-General Kofi Annan, in 2005, established the United Nations Democracy Fund (*www.un.org/democracyfund*). Its aim is to promote democracy throughout the world by providing assistance for projects that consolidate and strengthen democratic institutions and facilitate democratic governance—complementing UN efforts on elections, human rights, support to civil society, pluralistic media and the rule of law.

The Fund does not promote any single model of democracy. Rather, it reflects the view expressed in the outcome document of the 2005 World Summit that "democracy is a universal value based on the freely expressed will of people to determine their own political, economic, social and cultural system and their full participation in all aspects of their lives".

---

social security, and their right to travel documents. The *Protocol relating to the Status of Refugees* (1967) ensures the universal application of the Convention, which was originally designed for people who became refugees as a result of the Second World War. The *Convention* and the *Protocol* had 147 states parties at the end of 2010.

In parallel to the *International Covenants*, seven more so-called 'core' international human rights treaties (*www2.ohchr.org/english/law/index.htm#core*) are monitored for compliance by states parties. Each of the following treaties has established a committee of experts—usually referred to as 'treaty body'—to monitor implementation of treaty provisions by its states parties. Some of these treaties are supplemented by optional protocols dealing with specific concerns—including the possibility for individual persons to file a complaint if they believe they have been a victim of a human rights violation.

- The *International Convention on the Elimination of All Forms of Racial Discrimination* (1966) is accepted by 174 states parties. Based on the premise that any policy of superiority based on racial differences is unjustifiable, scientifically false and morally and legally condemnable, it defines 'racial discrimination' and commits states parties to take measures to abolish it in both law and practice. The *Convention* established a treaty body, the **Committee on the Elimination of Racial Discrimination**, to consider reports from states parties, as well as petitions from individuals alleging a violation of the *Convention*, if the state concerned has accepted this optional procedure of the *Convention*.

- The *Convention on the Elimination of All Forms of Discrimination against Women* (1979), with 186 states parties, guarantees women's equality before the law and specifies measures to eliminate discrimination against women with respect to political and public life, nationality, education, employment, health, marriage and the family. The **Committee on the Elimination of Discrimination against Women** is the treaty body that monitors implementation and considers reports from states parties. The *Optional Protocol* to the *Convention* (1999), with 100 states parties, allows individuals to submit to the Committee complaints on violations and provides the Committee with a mandate to conduct inquiries if information indicates grave or systematic violations of the *Convention*.

- The *Convention against Torture and Other Inhuman or Degrading Treatment or Punishment* (1984), with 147 states parties, defines torture as an international crime, holds states parties accountable for preventing it and requires them to punish perpetrators. No exceptional circumstances may be invoked to justify torture, nor may a torturer offer a defence of having acted under orders. The *Convention's* monitoring treaty body is the **Committee against Torture**. It reviews reports of states parties, receives and considers petitions from individuals whose states have accepted this procedure, and initiates investigations regarding countries where it believes that torture is serious and systematic. The *Optional Protocol* to the *Convention* (2002) created the **Subcommittee on Prevention of Torture** and allows in-country inspections of places of detention. The *Protocol* also provides for the establishment of national preventive mechanisms. It has 57 states parties.

- The *Convention on the Rights of the Child* (1989) recognizes the particular vulnerability of children. It brings together in one comprehensive code protections for children in all categories of human rights. The *Convention* guarantees non-discrimination and recognizes that the best interests of the child must guide all actions. Special attention is paid to children who are refugees or members of minorities. States parties are to provide guarantees for children's survival, development, protection and participation. The *Convention* is the most broadly ratified treaty, with 193 states parties. The **Committee on the Rights of the Child**, established by the *Convention*, oversees implementation and considers reports submitted by states parties. The *Convention* has two optional protocols, one on the involvement of children in armed conflict and the other on the sale of children, child prostitution and child pornography.

- The *International Convention on the Protection of the Rights of All Migrant Workers and Members of Their Families* (1990) defines basic rights of, and measures to protect, migrant workers, whether documented or undocumented, throughout the process of migration. It entered into force in 2003 and has 44 states parties. Its monitoring treaty body is the **Committee on Migrant Workers**.

- The *Convention on the Rights of Persons with Disabilities* (2006) outlaws discrimination against the world's 650 million persons with disabilities in all areas of life, including employment, education, health services, transportation and access to justice. It entered into force in 2008 and had 96 states parties at the end of 2010. Its monitoring body is the **Committee on Rights of Persons with Disabilities**. An *Optional Protocol* to the *Convention* gives individuals recourse to that Committee when all national options have been exhausted. The *Optional Protocol* had 60 parties at the end of 2010.

- The *International Convention for the Protection of All Persons from Enforced Disappearance* (2006) prohibits the practice of enforced disappearance and calls on states parties to make it an offence under law. It also affirms the right of victims and their families to know the circumstances of such disappearances and the fate of the disappeared person, as well as to claim reparations. It entered into force in 2010 and by the end of that year had 21 states parties.

The *Universal Declaration* and other UN instruments have also formed part of the background to several regional agreements, such as the *European Convention on Human Rights,* the *American Convention on Human Rights* and the *African Charter of Human and Peoples' Rights.*

Other standards

The United Nations has adopted many other standards and rules on the protection of human rights. These 'declarations', 'codes of conduct' and 'principles' are not treaties to which states become party. Nevertheless, they have a profound influence, not least because they are carefully drafted by states and adopted by consensus. Among the most important of these:

- The *Declaration on the Elimination of All Forms of Intolerance and of Discrimination Based on Religion and Belief* (1981) affirms the right of everyone to freedom of thought, conscience and religion and the right not to be subject to discrimination on the grounds of religion or other beliefs.

  The *Declaration on the Right to Development* (1986) established that right as "an inalienable human right by virtue of which each person and all peoples are entitled to participate in, contribute to and enjoy economic, social, cultural and political development in which all human rights and fundamental freedoms can be fully realized". It adds that "equality of opportunity for development is a prerogative both of nations and of individuals".

- The *Declaration on the Rights of Persons Belonging to National or Ethnic, Religious and Linguistic Minorities* (1992) proclaims the right of minorities to enjoy their own culture; to profess and practise their own religion; to use their own language; and to leave any country, including their own, and to return to their country. The *Declaration* calls for action by states to promote and protect these rights.

- The *Declaration on Human Rights Defenders* (1998) seeks to recognize, promote and protect the work of human rights activists all over the world. It enshrines the right of everyone—individually and in association with others—to promote and strive to protect human rights at the national and international levels, and to participate in peaceful activities against human rights violations. States are to take all necessary measures to protect human rights defenders against any violence, threat, retaliation, pressure or other arbitrary action.

- The *Declaration on the Rights of Indigenous Peoples* (2007) sets out the individual and collective rights of indigenous peoples, as well as their rights to culture, identity, language, employment, health, education and other benefits. It emphasizes the rights of indigenous peoples to maintain and strengthen their own institutions, cultures and traditions, and models of development. It prohibits discrimination against them and promotes their participation in public affairs.

Other important non-treaty standards include the *Standard Minimum Rules for the Treatment of Prisoners* (1957), the *Basic Principles on the Independence of the Judiciary* (1985), the *Basic Principles on the Role of Lawyers* (1990) and the *Body of Principles for the Protection of All Persons under Any Form of Detention or Imprisonment* (1988), among many others.

Human rights machinery

Human Rights Council

The **Human Rights Council** (*www.ohchr.org/english/bodies/hrcouncil*) is the main United Nations intergovernmental body responsible for promoting and protecting all human rights and fundamental freedoms. It was established by the General Assembly in 2006 to replace the 60-year-old Commission on Human Rights. The Council addresses human rights violations and makes corresponding recommendations. It responds to human rights emergencies, works to prevent abuses, provides overall policy guidance, develops new international norms, monitors the observance of human rights around the world, and assists states in fulfilling their human rights obligations. It provides an international forum where states (members and observers), intergovernmental organizations, national human rights institutions and NGOs can voice their concerns about human rights issues.

The Council's 47 members are elected directly and individually by secret ballot by the majority of the 192 members of the UN General Assembly. They serve for a three-year renewable term and cannot seek immediate re-election after two consecutive terms. The membership is based on equitable geographical distribution. Thirteen seats each are devoted to the Group of African States and the Group of Asian States; eight to the Group of Latin American and Caribbean States; seven to the Group of Western European and other States; and six to the Group of Eastern European States.

All members are required to uphold the highest standards in the promotion and protection of human rights and to fully cooperate with the Council. Together with all 192 UN member states, they are subject to a universal periodic review ensuring that they are themselves upholding the standards they seek to enforce. They can be suspended for gross and systemic human rights violations by a two-thirds vote of the members of the General Assembly.

The Council meets regularly throughout the year. It holds no fewer than three sessions per year, for no less than 10 weeks in total. Special sessions can be requested at any time by a member state with the support of one third of the Council's members. In 2010, two special sessions were held to support the recovery process in Haiti, following the massive January earthquake, and to address the human rights situation in Côte d'Ivoire following the November presidential elections.

The most innovative feature of the Human Rights Council is the Universal Periodic Review. This unique mechanism involves a review of the human rights records of all 192 UN member states once every four years. The Review is a cooperative, state-driven process, under the auspices of the Council, which provides the opportunity for each state to present measures taken and challenges to be met to improve the human rights situation in their country and to meet their international obligations. The Review is designed to ensure universality and equality of treatment for every country.

Special rapporteurs and working groups

The special rapporteurs and working groups on human rights (*www2.ohchr.org/english/bodies/chr/special/index.htm*) are on the front lines in the protection of human rights. They investigate violations and intervene in individual cases and emergency situations, in what are referred to as 'special procedures'. Human rights experts are independent. They serve in their personal capacity for a maximum of six years and are not remunerated. The number of such experts has grown steadily over the years. At the end of 2010, there were 31 thematic and eight country-specific special procedure mandates.

In preparing their reports to the Human Rights Council and the General Assembly, these experts use all reliable resources, including individual complaints and information from NGOs. They may also initiate 'urgent-action procedures' to intercede with governments at the highest level. A significant portion of their research is done in the field, where they meet with both authorities and victims, and gather on-site evidence. Their reports are made public, thus helping to publicize violations and to emphasize the responsibility of governments for the protection of human rights.

These experts examine, monitor and publicly report on human rights situations in specific countries, or on major human rights violations worldwide.

- Country-specific special rapporteurs, independent experts and representatives currently report on Burundi, Cambodia, the Democratic People's Republic of Korea, Haiti, Myanmar, Palestinian territories occupied since 1967, Somalia and the Sudan.
- Thematic special rapporteurs, representatives and working groups currently report on adequate housing, people of African descent, arbitrary detention, the sale of children, cultural rights, education, enforced or involuntary disappearances, summary executions, extreme poverty, the right to food, the effects of foreign debt on human rights, freedom of opinion and expression, freedom of religion or belief, physical and mental health, human rights defenders, independence of the judiciary, indigenous people, internally displaced persons, mercenaries, migrants, minority issues, racism and racial discrimination, slavery, solidarity and human rights, terrorism, torture, the illicit movement and dumping of toxic and dangerous products and wastes, trafficking in persons, transnational corporations, water and sanitation, and violence against women.

The Council can rely on the independence and expertise of a wide range of experts and working groups. It can set up fact-finding missions to investigate alleged violations of human rights, provide assistance to states, engage in dialogue with governments to bring about needed improvements and condemn abuses. Through its complaint procedure, it can be seized of gross and systematic human rights violations by individuals, groups or NGOs.

The work of the Human Rights Council is also supported by the **Advisory Committee**. Composed of 18 experts, the Committee serves as the Council's 'think-tank' and provides it with expertise and advice on human rights issues such as missing persons, the right to food, leprosy-related discrimination and human rights education and training. In the performance of its mandate, the Committee interacts with states, intergovernmental organizations, national human rights institutions, NGOs and other civil society entities.

UN High Commissioner for Human Rights

The **United Nations High Commissioner for Human Rights** exercises principal responsibility for UN human rights activities. Appointed for a four-year term, the High Commissioner is charged with many tasks, including: promoting and protecting the effective enjoyment by all of all human rights; promoting international cooperation for human rights; stimulating and coordinating action on human rights in the UN system; assisting in the development of new human rights standards; and promoting the ratification of human rights treaties. The High Commissioner is also mandated to respond to serious violations of human rights and to undertake preventive action.

Under the direction and authority of the Secretary-General, the High Commissioner reports to the Human Rights Council and the General Assembly. With the aim of securing respect for human rights and preventing violations, the High Commissioner engages in dialogue with governments. Within the UN system, the High Commissioner works to strengthen and streamline the United Nations human rights machinery to make it more efficient and effective.

The **Office of the High Commissioner for Human Rights (OHCHR)** (*www.ohchr. org*) is the focal point for United Nations human rights activities. It serves as the secretariat for the Human Rights Council, the treaty bodies (expert committees that monitor treaty compliance) and other UN human rights organs. It also undertakes human rights field activities, and provides advisory services and technical assistance. In addition to its regular budget, some of the Office's activities are financed through extrabudgetary resources. The High Commissioner has taken specific steps to institutionalize cooperation and coordination with other UN bodies involved in human rights, such as the United Nations Children's Fund (UNICEF), the United Nations Educational, Scientific and Cultural Organization (UNESCO), the United Nations Development Programme (UNDP), the Office of the United Nations High Commissioner for Refugees (UNHCR) and the United Nations Volunteers (UNV). Similarly, the Office works in the area of peace and security in close cooperation with the corresponding departments of the UN Secretariat. The Office is also part of the Inter-Agency Standing Committee (IASC), which oversees the international response to humanitarian emergencies.

Promoting and protecting human rights

The role and scope of UN action in promoting and protecting human rights continue to expand. The central mandate of the Organization is to ensure full respect for the human dignity of the "peoples of the United Nations", in whose name the *Charter* was written.

For the United Nations, education is a fundamental human right and one of the most effective instruments for the promotion of human rights. Human rights education, whether in formal or non-formal settings, seeks to advance a universal culture of human rights through innovative teaching methods, the spreading of knowledge and the modification of attitudes. During the United Nations Decade for Human Rights Education (1995–2004), for example, particular efforts were made to increase global awareness and foster a universal culture of human rights. The Decade led many countries to promote human rights education by including it in their school curriculums and adopting national action plans.

Through its international machinery, the United Nations is working on many fronts:

- as *global conscience*—setting the pace in establishing international standards of acceptable behaviour by nations. It has kept the world's attention focused on practices that threaten to undermine human rights standards. The General Assembly, through a wide range of declarations and conventions, has underscored the universality of human rights principles.

- as *lawmaker*—giving impetus to an unprecedented codification of international law. Human rights pertaining to women, children, prisoners, detainees and persons with mental disabilities, as well as to such violations as genocide, racial discrimination and torture, are now a major feature of international law, which once focused almost exclusively on inter-state relations.

- as *monitor*—playing a central role in ensuring that human rights are not only defined but also protected. The *International Covenant on Civil and Political Rights* and that on *Economic, Social and Cultural Rights* (1966) are among the earliest examples of treaties that empower international bodies to monitor how states live up to their commitments. Treaty bodies, special rapporteurs and working groups of the Human Rights Council each have procedures and mechanisms to monitor compliance with international standards and to investigate alleged violations. Their decisions on specific cases carry a moral weight that few governments are willing to defy.

- as *nerve centre*—OHCHR receives communications from groups and individuals claiming violations of their human rights. More than 100,000 complaints are received every year. OHCHR refers these communications to the appropriate UN bodies and mechanisms, taking into account the implementation procedures established by conventions and resolutions. Requests for urgent intervention can be addressed to OHCHR by fax (41-22-917-9008) and e-mail *(tb-petitions@ohchr.org).*

- as *defender*—when a rapporteur or the chairman of a working group learns that a serious human rights violation, such as torture or imminent extrajudicial execution, is about to occur, he or she may address an urgent message to the state concerned, requesting clarification and seeking guarantees that the alleged victim's rights will be protected.

- as *researcher*—compiling data that are indispensable to the development and application of human rights law. Studies and reports prepared by OHCHR at the request of UN bodies point the way towards new policies, practices and institutions to enhance respect for human rights.

- as *forum of appeal*—under the *First Optional Protocol to the International Covenant on Civil and Political Rights*, as well as the *International Convention on the Elimination of All Forms of Racial Discrimination*, the *Convention Against Torture*, the *Optional Protocol to the Convention on the Elimination of All Forms of Discrimination against Women*, the *Optional Protocol to the Convention on the Rights of Persons with Disabilities*, and the *International Convention for the Protection of All Persons from Enforced Disappearance*, individuals can bring complaints against states that have accepted the relevant appeal procedure, once all domestic remedies have been exhausted. The same will be possible in the future once the *Optional Protocol to the International Covenant on Economic, Social and Cultural Rights* enters into force. An optional protocol to the *Convention on the Rights of the Child* is also being negotiated. In addition, the special procedures of the Human Rights Council deal with numerous complaints submitted annually by NGOs or individuals.

- as *fact-finder*—the Human Rights Council has mechanisms to monitor and report on the incidence of certain kinds of abuses, as well as on violations in a specific country. The special rapporteurs, representatives and working groups are entrusted with this politically sensitive, humanitarian and sometimes dangerous task. They gather facts, keep contact with local groups and government authorities, conduct on-site visits when governments permit, and make recommendations on how respect for human rights might be strengthened.

- as *discreet diplomat*—the Secretary-General and the UN High Commissioner for Human Rights raise human rights concerns with member states on a confidential basis on such issues as the release of prisoners and the commutation of death sentences. The Human Rights Council may ask the Secretary-General to intervene or send an expert to examine a specific human rights situation, with a view to preventing flagrant violations. The Secretary-General may also undertake quiet diplomacy in the exercise of his 'good offices' to communicate the United Nations' legitimate concerns and curb abuses.

The right to development

The principle of equality of opportunity for development is deeply embedded in the *Charter of the United Nations* and the *Universal Declaration on Human Rights*. The *Declaration on the Right to Development,* adopted by the General Assembly in 1986, marked a turning point by proclaiming this an inalienable human right, by which each person and all peoples are entitled to participate in, contribute to and enjoy economic, social, cultural and political development. The right to development is given prominence in the 1993 *Vienna Declaration and Programme of Action* of the Second World Conference on Human Rights, and is cited in the outcomes of other major UN summits and conferences as well, including the 2000 *Millennium Declaration.* In 1998, the Commission on Human Rights established a working group to monitor progress, analyse obstacles and develop strategies for implementing the right to development.

The right to food

The right to food is a particular focus of the **Food and Agriculture Organization of the United Nations (FAO)** (*www.fao.org*). In support of that right, the FAO Council, in 2004, adopted its *Voluntary Guidelines to Support the Progressive Realisation of the Right to Adequate Food in the Context of National Food Security.* These 'Right to Food Guidelines' cover the full range of actions governments can consider in creating an environment that enables people to feed themselves in dignity—and to establish safety nets for those who are unable to do so. They also recommend measures to strengthen government accountability, while promoting integration of the human rights dimension in the work of agencies dealing with food and agriculture.

Labour rights

The **International Labour Organization (ILO)** (*www.ilo.org*) is the UN specialized agency entrusted with defining and protecting the rights of labour. Its tripartite **International Labour Conference**—made up of government, employer and worker

Technical cooperation programme

Since human rights are best protected when they are rooted in the local culture, the United Nations has increased its efforts to promote and protect these rights at the national and local level. International human rights norms cannot be applied unless they are incorporated in national legislation and supported by national institutions.

Many obstacles at the national level still hinder the universal enjoyment of human rights. Various member states do not have the infrastructure that would allow them to effectively promote and protect the rights of their citizens. This is particularly true of countries that are just recovering from deadly civil wars or emerging from humanitarian crises.

United Nations advisory services to governments and technical cooperation programmes aim to promote democracy, development and human rights, and strengthen the capacity of states to advance such rights in their laws and practice. The Programme of Technical Cooperation for Human Rights, supervised by the Office of the High Commissioner for Human Rights, manages a range of such projects. It is funded primarily by contributions from the Voluntary Fund for Technical Cooperation in the Field of Human Rights (*www2.ohchr.org/ english/about/funds/coop*).

The programme encourages ratification and supports implementation of international human rights instruments. It focuses on four core areas: the administration of justice; human rights education; national institutions; and national plans of action. Special attention is paid to economic, social and cultural rights; the right to development; racism; the rights of indigenous people; trafficking of women and children; the human rights of women; and the rights of the child.

OHCHR has also developed regional strategies through which intergovernmental cooperation is fostered, experience is shared, and common policies and programmes are developed. OHCHR regional offices serve as resource centres responding to country-level demands. In keeping with the UN reform programme, which identifies human rights as a cross-cutting element of UN system activities, OHCHR supports the integration of human rights standards into assessment and planning, as well as into the development of policy and methodology.

representatives—had adopted 188 conventions and 200 recommendations as of December 2010 on all aspects of work life, comprising a system of international labour law. While its recommendations provide guidance on policy, legislation and practice, its conventions create binding obligations for those states that ratify them.

Conventions and recommendations have been adopted on such matters as labour administration, industrial relations, employment policy, working conditions, social security, occupational safety and health. Some seek to ensure basic human rights in the workplace, while others address such issues as the employment of women and children, and such special categories as migrant workers and persons with disabilities (see *www.ilo.org/ilolex/english/index.htm*).

The ILO's supervisory procedure to ensure that its conventions are applied both in law and in practice is based on objective evaluations by independent experts, and on the examination of cases by the ILO's tripartite bodies. There is also a special procedure for investigating complaints of infringement of the freedom of association (see *www.ilo.org/global/What_we_do/InternationalLabourStandards/lang--en/index.htm*).

The ILO has brought about many landmark conventions, including the following:

- *on forced labour* (1930); requires the suppression of forced or compulsory labour in all its forms;
- *on freedom of association and protection of the right to organize* (1948); establishes the right of workers and employers to form and join organizations without prior authorization, and lays down guarantees for the free functioning of such organizations;
- *on the right to organize and collective bargaining* (1949); provides for protection against anti-union discrimination, protection of workers' and employers' organizations, and measures to promote collective bargaining;
- *on equal remuneration* (1951); calls for equal pay and benefits for work of equal value;
- *on discrimination* (1958); calls for national policies to promote equality of opportunity and treatment, and to eliminate discrimination in the workplace on grounds of race, colour, sex, religion, political opinion, extraction or social origin;
- *on minimum age* (1973); aims at the abolition of child labour, stipulating that the minimum age for employment shall not be less than the age of completion of compulsory schooling;
- *on the worst forms of child labour* (1999); prohibits child slavery, debt bondage, prostitution and pornography, dangerous work, and forcible recruitment for armed conflict;
- *on maternity protection* (2000); provides standards for maternity leave, employment protection, medical benefits and breaks for breastfeeding.

In 2010, the ILO Conference adopted a groundbreaking new international labour standard on HIV/AIDS—the first international human rights instrument to focus specifically on this issue in the world of work. It provides for antidiscrimination measures and emphasizes the importance of employment and income-generating activities for workers and people living with HIV, particularly in terms of continuing treatment.

The General Assembly has also taken a number of measures to protect the rights of migrant workers.

The struggle against discrimination

Apartheid

One of the great successes of the United Nations was the abolition of apartheid in South Africa, which demonstrated ways in which it can bring an end to major injustices in the world. Practically from its inception, the UN was involved in the struggle against apartheid, a system of institutionalized racial segregation and discrimination imposed by the South African government from 1948 until the early 1990s. When, in 1994, the newly elected President, Nelson Mandela, addressed the General Assembly, he noted that this was the first time in its 49 years that the Assembly had been addressed by a South African head of state drawn from among the African majority. Welcoming the vanquishing of apartheid, he observed: "That historic change has come about not least because of the great efforts in which the United Nations engaged to ensure the suppression of the apartheid crime against humanity."

Condemned by the UN in 1966 as a "crime against humanity" incompatible with the *Charter* and the *Universal Declaration of Human Rights*, apartheid remained on the General Assembly's agenda from 1948 until its demise:

- During the 1950s, the General Assembly repeatedly appealed to the South African government to abandon apartheid in the light of the principles of the *Charter*.
- In 1962, it established the United Nations **Special Committee against Apartheid**, to keep the racial policies of South Africa under review. The Special Committee became the focal point of international efforts to promote a comprehensive programme of action against apartheid.
- In 1963, the Security Council instituted a voluntary arms embargo against South Africa.
- The Assembly refused to accept South Africa's credentials to its regular sessions from 1970 through 1974. Following this ban, South Africa did not participate in further proceedings of the Assembly until the end of apartheid in 1994.
- In 1971, the Assembly called for a sports boycott of South Africa, a move that had strong impact on public opinion within the country and abroad.
- In 1973, the Assembly adopted the *International Convention on the Suppression and Punishment of the Crime of Apartheid*.
- In 1977, the Council made its arms embargo against South Africa mandatory, after determining that the country's aggressions against its neighbours and its potential nuclear capability constituted a threat to international peace and security. This was the first such action by the Council against a member state.
- In 1985, the Assembly adopted the *International Convention Against Apartheid in Sports*.
- Also in 1985, when the South African government proclaimed a state of emergency and escalated repression, the Security Council, for the first time, called on governments to take significant economic measures against South Africa under Chapter VII of the *Charter*.

The transition from the apartheid government to a non-racial democracy was facilitated by a 1990 national peace accord between the government and major political parties, with the full support of the UN. Two Security Council resolutions in 1992 emphasized the involvement of the international community in that transition. To strengthen the structures of the accord, the Security Council in 1992 deployed the **United Nations Observer Mission in South Africa (UNOMSA)**, which observed the 1994 elections that led to the establishment of a non-racial, democratic government. With the installation of that government and the adoption of the country's first non-racial, democratic constitution, apartheid came to an end.

Racism

In 1963, the General Assembly adopted the *United Nations Declaration on the Elimination of All Forms of Racial Discrimination*. The *Declaration* affirms the fundamental equality of all persons and confirms that discrimination between human beings on the grounds of race, colour or ethnic origin is a violation of the human rights proclaimed in the *Universal Declaration* and an obstacle to friendly and peaceful relations among nations and peoples. Two years later, the Assembly adopted the *International Convention on the Elimination of All Forms of Racial Discrimination,* which obliges states parties to adopt legislative, judicial, administrative and other measures to prevent and punish racial discrimination.

In 1993, the General Assembly proclaimed the Third Decade to Combat Racism and Racial Discrimination (1993–2003) and called on all states to take measures to combat new forms of racism, especially through laws, administrative measures, education and information. Also in 1993, the Commission on Human Rights appointed a special rapporteur on contemporary forms of racism, racial discrimination, xenophobia and related intolerance. The special rapporteur's mandate is to examine incidents of contemporary forms of racism worldwide; racial discrimination; any form of discrimination against Arabs, Muslims, Africans and people of African descent; xenophobia; antisemitism; and related expressions of intolerance, as well as governmental measures to overcome them.

The third **World Conference against Racism, Racial Discrimination, Xenophobia and Related Intolerance,** held in 2001, focused on practical measures to eradicate racism, including measures of prevention, education and protection; and adopted the *Durban Declaration and Programme of Action.* The **Durban Review Conference**, held in 2009, resulted in a 143-point declaration to combat racism and discrimination against minorities. It also warned against stereotyping people because of their religion and condemned antisemitism, islamophobia and christianophobia.

The rights of women

Equality for women has been a focus of the work of the United Nations since its founding in 1945. The UN has played a leading role in the global struggle for the promotion and protection of women's human rights; the elimination of all forms of discrimination and violence against women; and efforts to ensure that women have full and equal access to, and opportunities for participation in, politics and public life, including all aspects of economic and social development and decision-making.

In 2010, the General Assembly created UN-Women (*www.unwomen.org*), the **United Nations Entity for Gender Equality and the Empowerment of Women.** The move came as part of the UN reform agenda, bringing together resources and mandates for greater impact. UN-Women aims to significantly boost UN efforts to expand opportunities for women and girls and tackle discrimination around the globe. Involvement in the formulation of global standards and norms is one of UN-Women's principal roles.

The **Commission on the Status of Women** has elaborated international guidelines and laws for women's equality and non-discrimination—notably, the 1979 *Convention on the Elimination of Discrimination against Women* and the 1999 *Optional Protocol* to the *Convention.* It also prepared the *Declaration on the Elimination of All Forms of Violence against Women,* adopted by the General Assembly in 1993, which, among other things, defined violence against women as physical, sexual or psychological violence occurring in the family or the community and perpetrated or condoned by the state.

The **Committee on the Elimination of Discrimination against Women,** a body made up of 23 independent experts, monitors implementation of the 1979 *Convention on the Elimination of Discrimination against Women* by states parties. It con-

Women in national parliaments

Percentage in single house or lower house as of 31 December 2010

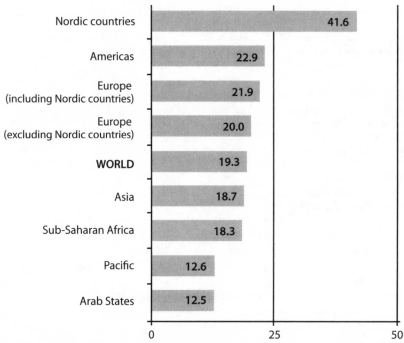

Nordic countries	41.6
Americas	22.9
Europe (including Nordic countries)	21.9
Europe (excluding Nordic countries)	20.0
WORLD	19.3
Asia	18.7
Sub-Saharan Africa	18.3
Pacific	12.6
Arab States	12.5

Source: Inter-Parliamentary Union, *www.ipu.org/wmn-e/world.htm.*

siders reports submitted by states parties to assess their progress in giving form to the principle of equality of women and men. The Committee can also examine individual communications and carry out inquiries under the provisions of the *Convention's Optional Protocol.* It makes recommendations on any issues affecting women to which it believes states parties should devote more attention, such as violence against women.

The rights of children

Millions of children die every year from malnutrition and disease. Countless others become victims of war, natural disaster, HIV/AIDS and extreme forms of violence, exploitation and abuse. Millions of children, especially girls, do not have access to quality education. The **United Nations Children's Fund (UNICEF)**, as well as the **Office of the High Commissioner for Human Rights (OHCHR)** and other UN agencies, strive to sustain global commitment to the *Convention on the Rights of the Child*, which embodies universal ethical principles and international legal standards of behaviour towards children.

The **Committee on the Rights of the Child**, established under the *Convention*, is a body of 18 independent experts that meets regularly to monitor the progress made by states parties in fulfilling their obligations under the *Convention* and makes recommendations to governments on ways to meet those obligations. The Committee also issues its interpretation of the *Convention's* provisions in the form of general comments.

UNiTE to End Violence against Women

"We must unite. Violence against women cannot be tolerated, in any form, in any context, in any circumstance, by any political leader or by any government."

"Men must teach each other that real men do not violate or oppress women— and that a woman's place is not just in the home or the field, but in schools and offices and boardrooms."

— Secretary-General Ban Ki-moon

Launched in 2008, the UNiTE to End Violence against Women campaign (*www. un.org/en/women/endviolence*) brings together a host of UN agencies and offices to galvanize action across the UN system to prevent and punish violence against women and girls. Through UNiTE, the UN joins forces with individuals, civil society and governments to put an end to violence against women in all its forms, and calls on all governments to adopt laws that criminalize violence against women.

The campaign runs until 2015. By 2015, UNiTE aims to achieve the following five goals in all countries:

- adoption and enforcement of national laws to address and punish all forms of violence against women and girls;
- adoption and implemention of national action plans;
- strengthing data collection on the prevalence of violence against women and girls;
- increasing public awareness and social mobilization;
- addressing the problem of sexual violence in conflict.

The General Assembly in 2000 adopted two *Optional Protocols* to the *Convention*: one prohibits the recruitment of children under 18 into armed forces or their participation in hostilities; the other strengthens prohibitions and penalties concerning the sale of children, child prostitution and child pornography. Although the Committee cannot consider individual complaints, a working group of the Human Rights Council is exploring the possibility of elaborating an optional protocol to the *Convention* to provide a communications/complaints procedure. Such a mechanism would further strengthen the protection of children's rights.

Concerning child labour, the UN seeks to protect children from exploitation and hazardous conditions that endanger their physical and mental development; to ensure children's access to quality education, nutrition and health care; and, in the long term, progressively eliminate child labour. The **International Programme on the Elimination of Child Labour**, an initiative of the ILO, seeks to raise awareness and mobilize action through the provision of technical cooperation. Direct interventions focus on the prevention of child labour; the search for alternatives, including decent employment for parents; and rehabilitation, education and vocational training for children. UNICEF supports programmes providing education, counselling and care to children working in very hazardous or abusive conditions and vigorously advocates against the violation of their rights.

Both the General Assembly and the Human Rights Council have urged governments to take action to protect and promote the rights of children, particularly children in difficult situations. They have called on states to implement programmes and measures that provide children with special protection and assistance, including access to health care, education and social services, as well as (where appropriate) voluntary repatriation, reintegration, family tracing and family reunification, in particular for children who are unaccompanied. The two bodies have also called on States to ensure that the best interests of the child are accorded primary consideration.

The special rapporteur on the sale of children, child prostitution and child pornography, as well as the special representatives of the Secretary-General on violence against children and for children and armed conflict, report regularly to the General Assembly and to the Human Rights Council. The latter also reports to the Security Council.

The post of special representative of the Secretary-General on violence against children was established in 2007, in the wake of the *World Report on Violence against Children*, which was presented to the General Assembly the previous year. The *Report* exposed for the first time the horrendous scale and impact of all forms of violence against children, highlighting the universality and magnitude of the problem in different settings: the home and family; schools; care and justice institutions; the workplace; and the community. Its 12 overarching recommendations and a number of specific recommendations have provided a comprehensive framework for follow-up action. The mandate of the special representative of the Secretary-General for children and armed conflict, established in 1996 by the Assembly for a period of three years, has been renewed ever since, most recently in 2008, for a further three-year period.

The rights of minorities

Some 1 billion people worldwide belong to minority groups, many of which are subject to discrimination and exclusion, and are often the victims of conflict. Meeting the legitimate aspirations of national, ethnic, religious and linguistic groups strengthens the protection of basic human rights, protects and accommodates cultural diversity, and increases the stability of society as a whole. The United Nations has from its inception placed minority rights high on its human rights agenda. The protection of the human rights of members of minority groups is guaranteed specifically in article 27 of the *International Covenant on Civil and Political Rights*, as well as in the principles of non-discrimination and participation, which are basic to all United Nations human rights law. The adoption of the *Declaration on the Rights of Persons Belonging to National or Ethnic, Religious and Linguistic Minorities* by the General Assembly in 1992 gave new impetus to the UN human rights agenda.

The **Forum on Minority Issues** was established in 2007 to provide a platform for promoting dialogue and cooperation on issues pertaining to national or ethnic, religious and linguistic minorities, as well as for providing thematic contributions and expertise to the work of the Independent Expert on minority issues. The Forum identifies and analyses best practices, challenges, opportunities and initiatives for the further implementation of the *Declaration*. It meets annually for two days of thematic discussions. The independent expert on minority issues guides the work of the Forum and reports its recommendations to the Human Rights Council. The president of the Human Rights Council appoints for each session, on the basis of regional rotation and in consultation with regional groups, a Forum chairperson selected from experts on minority issues.

Indigenous peoples

The United Nations has increasingly taken up the cause of indigenous peoples, who constitute one of the world's most disadvantaged groups. Indigenous peoples are also called first peoples, tribal peoples, aboriginals and autochthons. There are at least 5,000 indigenous peoples, made up of some 370 million individuals living in over 70 countries on five continents. Often excluded from decision-making processes, many have been marginalized, exploited, forcefully assimilated, and subjected to repression, torture and murder when they speak out in defence of their rights. Fearing persecution, they often become refugees and sometimes must hide their identity, abandoning their languages and traditional way of life.

In 1982, the Subcommission on Human Rights established a working group on indigenous populations, which prepared a draft *Declaration on the Rights of Indigenous Peoples*. In 1992, the Earth Summit heard the collective voice of indigenous peoples as they expressed their concerns about the deteriorating state of their lands, territories and environment. Various UN bodies—including UNDP, UNICEF, IFAD, UNESCO, the World Bank and the WHO—developed programmes to improve their health and literacy and combat degradation of their ancestral lands and territories. Subsequently, the General Assembly proclaimed 1993 as the International Year of the World's Indigenous People, followed by the International Decade of the World's Indigenous People (1995–2004) and the **Second International Decade of the World's Indigenous People (2005–2015)** (*www.un.org/esa/socdev/unpfii/en/second.html*).

This increased focus on indigenous issues led, in 2000, to the establishment of the **Permanent Forum on Indigenous Issues** (*www.un.org/esa/socdev/unpfii*) as a subsidiary organ of ECOSOC. This 16-expert forum, composed of an equal number of governmental and indigenous experts, advises ECOSOC; helps coordinate related UN activities; and considers indigenous concerns relating to economic and social development, culture, education, the environment, health and human rights. In addition, an Inter-Agency Support Group on Indigenous Issues was established.

The year 2007 saw the adoption of the landmark *Declaration on the Rights of Indigenous Peoples* by the General Assembly. The *Declaration* sets out the individual and collective rights of indigenous peoples, including their rights to culture, identity, language, employment, health and education. It emphasizes their rights to maintain and strengthen their own institutions, cultures and traditions, and to pursue their development in keeping with their own needs and aspirations. It also prohibits discrimination against them, and promotes their full and effective participation in all matters that concern them—including their right to remain distinct and to pursue their own visions of economic and social development.

OHCHR has played a pivotal role in these developments, and the implementation of the *Declaration* remains a priority for the Office. The Office contributes actively to the UN Inter-agency Support Group on Indigenous Issues. It conducts training on indigenous issues for UN country teams and for OHCHR field presences. OHCHR builds capacities among indigenous peoples. It services the Board of Trustees of the Voluntary Fund for Indigenous Populations, composed of five indigenous representatives. (The Fund supports the participation of representatives of indigenous communities and organizations in the annual sessions of the Permanent Forum on Indigenous Issues and the Expert Mechanism on the Rights of Indigenous Peoples.)

The Office also assists the special rapporteur on the situation of human rights and fundamental freedoms of indigenous peoples, and supports the **Expert Mechanism on the Rights of Indigenous Peoples**. Established in 2007, the five-expert Mechanism assists the Human Rights Council on issues related to indigenous rights. Following the first session of the Mechanism in 2008, OHCHR worked with it on a study on the right of indigenous peoples to education submitted to the Human Rights Council in 2009. The Office also carries out a range of country-specific and regional activities to advance the rights of indigenous peoples. It provides support for legislative initiatives and pursues thematic work on issues such as extractive industries and the rights of isolated indigenous peoples.

Persons with disabilities

Some 650 million persons—approximately 10 per cent of the world's population, of which some 80 per cent lives in the developing world—have some type of physical, mental or sensory impairment. Persons with disabilities are often excluded from the mainstream of society. Discrimination takes various forms, ranging from the denial of education or work opportunities to more subtle forms, such as segregation and isolation through the imposition of physical and social barriers. Society also suffers, since the loss of their enormous potential impoverishes the world. Changing the perception and concept of disability requires changing values and increasing understanding at all levels of society.

Since its inception, the United Nations has sought to advance the status of persons with disabilities and to improve their lives (see *www.un.org/disabilities*). Its concern for the well-being and rights of persons with disabilities is rooted in its founding principles of human rights, fundamental freedoms and equality of all human beings.

In the 1970s, the concept of human rights for persons with disabilities gained wider international acceptance. Through its adoption of the *Declaration on the Rights of Mentally Retarded Persons* (1971) and the *Declaration on the Rights of Disabled Persons* (1975), the General Assembly established the standards for equal treatment and equal access to services, thus accelerating the social integration of persons with disabilities. The International Year of Disabled Persons (1981) led to the adoption by the General Assembly of the *World Programme of Action Concerning Disabled Persons,* a policy framework for promoting the rights of persons with disabilities. The programme identifies two goals for international cooperation: equality of opportunity; and full participation of persons with disabilities in social life and development.

A major outcome of the United Nations Decade of Disabled Persons (1983–1992) was the adoption by the General Assembly in 1993 of the *Standard Rules on the Equalization of Opportunities for Persons with Disabilities,* which serve as an instrument for policymaking and provide a basis for technical and economic cooperation. A special rapporteur monitors the implementation of the *Rules* and reports annually to the **Commission for Social Development**, a subsidiary body of ECOSOC.

A further set of standards for the protection of people with mental illness— the *Principles for the Protection of Persons with Mental Illness and the Improvement of Health Care*—was adopted by the General Assembly in 1991. Three years later the Assembly endorsed a long-term strategy to further the implementation of the *World Programme of Action,* with the goal of "a society for all".

The *Convention on the Rights of Persons with Disabilities* and its *Optional Protocol* were adopted in 2006, and opened for signature in 2007. By the end of 2010, there were 147 signatories to the *Convention*, 90 signatories to the *Optional Protocol*, 96 ratifications of the *Convention* and 60 of the *Optional Protocol*. This is the highest number in history of signatures and ratifications to a UN convention since its opening day. The *Convention* entered into force in 2008. It is the first comprehensive human rights treaty of the 21st century and the first human rights convention to be open for signature by regional integration organizations.

The *Convention* marks a paradigm shift in attitudes and approaches to persons with disabilities. It takes the movement to new heights from viewing persons with disabilities as 'objects' of charity, medical treatment and social protection towards viewing them as 'subjects' with rights who are capable of making decisions based on their free and informed consent, as well as being active members of society. The secretariat for the *Convention's* international monitoring mechanisms, including the Committee on the Rights of Persons with Disabilities, lies with OHCHR, while the UN Department for Economic and Social Affairs organizes the conference of states parties in New York.

A growing body of data suggests the need to address disability issues in the context of national development, within the broad framework of human rights. The UN works with governments, NGOs, academic institutions and professional societies to promote awareness and build national capacities for broad human rights approaches to persons with disabilities. In doing so, it links disability issues with the international development agenda, including the Millennium Development Goals. Growing public support for disability action has focused on the need to improve information services, outreach and institutional mechanisms to promote equal opportunity. The UN is involved in helping countries strengthen their national capacities to promote such action in their overall development plans.

Migrant workers

More than 175 million people—including migrant workers, refugees, asylum-seekers, permanent immigrants and others—live and work in a country other than that of their birth or citizenship. Many of them are migrant workers. The term 'migrant worker' is defined in Article 2 of the *International Convention on the Protection of the Rights of All Migrant Workers and Members of Their Families (Migrant Workers Convention)* as: "a person who is to be engaged or has been engaged in a remunerated activity in a State of which he or she is not a national". The *Convention* breaks new ground in defining those rights that apply to certain categories of migrant workers and their families, including: frontier workers; seasonal workers; seafarers; workers on offshore installations; itinerant workers; migrants employed for a specific project; and self-employed workers.

The *Migrant Workers Convention* was adopted by the General Assembly in 1990, following 10 years of negotiations. It covers the rights of both documented and undocumented migrant workers and their families. It makes it illegal to expel migrant workers on a collective basis or to destroy their identity documents, work permits or passports. It entitles migrant workers to receive the same remuneration, social benefits and medical care as nationals; to join or take part in trade unions; and, upon ending their employment, to transfer earnings, savings and personal belongings. It also grants children of migrant workers the right to registration of birth and nationality, as well as access to education. The *Convention* entered into force in 2003. States parties monitor its implementation through the **Committee on Migrant Workers**.

The **Global Migration Group** is an inter-agency group bringing together 14 partners (12 UN agencies, the World Bank and the International Organization for Migration) to promote the application of international instruments and norms relating to migration, and to encourage the adoption of coherent, comprehensive and better coordinated approaches to international migration. In 2010, the Group voiced deep concern about the human rights of international migrants in an irregular situation and called upon all states to ensure that their laws and regulations conformed with and promoted the realization of applicable international human rights standards and guarantees at all stages of the migration process.

Administration of justice

The United Nations is committed to strengthening the protection of human rights in the judicial process. When individuals are under investigation by state authorities, or when they are arrested, detained, charged, tried or imprisoned, there is a need to ensure that the law is applied with due regard for the protection of human rights.

The UN has worked to develop standards and codes that serve as models for national legislation. They cover such issues as the treatment of prisoners, the protection of detained juveniles, the use of firearms by police, the conduct of law enforcement officials, the role of lawyers and prosecutors, and the independence of the judiciary. Many of these standards have been developed through the United Nations Commission on Crime Prevention and Criminal Justice and the Centre for International Crime Prevention.

OHCHR has a programme of technical assistance that focuses on human rights training for legislators, judges, lawyers, law enforcement officers, prison officials and the military.

At the end of 2010, there were 24 international instruments relating to the administration of justice. These include: *Standard Minimum Rules for the Treatment of Prisoners; Basic Principles for the Treatment of Prisoners; Body of Principles for the Protection of All Persons under Any Form of Detention or Imprisonment; United Nations Rules for the Protection of Juveniles Deprived of their Liberty; Safeguards Guaranteeing Protection of the Rights of those Facing the Death Penalty; Code of Conduct for Law Enforcement Officials; Basic Principles on the Use of Force and Firearms by Law Enforcement Officials; Basic Principles on the Role of Lawyers; Guidelines on the Role of Prosecutors; Basic Principles and Guidelines on the Right to a Remedy and Reparation;* and the *International Convention for the Protection of All Persons from Enforced Disappearance.* (For a complete list, see *www2.ohchr.org/english/law/index.htm.*)

Future priorities

Despite the efforts of the United Nations, massive and widespread violations of human rights continue worldwide. More than six decades after the adoption of the *Universal Declaration of Human Rights*, violations across the broad spectrum of human rights still dominate the news. At least part of this can be attributed to the heightened awareness of human rights and the stepped-up monitoring of problem areas. Particular examples are child abuse, violence against women and abuses that until only recently were considered acceptable behaviour by traditional standards.

Indeed, measures to promote and protect human rights are stronger than ever, and are increasingly linked to the fight for social justice, economic development and democracy. Human rights has become a cross-cutting theme in all UN policies and programmes. The vigorous actions taken by OHCHR, together with enhanced cooperation and coordination among UN partners, are tangible expressions of the strengthened ability of the UN system to fight for human rights.

The OHCHR's Strategic Management Plan for 2010–2011 prioritizes:

- countering discrimination, in particular racial discrimination, discrimination on the grounds of sex, religion and against others who are marginalized;
- combating impunity and strengthening accountability, the rule of law and democratic society;
- pursuing economic, social and cultural rights and combating inequalities and poverty, including in the context of the economic, food and climate crises;
- protecting human rights in the context of migration;
- protecting human rights in situations of armed conflict, violence and insecurity;
- strengthening human rights mechanisms and the progressive development of international human rights law.

V. HUMANITARIAN ACTION

UN Mission in Haiti assists earthquake victim
Haitian locals and peacekeepers from the United Nations Stabilization Mission in Haiti (MINUSTAH) rush a wounded woman to a UN helicopter in the aftermath of the powerful earthquake that levelled the country's capital, Port-au-Prince, and devastated the UN as well (13 January 2010, UN Photo/Logan Abassi).

V. HUMANITARIAN ACTION

Since it first coordinated humanitarian relief operations in Europe following the devastation and massive displacement of people in the Second World War, the United Nations has led the international community in responding to natural and man-made disasters that are beyond the capacity of national authorities alone. Today, the Organization is a major provider of emergency relief and longer-term assistance, a catalyst for action by governments and relief agencies, and an advocate on behalf of people struck by emergencies (see *www.un.org/ha*).

Man-made disasters and natural calamities have driven millions from their homes in the past few years. The displacement of entire populations as a result of war and insurgency in Afghanistan, Iraq, Somalia and other countries continues to concern the international community. Moreover, three of the 10 deadliest natural disasters of the past century occurred in the past decade alone—the 2004 Indian Ocean tsunami, the 2008 Nargis cyclone in Myanmar, and the 2010 earthquake in Haiti. Together, these calamities claimed over 600,000 lives.

Natural disasters, mostly weather-related, affect hundreds of millions of people every year. The Secretary-General has reported that, in 2009, some 92 per cent of natural disasters were caused by cyclones, floods, earthquakes and drought, with heat waves and forest fires also taking a toll in human suffering. More than 98 per cent of those killed in natural disasters in the last decade were in developing countries—an overwhelming figure that indicates how poverty, population pressures and environmental degradation exacerbate human suffering.

Confronted with conflict and the escalating human and financial cost of natural disasters, the UN engages on two fronts. On one hand, it brings immediate relief to the victims, primarily through its operational agencies; on the other hand, it seeks more effective strategies to prevent emergencies from arising in the first place.

When disaster strikes, the UN and its agencies rush to deliver humanitarian assistance. For example, in 2009, the World Food Programme (WFP) fed 101.8 million people in 75 countries, including most of the world's refugees and internally displaced persons. Of these, 84.1 million were women and children. In Pakistan, at the end of 2010, hundreds of thousands of the displaced remained in camps after the summer's floods, and thousands more were still cut off from assistance. In the wake of the floods, the United Nations Children's Fund (UNICEF) and its partners provided clean water to 2.8 million people daily, as well as sanitation facilities for 1.5 million. UNICEF also set up 1,550 temporary learning centres to educate children. Together with the World Health Organization (WHO), it supplied vaccines for more than 9 million children, while the United Nations Population Fund (UNFPA) coordinated interventions to prevent and respond to gender-based violence among the affected population.

After the March 2011 earthquake and tsunami that struck Japan and the Fukushima nuclear plant, the UN sent a disaster team to assist the government with relief efforts. The WFP supported government delivery of relief items and IAEA helped monitor radiation near the plant. The FAO, IAEA and WHO moved to address related food safety issues.

The Indian Ocean earthquake-tsunami of December 2004

In the early hours of 26 December 2004, a massive earthquake measuring 9.0 on the Richter scale struck the west coast of northern Sumatra, Indonesia, triggering a powerful tsunami up to 10 metres (33 feet) in height. It moved through the Indian Ocean at up to 800 kilometres (500 miles) an hour.

The tsunami was unprecedented in modern history. It wrecked coastal areas in India, Indonesia, Maldives, Myanmar, Seychelles, Somalia, Sri Lanka and Thailand, travelling as far as 2,000 miles inland in places. It caused deaths as far away as South Africa, with more than half of them in Indonesia alone. Official tallies a year later recorded 181,516 dead and 49,936 missing in 12 countries. More than 1.7 million people lost their homes, while 5 to 6 million were in need of food, water and medical supplies.

The UN system immediately sprang into action. With programmes already on the ground in each of the affected countries, the massive and rapid UN response ensured that survivors had sufficient access to food, shelter and medical attention, thus preventing a second disaster: an outbreak of disease and hunger. On 5 January 2005, a 'flash appeal' was issued for $977 million to fund the efforts of some 40 UN agencies and NGOs addressing a wide range of humanitarian needs—including agriculture, support services, economic recovery and infrastructure, education, family shelter, mine action, security, protection of human rights and the rule of law, and water and sanitation.

In 2010 alone, in response to emergencies, the Central Emergency Response Fund (CERF), managed by the Office for the Coordination of Humanitarian Affairs (OCHA), allocated around $400 million for rapid response operations. Some $35.5 million were allocated to Haiti in response to the January 2010 earthquake—the largest amount ever allocated by CERF to one emergency. Through other means, such as the **Humanitarian Early Warning Service** (*www.hewsweb.org*) and the **United Nations International Strategy for Disaster Reduction (ISDR)** (*www.unisdr. org*), the UN works to prevent humanitarian crises and mitigate their effects. The FAO monitors impending famines, as well as other food and agricultural concerns, while the World Meteorological Organization (WMO) carries out tropical cyclone forecasting and drought monitoring. The United Nations Development Programme (UNDP) assists disaster-prone countries in developing contingency planning and other preparedness measures.

Coordinating humanitarian action

Since the 1990s, the world has seen an upsurge in the number and intensity of civil wars. These have caused large-scale humanitarian crises—with extensive loss of life, massive displacements of people and widespread damage to societies in complicated political and military environments. To address these complex emergencies, the United Nations has considerably upgraded its capacity to respond quickly and effectively. In 1991, the General Assembly established an inter-agency standing committee to coordinate the international response to humanitarian crises. The **United Nations Emergency Relief Coordinator** is the Organization's focal point for this endeavour, acting as the system's principal policy adviser, coordinator and advocate on humanitarian emergencies. The Emergency

Haiti rebuilds after January 2010 earthquake

On 12 January 2010, a devastating earthquake struck Haiti, killing 220,000 people and rendering 1.5 million others homeless. Despite its own loss of 102 staff members, the United Nations completed an initial needs assessment within 72 hours, and within four days it had deployed relief teams to the field.

In the first four months after the disaster, through a response coordinated by the UN and its Stabilization Mission in Haiti (MINUSTAH), working together with thousands of international humanitarian partners, 1.5 million people were provided with shelter, many millions received food and medical assistance, and 1.7 million had basic water and sanitation made available. Donors came to fund 72 per cent of emergency needs, with almost $1 billion received. More than 300,000 Haitians were employed through Cash for Work or Food for Work programmes between February and November 2010.

As of January 2011, some 700,000 people had left the camps, 100,000 of these having been relocated to 31,000 transitional shelters. An estimated 810,000 people were still living in around 1,150 camps. Some 95 per cent of children in the earthquake zones who had been attending school before the quake had returned to the classroom. About $3 billion in projects for 2011 had been approved, with $1.28 billion already funded and $1.63 billion committed and earmarked.

Relief Coordinator heads the **Office for the Coordination of Humanitarian Affairs (OCHA)** (*www.ochaonline.un.org*), which coordinates assistance in humanitarian crises that go beyond the capacity and mandate of any single agency.

Usually there are many actors in the international community—including governments, non-governmental organizations (NGOs) and UN agencies—who seek to respond simultaneously to complex emergencies. OCHA works with them to ensure that there is a coherent framework within which everyone can contribute promptly and effectively to the overall effort. When an emergency strikes, OCHA coordinates the international response. It determines priorities for action through consultations with member states and with the **Inter-Agency Standing Committee (IASC)** (*www.humanitarianinfo.org/iasc*) at Headquarters and in the field. As the primary mechanism for the inter-agency coordination of humanitarian assistance, the IASC engages key UN and non-UN humanitarian partners in the international community. OCHA then provides support for the coordination of activities in the affected country. For example, OCHA ensures that military resources—when available and appropriate—are effectively used to respond to humanitarian emergencies.

OCHA maintains an in-house emergency response capacity, supported by a 24-hour monitoring and alert system. UN disaster assessment and coordination teams can be dispatched within 12 to 24 hours of a natural disaster or sudden-onset emergency to gather information, assess needs and coordinate international assistance. It also operates through a network of regional offices and field offices, humanitarian coordinators and country teams. The humanitarian coordinator has overall responsibility for ensuring coherence of relief efforts in the field. By bringing together needs assessments, contingency planning and the formulation of programmes, OCHA supports the humanitarian coordinator and the operational agencies that deliver assistance.

Coordinating emergency relief

The Inter-Agency Standing Committee (IASC) brings together all major humanitarian agencies, both within and outside the United Nations. It is chaired by the United Nations Emergency Relief Coordinator.

The IASC develops humanitarian policies, agrees on a clear division of responsibility for the various aspects of humanitarian assistance, identifies and addresses gaps in response, and advocates for effective application of humanitarian principles. Its 'cluster approach' to humanitarian assistance aims to strengthen humanitarian response by ensuring high standards of predictability, accountability and partnership. Any major new or ongoing emergency is now addressed in terms of the following clusters, each with its own lead agency or agencies, and a range of UN and non-UN partners:

- agriculture (FAO);
- camp coordination and management (UNHCR for conflict IDPs; International Organization for Migration for disaster situations);
- early recovery (UNDP);
- education (UNICEF and Save the Children);
- emergency shelter (UNHCR and the International Federation of Red Cross and Red Crescent Societies);
- emergency telecommunications (WFP);
- health (WHO);
- logistics (WFP);
- nutrition (UNICEF);
- protection (UNHCR for conflict IDPs and UNHCR/OHCHR/UNICEF for disasters and civilians affected by conflict other than IDPs);
- water sanitation and hygiene (UNICEF).

The Office also helps its IASC partners and the humanitarian coordinator to mobilize resources by launching consolidated inter-agency appeals for contributions. It organizes donor meetings and follow-up arrangements, monitors the status of contributions in response to its appeals, and issues situation reports to keep donors and others updated on developments. Since 1992, OCHA has raised more than $42 billion for emergency assistance, through a total of 330 consolidated and flash appeals.

OCHA's **Central Emergency Response Fund (CERF)** was launched in March 2006 as an improved financing mechanism to facilitate immediate response to humanitarian emergencies. It was established in the aftermath of a string of extremely destructive recent natural disasters that occurred with little warning and demanded rapid response for emergency relief and recovery. These included the December 2004 Indian Ocean earthquake-tsunami, the October 2005 South Asian earthquake, a record-breaking hurricane season, and a major landslide in the Philippines in February 2006. Some 59 UN member states, together with other public and private donors, pledged more than $358 million for 2011 during the annual CERF High-Level Conference in December 2010. Since its establishment in 2006, CERF has committed more than $1.8 billion to humanitarian partners in 78 countries and territories.

Protecting children in war

Today, in more than 30 conflict situations worldwide, more than 250,000 young persons under 18 are ruthlessly exploited as soldiers—some as young as seven or eight. It is estimated that 40 per cent of all child soldiers are girls. More than 2 million children have been killed in wars and civil strife, and 6 million have been maimed or permanently disabled. Thousands of girls are subject to sexual violence and exploitation. Some boys and girls are abducted from their homes and separated from their parents, while others have been orphaned by war.

To tackle this tragedy, the Security Council has called for stronger efforts to end the use of children as soldiers and to protect children in armed conflict. Peacekeeping operations now include the protection of children in their mandate, and several peacekeeping missions include civilian specialists on the protection of children.

The UN has been at the forefront in developing norms and standards for the protection of children in conflict (*www.un.org/children/conflict*):

- The *Rome Statute* of the International Criminal Court classifies conscription, enlistment or use in hostilities of children under 15 as a war crime.
- The *Optional Protocol to the Convention on the Rights of the Child* sets an age limit of 18 years for compulsory recruitment and direct participation in hostilities, and requires states parties to raise the minimum age for voluntary recruitment to at least 16.
- Seven Security Council resolutions—1261(1999), 1314(2000), 1379(2001), 1460(2003), 1539(2004), 1612(2005) and 1882(2009)—address the protection of children in conflict.
- ILO *Convention 182* defines child soldiering as one of the worst forms of child labour and sets 18 as the minimum age for forced or compulsory recruitment.
- The *Geneva Conventions* and their *Additional Protocols* stipulate that children shall be the object of special respect and shall be protected against any form of assault during conflict, and that they should be provided "with the care and aid they require".

The Secretary-General's special representative for children and armed conflict works to increase global awareness and mobilize the political support of governments and civil society. The special representative is a key advocate for strengthening the monitoring and reporting mechanisms on violations of children's rights in armed conflict; placing their welfare on peace agendas; and putting their needs at the centre of post-conflict recovery programmes.

The "Zero Under 18" campaign (*http://zerounder18.org*) was launched in 2010 by the Office of the Special Representative for Children and Armed Conflict in cooperation with the Special Representative on violence against children, UNICEF, OHCHR and the Committee on the Rights of the Child. Its aim is to achieve universal ratification of the *Optional Protocol on the Involvement of Children in Armed Conflict* by 2012. By the end of the year, it had been ratified by 139 UN member states. UNICEF, for its part, works with governments and rebel movements to demobilize child soldiers, reunite them with their families, and foster their social reintegration.

OCHA also works with its partners in the humanitarian community to build consensus around policies, and to identify specific humanitarian issues arising from operational experiences in the field. It tries to ensure that major humanitarian issues are addressed—including those that fall between the mandates of humanitarian bodies. By advocating on humanitarian issues, OCHA gives voice to the silent victims of crises, and ensures that the views and concerns of the humanitarian community are reflected in overall efforts towards recovery and peacebuilding. In this way, OCHA also promotes greater respect for humanitarian norms and principles, and draws attention to such specific issues as access to affected populations; the humanitarian impact of sanctions; anti-personnel landmines; and the unchecked proliferation of small arms.

To support humanitarian advocacy, policy making and emergency coordination, OCHA has developed a robust set of online tools. OCHA manages **ReliefWeb** (*www.reliefweb.int)*—the world's foremost humanitarian website—providing the latest information on emergencies worldwide. It also hosts IRIN (*www.irinnews. org*), a news service that offers accurate and impartial reporting and analysis about sub-Saharan Africa, the Middle East, Asia and the Americas for the humanitarian community.

Humanitarian assistance and protection

Three United Nations entities—UNICEF, WFP and UNHCR—have primary roles in providing protection and assistance in humanitarian crises.

Children and women constitute the majority of refugees and displaced persons. In acute emergencies, the **United Nations Children's Fund (UNICEF)** works alongside other relief agencies to help re-establish basic services such as water and sanitation, set up schools, and provide immunization services, medicines and other supplies to uprooted populations. UNICEF also consistently urges governments and warring parties to act more effectively to protect children. Its programmes in conflict zones have included the negotiation of ceasefires to facilitate the provision of key services such as child immunization. To this end, UNICEF has pioneered the concept of 'children as zones of peace' and created 'days of tranquillity' and 'corridors of peace' in war-affected regions. Special programmes assist traumatized children and help reunite unaccompanied children with parents or extended families. In 2009, UNICEF provided nearly $3 billion in humanitarian assistance for emergencies.

The **World Food Programme (WFP)** provides fast, efficient relief to millions of people who are victims of natural or man-made disasters, including most of the world's refugees and internally displaced persons. Such crises consume the largest part of WFP's financial and human resources. A decade ago, two out of three tons of food aid provided by the WFP was used to help people become self-reliant. Today, the picture is reversed, with three quarters of WFP resources going to victims of humanitarian crises. In 2009, WFP assistance reached 101.8 million people in 75 countries, with an unprecedented 4.6 million metric tons of food aid. In 2010, the WFP assisted more than 90 million people in over 70 countries, including internally displaced persons, refugees, children orphaned by AIDS, and victims of conflict and natural disasters such as floods, drought and earthquakes. When war or disaster strikes, the WFP responds quickly with emergency relief, then mounts programmes to facilitate smooth and effective recovery aimed at rebuilding lives and livelihoods. The WFP is also responsible for mobilizing food and funds for all large-scale refugee-feeding operations managed by the UNHCR.

Rural populations in the developing world are often the most vulnerable to disasters, with most of these communities dependent on agriculture for their food security and livelihoods. The expertise of the **Food and Agriculture Organization of the United Nations (FAO)** in farming, livestock, fisheries and forestry is crucial

Protecting humanitarian workers

United Nations personnel and other humanitarian workers in the field continue to be subject to attacks. Over the years, scores have been killed, taken hostage or detained while working in conflict areas. Violent incidents against UN staff have included armed robbery, assault and rape. The heightened visibility of UN personnel as representatives of the international community places them at substantial risk of being targeted. This was brought home on 19 August 2003, when the terrorist bombing of the UN headquarters in Baghdad left 22 dead and 150 injured. Among those killed was UN High Commissioner for Human Rights Sergio Vieira de Mello, on assignment as head of the UN mission there. It was the most devastating single attack on UN civilian staff in the Organization's history.

Another deadly bomb attack occurred on 11 December 2007 in Algiers that claimed the lives of 17 UN staff members and left 40 injured. The Secretary-General set up an independent panel to investigate the atrocity and make recommendations to improve the security of UN employees around the world.

The 1994 *Convention on the Safety of United Nations and Associated Personnel* obliges the governments of countries where the UN is at work to safeguard its staff, and to take preventive measures against murders and abductions. From Afghanistan to Darfur, and from Somalia to Pakistan, however, still too many UN staff and associated personnel lost their lives or were wounded in a string of random or premeditated attacks over 2009–2010.

In his 2009 report to the General Assembly on the protection of UN staff and the security of humanitarian personnel, Secretary-General Ban Ki-moon expressed his concern over the increased number of security incidents, and by "the trend of politically or criminally motivated targeting of humanitarian workers, which is most evident in Somalia, the Sudan and Haiti".

"I am profoundly distressed by the number of lost lives during the reporting period—63 United Nations and humanitarian personnel deaths as a result of acts of violence", he said. "United Nations personnel are regularly confronted with threats from armed conflict, terrorism, kidnapping, harassment, banditry and intimidation, and they are asked to work under extremely difficult circumstances."

"While not abrogating the responsibility of host Governments, it is recognized that the United Nations must, at times, operate in areas where the host Governments' capacities are limited", the Secretary-General said. He was therefore encouraged by the vigour with which the humanitarian community had embraced the Saving Lives Together framework for improving security arrangements among international organizations, NGOs and the UN.

---

in emergency relief and rehabilitation. The FAO assists countries in preventing, mitigating, preparing for and responding to disasters. Its **Global Information and Early Warning System** (*www.fao.org/giews*) provides regular and updated information on the global food situation. Together with the WFP, the FAO carries out assessments of the food situation in food-insecure countries following man-made or natural disasters. Based on these assessments, emergency food aid operations are prepared and jointly approved. Its work in post-disaster and complex emergency situations emphasizes the protection and rehabilitation of agricultural livelihoods. The FAO aims to restore local food production, providing an exit from food aid and other forms of assistance, bolstering self-reliance and reducing the need for relief and harmful coping strategies.

The **World Health Organization (WHO)** focuses on assessing the health needs of those affected by emergencies and disasters, providing health information and assisting in coordination and planning. The WHO carries out emergency programmes in such areas as nutritional and epidemiological surveillance, control of epidemics, immunizations, management of essential drugs and medical supplies, reproductive health and mental health. It makes special efforts to eradicate polio and to control tuberculosis and malaria in countries affected by emergencies.

The **United Nations Population Fund (UNFPA)** also moves quickly when emergency strikes. Pregnancy-related deaths and sexual violence soar in times of upheaval, while reproductive health services often become unavailable. Young people become more vulnerable to HIV infection and sexual exploitation, and many women lose access to family planning services. In emergencies, the UNFPA acts to protect the reproductive health of communities in crisis, and continues to provide assistance as these communities move beyond the acute phase into reconstruction efforts.

The **United Nations Development Programme (UNDP)** is the agency responsible for coordinating activities for natural disaster mitigation, prevention and preparedness. Governments frequently call on the UNDP to help design rehabilitation programmes and direct donor aid. The UNDP and humanitarian agencies work together to integrate concern for recovery, and transitional and long-term development in their relief operations. The UNDP also supports programmes for the demobilization of former combatants, comprehensive mine action, the return and reintegration of refugees and internally displaced persons, and the restoration of the institutions of governance.

To ensure that resources provided have maximum impact, each project is carried out in consultation with local and national government officials. UNDP offers rapid assistance to entire communities, while helping to establish the social and economic foundations for lasting peace, development and the alleviation of poverty. This community-based approach has helped provide urgent and lasting relief for hundreds of thousands of victims of war and civil upheaval. Today, many conflict-scarred communities have improved their living standards thanks to UN-led training programmes, credit schemes and infrastructure projects.

Protecting and assisting refugees

In 2010, the **Office of the United Nations High Commissioner for Refugees (UNHCR)** (*www.unhcr.org*) counted 43.3 million forcibly displaced people worldwide—the highest number since the mid-1990s. This included 27.1 million internally displaced persons (IDPs), 15.2 million refugees and 983,000 asylum-seekers. Of the 15.2 million refugees, 10.4 million were under UNHCR's responsibility, and 4.7 million were Palestinian refugees under the mandate of the United Nations Relief and Works Agency for Palestine Refugees in the Near East (UNRWA).

More than 26 million people—10.4 million refugees and 15.6 million IDPs—were receiving protection or assistance from UNHCR at the end of 2009, one million more than in 2008. By 2010, UNHCR had identified some 6.6 million stateless persons in 60 countries. Yet it estimated that the overall number of stateless persons worldwide could be far higher, at around 12 million.

Refugees in their own country

Internally displaced persons (IDPs) are those who have been forced to flee their homes to escape war, generalized violence, human rights violations or natural and man-made disasters, but who have not crossed an international border. Civil wars have created large groups of such persons all over the world. There were an estimated 27.1 million IDPs in 2010—nearly double the number of refugees. While refugees often find safety, food and shelter in a second country and are protected by a well-defined body of international laws, the internally displaced may be trapped in an ongoing internal conflict at the mercy of warring parties, making the provision of relief hazardous or impossible. Primary responsibility for such persons lies with the government, which is often unable—or unwilling—to help, and may even view them as 'enemies of the state'.

Yet like refugees, IDPs need immediate protection and assistance, as well as long-term solutions, such as return or resettlement. UNHCR has increasingly been called on to aid such persons in various regions and countries—including, Colombia, Côte d'Ivoire, the Democratic Republic of the Congo, Iraq, Lebanon, Somalia, Sri Lanka, Timor-Leste, Uganda and elsewhere—providing assistance on the basis of humanitarian need rather than refugee status. The task has been daunting. In Somalia alone, there were an estimated 1.5 million IDPs in 2010. In Pakistan, an estimated 1.6 million people were internally displaced because of conflict and natural disasters.

Recognizing that no UN agency had the mandate and resources to protect and assist IDPs single-handedly, the Inter-Agency Standing Committee (IASC) in 2005 developed a collaborative model by which agencies pool their resources in responding to humanitarian crises. Under this innovative 'cluster approach', UNHCR exercises leadership responsibility and accountability for three of the eleven clusters, namely protection; emergency shelter; and camp coordination and management.

Developing countries were host to four fifths of the world's refugees. Women and girls represented, on average, 49 per cent of persons of concern to UNHCR. They constituted 47 per cent of refugees and asylum-seekers, and half of all IDPs and returnees (former refugees). Forty-one per cent of refugees and asylum-seekers were children less than 18 years of age.

Afghan and Iraqi refugees accounted for nearly 50 per cent of the refugees under UNHCR's responsibility worldwide in 2009. One out of four refugees in the world was from Afghanistan (2.9 million); they were located in 71 different countries of asylum. Iraqis constituted the second largest refugee group, with 1.8 million having sought refuge primarily in neighbouring countries. Refugees from Somalia were third, with some 27 per cent of its population in need of humanitarian assistance. An estimated 1.5 million Somalis were internally displaced, a fifth of whom were uprooted in 2010 alone.

UNHCR has been one of the lead humanitarian agencies for some of the major emergencies in post-war history—in the Balkans, which produced the largest refugee flows in Europe since the Second World War; in the aftermath of the Gulf War; in Africa's Great Lakes region; in the massive exoduses in Kosovo and Timor-Leste; in repatriation in Afghanistan; and, more recently, in the exodus from conflict-ridden Iraq and from southern and central Somalia.

Global warming and environmental refugees

In increasing numbers, scholars and international organizations are predicting that millions of people worldwide might be displaced because of global warming leading to rising sea levels, desertification, dried-up aquifers, weather-induced flooding and other serious environmental changes. The plight of the Carteret Islanders in the South Pacific, whose islands are disappearing under the ocean, is one example of a growing problem.

According to the Tokyo-based United Nations University (UNU), environmental problems have already contributed to large permanent migrations and could eventually displace hundreds of millions of people. But environmental refugees are not yet recognized under existing international instruments. The situation is highly complex, with global organizations fully engaged in meeting the needs of refugees as defined under the 1951 *Convention*. The international community must prepare to respond to this new kind of refugee with effective measures secured by international frameworks.

Refugees are defined as those who have fled their countries because of a well-founded fear of persecution due to their race, religion, nationality, political opinion or membership in a particular social group, and who cannot or do not want to return. It also includes persons who have fled war or other violence in their country. The legal status of refugees is defined in two international treaties, the 1951 *Convention Relating to the Status of Refugees* and its 1967 *Protocol*, which spell out their rights and obligations. There are 147 states parties to one or both of these instruments.

UNHCR's most important function is international protection—trying to ensure respect for refugees' basic human rights, including their ability to seek asylum, and to ensure that no one is returned involuntarily to a country where he or she has reason to fear persecution. Other types of assistance include:

- help during major emergencies involving the movement of large numbers of refugees;
- regular programmes in such fields as education, health and shelter;
- assistance to promote the self-sufficiency of refugees and their integration in host countries;
- voluntary repatriation; and
- resettlement in third countries for refugees who cannot return to their homes and who face protection problems in the country where they first sought asylum.

Although UNHCR's mandate is to protect and assist refugees, it has increasingly been called upon to come to the aid of a wider range of people living in refugee-like situations. These include people displaced within their own countries, former refugees who may need UNHCR monitoring and assistance once they have returned home, stateless persons, and those who receive temporary protection outside their home countries but do not receive the full legal status of refugees. Today, refugees comprise the second largest group of people of concern to UNHCR.

Asylum-seekers are persons who have left their countries of origin and have applied for recognition as refugees in other countries, and whose applications are still pending. At the beginning of 2010, UNHCR was assisting close to 1 million

People in flight

By region

Africa	10,636,239
Asia	13,624,502
Europe	1,087,700
Latin America and Caribbean	3,898,344
North America	3,934
Oceania	2,519
Various	7,207,568
Total:	**36,460,806**

NOTE: This listing of the number of persons of concern to UNHCR as of 1 January 2010 includes refugees, asylum-seekers, returnees, internally displaced persons and others of concern. It does not include the 4.7 million Palestinians assisted by UNRWA. Palestinians outside the UNRWA area of operations, such as those in Iraq or Libya, however, are of concern to UNHCR.

people in this category. South Africa was the main destination for asylum-seekers, with some 222,000 new claims just in 2009—followed by the United States, Kenya, France, Canada, the United Kingdom, and Germany. Afghanistan was the main country of origin of asylum-seekers, with some 26,800 Afghans requesting refugee status in 2009—45 per cent more than in 2008, when there were around 18,500 requests. Afghans represented some 7 per cent of all asylum applications lodged. After Afghanistan, Iraq, Somalia, Russia and China were the main source countries of those seeking asylum.

During 2009, some 2.2 million IDPs were able to return home, but only 251,000 refugees were voluntarily repatriated—the lowest level since 1990. The three main durable solutions for refugees are voluntary repatriation to their home country in safety and dignity; local integration in the country of asylum, where feasible; or resettlement in a third country. Voluntary repatriation is generally considered the preferred option. The sudden return of large numbers of people to their home country, however, can quickly overwhelm fragile economic and social infrastructures. To ensure that returnees can rebuild their lives after they return home, UNHCR works with a range of organizations to facilitate their reintegration. This requires emergency assistance for those in need, development programmes for the areas that have been devastated, and job-creation schemes. For all of these reasons, the development of effective links between peace, stability, security, respect for human rights and sustainable development is increasingly seen as crucial for the achievement of durable solutions to the refugee problem.

Palestine refugees

Since 1950, the **United Nations Relief and Works Agency for Palestine Refugees in the Near East (UNRWA)** has been providing education, health, relief and social services to Palestine refugees. The General Assembly created UNRWA to provide emergency relief to some 750,000 Palestine refugees who had lost their homes and livelihoods as a result of the 1948 Arab-Israeli conflict. By the end of 2010, UNRWA was providing essential basic services to assist 4.7 million registered Palestine refugees in Jordan, Lebanon, Syria, and the occupied Palestinian territory (comprised of the West Bank and the Gaza Strip). In the past decade, the need for UNRWA's humanitarian role has been reinforced by recurrent conflicts in the region.

Education is UNRWA's largest area of activity, accounting for nearly 60 per cent of its regular budget. The Agency operates one of the largest school systems in the Middle East, with 691 schools, 22,000 educational staff, 483,000 enrolled pupils (49.8 per cent female), 10 vocational training centres, 6,395 training sites, three educational science faculties, 900 teachers in training, and 1,400 student teachers. The Agency's network of 137 health care centres performed 11 million medical consultations in 2009. Its environmental health programme controls the quality of drinking water, provides sanitation, and carries out vector and rodent control in refugee camps.

In 2009, some 257,000 of the poorest refugees, unable to support themselves, received special hardship assistance, including the provision of food and shelter rehabilitation. Meanwhile, an income-generation programme in 2009 provided more than 12,000 small loans worth $15 million to vulnerable refugees in the occupied Palestinian territory, Jordan and Syria. The same year, some 265,000 people received special hardship assistance, intended to ensure minimum standards of nutrition and shelter, as well as promote self-reliance. An income-generation programme in the West Bank and Gaza Strip provides loans ranging from $3,000 to $75,000 to small businesses and micro-enterprises, with most of the beneficiaries being women.

The Agency's continuing efforts have helped to upgrade infrastructure, create employment and improve socio-economic conditions. Unlike other UN organizations that work through local authorities or executing agencies, UNRWA provides its services directly to refugees. It plans and carries out its own activities and projects, and builds and administers facilities such as schools and clinics. The international community considers UNRWA a stabilizing factor in the Middle East. The refugees themselves look upon its programmes as a symbol of the international community's commitment to attaining a lasting solution of the Palestine refugee issue.

VI. INTERNATIONAL LAW

Public hearings of the International Court of Justice
(March 2006, ICJ/Jeroen Bouman)

VI. INTERNATIONAL LAW

Among the greatest and most wide-reaching achievements of the United Nations is the development of a body of international law—conventions, treaties and standards—central to promoting economic and social development, as well as to advancing international peace and security (see *www.un.org/law*). Many of the treaties brought about by the United Nations form the basis of the law that governs relations among nations. While the work of the UN in this area does not always receive attention, it has a daily impact on the lives of people everywhere.

The *Charter of the United Nations* specifically calls on the Organization to help in the settlement of international disputes by peaceful means, including arbitration and judicial settlement (Article 33), and to encourage the progressive development of international law and its codification (Article 13). Over the years, the United Nations has sponsored over 500 multilateral agreements treating a broad range of common concerns among states and legally binding for the countries that ratify them.

In many areas, the legal work of the United Nations has been pioneering, addressing problems as they take on an international dimension. The UN has been in the forefront of efforts to provide a legal framework in such areas as protecting the environment, regulating migrant labour, curbing drug trafficking and combating terrorism. This work continues today, as international law assumes a more central role across a wider spectrum of issues, including human rights law and international humanitarian law.

Judicial settlement of disputes

The primary United Nations organ for the settlement of disputes is the **International Court of Justice** (*www.icj-cij.org*). Popularly known as the World Court, it was founded in 1946. Since its founding, the Court has considered some 150 cases, issued numerous judgments on disputes brought to it by states and issued advisory opinions in response to requests by UN organizations. Most cases have been dealt with by the full Court, but since 1981 six cases have been referred to special chambers at the request of the parties.

In its judgments, the Court has addressed international disputes involving economic rights, rights of passage, the non-use of force, non-interference in the internal affairs of states, diplomatic relations, hostage-taking, the right of asylum and nationality. States bring such disputes before the Court in search of an impartial solution to their differences on the basis of law. By achieving peaceful settlement on such questions as land frontiers, maritime boundaries and territorial sovereignty, the Court has often helped to prevent the escalation of disputes.

In a typical case of territorial rights, the Court in 2002 settled a sovereignty dispute between Cameroon and Nigeria over the oil-rich Bakassi peninsula, and then over the whole land and sea boundary between the two states. Earlier that year, it resolved a sovereignty dispute between Indonesia and Malaysia over two islands in the Celebes Sea, granting them to Malaysia. In 2001, the Court ended a maritime and territorial dispute between Qatar and Bahrain that had been a strain on their relations.

In 1999, the Court resolved a sensitive frontier dispute between Botswana and Namibia, with a ruling accepted by both countries. In 1992, it settled a nearly century-old dispute between El Salvador and Honduras, which had led to a short but bloody war in 1969. In 1994, the Court acted on a dispute that had been jointly referred to it by Libya and Chad, ruling that their territory was defined by a 1955 treaty between Libya and France. As a result, Libya withdrew its forces from an area along its southern border with Chad.

Various cases have been referred to the Court against the background of conflict or political upheaval. In 1980, the United States brought a case arising from the seizure of its Tehran embassy and the detention of its staff. The Court held that Iran must release the hostages, hand back the embassy and make reparation. However, before the Court could set the amount of reparation, the case was withdrawn due to an agreement between the two countries. In 1989, Iran asked the Court to condemn the shooting down of an Iranian airliner by a United States warship, and to find the United States responsible for the payment of compensation to Iran. The case was closed in 1996, following a compensation settlement between the parties.

Bosnia and Herzegovina brought a case concerning the application of the *Convention on the Prevention and Punishment of the Crime of Genocide* against the Federal Republic of Yugoslavia regarding, among other things, the massacres that took place at Srebrenica in July 1995. In its judgment, issued in 2007, the Court said it had not been established that the massacres had taken place on the instructions, under the control, or with the foreknowledge of the Federal Republic. Therefore, under international law, it had not committed genocide.

Nonetheless, the Court found that "the authorities of the Respondent could not have been unaware of the grave risk of genocide once the VRS forces"—the army of the Republika Srpska—"had decided to take possession of the Srebrenica enclave". The Court held that despite this awareness, "the Respondent did nothing to prevent the Srebrenica massacres, claiming that they were powerless to do so, which hardly tallies with their known influence over the VRS". It was therefore in breach of its obligation under the *Convention* to take whatever action it could to prevent the genocide.

The Court in 1996 rejected objections by the United States to its jurisdiction in a 1992 case concerning the destruction of Iranian oil platforms by United States warships. In November 2003, the Court held that the United States' actions could not be justified as necessary to protect its national security interests. As those actions did not constitute a breach of its obligations regarding freedom of commerce, however, Iran's claim for reparation could not be upheld. The Court also refused to uphold a United States counterclaim.

States often submit questions relating to economic rights. In 1995, in the midst of a dispute over fisheries jurisdiction between Canada and the European Union, Spain instituted a case against Canada after that country seized a Spanish fishing trawler on the high seas. A case involving environmental protection was brought by Hungary and Slovakia concerning the validity of a 1997 treaty they had concluded on the building of a barrage system on the Danube River. In 1997, the Court found both states in breach of their legal obligations, and called on them to carry out that treaty.

The number of judicial cases submitted to the Court has increased significantly since the 1970s, when it had only one or two cases on its docket at any one time.

At the beginning of 2011, there were 16 pending cases on the Court's docket, including three under active consideration—Nicaragua v. Colombia, concerning a territorial and maritime dispute; Georgia v. Russian Federation, concerning the question of the application of the *International Convention on the Elimination of All Forms of Racial Discrimination*; and Costa Rica v. Nicaragua, concerning certain activities carried out by Nicaragua in the border area joining the two countries.

The Court's advisory opinions have dealt with, among other things, admission to United Nations membership, reparation for injuries suffered in the service of the United Nations and the territorial status of Western Sahara. Two opinions, rendered in 1996 at the request of the General Assembly and the World Health Organization, concerned the legality of the threat or use of nuclear weapons. In a 1971 advisory opinion requested by the Security Council, the Court stated that the continued presence of South Africa in Namibia was illegal and that South Africa was under obligation to withdraw its administration and end its occupation—clearing the way for the independence of Namibia in March 1990.

Development and codification of international law

The **International Law Commission** (*www.un.org/law/ilc*) was established by the General Assembly in 1947 to promote the progressive development of international law and its codification. The Commission, which meets annually, is composed of 34 members elected by the General Assembly for five-year terms. Collectively, the members represent the world's principal legal systems, and serve as experts in their individual capacity, not as representatives of their governments. They address a wide range of issues relevant to the regulation of relations among states, and frequently consult with the International Committee of the Red Cross, the International Court of Justice and UN specialized agencies, depending on the subject being examined.

Most of the Commission's work involves the preparation of drafts on aspects of international law. Some topics are chosen by the Commission, others are referred to it by the General Assembly. When the Commission completes work on a topic, the General Assembly sometimes convenes an international conference of plenipotentiaries to incorporate the draft into a convention. The convention is then opened to states to become parties—meaning that such countries formally agree to be bound by its provisions. Some of these conventions form the very foundation of the law governing relations among states. Examples include:

- the *Convention on the Non-navigational Uses of International Watercourses*, adopted by the General Assembly in 1997, which regulates the equitable and reasonable utilization of watercourses shared by two or more countries;
- the *Convention on the Law of Treaties between States and International Organizations or between International Organizations*, adopted at a conference in Vienna in 1986;
- the *Convention on the Succession of States in Respect of State Property, Archives and Debts*, adopted at a conference in Vienna in 1983;
- the *Convention on the Prevention and Punishment of Crimes against Internationally Protected Persons, including Diplomatic Agents*, adopted by the General Assembly in 1973;

- the *Convention on the Law of Treaties*, adopted at a conference in Vienna in 1969;
- the *Convention on Diplomatic Relations* and the *Convention on Consular Relations*, adopted at conferences held in Vienna in 1961 and 1963, respectively.

In 1999, the Commission adopted a draft declaration aimed at preventing people from becoming stateless in such situations as dissolution of a state or separation of a territory. State responsibility had been a major subject of study by the Commission since its first session in 1949. In 2001, it completed its study of the subject with the adoption of draft articles on the "Responsibility of States for internationally wrongful acts". Also in 2001, the Commission adopted draft articles on the prevention of transboundary damage resulting from hazardous activities.

In 2006, the Commission adopted a set of draft articles on diplomatic protection and draft principles on the allocation of loss in the case of transboundary harm arising out of hazardous activities. In 2008, it adopted two sets of draft articles—on reservations to treaties and on the law of transboundary aquifers. In 2009, the Commission adopted a set of draft articles on the responsibility of international organizations.

Other topics currently being considered by the Commission include: the effects of armed conflicts on treaties; expulsion of aliens; obligation to extradite or prosecute; and protection of persons in the event of disasters.

International trade law

The **United Nations Commission on International Trade Law (UNCITRAL)** (*www. uncitral.org*) facilitates world trade by developing conventions, model laws, rules and legal guides designed to harmonize international trade law. Established by the General Assembly in 1966, UNCITRAL has become the core legal body of the UN system in the field of international trade law. The international trade law division of the United Nations Office of Legal Affairs serves as its secretariat. The Commission is composed of 60 member state representatives elected by the General Assembly. Membership is structured so as to be representative of the world's various geographic regions and its principal economic and legal systems. Members of the Commission are elected for six-year terms. The terms of half the members expire every three years.

In the past 45 years, the Commission has developed widely accepted texts that are viewed as landmarks in various fields of law. These include the *UNCITRAL Arbitration Rules* (1976); the *UNCITRAL Conciliation Rules* (1980); the *United Nations Convention on Contracts for the International Sale of Goods* (1980); the *UNCITRAL Model Law on International Commercial Arbitration* (1985); the *Model Law on Electronic Commerce* (1996); and the *United Nations Convention on Contracts for the International Carriage of Goods Wholly or Partly by Sea* (2008).

The Commission is also continuing its work on issues of insolvency in groups of companies (enterprise groups); the revision of the *UNCITRAL Model Law on Procurement* and the *UNCITRAL Arbitration Rules*; and the compilation and publication of Case Law on UNCITRAL Texts (CLOUT).

Environmental law

The UN has pioneered the development of international environmental law, brokering major treaties that have advanced environmental protection everywhere. The **United Nations Environment Programme (UNEP)** (*www.unep.org*) administers many of these treaties, while the rest are administered by other bodies, including treaty secretariats:

- The *Convention on Wetlands of International Importance Especially as Waterfowl Habitat* (1971) obligates states parties to use wisely all wetlands under their jurisdiction (promoted by UNESCO);
- The *Convention Concerning the Protection of the World Cultural and Natural Heritage* (1972) obligates states parties to protect unique natural and cultural areas (promoted by UNESCO);
- The *Convention on International Trade in Endangered Species of Wild Fauna and Flora* (1973) controls international trade in selected wild animal and plant species or products through quotas or outright bans, to ensure their survival;
- The *Bonn Convention on the Conservation of Migratory Species of Wild Animals* (1979) and a series of associated regional and species-specific agreements aim to conserve terrestrial, marine and avian migratory species and their habitats;
- The *Convention on Long-range Transboundary Air Pollution (Acid Rain Convention)* (1979) and its protocols, negotiated under the auspices of the United Nations Economic Commission for Europe (ECE), provide for the control and reduction of air pollution in Europe and North America;
- The *United Nations Convention on the Law of the Sea* (1982) regulates in a comprehensive way numerous maritime issues, including the protection and preservation of coasts and the marine environment; the prevention and control of marine pollution; rights to living and non-living resources; and the management and conservation of living resources;
- The *Vienna Convention for the Protection of the Ozone Layer* (1985), the *Montreal Protocol* (1987) and its amendments seek to reduce damage to the ozone layer, which shields life from the sun's harmful ultraviolet radiation;
- The *Basel Convention on the Control of Transboundary Movement of Hazardous Wastes and their Disposal* (1989) and its amendments, along with its 1999 *Protocol* on liability and compensation resulting from cross-border movement of hazardous wastes, obligate states parties to reduce shipping and dumping of dangerous wastes across borders and minimize their toxic potential;
- The *Agreement on the Conservation of Small Cetaceans of the Baltic and North Seas* (1991) aims to promote cooperation among parties for the conservation of small cetaceans and their habitats;
- The *Convention on Biological Diversity* (1992) seeks to conserve biological diversity, promote the sustainable use of its components, and encourage equitable sharing of the benefits arising from the use of genetic resources. Its *Cartagena Protocol* on biosafety (2000) seeks to protect biological diversity from potential risks posed by living modified organisms (LMOs);
- The *Framework Convention on Climate Change* (1992) obligates states parties to reduce emissions of greenhouse gases that cause global warming and related atmospheric problems. The Convention's *Kyoto Protocol* (1997) strengthens the international response to climate change by setting legally binding emission targets for the period 2008–2012;
- The *International Convention to Combat Desertification in those Countries Experiencing Serious Drought and/or Desertification, Particularly in Africa* (1994) seeks to promote international cooperation to combat desertification and to mitigate the effects of drought;

- The *Agreement on the Conservation of Cetaceans in the Black Sea, Mediterranean Sea and Contiguous Atlantic Area* (1996) seeks to reduce the threat to cetaceans in Mediterranean and Black Sea waters, and requires that states ban the deliberate capture of cetaceans and create protected zones;
- The *Rotterdam Convention on the Prior Informed Consent Procedure for Certain Hazardous Chemicals and Pesticides in International Trade* (1998) obligates exporters of hazardous chemicals or pesticides to inform importing states on the potential dangers of these substances;
- The *Stockholm Convention on Persistent Organic Pollutants* (2001) aims to reduce and eliminate releases of certain highly toxic pesticides, industrial chemicals and by-products—such as DDT, PCBs and dioxin—that are highly mobile and accumulate in the food chain;
- The *Kyiv Protocol on Strategic Environmental Assessment* (2003) requires states parties to evaluate the environmental consequences of their draft plans and programmes.

The UNEP Regional Seas Programme (*www.unep.org/regionalseas*) helps more than 140 participating countries in 13 regions counteract the accelerating degradation of the world's oceans and coastal areas through the sustainable management and use of the marine and coastal environment. In most cases, it does so on the basis of a strong legal framework in the form of a regional convention and associated protocols on specific problems. UN partners include UNDP, FAO, the International Oceanographic Commission of UNESCO, the IMO and the IAEA.

Law of the sea

The *United Nations Convention on the Law of the Sea* (*www.un.org/depts/los*) is one of the world's most comprehensive instruments of international law. Its 320 articles and nine annexes contain an all-encompassing legal regime for our oceans and seas, establishing rules governing all activities in the oceans and the use of their resources—including navigation and overflight, exploration and exploitation of minerals, conservation and management of living resources, protection of the marine environment, and marine scientific research. It enshrines the notion that all problems of ocean space are interrelated and need to be addressed as a whole. It embodies in one instrument the codification of traditional rules for the use of the oceans, as well as the development of new rules governing emerging concerns. It is a unique instrument, often referred to as a 'constitution for the oceans'.

It is now almost universally accepted that all activities in the oceans and the seas must be carried out in conformity with the provisions of the *Convention*. Like other such instruments, its authority resides in its acceptance. As of December 2010, the *Convention* had 161 states parties, along with the European Union and two non-independent territories. Other states are in the process of becoming party to it. Nearly all states recognize and adhere to its provisions.

Impact of the Convention

Through national and international legislation and related decision-making, states have consistently upheld the *Convention* as the pre-eminent international legal instrument in the field. Its authority is found in the near-universal acceptance of some of its key provisions, including: 12 nautical miles as the limit of the territorial sea; coastal states' sovereign rights and jurisdiction in an "exclusive economic zone" up to the limit of 200 nautical miles; and their sovereign rights over the continental shelf extending up to a distance of 200 nautical miles or, under certain circumstances, beyond that limit. The *Convention* has also brought stability in the area of navigation, establishing the rights of innocent passage through the territorial sea; transit passage through narrow straits used for international navigation; sea lanes passage through archipelagic waters; and freedom of navigation in the exclusive economic zone.

The near-universal acceptance of the *Convention* was facilitated in 1994 by the General Assembly's adoption of the *Agreement Relating to the Implementation of Part XI of the Convention*, which removed certain obstacles relating to the seabed area that had prevented mainly industrialized countries from signing the *Convention*. The Part XI Agreement is now widely accepted, with 140 states parties as of December 2010.

The *Convention* has also been acknowledged for its provisions on the rights of coastal states, in the exercise of their jurisdiction, to regulate, authorize and conduct marine scientific research, as well as their duties relating to the prevention, reduction and control of pollution of the marine environment, and on the rights of landlocked states to participate in the exploitation of the living marine resources of the exclusive economic zones of coastal states. Moreover, the *Convention* is recognized as the framework and foundation for any future instruments that seek to further clarify the rights and obligations of states in the oceans.

One such instrument, the 1995 *Agreement on Straddling Fish Stocks and Highly Migratory Fish Stocks*, implements provisions in the *Convention* relating to these fish stocks, setting out the legal regime for their conservation and management. It requires states to cooperate in adopting measures to ensure their long-term sustainability and to promote their optimum utilization. States are also required to cooperate to achieve compatibility of measures with respect to these stocks for areas under national jurisdiction and the adjacent high seas. As of December 2010, the *Agreement* had 78 parties.

Bodies established under the Convention

The *Convention* established three specific organs to deal with various aspects of the law of the sea.

The **International Seabed Authority** (*www.isa.org.jm*) is the organization through which states parties organize and control activities relating to the deep seabed's mineral resources in the international seabed area, beyond the limits of national jurisdiction. Inaugurated in 1994, it is located in Kingston, Jamaica. In 2002, the Authority adopted regulations on prospecting and exploration for polymetallic nodules in the Area (defined as "the seabed and ocean floor and subsoil thereof, beyond the limits of national jurisdiction").

Following adoption of these regulations, which include standard clauses for exploration contracts, the first 15-year contracts for exploration for polymetallic nodules in the deep seabed were signed in 2001 with the registered pioneer investors from various countries. These pioneer investors are state-owned enterprises or multinational consortia that—having undertaken prospecting activities and having located economically exploitable deposits of polymetallic nodules in the Area before the adoption of the *Convention*—were accorded preferential treatment in the granting of production authorizations over other applicants, with the exception of 'the Enterprise'. The Enterprise is the organ of the International Seabed Authority that carries out activities in the Area as enumerated in the *Convention*, as well as the transport, processing and marketing of minerals recovered from the Area—functions currently being carried out by the Legal and Technical Commission of the Authority.

The **International Tribunal for the Law of the Sea** (*www.itlos.org*), operational since 1996, was established to settle disputes relating to the interpretation or application of the *Convention*. Composed of 21 judges elected by the states parties, it is located in the German seaport of Hamburg. It received its first application instituting a case in 2001.

As of December 2010, 18 cases had been submitted to the Tribunal, most of them seeking the prompt release of vessels and crews allegedly arrested in breach of the *Convention*. Some, such as *New Zealand v. Japan* and *Australia v. Japan*, concerning southern blue-fin tuna stocks, have dealt with the conservation of living resources. Another case, *Ireland v. United Kingdom*, dealt with the prevention of land-based pollution from a plant designed to reprocess spent nuclear fuel. Of these 18 cases, two were still on the court's docket at the end of 2010. One concerned a dispute on delimitation of the maritime boundary between Bangladesh and Myanmar in the Bay of Bengal. The other was a case brought by Saint Vincent and the Grenadines against Spain concerning a vessel arrested by Spain.

The purpose of the **Commission on the Limits of the Continental Shelf** (*www.un.org/depts/los/clcs_new/clcs_home.htm*) is to facilitate implementation of the *Convention* with respect to delineation of the outer limits of the continental shelf when that submerged portion of the land territory of a coastal state extends beyond the 200 nautical miles from its coastline—established as the minimal legal distance under the *Convention*. Under its article 76, the coastal state may establish the outer limits of its *juridical* continental shelf in such cases through the application of specified scientific and technical formulas. The Commission held its first session at United Nations Headquarters in 1997. Its 21 members, elected by the states parties to the *Convention*, serve in their personal capacity. They are experts in geology, geophysics, hydrography and geodesy. The Commission received its first submission by a state party, the Russian Federation, in December 2001.

Meetings of states parties and General Assembly processes

Although the *Convention* does not provide for a periodic conference of states parties, the annual meeting of states parties, which is convened by the UN Secretary-General, has served as a forum where issues of concern have been discussed. This is in addition to its assigned administrative functions, such as election of members of the Tribunal and the Commission, as well as other budgetary and administrative actions. The Secretary-General has also convened annual informal consultations of the states parties to the *Fish Stocks Agreement* since its entry into force in 2001, to monitor its implementation.

The General Assembly performs an oversight function with respect to ocean affairs and the law of the sea. In 2000, it established an open-ended, informal, consultative process to facilitate its own annual review of developments in the field. That process, convened annually, makes suggestions to the Assembly on particular issues, with an emphasis on identifying areas where coordination and cooperation among governments and agencies should be enhanced. Such topics have included safety of navigation and the protection of vulnerable marine ecosystems. The consultative process has been repeatedly extended because of the positive results it has achieved. In 2004, the General Assembly also established an open-ended, informal, ad hoc working group to study issues relating to the conservation and sustainable use of marine biological diversity beyond areas of national jurisdiction.

International humanitarian law

International humanitarian law encompasses the principles and rules that regulate the means and methods of warfare, as well as the humanitarian protection of civilian populations, sick and wounded combatants, and prisoners of war. Major instruments include the 1949 *Geneva Conventions for the Protection of War Victims* and two additional protocols concluded in 1977 under the auspices of the International Committee of the Red Cross (*www.icrc.org*).

The United Nations has taken a leading role in efforts to advance international humanitarian law. The Security Council has become increasingly involved in protecting civilians in armed conflict, promoting human rights and protecting children in wars. The establishment of the **International Criminal Tribunals for the former Yugoslavia (1993)** and for **Rwanda (1994)** have served both to ensure accountability, and to strengthen and enhance the wider appreciation of humanitarian law. This applies as well to three courts established by the states concerned but with substantial UN support: the **Special Court for Sierra Leone (2002)**, the **Extraordinary Chambers in the Courts of Cambodia (2006)** and the **Special Tribunal for Lebanon (2007)**. Sometimes referred to as 'hybrid' courts, they are non-permanent institutions which will cease to exist once all their cases have been heard.

The General Assembly, as a political forum of the United Nations, has contributed to elaborating a number of instruments that have significantly advanced the scope and application of international humanitarian law. Among them are the *Convention on the Prevention and Punishment of the Crime of Genocide* (1948); the *Convention on the Non-Applicability of Statutory Limitations to War Crimes and Crimes Against Humanity* (1968); the *Convention on Prohibition and Restrictions on the Use of Certain Conventional Weapons which may be deemed to be Excessively Injurious or to have Indiscriminate Effects* (1980) and its five protocols; the *Principles of International Cooperation in the Detection, Arrest, Extradition and Punishment of Persons Guilty of War Crimes and Crimes Against Humanity,* which the Assembly adopted in 1973; and the *Convention on Cluster Munitions* (2008).

The Assembly also facilitated the convening of the diplomatic conference that adopted the **Rome Statute of the International Criminal Court** in 1998. Even prior to this landmark event, the preparatory commission for the Court had elaborated the "elements of crimes" with respect to genocide, war crimes and crimes against humanity—a major contribution to international humanitarian law.

International terrorism

The United Nations has consistently addressed the problem of terrorism at both the legal and political level. It has also been the target of terrorism. From Afghanistan to Algeria, from Iraq to Pakistan, UN staff members have lost their lives in the line of duty, in the service of peace, human rights and development.

The International Criminal Court

The idea of a permanent international court to prosecute crimes against humanity was first considered at the United Nations in the context of the adoption of the *Genocide Convention* of 1948. For many years, differences of opinions forestalled further developments. In 1992, the General Assembly directed the International Law Commission to prepare a draft statute for such a court. The massacres in Cambodia, the former Yugoslavia and Rwanda made the need for it even more urgent.

Established by the *Rome Statute of the International Criminal Court (www.un.org/law/icc)* adopted at a plenipotentiary conference in Rome on 17 July 1998, the International Criminal Court (ICC) (*www.icc-cpi.int*) has jurisdiction to prosecute individuals who commit genocide, war crimes and crimes against humanity. It will also have jurisdiction over the crime of aggression when agreement is reached on the definition of such a crime. The ICC is legally and functionally independent from the United Nations, and is not a part of the UN system. The *Statute* entered into force on 1 July 2002. As of December 2010, the *Statute* had 114 states parties. The cooperation between the UN and the ICC is governed by a *Negotiated Relationship Agreement*. The Security Council can initiate proceedings before the ICC, and can refer to the ICC situations that would not otherwise fall under the Court's jurisdiction.

The Court has 18 judges, elected by the states parties for a term limited to nine years, except that a judge shall remain in office to complete any trial or appeal which has already begun. No two judges can be from the same country.

As of February 2011, three states parties to the *Rome Statute*—Uganda, the Democratic Republic of the Congo and the Central African Republic—had referred situations occurring in their territories to the Court. In addition, the Security Council referred the situation in Darfur, Sudan, a non-state party. After a thorough analysis of available information, the Prosecutor opened and was conducting investigations in all of these situations.

President: Sang-Hyun Song (Republic of Korea)
Prosecutor: Luis Moreno-Ocampo (Argentina)
Registrar: Silvana Arbia (Italy)
Headquarters: Secretariat of the Assembly of States Parties, International Criminal
     Court, Maanweg 174, 2516 AB The Hague, The Netherlands
Tel.: (31-70) 515 98 06; Fax: (31-70) 515 83 76

The UN and its related bodies—such as the International Civil Aviation Organization (ICAO), the International Maritime Organization (IMO) and the International Atomic Energy Agency (IAEA)—have developed a network of international agreements that constitute the basic legal instruments against terrorism. These include the following:

- *Convention on Offences and Certain Other Acts Committed on Board Aircraft* (Tokyo, 1963);
- *Convention for the Suppression of Unlawful Seizure of Aircraft* (The Hague, 1970);
- *Convention for the Suppression of Unlawful Acts against the Safety of Civil Aviation* (Montreal, 1971);
- *Convention on the Prevention and Punishment of Crimes against Internationally Protected Persons, including Diplomatic Agents* (New York, 1973);
- *Convention on the Physical Protection of Nuclear Material* (Vienna, 1980);
- *Protocol for the Suppression of Unlawful Acts of Violence at Airports Serving International Civil Aviation* (Montreal, 1988);

- *Convention for the Suppression of Unlawful Acts against the Safety of Maritime Navigation* (Rome, 1988);
- *Protocol for the Suppression of Unlawful Acts against the Safety of Fixed Platforms Located on the Continental Shelf* (Rome, 1988);
- *Convention on the Marking of Plastic Explosives for the Purpose of Detection* (Montreal, 1991).

The General Assembly has also concluded the following five conventions:

- *International Convention against the Taking of Hostages* (1979), in which states parties agree to make the taking of hostages punishable by appropriate penalties. They also agree to prohibit certain activities within their territories, to exchange information and to enable any criminal or extradition proceedings to take place. If a state party does not extradite an alleged offender, it must submit the case to its own authorities for prosecution;
- *Convention on the Safety of United Nations and Associated Personnel* (1994), adopted by the Assembly following many instances of attacks against UN personnel in the field which resulted in injury and death;
- *International Convention for the Suppression of Terrorist Bombings* (1997). It is aimed at denying 'safe havens' to persons wanted for terrorist bombings by obligating each state party to prosecute such persons if it does not extradite them to another state that has issued an extradition request;
- *International Convention for the Suppression of the Financing of Terrorism* (1999) obligates states parties either to prosecute or extradite persons accused of funding terrorist activities, and requires banks to enact measures to identify suspicious transactions;
- *International Convention for the Suppression of Acts of Nuclear Terrorism* (2005) covers a broad range of acts and possible targets, in crisis and post-crisis situations. It also covers threats and attempts to commit or participate in such acts, including as an accomplice. The *Convention*, which stipulates that offenders be either prosecuted or extradited, entered into force in 2007.

In 1994, the General Assembly adopted a *Declaration on Measures to Eliminate International Terrorism*. In 1996, in a *Declaration to Supplement the 1994 Declaration*, the Assembly condemned all acts and practices of terrorism as criminal and unjustifiable, wherever and by whomever committed. It also urged states to take measures at the national and international levels to eliminate international terrorism. An *ad hoc* committee established by the Assembly in 1996 is currently negotiating a comprehensive convention against international terrorism to fill in gaps left by existing treaties.

Soon after the 11 September 2001 terrorist attacks on the United States, the Security Council that same month established its **Counter-Terrorism Committee** (*www.un.org/sc/ctc*). Among its functions, the Committee monitors implementation of Council resolutions 1624(2005) and 1373(2001), which imposed certain obligations on member states. These include: criminalization of terrorism-related activities, including the provision of assistance to carry them out; denial of funding and safe haven to terrorists; and the exchange of information on terrorist groups.

In 2006, the **United Nations Global Counter-Terrorism Strategy** (see *www.un.org/terrorism*) was launched, following its unanimous adoption by the General Assembly. Based on the fundamental conviction that terrorism in all its forms is unacceptable and can never be justified, the Strategy outlines a range of measures to address terrorism in all its aspects at the national, regional and international levels. In 2010, in its second biennial review of the Strategy, the Assembly reaffirmed the primary responsibility of member states for its implementation.

Addressing the Security Council in September 2010, Secretary-General Ban Ki-moon made particular reference to the "Alliance of Civilizations", describing it as "a central part of the UN's response to extremism and intolerance—a necessary voice of moderation to counter the incitement and hate that are such prominent parts of terrorism's playbook".

Other legal questions

The General Assembly has adopted legal instruments on various other questions concerning the international community and the peoples of the world. Among these are the *International Convention against the Recruitment, Use, Financing and Training of Mercenaries* (1989); the *Body of Principles for the Protection of All Persons under Any Form of Detention or Imprisonment* (1988); and the *Declaration on the Enhancement of the Effectiveness of the Principle of Refraining from the Threat or Use of Force in International Relations* (1987).

The Assembly has adopted many international instruments having to do with the work of the UN itself on the recommendation of the **Special Committee on the Charter of the United Nations and on the Strengthening of the Role of the Organization**, established by the Assembly in 1974. These include the *United Nations Model Rules for the Conciliation of Disputes between States* (1995); the *Declaration on the Enhancement of Cooperation between the United Nations and Regional Arrangements or Agencies in the Maintenance of International Peace and Security* (1994); the *Declaration on Fact-finding by the United Nations in the Field of the Maintenance of International Peace and Security* (1991); the *Declaration on the Prevention and Removal of Disputes and Situations Which May Threaten International Peace and Security and on the Role of the United Nations in this Field* (1988); and the *Declaration on the Peaceful Settlement of International Disputes* (1982).

Under Article 102 of the *Charter of the United Nations*, every international agreement entered into by any member state shall be registered with the United Nations Secretariat and published by it. The United Nations **Office of Legal Affairs** is responsible for the registration and publication of treaties. It publishes the *United Nations Treaty Series,* which contains the texts of more than 158,000 treaties and related subsequent actions. It also discharges the functions of the Secretary-General as depositary of multilateral treaties. In that role, the Office maintains the status of over 500 major multilateral treaties in the publication *Multilateral Treaties Deposited with the Secretary-General.* Updated daily in electronic format and available in the United Nations Treaty Collection on the Internet (*untreaty.un.org*), this documentation is also available in hard copy.

Timorese celebrate International Day of Peace
Timorese in traditional dress take part in a ceremony for the International Day of Peace that also marked the resumption of policing responsibilities in the district of Alieu by the Polícia Nacional de Timor-Leste (PNTL), which took over from UN Police forces (21 September 2010, UN Photo/Martine Perret).

VII. DECOLONIZATION

Nearly 100 nations whose peoples were formerly under colonial rule or a trusteeship arrangement have joined the United Nations as sovereign independent states since the Organization was founded in 1945. Additionally, many other Territories have achieved self-determination through political association or integration with an independent state. The United Nations has played a crucial role in that historic change by encouraging the aspirations of dependent peoples and by setting goals and standards to accelerate their attainment of independence. United Nations missions have supervised elections leading to independence—in Togoland (1956 and 1968), Western Samoa (1961), Namibia (1989) and, most recently, in Timor-Leste (formerly East Timor).

The decolonization efforts of the United Nations derive from the *Charter* principle of "equal rights and self-determination of peoples", as well as from three specific chapters in the *Charter*—Chapters XI, XII and XIII—which are devoted to the interests of dependent peoples. Since 1960, the United Nations has also been guided by the General Assembly's *Declaration on the Granting of Independence to Colonial Countries and Peoples*, also known as the *Declaration on Decolonization*, by which member states proclaimed the necessity of bringing colonialism to a speedy end. The United Nations has also been guided by General Assembly resolution 1541(XV) of 1960, which defined three options offering full self-government for Non-Self-Governing Territories.

Despite the great progress made against colonialism, more than 1 million people still live under colonial rule, and the United Nations continues its efforts to help achieve self-determination in the remaining Non-Self-Governing Territories (see *www.un.org/depts/dpi/decolonization*).

International trusteeship system

Under Chapter XII of the *Charter*, the United Nations established an international trusteeship system for the supervision of Trust Territories placed under it by individual agreements with the states administering them. The system applied to: Territories held under mandates established by the League of Nations after the First World War; Territories detached from "enemy states" as a result of the Second World War; and Territories voluntarily placed under the system by states responsible for their administration. The goal of the system was to promote the political, economic and social advancement of the Territories and their development towards self-government and self-determination.

The **Trusteeship Council** was established under Chapter XIII of the *Charter* to supervise the administration of Trust Territories and to ensure that governments responsible for their administration took adequate steps to prepare them for the achievement of the *Charter* goals.

In the early years of the United Nations, 11 Territories were placed under the trusteeship system. Over the years, all 11 Territories either became independent states or voluntarily associated themselves with a state. The last one to do so was the Trust Territory of the Pacific Islands (Palau), administered by the United States. The Security Council in 1994 terminated the United Nations Trusteeship Agreement for that Territory after it chose free association with the United States in a 1993 plebiscite. Palau became independent in 1994, joining the United Nations as its 185th member state. With no Territories left on its agenda, the trusteeship system had completed its historic task.

Territories to which the Declaration on the Granting of Independence to Colonial Countries and Peoples continues to apply

Territory	*Administering authority*
Africa	
Western Sahara[1]	—
Asia and the Pacific	
American Samoa	United States
Guam	United States
New Caledonia[2]	France
Pitcairn	United Kingdom
Tokelau	New Zealand
Atlantic Ocean, Caribbean and Mediterranean	
Anguilla	United Kingdom
Bermuda	United Kingdom
British Virgin Islands	United Kingdom
Cayman Islands	United Kingdom
Falkland Islands (Malvinas)	United Kingdom
Gibraltar	United Kingdom
Montserrat	United Kingdom
Saint Helena	United Kingdom
Turks and Caicos Islands	United Kingdom
United States Virgin Islands	United States

[1] On 26 February 1976, Spain informed the Secretary-General that as of that date it had terminated its presence in the Territory of the Sahara, and deemed it necessary to place on record that Spain considered itself thenceforth exempt from any international responsibility in connection with its administration, in view of the cessation of its participation in the temporary administration established for the Territory. In 1990, the General Assembly reaffirmed that the question of Western Sahara was a question of decolonization that remained to be completed by the people of Western Sahara.

[2] On 2 December 1986, the General Assembly determined that New Caledonia was a Non-Self-Governing Territory.

Non-Self-Governing Territories

The *Charter of the United Nations* also addresses the issue of other Non-Self-Governing Territories not brought into the trusteeship system. Chapter XI of the *Charter*—the *Declaration regarding Non-Self-Governing Territories*—provides that member states administering such Territories recognize "that the interests of the inhabitants of these Territories is paramount" and accept the obligation to promote their well-being as a "sacred trust". To this end, administering powers, in addition to ensuring the political, economic, social and educational advancement of those peoples, undertake to assist them in developing self-government and democratic political institutions. Administering powers have an obligation to transmit regularly to the Secretary-General information on the economic, social and educational conditions in the Territories under their administration.

In 1946, eight member states—Australia, Belgium, Denmark, France, the Netherlands, New Zealand, the United Kingdom and the United States—identified the non-self-governing Territories under their administration. There were 72 such Territories in all, of which eight became independent before 1959. In 1963, the Assembly approved a revised list of 64 Territories to which the 1960 *Declaration on Decolonization* applied. Today, 16 such Territories remain, with France, New Zealand, the United Kingdom and the United States as administering powers.

In 2005, Tokelau's national representative body, the General Fono, approved a draft treaty of free association between Tokelau and New Zealand, and then a draft constitution. In a 2006 referendum, 60 per cent of registered Tokelauans voted in favour of free association, falling just short of the required two-thirds majority. A second referendum, held in 2007, fell 16 votes short of the required majority, with 446 votes in favour out of 692 votes cast.

Declaration on the Granting of Independence to Colonial Countries and Peoples

The desire of the peoples of dependent Territories to achieve self-determination, and the international community's perception that *Charter* principles were being too slowly applied, led the General Assembly to proclaim in 1960 the *Declaration on the Granting of Independence to Colonial Countries and Peoples* (resolution 1514(XV)). The *Declaration* states that subjecting peoples to alien subjugation, domination and exploitation constitutes a denial of fundamental human rights; is contrary to the *Charter*; and is an impediment to the promotion of world peace and cooperation. It adds that "immediate steps shall be taken, in Trust and Non-Self-Governing Territories or all other Territories which have not yet attained independence, to transfer all powers to the peoples of those Territories, without any conditions or reservations, in accordance with their freely expressed will and desire, without any distinction as to race, creed or colour in order to enable them to enjoy complete independence and freedom". Also in 1960, the Assembly approved resolution 1541(XV), defining the three legitimate political status options offering full self-government—free association with an independent state, integration into an independent state, or independence.

In 1961, the Assembly established a special committee to examine the application of the *Declaration* and make recommendations on its implementation. Commonly referred to as the **Special Committee on Decolonization**, its full title is the Special Committee on the Situation with Regard to the Implementation of the Declaration on the Granting of Independence to Colonial Countries and Peoples. It meets annually, hears petitioners and representatives of the Territories, dispatches visiting missions to the Territories, and organizes annual seminars on the political, social, economic and educational situations in the Territories.

In the years following the adoption of the *Declaration*, some 60 colonial Territories, inhabited by more than 80 million people, attained self-determination through independence, and joined the United Nations as sovereign members. The Assembly has called upon the administering powers to take all necessary steps to enable the peoples of the Non-Self-Governing Territories to exercise fully their right to self-determination and independence. It has also called upon the administering powers to complete the withdrawal of remaining military bases from those Territories, and to ensure that no activity of foreign economic and other interests hinders the implementation of the *Declaration*.

In this respect, New Zealand has extended continuous cooperation to the Special Committee regarding Tokelau. France began cooperating with the Committee in 1999, following the signing of an agreement on the future of New Caledonia. In recent years, two administering powers have not participated formally in the Committee's work. The United States has maintained that it remains conscious of its role as an administering power and will continue to meet its responsibilities under the *Charter*. The United Kingdom has repeatedly stated that while most of the Territories under its administration chose independence, a small number have preferred to remain associated with it.

At the end of the first International Decade for the Eradication of Colonialism (1991–2000), the General Assembly declared a Second International Decade for the Eradication of Colonialism (2001–2010), calling on member states to redouble their efforts to achieve complete decolonization. In the case of certain Territories, such as Western Sahara, the Assembly has entrusted the Secretary-General with specific tasks to facilitate the process of decolonization, in accordance with the *Charter* and the objectives of the *Declaration*.

Namibia

The United Nations helped bring about the independence of Namibia in 1990— a case history revealing the complexity of the efforts needed to ensure the peaceful transition of a Territory to independence. Formerly known as South West Africa, Namibia was an African Territory under the League of Nations mandate system.

In 1946, the General Assembly asked South Africa to administer the Territory under the trusteeship system. South Africa refused, and in 1949 informed the United Nations that it would no longer transmit information on the Territory, maintaining that the mandate had ended with the demise of the League. The General Assembly, stating that South Africa had not fulfilled its obligations, terminated that mandate in 1966 and placed the Territory under the responsibility of the United Nations Council for South West Africa, which was renamed the Council for Namibia in 1968. In 1976, the Security Council demanded that South Africa accept elections for the Territory under UN supervision. The General Assembly stated that independence talks would have to involve the South West Africa People's Organization (SWAPO)—the sole representative of the Namibian people.

In 1978, Canada, France, the Federal Republic of Germany, the United Kingdom and the United States submitted to the Security Council a settlement proposal providing for elections for a constituent assembly under UN auspices. The Council endorsed the Secretary-General's recommendations for implementing the proposal, asked him to appoint a special representative for Namibia, and established the **United Nations Transition Assistance Group (UNTAG)**. Years of negotiations by the Secretary-General and his special representative, as well as United States mediation, led in 1988 to agreements for the achievement of peace in southern Africa, by which South Africa agreed to cooperate with the Secretary-General to ensure Namibia's independence through elections.

The operation that led to Namibia's independence started in 1989. UNTAG supervised and controlled the entire electoral process, which was conducted by the Namibian authorities. It monitored the ceasefire between SWAPO and South Africa and the demobilization of all military forces, and ensured a smooth electoral process, including the monitoring of local police.

The elections for the constituent assembly were won by SWAPO and were declared "free and fair" by the Secretary-General's special representative. Following the elections, South Africa withdrew its remaining troops. The constituent assembly drafted a new constitution, approved in February 1990, and elected SWAPO leader Sam Nujoma as President for a five-year term. In March, Namibia became independent, with the Secretary-General administering the oath of office to Namibia's first President. In April of the same year, it joined the United Nations.

Timor-Leste

Another United Nations success story is the process that led to the independence of Timor-Leste—formerly known as East Timor. A major UN operation oversaw its transition towards independence, after the East Timorese people voted in favour of independence in a popular consultation conducted by the UN in 1999.

The island of Timor lies to the north of Australia, in the south-central part of the chain of islands forming Indonesia. Its western part had been a Dutch colony, and became part of Indonesia when that country attained independence. East Timor was a Portuguese colony.

In 1960, the General Assembly placed East Timor on the list of Non-Self-Governing Territories. In 1974, recognizing its right to self-determination, Portugal sought to establish a provisional government and popular assembly to determine East Timor's status. In 1975, however, civil war broke out between the Territory's newly formed political parties. Portugal withdrew, stating it could not control the situation. One East Timorese side declared independence as a separate country, while another proclaimed independence and integration with Indonesia.

In December, Indonesian troops landed in East Timor, and a provisional government was formed. Portugal broke off relations with Indonesia and brought the matter before the Security Council, which called on Indonesia to withdraw its forces and urged all states to respect the right of the East Timorese people to self-determination. In 1976, the provisional government held elections for an assembly, which then called for integration with Indonesia. When Indonesia issued a law supporting that decision, the pro-independence movement began an armed resistance. In 1983, the Secretary-General started talks with Indonesia and Portugal, but it was only in 1999, through the good offices of the Secretary-General, that agreements were reached, paving the way for a popular consultation.

On the basis of those agreements, the **United Nations Mission in East Timor (UNAMET)** organized and conducted voter registration and an official ballot. In August 1999, however, when 78.5 per cent of 450,000 registered voters rejected autonomy within Indonesia, militias opposing independence unleashed a campaign of systematic destruction and violence, killing many and forcing more than 200,000 East Timorese to flee their homes. After intensive talks, Indonesia accepted the deployment of a UN-authorized multinational force. In September, acting under Chapter VII of the *Charter*, the Security Council authorized the dispatch of the **International Force in East Timor (INTERFET)**, which helped restore peace and security. Immediately following that action, the Council, in October, established the **United Nations Transitional Administration in East Timor (UNTAET)**, giving it full executive and legislative authority during the country's transition to independence.

In August 2001, more than 91 per cent of East Timor's eligible voters went to the polls to elect an 88-member constituent assembly, tasked with writing and adopting a new constitution and establishing the framework for future elections and the transition to full independence. In March 2002, the constituent assembly signed into force the Territory's first constitution. The following month, after winning 82.7 per cent of the vote, Xanana Gusmão was appointed president-elect. On 20 May 2002, the Territory attained independence. The constituent assembly was transformed into the national parliament, and the new country adopted the name Timor-Leste. In September of that year, it became the 191st member state of the United Nations.

Following the successful decolonization of East Timor, the UN has remained committed to supporting the independent country of Timor-Leste in consolidating democratic institutions and advancing socio-economic development.

Western Sahara

The United Nations has been dealing with an ongoing dispute concerning Western Sahara—a Territory on the north-west coast of Africa bordering Algeria, Mauritania and Morocco—since 1963.

Western Sahara became a Spanish colony in 1884. In 1963, both Mauritania and Morocco laid claim to it. The International Court of Justice, in a 1975 opinion requested by the General Assembly, rejected the claims of territorial sovereignty by Mauritania and Morocco.

The United Nations has been seeking a settlement in Western Sahara since the withdrawal of Spain in 1976 and the ensuing fighting between Morocco—which had 'reintegrated' the Territory—and the Popular Front for the Liberation of Saguia el-Hamra and Río de Oro (Frente Polisario), supported by Algeria. In 1979, the Organization of African Unity (OAU) called for a referendum to enable the people of the Territory to exercise their right to self-determination. By 1982, 26 OAU member states had recognized the "Saharawi Arab Democratic Republic" (SADR) proclaimed by Polisario in 1976. When SADR was seated at the 1984 OAU summit, Morocco withdrew from the OAU.

A joint good offices mission by the Secretary-General and the OAU Chairman led to 1988 settlement proposals calling for a ceasefire, and for a referendum to choose between independence and integration with Morocco, to which the parties agreed in principle. By resolution 690(1991), the Security Council created the **United Nations Mission for the Referendum in Western Sahara (MINURSO)** in 1991 to assist the Secretary-General's special representative in all matters related to the organization and conduct of a referendum of self-determination for the people of Western Sahara. All Western Saharans aged 18 and over counted in the 1974 Spanish census would have the right to vote, whether living in the Territory or outside. An identification commission would update the census list and identify voters. Refugees living outside the Territory would be identified with the assistance of the Office of the United Nations High Commissioner for Refugees (UNHCR).

In September 1991, the ceasefire came into effect. It has been observed ever since by MINURSO's military observers, with no major violations. However, the parties have continued to differ on implementation of the settlement plan—particularly with respect to voter eligibility for the referendum. In 1997, a compromise was brokered by the Secretary-General's personal envoy for Western Sahara, and the identification process was completed at the end of 1999. Nevertheless, despite continuing consultations and negotiations, disagreements persisted over implementation of the plan.

In 2004, Morocco rejected a proposal put forward by the special envoy as well as the settlement plan itself. Despite the continuing stalemate, there were some positive developments over the ensuing years, including the Frente Polisario's release of all remaining Moroccan prisoners of war in August 2005, and the 2004 establishment of a UNHCR-sponsored 'family visits' programme between Western Saharan refugees living in the camps in Tindouf, Algeria, and their relatives in Western Sahara Territory—some of whom had not seen each other for 30 years.

In 2007, the Secretary-General's personal envoy observed that there were two options left: indefinite prolongation of the impasse, or direct negotiations. The Security Council called for good faith negotiations without preconditions. The envoy then facilitated meetings with the parties in New York, also attended by Algeria and Mauritania. At the second meeting, the parties acknowledged that the status quo was unacceptable and committed themselves to continuing the negotiations in good faith.

Despite the continued divergence in positions, this renewed dialogue marked the first direct negotiations between the parties in more than seven years. A third round was held in 2008, and the parties came together for further informal meetings in 2009 and 2010. None of the meetings, however, produced any movement on the core substantive issues. Meanwhile, MINURSO continued to support a range of assistance programmes for the displaced and separated Sahrawi families. It also assisted both parties in maintaining the ceasefire across the buffer strip, which stretches along the entire length of the disputed territory and separates the Moroccan-administered portion in the west from the area that is controlled by the Frente Polisario in the east.

APPENDICES

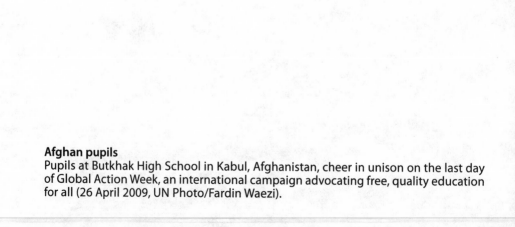

Afghan pupils
Pupils at Butkhak High School in Kabul, Afghanistan, cheer in unison on the last day of Global Action Week, an international campaign advocating free, quality education for all (26 April 2009, UN Photo/Fardin Waezi).

UNITED NATIONS MEMBER STATES

Member state	Date of admission	Scale of assessments for 2010–2012 (per cent)	Population
Afghanistan	19 November 1946	0.004	29,117,000
Albania	14 December 1955	0.010	3,169,000
Algeria	8 October 1962	0.128	35,423,000
Andorra	28 July 1993	0.007	87,000
Angola	1 December 1976	0.010	18,993,000
Antigua and Barbuda	11 November 1981	0.002	89,000
Argentina	24 October 1945	0.287	40,666,000
Armenia	2 March 1992	0.005	3,090,000
Australia	1 November 1945	1.933	21,512,000
Austria	4 December 1955	0.851	8,387,000
Azerbaijan	2 March 1992	0.015	8,934,000
Bahamas	18 September 1973	0.018	346,000
Bahrain	21 September 1971	0.039	807,000
Bangladesh	17 September 1974	0.010	164,425,000
Barbados	9 December 1966	0.008	257,000
Belarus[1]	24 October 1945	0.042	9,588,000
Belgium	27 December 1945	1.075	10,698,000
Belize	25 September 1981	0.001	313,000
Benin	20 September 1960	0.003	9,212,000
Bhutan	21 September 1971	0.001	708,000
Bolivia (Plurinational State of)	14 November 1945	0.007	10,031,000
Bosnia and Herzegovina[2]	22 May 1992	0.014	3,760,000
Botswana	17 October 1966	0.018	1,978,000
Brazil	24 October 1945	1.611	195,423,000
Brunei Darussalam	21 September 1984	0.028	407,000
Bulgaria	14 December 1955	0.038	7,497,000
Burkina Faso	20 September 1960	0.003	16,287,000
Burundi	18 September 1962	0.001	8,519,000
Cambodia	14 December 1955	0.003	15,053,000
Cameroon	20 September 1960	0.011	19,958,000
Canada	9 November 1945	3.207	33,890,000
Cape Verde	16 September 1975	0.001	513,000
Central African Republic	20 September 1960	0.001	4,506,000
Chad	20 September 1960	0.002	11,506,000
Chile	24 October 1945	0.236	17,135,000
China	24 October 1945	3.189	1,354,146,000
Colombia	5 November 1945	0.144	46,300,000
Comoros	12 November 1975	0.001	691,000
Congo	20 September 1960	0.003	3,759,000
Costa Rica	2 November 1945	0.034	4,640,000
Côte d'Ivoire	20 September 1960	0.010	21,571,000
Croatia[2]	22 May 1992	0.097	4,410,000
Cuba	24 October 1945	0.071	11,204,000
Cyprus	20 September 1960	0.046	880,000
Czech Republic[3]	19 January 1993	0.349	10,411,000

Member state	Date of admission	Scale of assessments for 2010–2012 (per cent)	Population
Democratic People's Republic of Korea	17 September 1991	0.007	23,991,000
Democratic Republic of the Congo [4]	20 September 1960	0.003	67,827,000
Denmark	24 October 1945	0.736	5,481,000
Djibouti	20 September 1977	0.001	879,000
Dominica	18 December 1978	0.001	67,000
Dominican Republic	24 October 1945	0.042	10,225,000
Ecuador	21 December 1945	0.040	13,775,000
Egypt [5]	24 October 1945	0.094	84,474,000
El Salvador	24 October 1945	0.019	6,194,000
Equatorial Guinea	12 November 1968	0.008	693,000
Eritrea	28 May 1993	0.001	5,224,000
Estonia	17 September 1991	0.040	1,339,000
Ethiopia	13 November 1945	0.008	84,976,000
Fiji	13 October 1970	0.004	854,000
Finland	14 December 1955	0.566	5,346,000
France	24 October 1945	6.123	62,637,000
Gabon	20 September 1960	0.014	1,501,000
Gambia	21 September 1965	0.001	1,751,000
Georgia	31 July 1992	0.006	4,219,000
Germany [6]	18 September 1973	8.018	82,057,000
Ghana	8 March 1957	0.006	24,333,000
Greece	25 October 1945	0.691	11,183,000
Grenada	17 September 1974	0.001	104,000
Guatemala	21 November 1945	0.028	14,377,000
Guinea	12 December 1958	0.002	10,324,000
Guinea-Bissau	17 September 1974	0.001	1,647,000
Guyana	20 September 1966	0.001	761,000
Haiti	24 October 1945	0.003	10,188,000
Honduras	17 December 1945	0.008	7,616,000
Hungary	14 December 1955	0.291	9,973,000
Iceland	19 November 1946	0.042	329,000
India	30 October 1945	0.534	1,214,464,000
Indonesia [7]	28 September 1950	0.238	232,517,000
Iran (Islamic Republic of)	24 October 1945	0.233	75,078,000
Iraq	21 December 1945	0.020	31,467,000
Ireland	14 December 1955	0.498	4,589,000
Israel	11 May 1949	0.384	7,285,000
Italy	14 December 1955	4.999	60,098,000
Jamaica	18 September 1962	0.014	2,730,000
Japan	18 December 1956	12.530	126,995,000
Jordan	14 December 1955	0.014	6,472,000
Kazakhstan	2 March 1992	0.076	15,753,000
Kenya	16 December 1963	0.012	40,863,000
Kiribati	14 September 1999	0.001	100,000
Kuwait	14 May 1963	0.263	3,051,000
Kyrgyzstan	2 March 1992	0.001	5,550,000

Member state	Date of admission	Scale of assessments for 2010–2012 (per cent)	Population
Lao People's Democratic Republic	14 December 1955	0.001	6,436,000
Latvia	17 September 1991	0.038	2,240,000
Lebanon	24 October 1945	0.033	4,255,000
Lesotho	17 October 1966	0.001	2,084,000
Liberia	2 November 1945	0.001	4,102,000
Libyan Arab Jamahiriya	14 December 1955	0.129	6,546,000
Liechtenstein	18 September 1990	0.009	36,000
Lithuania	17 September 1991	0.065	3,255,000
Luxembourg	24 October 1945	0.090	492,000
Madagascar	20 September 1960	0.003	20,146,000
Malawi	1 December 1964	0.001	15,692,000
Malaysia [8]	17 September 1957	0.253	27,914,000
Maldives	21 September 1965	0.001	314,000
Mali	28 September 1960	0.003	13,323,000
Malta	1 December 1964	0.017	410,000
Marshall Islands	17 September 1991	0.001	63,000
Mauritania	27 October 1961	0.001	3,366,000
Mauritius	24 April 1968	0.011	1,297,000
Mexico	7 November 1945	2.356	110,645,000
Micronesia (Federated States of)	17 September 1991	0.001	111,000
Monaco	28 May 1993	0.003	33,000
Mongolia	27 October 1961	0.002	2,701,000
Montenegro [2]	28 June 2006	0.004	626,000
Morocco	12 November 1956	0.058	32,381,000
Mozambique	16 September 1975	0.003	23,406,000
Myanmar	19 April 1948	0.006	50,496,000
Namibia	23 April 1990	0.008	2,212,000
Nauru	14 September 1999	0.001	10,000
Nepal	14 December 1955	0.006	29,853,000
Netherlands	10 December 1945	1.855	16,653,000
New Zealand	24 October 1945	0.273	4,303,000
Nicaragua	24 October 1945	0.003	5,822,000
Niger	20 September 1960	0.002	15,891,000
Nigeria	7 October 1960	0.078	158,259,000
Norway	27 November 1945	0.871	4,855,000
Oman	7 October 1971	0.086	2,905,000
Pakistan	30 September 1947	0.082	184,753,000
Palau	15 December 1994	0.001	21,000
Panama	13 November 1945	0.022	3,508,000
Papua New Guinea	10 October 1975	0.002	6,888,000
Paraguay	24 October 1945	0.007	6,460,000
Peru	31 October 1945	0.090	29,496,000
Philippines	24 October 1945	0.090	93,617,000
Poland	24 October 1945	0.828	38,038,000
Portugal	14 December 1955	0.511	10,732,000
Qatar	21 September 1971	0.135	1,508,000
Republic of Korea	17 September 1991	2.260	48,501,000

Member state	Date of admission	Scale of assessments for 2010–2012 (per cent)	Population
Republic of Moldova	2 March 1992	0.002	3,576,000
Romania	14 December 1955	0.177	21,190,000
Russian Federation [9]	24 October 1945	1.602	140,367,000
Rwanda	18 September 1962	0.001	10,277,000
Saint Kitts and Nevis	23 September 1983	0.001	52,000
Saint Lucia	18 September 1979	0.001	174,000
Saint Vincent and the Grenadines	16 September 1980	0.001	109,000
Samoa	15 December 1976	0.001	179,000
San Marino	2 March 1992	0.003	32,000
Sao Tome and Principe	16 September 1975	0.001	165,000
Saudi Arabia	24 October 1945	0.830	26,246,000
Senegal	28 September 1960	0.006	12,861,000
Serbia [2]	1 November 2000	0.037	9,856,000
Seychelles	21 September 1976	0.002	85,000
Sierra Leone	27 September 1961	0.001	5,836,000
Singapore [8]	21 September 1965	0.335	4,837,000
Slovakia [3]	19 January 1993	0.142	5,412,000
Slovenia [2]	22 May 1992	0.103	2,025,000
Solomon Islands	19 September 1978	0.001	536,000
Somalia	20 September 1960	0.001	9,359,000
South Africa	7 November 1945	0.385	50,492,000
Spain	14 December 1955	3.177	45,317,000
Sri Lanka	14 December 1955	0.019	20,410,000
Sudan	12 November 1956	0.010	43,192,000
Suriname	4 December 1975	0.003	524,000
Swaziland	24 September 1968	0.003	1,202,000
Sweden	19 November 1946	1.064	9,293,000
Switzerland	10 September 2002	1.130	7,595,000
Syrian Arab Republic [5]	24 October 1945	0.025	22,505,000
Tajikistan	2 March 1992	0.002	7,075,000
Thailand	16 December 1946	0.209	68,139,000
The former Yugoslav Republic of Macedonia [2]	8 April 1993	0.007	2,043,000
Timor-Leste	27 September 2002	0.001	1,171,000
Togo	20 September 1960	0.001	6,780,000
Tonga	14 September 1999	0.001	104,000
Trinidad and Tobago	18 September 1962	0.044	1,344,000
Tunisia	12 November 1956	0.030	10,374,000
Turkey	24 October 1945	0.617	75,705,000
Turkmenistan	2 March 1992	0.026	5,177,000
Tuvalu	5 September 2000	0.001	10,000
Uganda	25 October 1962	0.006	33,796,000
Ukraine	24 October 1945	0.087	45,433,000
United Arab Emirates	9 December 1971	0.391	4,707,000
United Kingdom of Great Britain and Northern Ireland	24 October 1945	6.604	61,899,000
United Republic of Tanzania [10]	14 December 1961	0.008	45,040,000
United States of America	24 October 1945	22.000	317,641,000
Uruguay	18 December 1945	0.027	3,372,000

Member state	Date of admission	Scale of assessments for 2010–2012 (per cent)	Population
Uzbekistan	2 March 1992	0.010	27,794,000
Vanuatu	15 September 1981	0.001	246,000
Venezuela (Bolivarian Republic of)	15 November 1945	0.314	29,044,000
Viet Nam	20 September 1977	0.033	89,029,000
Yemen[11]	30 September 1947	0.010	24,256,000
Zambia	1 December 1964	0.004	13,257,000
Zimbabwe	25 August 1980	0.003	12,644,000

The following state, not a member of the United Nations but participating in certain of its activities, contributes towards the expenses of the Organization on the basis of the percentage rate indicated:

Holy See	0.001	1,000

NOTES

[1] On 19 September 1991, the Byelorussian Soviet Socialist Republic informed the United Nations that it had changed its name to Belarus.

[2] The Socialist Federal Republic of Yugoslavia was an original member of the United Nations, the *Charter* having been signed on its behalf on 26 June 1945 and ratified 19 October 1945, until its dissolution following the establishment and subsequent admission, as new members, of Bosnia and Herzegovina, the Republic of Croatia, the Republic of Slovenia, The former Yugoslav Republic of Macedonia, and the Federal Republic of Yugoslavia. The Republic of Bosnia and Herzegovina, the Republic of Croatia and the Republic of Slovenia were admitted as members of the United Nations on 22 May 1992. On 8 April 1993, the General Assembly decided to admit as a member of the United Nations the state provisionally referred to for all purposes within the United Nations as 'The former Yugoslav Republic of Macedonia' pending settlement of the difference that had arisen over its name. The Federal Republic of Yugoslavia was admitted as a member of the United Nations on 1 November 2000. On 12 February 2003, it informed the United Nations that it had changed its name to Serbia and Montenegro, effective 4 February 2003. In a letter dated 3 June 2006, the President of the Republic of Serbia informed the Secretary-General that the membership of Serbia and Montenegro was being continued by the Republic of Serbia following Montenegro's declaration of independence from Serbia on 3 June 2006. On 28 June 2006, Montenegro was accepted as a United Nations member state by the General Assembly.

[3] Czechoslovakia, an original member of the United Nations from 24 October 1945, changed its name to the Czech and Slovak Federal Republic on 20 April 1990. It was dissolved on 1 January 1993 and succeeded by the Czech Republic and Slovakia, both of which became members of the United Nations on 19 January 1993.

[4] The Republic of Zaire informed the United Nations that, effective 17 May 1997, it had changed its name to the Democratic Republic of the Congo.

[5] Egypt and Syria were original members of the United Nations from 24 October 1945. Following a plebiscite on 21 February 1958, the United Arab Republic was established by a union of Egypt and Syria and continued as a single member. On 13 October 1961, Syria, having resumed its status as an independent state, resumed its separate membership in the United Nations; it changed its name to the Syrian Arab Republic on 14 September 1971. On 2 September 1971, the United Arab Republic changed its name to the Arab Republic of Egypt.

[6] The Federal Republic of Germany and the German Democratic Republic were admitted to membership in the United Nations on 18 September 1973. Through the accession of the German Democratic Republic to the Federal Republic of Germany, effective 3 October 1990, the two German states united to form one sovereign state. As of that date, the Federal Republic of Germany has acted in the United Nations under the designation Germany.

[7] By a letter of 20 January 1965, Indonesia announced its decision to withdraw from the United Nations "at this stage and under the present circumstances". By a telegram of 19 September 1966, it announced its decision "to resume full cooperation with the United Nations and to resume participation in its activities". On 28 September 1966, the General Assembly took note of this decision, and the President invited representatives of Indonesia to take their seats in the Assembly.

[8] The Federation of Malaya joined the United Nations on 17 September 1957. On 16 September 1963, its name was changed to Malaysia, following the admission to the new federation of Sabah (North Borneo), Sarawak and Singapore. Singapore became an independent state on 9 August 1965 and a member of the United Nations on 21 September 1965.

[9] The Union of Soviet Socialist Republics was an original member of the United Nations from 24 October 1945. On 24 December 1991, the President of the Russian Federation informed the Secretary-General that the membership of the Soviet Union in the Security Council and all other UN organs was being continued by the Russian Federation with the support of the 11 member countries of the Commonwealth of Independent States.

[10] Tanganyika was a member of the United Nations from 14 December 1961 and Zanzibar from 16 December 1963. Following the ratification on 26 April 1964 of Articles of Union between Tanganyika and Zanzibar, the United Republic of Tanganyika and Zanzibar continued as a single member, changing its name to the United Republic of Tanzania on 1 November 1964.

[11] Yemen was admitted to membership in the United Nations on 30 September 1947 and Democratic Yemen on 14 December 1967. On 22 May 1990, the two countries merged and have since been represented as one member of the United Nations with the name Yemen.

GROWTH IN UNITED NATIONS MEMBERSHIP

Year	Number	Member states
1945	51	Argentina, Australia, Belarus[1], Belgium, Bolivia, Brazil, Canada, Chile, China, Colombia, Costa Rica, Cuba, Czechoslovakia[2], Denmark, Dominican Republic, Ecuador, Egypt[3], El Salvador, Ethiopia, France, Greece, Guatemala, Haiti, Honduras, India, Iran, Iraq, Lebanon, Liberia, Luxembourg, Mexico, Netherlands, New Zealand, Nicaragua, Norway, Panama, Paraguay, Peru, Philippines, Poland, Russian Federation[4], Saudi Arabia, South Africa, Syrian Arab Republic[3], Turkey, Ukraine, United Kingdom of Great Britain and Northern Ireland, United States of America, Uruguay, Venezuela, Yugoslavia
1946	55	Afghanistan, Iceland, Sweden, Thailand
1947	57	Pakistan, Yemen[5]
1948	58	Myanmar
1949	59	Israel
1950	60	Indonesia[6]
1955	76	Albania, Austria, Bulgaria, Cambodia, Finland, Hungary, Ireland, Italy, Jordan, Lao People's Democratic Republic, Libyan Arab Jamahiriya, Nepal, Portugal, Romania, Spain, Sri Lanka
1956	80	Japan, Morocco, Sudan, Tunisia
1957	82	Ghana, Malaysia[7]
1958	82[3]	Guinea
1960	99	Benin, Burkina Faso, Cameroon, Central African Republic, Chad, Congo, Côte d'Ivoire, Cyprus, Democratic Republic of the Congo[8], Gabon, Madagascar, Mali, Niger, Nigeria, Senegal, Somalia, Togo
1961	104[3]	Mauritania, Mongolia, Sierra Leone, United Republic of Tanzania[9]
1962	110	Algeria, Burundi, Jamaica, Rwanda, Trinidad and Tobago, Uganda
1963	113	Kenya, Kuwait, Zanzibar[9]
1964	115[9]	Malawi, Malta, Zambia
1965	117[6]	Gambia, Maldives, Singapore[7]
1966	122[6]	Barbados, Botswana, Guyana, Lesotho
1967	123	Democratic Yemen[5]
1968	126	Equatorial Guinea, Mauritius, Swaziland
1970	127	Fiji
1971	132	Bahrain, Bhutan, Oman, Qatar, United Arab Emirates
1973	135	Bahamas, Federal Republic of Germany[10], German Democratic Republic[10]
1974	138	Bangladesh, Grenada, Guinea-Bissau
1975	144	Cape Verde, Comoros, Mozambique, Papua New Guinea, Sao Tome and Principe, Suriname
1976	147	Angola, Samoa, Seychelles
1977	149	Djibouti, Viet Nam
1978	151	Dominica, Solomon Islands
1979	152	Saint Lucia
1980	154	Saint Vincent and the Grenadines, Zimbabwe
1981	157	Antigua and Barbuda, Belize, Vanuatu
1983	158	Saint Kitts and Nevis
1984	159	Brunei Darussalam

Year	Number	Member states
1990	159[4,10]	Liechtenstein, Namibia
1991	166	Democratic People's Republic of Korea, Estonia, Federated States of Micronesia, Latvia, Lithuania, Marshall Islands, Republic of Korea
1992	179	Armenia, Azerbaijan, Bosnia and Herzegovina[11], Croatia[11], Georgia, Kazakhstan, Kyrgyzstan, Republic of Moldova, San Marino, Slovenia[11], Tajikistan, Turkmenistan, Uzbekistan
1993	184	Andorra, Czech Republic[2], Eritrea, Monaco, Slovakia[2], The former Yugoslav Republic of Macedonia[11]
1994	185	Palau
1999	188	Kiribati, Nauru, Tonga
2000	189	Serbia[11], Tuvalu
2002	191	Switzerland, Timor-Leste
2006	192	Montenegro[11]

NOTES

[1] On 19 September 1991, the Byelorussian Soviet Socialist Republic informed the United Nations that it had changed its name to Belarus.

[2] Czechoslovakia, an original member of the United Nations from 24 October 1945, changed its name to the Czech and Slovak Federal Republic on 20 April 1990. It was dissolved on 1 January 1993 and succeeded by the Czech Republic and Slovakia, both of which became members of the United Nations on 19 January 1993.

[3] Egypt and Syria were original members of the United Nations from 24 October 1945. Following a plebiscite on 21 February 1958, the United Arab Republic was established by a union of Egypt and Syria and continued as a single member. On 13 October 1961, Syria, having resumed its status as an independent state, resumed its separate membership in the United Nations; it changed its name to the Syrian Arab Republic on 14 September 1971. On 2 September 1971, the United Arab Republic changed its name to the Arab Republic of Egypt.

[4] The Union of Soviet Socialist Republics was an original member of the United Nations from 24 October 1945. On 24 December 1991, the President of the Russian Federation informed the Secretary-General that the membership of the Soviet Union in the Security Council and all other UN organs was being continued by the Russian Federation with the support of the 11 member countries of the Commonwealth of Independent States.

[5] Yemen was admitted to membership in the United Nations on 30 September 1947 and Democratic Yemen on 14 December 1967. On 22 May 1990, the two countries merged and have since been represented as one member of the United Nations with the name Yemen.

[6] By a letter of 20 January 1965, Indonesia announced its decision to withdraw from the United Nations "at this stage and under the present circumstances". By a telegram of 19 September 1966, it announced its decision "to resume full cooperation with the United Nations and to resume participation in its activities". On 28 September 1966, the General Assembly took note of this decision, and the President invited representatives of Indonesia to take their seats in the Assembly.

[7] The Federation of Malaya joined the United Nations on 17 September 1957. On 16 September 1963, its name was changed to Malaysia, following the admission to the new federation of Sabah (North Borneo), Sarawak and Singapore. Singapore became an independent state on 9 August 1965 and a member of the United Nations on 21 September 1965.

[8] The Republic of Zaire informed the United Nations that, effective 17 May 1997, it had changed its name to the Democratic Republic of the Congo.

[9] Tanganyika was a member of the United Nations from 14 December 1961 and Zanzibar from 16 December 1963. Following the ratification on 26 April 1964 of Articles of Union between Tanganyika and Zanzibar, the United Republic of Tanganyika and Zanzibar continued as a single member, changing its name to the United Republic of Tanzania on 1 November 1964.

[10] The Federal Republic of Germany and the German Democratic Republic were admitted to membership in the United Nations on 18 September 1973. Through the accession of the German Democratic Republic to the Federal Republic of Germany, effective 3 October 1990, the two German states united to form one sovereign state. As of that date, the Federal Republic of Germany has acted in the United Nations under the designation Germany.

[11] The Socialist Federal Republic of Yugoslavia was an original member of the United Nations, the *Charter* having been signed on its behalf on 26 June 1945 and ratified 19 October 1945, until its dissolution following the establishment and subsequent admission, as new members, of Bosnia and Herzegovina, the Republic of Croatia, the Republic of Slovenia, The former Yugoslav Republic of Macedonia, and the Federal Republic of Yugoslavia. The Republic of Bosnia and Herzegovina, the Republic of Croatia and the Republic of Slovenia were admitted as members of the United Nations on 22 May 1992. On 8 April 1993, the General Assembly decided to admit as a member of the United Nations the state provisionally referred to for all purposes within the United Nations as 'The former Yugoslav Republic of Macedonia' pending settlement of the difference that had arisen over its name. The Federal Republic of Yugoslavia was admitted as a member of the United Nations on 1 November 2000. On 12 February 2003, it informed the United Nations that it had changed its name to Serbia and Montenegro, effective 4 February 2003. In a letter dated 3 June 2006, the President of the Republic of Serbia informed the Secretary-General that the membership of Serbia and Montenegro was being continued by the Republic of Serbia following Montenegro's declaration of independence from Serbia on 3 June 2006. On 28 June 2006 Montenegro was accepted as a United Nations member state by the General Assembly.

PEACEKEEPING OPERATIONS: PAST AND PRESENT

UNTSO*	United Nations Truce Supervision Organization (Jerusalem)	May 1948–
UNMOGIP*	United Nations Military Observer Group in India and Pakistan	January 1949–
UNEF I	First United Nations Emergency Force (Gaza)	November 1956–June 1967
UNOGIL	United Nations Observation Group in Lebanon	June–December 1958
ONUC	United Nations Operation in the Congo	July 1960–June 1964
UNSF	United Nations Security Force in West New Guinea (West Irian)	October 1962–April 1963
UNYOM	United Nations Yemen Observation Mission	July 1963–September 1964
UNFICYP*	United Nations Peacekeeping Force in Cyprus	March 1964–
DOMREP	Mission of the Special Representative of the Secretary-General in the Dominican Republic	May 1965–October 1966
UNIPOM	United Nations India-Pakistan Observation Mission	September 1965–March 1966
UNEF II	Second United Nations Emergency Force (Suez Canal and later Sinai Peninsula)	October 1973–July 1979
UNDOF*	United Nations Disengagement Observer Force (Syrian Golan Heights)	May 1974–
UNIFIL*	United Nations Interim Force in Lebanon	March 1978–
UNGOMAP	United Nations Good Offices Mission in Afghanistan and Pakistan	May 1988–March 1990
UNIIMOG	United Nations Iran-Iraq Military Observer Group	August 1988–February 1991
UNAVEM I	United Nations Angola Verification Mission I	December 1988–June 1991
UNTAG	United Nations Transition Assistance Group (Namibia and Angola)	April 1989–March 1990
ONUCA	United Nations Observer Group in Central America	November 1989–January 1992
MINURSO*	United Nations Mission for the Referendum in Western Sahara	April 1991–
UNIKOM	United Nations Iraq-Kuwait Observation Mission	April 1991–October 2003
UNAVEM II	United Nations Angola Verification Mission II	May 1991–February 1995
ONUSAL	United Nations Observer Mission in El Salvador	July 1991–April 1995
UNAMIC	United Nations Advance Mission in Cambodia	October 1991–March 1992
UNPROFOR	United Nations Protection Force (former Yugoslavia)	February 1992–December 1995
UNTAC	United Nations Transitional Authority in Cambodia	March 1992–September 1993

UNOSOM I	United Nations Operation in Somalia I	April 1992–March 1993
ONUMOZ	United Nations Operation in Mozambique	December 1992–December 1994
UNOSOM II	United Nations Operation in Somalia II	March 1993–March 1995
UNOMUR	United Nations Observer Mission Uganda-Rwanda	June 1993–September 1994
UNOMIG	United Nations Observer Mission in Georgia	August 1993–June 2009
UNOMIL	United Nations Observer Mission in Liberia	September 1993–September 1997
UNMIH	United Nations Mission in Haiti	September 1993–June 1996
UNAMIR	United Nations Assistance Mission for Rwanda	October 1993–March 1996
UNASOG	United Nations Aouzou Strip Observer Group (Chad/Libya)	May–June 1994
UNMOT	United Nations Mission of Observers in Tajikistan	December 1994–May 2000
UNAVEM III	United Nations Angola Verification Mission III	February 1995–June 1997
UNCRO	United Nations Confidence Restoration Operation in Croatia	March 1995–January 1996
UNPREDEP	United Nations Preventive Deployment Force (The former Yugoslav Republic of Macedonia)	March 1995–February 1999
UNMIBH	United Nations Mission in Bosnia and Herzegovina	December 1995–December 2002
UNTAES	United Nations Transitional Administration for Eastern Slavonia, Baranja and Western Sirmium (Croatia)	January 1996–January 1998
UNMOP	United Nations Mission of Observers in Prevlaka	February 1996–December 2002
UNSMIH	United Nations Support Mission in Haiti	July 1996–June 1997
MINUGUA	United Nations Verification Mission in Guatemala	January–May 1997
MONUA	United Nations Observer Mission in Angola	June 1997–February 1999
UNTMIH	United Nations Transition Mission in Haiti	August–November 1997
MIPONUH	United Nations Civilian Police Mission in Haiti	December 1997–March 2000
UNPSG	United Nations Civilian Police Support Group (Croatia)	January–October 1998
MINURCA	United Nations Mission in the Central African Republic	April 1998–February 2000
UNOMSIL	United Nations Observer Mission in Sierra Leone	July 1998–October 1999
UNMIK*	United Nations Interim Administration Mission in Kosovo	June 1999–
UNAMSIL	United Nations Mission in Sierra Leone	October 1999–December 2005
UNTAET	United Nations Transitional Administration in East Timor	October 1999–May 2002
MONUC	United Nations Observer Mission in the Democratic Republic of the Congo	December 1999–June 2010

UNMEE	United Nations Mission in Ethiopia and Eritrea	July 2000–July 2008
UNAMA**	United Nations Assistance Mission in Afghanistan	March 2002–
UNMISET	United Nations Mission of Support in East Timor	May 2002–May 2005
MINUCI	United Nations Mission in Côte d'Ivoire	May 2003–April 2004
UNMIL*	United Nations Mission in Liberia	September 2003–
UNOCI*	United Nations Operation in Côte d'Ivoire	April 2004–
MINUSTAH*	United Nations Stabilization Mission in Haiti	April 2004–
UNMIS*	United Nations Mission in the Sudan	March 2005–
ONUB	United Nations Operation in Burundi	May 2004–31 December 2006
UNMIT*	United Nations Integrated Mission in Timor-Leste	August 2006–
BINUB**	United Nations Integrated Office in Burundi	January 2007–
UNAMID*	African Union/United Nations Hybrid Operation in Darfur	July 2007–
MINURCAT*	United Nations Mission in the Central African Republic and Chad	September 2007–
MONUSCO*	United Nations Organization Stabilization Mission in the Democratic Republic of the Congo	July 2010–

NOTES

* Current operation.
** Current political mission directed and supported by DPKO.

For the most up-to-date listing of United Nations Peacekeeping Operations, please visit the website: *www.un.org/en/peacekeeping*.

DECOLONIZATION

**Trust and Non-Self-Governing Territories that have achieved independence
since the adoption of the *Declaration on the Granting of Independence to Colonial
Countries and Peoples* on 14 December 1960**

	Date of UN admission
AFRICA	
Algeria	8 October 1962
Angola	1 December 1976
Botswana	17 October 1966
Burundi	18 September 1962
Cape Verde	16 September 1975
Comoros	12 November 1975
Djibouti	20 September 1977
Equatorial Guinea	12 November 1968
Gambia	21 September 1965
Guinea-Bissau	17 September 1974
Kenya	16 December 1963
Lesotho	17 October 1966
Malawi	1 December 1964
Mauritius	24 April 1968
Mozambique	16 September 1975
Namibia	23 April 1990
Rwanda	18 September 1962
Sao Tome and Principe	26 September 1975
Seychelles	21 September 1976
Sierra Leone	27 September 1961
Swaziland	24 September 1968
Uganda	25 October 1962
United Republic of Tanzania[1]	14 December 1961
Zambia	1 December 1964
Zimbabwe	18 April 1980
ASIA	
Brunei Darussalam	21 September 1984
Democratic Yemen	14 December 1967
Oman	7 October 1971
Singapore	21 September 1965
CARIBBEAN	
Antigua and Barbuda	11 November 1981
Bahamas	18 September 1973
Barbados	9 December 1966
Belize	25 September 1981
Dominica	18 December 1978
Grenada	17 December 1974
Guyana	20 September 1966
Jamaica	18 September 1962
Saint Kitts and Nevis	23 September 1983
Saint Lucia	18 September 1979
Saint Vincent and the Grenadines	16 September 1980

Suriname[2]	4 December 1975
Trinidad and Tobago	18 September 1962
EUROPE	
Malta	1 December 1964
PACIFIC	
Federated States of Micronesia	17 September 1991
Fiji	13 October 1970
Kiribati	14 September 1999
Marshall Islands	17 September 1991
Nauru	14 September 1999
Palau	15 December 1994
Papua New Guinea	10 October 1975
Samoa	15 December 1976
Solomon Islands	19 September 1978
Timor-Leste	27 September 2002
Tuvalu	5 September 2000

NOTES

[1] The former Trust Territory of Tanganyika, which became independent in December 1961, and the former Protectorate of Zanzibar, which achieved independence in December 1963, united into a single state in April 1964.

[2] By resolution 945(X), the General Assembly accepted the cessation of the transmission of information regarding Suriname following constitutional changes in the relationship between the Netherlands, Suriname and the Netherlands Antilles.

Dependent Territories that have become integrated or associated with independent states since the adoption of the *Declaration on the Granting of Independence to Colonial Countries and Peoples* on 14 December 1960

Territory	
Cameroons (under British administration)	The northern part of the Trust Territory joined the Federation of Nigeria on 1 June 1961 and the southern part joined the Republic of Cameroon on 1 October 1961
Cook Islands	Fully self-governing in free association with New Zealand since August 1965
Ifni	Returned to Morocco in June 1969
Niue	Fully self-governing in free association with New Zealand since August 1974
North Borneo	North Borneo and Sarawak joined the Federation of Malaya in 1963 to form the Federation of Malaysia
São Joao Batista de Ajuda	Nationally united with Dahomey (now Benin) in August 1961
Sarawak	Sarawak and North Borneo joined the Federation of Malaya in 1963 to form the Federation of Malaysia
West New Guinea (West Irian)	United with Indonesia in 1963
Cocos (Keeling) Islands	Integrated with Australia in 1984

Trust Territories that have achieved self-determination

Territory

Togoland (under British administration)	United with the Gold Coast (Colony and Protectorate), a Non-Self-Governing Territory administered by the United Kingdom, in 1957 to form Ghana
Somaliland (under Italian administration)	United with British Somaliland Protectorate in 1960 to form Somalia
Togoland (under French administration)	Became independent as Togo in 1960
Cameroons (under French administration)	Became independent as Cameroon in 1960
Tanganyika (under British administration)	Became independent in 1961 (in 1964, Tanganyika and the former Protectorate of Zanzibar, which had become independent in 1963, united as a single state under the name of the United Republic of Tanzania)
Ruanda-Urundi (under Belgian administration)	Voted to divide into the two sovereign states of Rwanda and Burundi in 1962
Western Samoa (under New Zealand administration)	Became independent as Samoa in 1962
Nauru (administered by Australia on behalf of Australia, New Zealand and the United Kingdom)	Became independent in 1968
New Guinea (administered by Australia)	United with the Non-Self-Governing Territory of Papua, also administered by Australia, to become the independent state of Papua New Guinea in 1975

Trust Territories of the Pacific Islands

Territory

Federated States of Micronesia	Became fully self-governing in free Association with the United States in 1990
Republic of the Marshall Islands	Became fully self-governing in free Association with the United States in 1990
Commonwealth of the Northern Mariana Islands	Became fully self-governing as a Commonwealth of the United States in 1990
Palau	Became fully self-governing in free Association with the United States in 1994

UNITED NATIONS OBSERVANCES

International Decades

2011–2020	Decade of Action for Road Safety
2010–2020	United Nations Decade for Deserts and the Fight against Desert-ification
2008–2017	Second United Nations Decade for the Eradication of Poverty
2006–2016	Decade of Recovery and Sustainable Development of the Affect-ed Regions (third decade after the Chernobyl disaster)
2005–2015	International Decade for Action, "Water for Life" (from 22 March 2005)
2005–2014	Second International Decade of the World's Indigenous People
	United Nations Decade of Education for Sustainable Development
2003–2012	United Nations Literacy Decade: Education for All
2001–2010	Decade to Roll Back Malaria in Developing Countries, Particu-larly in Africa
	International Decade for a Culture of Peace and Non-violence for the Children of the World
	Second International Decade for the Eradication of Colonialism

International Years

2013	International Year of Water Cooperation
2012	International Year of Cooperatives
	International Year of Sustainable Energy for All
2011	International Year of Chemistry
	International Year of Forests
	International Year for People of African Descent
2010–2011	International Year of Youth (from 12 August 2010)

Annual Weeks

First week of February	World Interfaith Harmony Week
21–27 March	Week of Solidarity with the Peoples Struggling against Racism and Racial Discrimination
25–31 May	Week of Solidarity with the Peoples of Non-Self-Governing Territories
1–7 August	World Breastfeeding Week (WHO)
4–10 October	World Space Week
24–30 October	Disarmament Week
The week of 11 November	International Week of Science and Peace

Annual Days

27 January	International Day of Commemoration in Memory of the Victims of the Holocaust
4 February	World Cancer Day (WHO)
20 February	World Day of Social Justice
21 February	International Mother Language Day (UNESCO)
8 March	International Women's Day
21 March	International Day for the Elimination of Racial Discrimination
	International Day of Nowruz
	World Poetry Day (UNESCO)
22 March	World Water Day

23 March	World Meteorological Day (WMO)
24 March	International Day for the Right to the Truth concerning Gross Human Rights Violations and for the Dignity of Victims
	World Tuberculosis Day (WHO)
25 March	International Day of Remembrance of the Victims of Slavery and the Transatlantic Slave Trade
	International Day of Solidarity with Detained and Missing Staff Members
2 April	World Autism Awareness Day
4 April	International Day for Mine Awareness and Assistance in Mine Action
7 April	World Health Day (WHO)
	Day of Remembrance of the Victims in Rwanda Genocide
22 April	International Mother Earth Day
23 April	World Book and Copyright Day (UNESCO)
25 April	World Malaria Day (WHO)
26 April	World Intellectual Property Day (WIPO)
28 April	World Day for Safety and Health at Work (ILO)
3 May	World Press Freedom Day
8–9 May	Time of Remembrance and Reconciliation for Those Who Lost Their Lives during the Second World War
9–10 May	World Migratory Bird Day (UNEP)
15 May	International Day of Families
17 May	World Telecommunication and Information Society Day (ITU)
21 May	World Day for Cultural Diversity for Dialogue and Development
22 May	International Day for Biological Diversity
29 May	International Day of UN Peacekeepers
31 May	World No-Tobacco Day (WHO)
4 June	International Day of Innocent Children Victims of Aggression
5 June	World Environment Day (UNEP)
8 June	World Oceans Day
12 June	World Day Against Child Labour (ILO)
14 June	World Blood Donor Day (WHO)
17 June	World Day to Combat Desertification and Drought
20 June	World Refugee Day
23 June	International Widows' Day
	United Nations Public Service Day
25 June	Day of the Seafarer
26 June	International Day against Drug Abuse and Illicit Trafficking
	United Nations International Day in Support of Victims of Torture
First Saturday of July	International Day of Cooperatives
11 July	World Population Day
18 July	Nelson Mandela International Day
9 August	International Day of the World's Indigenous People
12 August	International Youth Day
19 August	World Humanitarian Day
23 August	International Day for the Remembrance of the Slave Trade and Its Abolition (UNESCO)
26 August	Namibia Day
29 August	International Day against Nuclear Tests
8 September	International Literacy Day (UNESCO)
10 September	World Suicide Prevention Day (WHO)

15 September	International Day of Democracy
16 September	International Day for the Preservation of the Ozone Layer
21 September	International Day of Peace
Last Sunday in September	World Heart Day (WHO)
27 September	World Tourism Day (UNWTO)
28 September	World Rabies Day (WHO)
Last week of September	World Maritime Day (IMO)
1 October	International Day of Older Persons
2 October	International Day of Non-Violence
First Monday in October	World Habitat Day
5 October	World Teachers' Day (UNESCO)
9 October	World Post Day (UPU)
10 October	World Mental Health Day (WHO)
13 October	International Day for Disaster Reduction
	World Sight Day (WHO)
15 October	International Day of Rural Women
16 October	World Food Day (FAO)
17 October	International Day for the Eradication of Poverty
20 October	World Statistics Day
24 October	United Nations Day
	World Development Information Day
27 October	World Day for Audiovisual Heritage (UNESCO)
6 November	International Day for Preventing the Exploitation of the Environment in War and Armed Conflict
10 November	World Science Day for Peace and Development (UNESCO)
14 November	World Diabetes Day (WHO)
16 November	International Day for Tolerance
Third Thursday in November	World Philosophy Day (UNESCO)
16 November	World Chronic Obstructive Pulmonary Disease Day (WHO)
Third Sunday in November	World Day of Remembrance for Road Traffic Victims (WHO)
20 November	Africa Industrialization Day
	Universal Children's Day
21 November	World Television Day
25 November	International Day for the Elimination of Violence against Women
29 November	International Day of Solidarity with the Palestinian People
1 December	World AIDS Day
2 December	International Day for the Abolition of Slavery
3 December	International Day of Persons with Disabilities
5 December	International Volunteer Day for Economic and Social Development
7 December	International Civil Aviation Day (ICAO)
9 December	International Anti-Corruption Day
10 December	Human Rights Day
11 December	International Mountain Day
18 December	International Migrants Day
19 December	United Nations Day for South-South Cooperation
20 December	International Human Solidarity Day

NOTE: For the most up-to-date listing of United Nations Observances, please visit the website: *www.un.org/observances.*

UN INFORMATION CENTRES, SERVICES AND OFFICES

AFRICA

Accra
United Nations Information Centre
Gamal Abdel Nasser/Liberia Roads
(P.O. Box GP 2339)
Accra, Ghana
Tel.: (233) 030 2 665511
Fax: (233) 030 2 665578
E-mail: unic.accra@unic.org
Website: *http://accra.unic.org*
Serving: Ghana, Sierra Leone

Algiers
United Nations Information Centre
41 rue Mohamed Khoudi, El Biar
El Biar, 16030 El Biar, Alger
(Boîte postale 444, Hydra-Alger)
Algiers, Algeria
Tel.: (213 21) 92 54 42
Fax: (213 21) 92 54 42
E-mail: unic.dz@undp.org
Website: *http://algiers.unic.org*
Serving: Algeria

Antananarivo
United Nations Information Centre
22 Rue Rainitovo, Antasahavola
(Boîte postale, 1348)
Antananarivo, Madagascar
Tel.: (261 20) 22 241 15
Fax: (261 20) 22 367 94
E-mail: unic.ant@moov.mg
Website: *http://antananarivo.unic.org*
Serving: Madagascar

Asmara
United Nations Information Centre
Hiday Street, Airport Road
(P.O. Box 5366)
Asmara, Eritrea
Tel.: (291 1) 15 11 66 ext. 311
Fax: (29 1) 15 10 81
E-mail: dpi.er@undp.org
Website: *http://asmara.unic.org*
Serving: Eritrea

Brazzaville
United Nations Information Centre
Avenue Foch, Case ortf 15
(Boîte postale 13210)
Brazzaville, Congo
Tel.: (242) 660 85 76
Fax: N/A
E-mail: unic.brazzaville@unic.org
Website: *http://brazzaville.unic.org*
Serving: Congo

Bujumbura
United Nations Information Centre
117 Avenue de la Révolution
(Boîte postale 2160)
Bujumbura, Burundi
Tel.: (257) 22 50 18
Fax: (257) 24 17 98
E-mail: unic.bujumbura@unic.org
Website: *http://bujumbura.unic.org*
Serving: Burundi

Cairo
United Nations Information Centre
1 Osiris Street, Garden City
(P.O. Box 262)
Cairo, Egypt
Tel.: (202) 27900022
Fax: (202) 27953705
E-mail: info@unic-eg.org
Website: *http://www.unic-eg.org*
Serving: Egypt, Saudi Arabia

Dakar
United Nations Information Centre
Immeuble Soumex, Mamelles-Almadies
(Boîte postale 154)
Dakar, Senegal
Tel.: (221) 33 869 99 11
Fax: (221) 33 860 51 48
E-mail: unic.dakar@unic.org
Website: *http://dakar.unic.org*
Serving: Cape Verde, Côte d'Ivoire, Gambia, Guinea-Bissau, Mauritania, Senegal

Dar es Salaam
United Nations Information Centre
Kings Way/Mafinga Street
Plot 134-140, Kinondoni
(P.O. Box 9224)
Dar es Salaam, United Republic of Tanzania
Tel.: (255 22) 219 9343
Fax: (255 22) 266 7633

E-mail: unic.daressalaam@unic.org
Website: *http://daressalaam.unic.org*
Serving: United Republic of Tanzania

Harare
United Nations Information Centre
Sanders House (2nd floor), cnr. First Street/
   Jason Moyo Avenue
(P.O. Box 4408)
Harare, Zimbabwe
Tel.: (263 4) 777 060
Fax: (263 4) 750 476
E-mail: unic.harare@unic.org
Website: *http://harare.unic.org*
Serving: Zimbabwe

Khartoum
United Nations Information Centre
United Nations Compound House #7, Blk 5
Gamma'a Avenue
(P.O. Box 1992)
Khartoum, Sudan
Tel.: (249 183) 783 755
Fax: (249 183) 773 772
E-mail: unic.sd@undp.org
Website: *http://khartoum.unic.org*
Serving: Somalia, Sudan

Lagos
United Nations Information Centre
17 Alfred Rewane Road (formerly
   Kingsway Road), Ikoyi
(P.O. Box 1068)
Lagos, Nigeria
Tel.: (234 1) 775 5989
Fax: (234 1) 463 0916
E-mail: lagos@unic.org
Website: *http://lagos.unic.org*
Serving: Nigeria

Lomé
United Nations Information Centre
468, Angle rue Atime
Avenue de la Libération
(Boîte postale 911)
Lomé, Togo
Tel.: (228) 221 2306
Fax: (228) 221 2306
E-mail: cinutogo@cafe.tg
Website: *http://lome.unic.org*
Serving: Benin, Togo

Lusaka
United Nations Information Centre
Revenue House (Ground floor)
Cairo Road (Northend)
(P.O. Box 32905, Lusaka 10101)
Lusaka, Zambia
Tel.: (260 211) 228 478
Fax: (260 211) 222 958
E-mail: unic.lusaka@unic.org
Website: *http://lusaka.unic.org*
Serving: Botswana, Malawi, Swaziland,
   Zambia

Maseru
United Nations Information Centre
United Nations Road
UN House
(P.O. Box 301, Maseru 100)
Maseru, Lesotho
Tel.: (266 22) 313 790
Fax: (266 22) 310 042
E-mail: unic.maseru@unic.org
Website: *http://maseru.unic.org*
Serving: Lesotho

Nairobi
United Nations Information Centre
United Nations Office, Gigiri
(P.O. Box 20552-00200)
Nairobi, Kenya
Tel.: (254 20) 762 3798
Fax: (254 20) 762 4349
E-mail: Nairobi.unic@unon.org
Website: *http://www.unicnairobi.org*
Serving: Kenya, Seychelles, Uganda

Ouagadougou
United Nations Information Centre
14 Avenue de la Grande Chancellerie
Secteur no. 4
(Bôite postale 135)
Ougadougou 01, Burkina Faso
Tel.: (226) 5030 6076
Fax: (226) 5031 1322
E-mail: unic.ouagadougou@unic.org
Website: *http://ouagadougou.unic.org*
Serving: Burkina Faso, Chad, Mali, Niger

Pretoria
United Nations Information Centre
Metro Park Building
351 Schoeman Street
(P.O. Box 12677), Tramshed

Pretoria, South Africa 0126
Tel.: (27 12) 354 8506
Fax: (27 12) 354 8501
E-mail: unic.pretoria@unic.org
Website: *http://pretoria.unic.org*
Serving: South Africa

Rabat
United Nations Information Centre
6 Angle Avenue Tarik Ibn Ziyad et Rue
  Roudana
(Boîte postale 601), Casier ONU,
  Rabat-Chellah)
Rabat, Morocco
Tel.: (212 537) 76 86 33
Fax: (212 37) 76 83 77
E-mail: unicmor@unicmor.ma
Website: *http://www.unicmor.ma*
Serving: Morocco

Tripoli
United Nations Information Centre
Khair Aldeen Baybers Street
Hay El-Andalous
(P.O. Box 286, Hay El-Andalous)
Tripoli, Libyan Arab Jamahiriya
Tel.: (218 21) 477 0521
Fax: (218 21) 477 7343
E-mail: tripoli@un.org
Website: *http://tripoli.unic.org*
Serving: Libyan Arab Jamahiriya

Tunis
United Nations Information Centre
41 Bis, Av. Louis Braille, Cité El Khadra
(Boîte postale 863)
1003 Tunis, Tunisia
Tel.: (216 71) 902 203
Fax: (216 71) 906 811
E-mail: unic.tunis@unic.org
Website: *http://www.unictunis.org.tn*
Serving: Tunisia

Windhoek
United Nations Information Centre
UN House, 38-44 Stein Street, Klein
(Private Bag 13351)
Windhoek, Namibia
Tel.: (264 61) 2046111
Fax: (264 61) 2046521
E-mail: unic.windhoek@unic.org
Website: *http://windhoek.unic.org*
Serving: Namibia

Yaoundé
United Nations Information Centre
Immeuble Tchinda
Rue 2044
Derrière camp SIC TSINGA
(Boîte postale 836)
Yaoundé, Cameroon
Tel.: (237) 2 221 23 67
Fax: (237) 2 221 23 68
E-mail: unic.cameroon@unic.org
Website: *http://yaounde.unic.org*
Serving: Cameroon, Central African Republic,
  Gabon

THE AMERICAS

Asunción
United Nations Information Centre
Avda. Mariscal López esq. Guillermo Saraví
Edificio Naciones Unidas
(Casilla de Correo 1107)
Asunción, Paraguay
Tel.: (595 21) 614 443
Fax: (595 21) 611 988
E-mail: unic.py@undp.org
Website: *http://asuncion.unic.org*
Serving: Paraguay

Bogotá
United Nations Information Centre
Calle 100 No. 8A-55 Piso 10
Edificio World Trade Center-Torre "C"
(Apartado, Aéreo 058964)
Bogotá 2, Colombia
Tel.: (57 1) 257 6044
Fax: (57 1) 257 6244
E-mail: unic.bogota@unic.org
Website: *http://www.nacionesunidas.org.co*
Serving: Colombia, Ecuador, Venezuela

Buenos Aires
United Nations Information Centre
Junín 1940, 1er piso
1113 Buenos Aires, Argentina
Tel.: (54 11) 4803 7671
Fax: (54 11) 4804 7545
E-mail: unic.buenosaires@unic.org
Website: *http://www.unic.org.ar*
Serving: Argentina, Uruguay

La Paz
United Nations Information Centre
Calle 14 esq. S. Bustamante

Edificio Metrobol II, Calacoto
(Apartado Postal 9072)
La Paz, Bolivia
Tel.: (591 2) 262 4512
Fax: (591 2) 279 5820
E-mail: unic.lapaz@unic.org
Website: *http://www.nu.org.bo*
Serving: Bolivia

Lima
United Nations Information Centre
Lord Cochrane 130
San Isidro (L-27)
(P.O. Box 14-0199)
Lima, Peru
Tel.: (511) 441 8745
Fax: (511) 441 8735
E-mail: unic.lima@unic.org
Website: *http://www.uniclima.org.pe*
Serving: Peru

Mexico City
United Nations Information Centre
Montes Urales 440, 3rd floor
Colonia Lomas de Chapultepec
Mexico City, D.F. 11000, Mexico
Tel.: (52 55) 4000 9600
Fax: (52 55) 5203 8638
E-mail: infounic@un.org.mx
Website: *http://www.cinu.org*
Serving: Cuba, Dominican Republic, Mexico

Panama City
United Nations Information Centre
UN House Bldg. 128, 1st Floor
Ciudad del Saber, Clayton
(P.O. Box 0819-01082)
Panama City, Panama
Tel.: (507) 301 0035/0036
Fax: (507) 301 0037
E-mail: unic.panama@unic.org
Website: *http://www.cinup.org*
Serving: Panama

Port of Spain
United Nations Information Centre
2nd floor, Bretton Hall
16 Victoria Avenue
(P.O. Box 130)
Port of Spain, Trinidad and Tobago, W.I.
Tel.: (868) 623 4813
Fax: (868) 623 4332
E-mail: unic.portofspain@unic.org

Website: *http://portofspain.unic.org*
Serving: Antigua and Barbuda, Aruba,
Bahamas, Barbados, Belize, Dominica,
Grenada, Guyana, Jamaica, Netherlands
Antilles, Saint Kitts and Nevis, Saint
Lucia, Saint Vincent and the Grenadines,
Suriname, Trinidad and Tobago

Rio de Janeiro
United Nations Information Centre
Palácio Itamaraty
Av. Marechal Floriano 196
20080-002 Rio de Janeiro RJ, Brazil
Tel.: (55 21) 2253 2211
Fax: (55 21) 2233 5753
E-mail: unic.brazil@unic.org
Website: *http://unicrio.org.br*
Serving: Brazil

Santiago
United Nations Information Service,
    Economic Commission for Latin America
    and the Caribbean
Edificio Naciones Unidas
Avenida Dag Hammarskjöld 3477
Vitacura (Casilla 179-D)
Santiago, Chile
Tel.: 56 2/210 2000
Fax: 56 2/208 1947
E-mail: dpisantiago@eclac.cl
Website: *http://www.eclac.org/prensa*
Serving: Chile, ECLAC

Washington, D.C.
United Nations Information Centre
1775 K Street, N.W., Suite 400
Washington, D.C. 20006
United States of America
Tel.: (202) 331 8670
Fax: (202) 331 9191
E-mail: unicdc@unicwash.org
Website: *http://www.unicwash.org*
Serving: United States of America

ASIA AND THE PACIFIC

Bangkok
United Nations Information Service,
    Economic and Social Commission
    for Asia and the Pacific
United Nations Building
Rajdamnern Nok Avenue
Bangkok 10200, Thailand

Tel.: (66) (0) 2 288 1866
Fax: (66) (0) 2 288 1052
E-mail: unisbkk.unescap@un.org
Website: *http://www.unescap.org/unis*
Serving: Cambodia, Lao People's Democratic
   Republic, Malaysia, Singapore, Thailand,
   Viet Nam, ESCAP

Beirut
United Nations Information Centre, United
   Nations Information Service, Economic
   and Social Commission for Western Asia
UN House, Riad El-Sohl Square
(P.O. Box 11-8575-4656)
Beirut, Lebanon
Tel.: (961 1) 981 301/311
   Ext. 1828/1829/1830/1832/1833
Fax: (961 1) 97 04 24
E-mail: unic-beirut@un.org
Website: *http://www.unicbeirut.org*
Serving: Jordan, Kuwait, Lebanon, Syrian
   Arab Republic, ESCWA

Canberra
United Nations Information Centre
Level 1 Barton, 7 National Circuit
(P.O. Box 5366, Kingston, ACT 2604)
Canberra ACT 2600, Australia
Tel.: (61 2) 627 09200
Fax: (61 2) 627 38206
E-mail: unic.canberra@unic.org
Website: *http://www.un.org.au*
Serving: Australia, Fiji, Kiribati, Nauru, New
   Zealand, Samoa, Tonga, Tuvalu, Vanuatu

Colombo
United Nations Information Centre
202/204 Bauddhaloka Mawatha
(P.O. Box 1505, Colombo)
Colombo 7, Sri Lanka
Tel.: (94 112) 580 791
Fax: (94 112) 501 396
E-mail: unic.lk@undp.org
Website: *http://colombo.unic.org*
Serving: Sri Lanka

Dhaka
United Nations Information Centre
IDB Bhaban (8th floor)
Sher-e-Banglanagar
(G.P.O. Box 3658, Dhaka-1000)
Dhaka-1207, Bangladesh

Tel.: (880 2) 8117 868 (Library)
Fax: (880 2) 8112 343
E-mail: unic.dhaka@undp.org
Website: *http://www.unicdhaka.org*
Serving: Bangladesh

Islamabad
United Nations Information Centre
Serena Business Complex,
   2nd Floor, Sector G-5/1
Khayaban-e-Suharwardy
(P.O. Box 1107)
Islamabad, Pakistan
Tel.: (0092 51) 8355 719/5720
Fax: (0092 51) 2271 856
E-mail: unic.islamabad@unic.org
Website: *http://www.un.org.pk/unic*
Serving: Pakistan

Jakarta
United Nations Information Centre
Menara Thamrin Building, 3A floor
Jalan MH Thamrin, Kav. 3
Jakarta 10250, Indonesia
Tel.: (6221) 3983 1011
Fax: (6221) 3983 1014
E-mail: unic-jakarta@unic-jakarta.org
Website: *http://www.unic-jakarta.org*
Serving: Indonesia

Kathmandu
United Nations Information Centre
Harihar Bhavan
(P.O. Box 107, UN House)
Kathmandu, Nepal
Tel.: (977 1) 552 3200 ext. 1600
Fax: (977 1) 554 3723
E-mail: unic.np@undp.org
Website: *http://kathmandu.unic.org*
Serving: Nepal

Manama
United Nations Information Centre
United Nations House
Bldg. 69, Road 1901, Block 319
(P.O. Box 26004, Manama)
Manama, Bahrain
Tel.: (973) 17 311 676
Fax: (973) 17 311 692
E-mail: unic.manama@unic.org
Website: *http://www.un.org.bh/unic.html*
Serving: Bahrain, Qatar, United Arab Emirates

Manila
United Nations Information Centre
GC Corporate Plaza (ex Jaka II Building)
5th floor, 150 Legaspi Street, Legaspi Village
(P.O. Box 7285 ADC (DAPO), Pasay City)
Makati City
1229 Metro Manila, Philippines
Tel.: (63 2) 338 5521
Fax: (63 2) 339 0177
E-mail: unic.manila@unic.org
Website: *http://www.unicmanila.org*
Serving: Papua New Guinea, Philippines,
  Solomon Islands

New Delhi
United Nations Information Centre
55 Lodi Estate
New Delhi 110 003, India
Tel.: (91 11) 4653 2333
Fax: (91 11) 2462 8508
E-mail: unicindia@unicindia.org
Website: *http://www.unic.org.in*
Serving: Bhutan, India

Sana'a
United Nations Information Centre
Street 5, Off Abawnya Area
Handhel Zone, beside Handhal Mosque
(P.O. Box 237)
Sana'a, Yemen
Tel.: (967 1) 274 000
Fax: (967 1) 274 043
E-mail: unicyem@y.net.ye
Website: *http://www.unicyem.org*
Serving: Yemen

Tehran
United Nations Information Centre
No. 8, Shahrzad Blvd. Darrous
(P.O. Box 15875-4557, Tehran)
Tehran, Iran
Tel.: (98 21) 2 286 0694
Fax: (98 21) 2 287 3395
E-mail: unic.tehran@unic.org
Website: *http://www.unic-ir.org*
Serving: Iran

Tokyo
United Nations Information Centre
UNU Building (8th floor)
53-70 Jingumae 5-Chome, Shibuya-Ku
Tokyo 150-0001, Japan

Tel.: (81 3) 5467 4454
Fax: (81 3) 5467 4455
E-mail: unic.tokyo@unic.org
Website: *http://www.unic.or.jp*
Serving: Japan

Yangon
United Nations Information Centre
6 Natmauk Road
Tamwe Township
(P.O. Box 230)
Yangon, Myanmar
Tel.: (95 1) 542 911
Fax: (95 1) 545 634
E-mail: unic.myanmar@undp.org
Website: *http://yangon.unic.org*
Serving: Myanmar

**EUROPE AND THE COMMMONWEALTH
OF INDEPENDENT STATES**

Almaty
United Nations Information Office
67, Tole Bi Street, 050000 Almaty
Republic of Kazakhstan
Tel.: (7 727) 258 2643 ext. 1416
Fax: (7 727) 258 2645
E-mail: kazakhstan@unic.org, dpi.kz@undp.org
Website: *http://kazakhstan.unic.org*
Serving: Kazakhstan

Ankara
United Nations Information Centre
Birlik Mahallesi, 415. Cadde No. 11
06610 Cankaya
Ankara, Turkey
Tel.: (90 312) 454 1052
Fax: (90 312) 496 1499
E-mail: unic.ankara@unic.org
Website: *http://www.unicankara.org.tr*
Serving: Turkey

Baku
United Nations Office
UN 50th Anniversary Street, 3
Baku, AZ1001
Azerbaijan
Tel.: (994 12) 498 98 88
Fax: (994 12) 498 32 35
E-mail: un-dpi@un-az.org
Website: *http://azerbaijan.unic.org*
Serving: Azerbaijan

Brussels
Regional United Nations Information Centre
Résidence Palace
Rue de la Loi/Westraat 155
Quartier Rubens, Block C2
1040 Brussels, Belgium
Tel.: (32 2) 788 8484
Fax: (32 2) 788 8485
E-mail: info@unric.org
Website: *http://www.unric.org*
Serving: Andorra, Belgium, Cyprus, Denmark,
   Finland, France, Germany, Greece, Holy
   See, Iceland, Ireland, Italy, Luxembourg,
   Malta, Monaco, Netherlands, Norway,
   Portugal, San Marino, Spain, Sweden,
   United Kingdom, European Union

Bucharest
United Nations Information Centre
48 A Primaverii Blvd.
011975 Bucharest 1, Romania
Tel.: (40 21) 201 78 77
Fax: (40 21) 201 78 80
E-mail: unic.romania@unic.org
Website: *http://www.onuinfo.ro*
Serving: Romania

Geneva
United Nations Information Service,
   United Nations Office at Geneva
Palais des Nations
1211 Geneva 10, Switzerland
Tel.: (41 22) 917 2302
Fax: (41 22) 917 0030
E-mail: press_geneva@unog.ch
Website: *http://www.unog.ch*
Serving: Switzerland

Kyiv
United Nations Office
Klovskiy Uzviz, 1
Kyiv, Ukraine
Tel.: (380 44) 253 93 63
Fax: (380 44) 253 26 07
E-mail: registry@un.org.ua
Website: *http://www.un.org.ua*
Serving: Ukraine

Minsk
United Nations Office
Kirov Street, 17, 6th Floor, 220030
Minsk, Belarus
Tel.: (375 17) 2278 149

Fax: (375 17) 226 0340
E-mail: dpi.staff.by@undp.org
Website: *http://www.un.by*
Serving: Belarus

Moscow
United Nations Information Centre
Glazovsky Pereulok, 4/16
Moscow, 119002 Russian Federation
Tel.: (7 499) 241 2894
Fax: (7 495) 695 2138
E-mail: dpi-moscow@unic.ru
Website: *http://www.unic.ru*
Serving: Russian Federation

Prague
United Nations Information Centre
nam. Kinskych 6
15000 Prague 5, Czech Republic
Tel.: (420) 257 199 831
Fax: (420) 257 316 761
E-mail: info@osn.cz
Website: *http://www.osn.cz*
Serving: Czech Republic

Tashkent
United Nations Office
4, T. Shevchenko Street,
Tashkent 100029, Uzbekistan
Tel.: (998 71) 1203 450
Fax: (998 71) 1203 485
E-mail: registry.uz@undp.org
Website: *http://www.un.uz*
Serving: Uzbekistan

Tbilisi
United Nations Office
9, Eristavi Street
0179 Tbilisi, Georgia
Tel.: 995 32 25 11 26
Fax: 995 32 25 02 71
E-mail: uno.tbilisi@unic.org
Website: *http://georgia.unic.org*
Serving: Georgia

Vienna
United Nations Information Service,
   United Nations Office at Vienna
Vienna International Centre
Wagramer Strasse 5
(P.O. Box 500, A-1400 Vienna)
A-1220 Vienna, Austria
Tel.: (43 1) 26060 4666

Fax: (43 1) 26060 5899
E-mail: unis@unvienna.org
Website: *http://www.unis.unvienna.org*
Serving: Austria, Hungary, Slovakia, Slovenia

Warsaw
United Nations Information Centre
Al. Niedpodleglosci 186
(UN Centre P.O. Box 1, 02-514 Warsaw 12)
00-608 Warszawa, Poland
Tel.: (48 22) 825 5784
Fax: (48 22) 825 7706
E-mail: unic.poland@unic.org
Website: *http://www.unic.un.org.pl*
Serving: Poland

Yerevan
United Nations Office
Petros Adamyan Street, 14, 1st Floor
0010 Yerevan, Armenia
Tel.: (374 10) 560 212
Fax: (374 10) 561 406
E-mail: uno.yerevan@unic.org
Website: *http://www.un.am*
Serving: Armenia

SELECTED UNITED NATIONS WEBSITES

United Nations   *www.un.org*
United Nations system   *www.unsystem.org*

Principal Organs

Economic and Social Council   *www.un.org/en/ecosoc*
General Assembly   *www.un.org/en/ga*
International Court of Justice   *www.icj-cij.org*
Secretariat   *www.un.org/en/mainbodies/secretariat*
Security Council   *www.un.org/docs/sc*
Trusteeship Council   *www.un.org/en/mainbodies/trusteeship*

Programmes and Funds

International Trade Center (ITC)   *www.intracen.org*
Office of the United Nations High Commissioner
   for Refugees (UNHCR)   *www.unhcr.org*
United Nations Capital Development Fund (UNCDF)   *www.uncdf.org*
United Nations Children's Fund (UNICEF)   *www.unicef.org*
United Nations Conference on Trade and Development (UNCTAD)   *www.unctad.org*
United Nations Development Programme (UNDP)   *www.undp.org*
United Nations Entity for Gender Equality
   and the Empowerment of Women (UN-Women)   *www.unwomen.org*
United Nations Environment Programme (UNEP)   *www.unep.org*
United Nations Human Settlements Programme (UN-HABITAT)   *www.unhabitat.org*
United Nations Office on Drugs and Crime (UNODC) *www.unodc.org*
United Nations Population Fund (UNFPA)   *www.unfpa.org*
United Nations Relief and Works Agency
   for Palestine Refugees in the Near East (UNRWA)   *www.un.org/unrwa*
United Nations Volunteers (UNV)   *www.unv.org*
World Food Programme (WFP)   *www.wfp.org*

Research and Training Institutes

United Nations Institute for Disarmament Research (UNIDIR)   *www.unidir.org*
United Nations Institute for Training and Research (UNITAR) *www.unitar.org*
United Nations Interregional Crime and Justice
   Research Institute (UNICRI)   *www.unicri.it*
United Nations Research Institute for Social Development (UNRISD)   *www.unrisd.org*
United Nations System Staff College (UNSSC)   *www.unssc.org*
United Nations University (UNU)   *www.unu.org*

Other Entities

Joint United Nations Programme on HIV/AIDS (UNAIDS)   *www.unaids.org*
United Nations International Strategy for Disaster Reduction (UNISDR)   *www.unisdr.org*
United Nations Office for Project Services (UNOPS)   *www.unops.org*

Subsidiary Bodies and Functional Commissions

Commission on Crime Prevention
   and Criminal Justice   *www.unodc.org/unodc/en/commissions/CCPCJ/index.html*

Commission on Narcotic Drugs   *www.unodc.org/unodc/en/commissions/CND/index.html*
Commission on Population
   and Development   *www.un.org/esa/population/cpd/aboutcom.htm*
Commission on Science
   and Technology for Development   *www.unctad.org/cstd*
Commission on Social Development   *www.un.org/esa/socdev/csd/index.html*
Commission on the Status of Women   *www.un.org/womenwatch/daw/csw*
Commission on Sustainable
   Development   *www.un.org/esa/dsd/csd/csd_aboucsd.shtml*
Counter-Terrorism Committee (CTC)   *www.un.org/en/sc/ctc*
Disarmament Commission (UNDC)   *www.un.org/Depts/ddar/discomm/undc*
Human Rights Council (HRC)   *www2.ohchr.org/english/bodies/hrcouncil*
International Criminal Tribunal for Rwanda (ICTR) *www.unictr.org*
International Criminal Tribunal for the former Yugoslavia (ICTY)   *www.icty.org*
International Law Commission (ILC)   *www.un.org/law/ilc*
Peacekeeping operations
   and political missions   *www.un.org/en/peacekeeping*
Permanent Forum on Indigenous Issues   *www.un.org/esa/socdev/unpfii*
Statistical Commission   *unstats.un.org/unsd/statcom/commission.htm*
United Nations Forum on Forests   *www.un.org/esa/forests*
United Nations Peacebuilding Commission   *www.un.org/peace/peacebuilding*

Regional Commissions

Economic Commission for Africa (ECA)   *www.uneca.org*
Economic Commission for Europe (ECE)   *www.unece.org*
Economic Commission for Latin America
   and the Caribbean (ECLAC)   *www.eclac.org*
Economic and Social Commission for Asia and the Pacific (ESCAP)   *www.unescap.org*
Economic and Social Commission for Western Asia (ESCWA)   *www.escwa.un.org*

Specialized Agencies

Food and Agriculture Organization of the United Nations (FAO)   *www.fao.org*
International Civil Aviation Organization (ICAO)   *www.icao.int*
International Fund for Agricultural Development (IFAD)   *www.ifad.org*
International Labour Organization (ILO)   *www.ilo.org*
International Maritime Organization (IMO)   *www.imo.org*
International Monetary Fund (IMF)   *www.imf.org*
International Telecommunication Union (ITU)   *www.itu.int*
United Nations Educational, Scientific
   and Cultural Organization (UNESCO)   *www.unesco.org*
United Nations Industrial Development Organization (UNIDO)   *www.unido.org*
Universal Postal Union (UPU)   *www.upu.int*
World Bank Group   *www.worldbank.org*
World Health Organization (WHO)   *www.who.int*
World Intellectual Property Organization (WIPO)   *www.wipo.int*
World Meteorological Organization (WMO)   *www.wmo.ch*
World Tourism Organization (UNWTO)   *www.unwto.org*

Related Organizations

International Atomic Energy Agency (IAEA)	*www.iaea.org*
Organization for the Prohibition of Chemical Weapons (OPCW)	*www.opcw.org*
Preparatory Committee for the Comprehensive Nuclear-Test-Ban Treaty Organization (CTBTO)	*www.ctbto.org*
World Trade Organization (WTO)	*www.wto.org*

INDEX